The Pretty Things

growing old disgracefully

Alan Lakey

FIRE FLY

PUBLISHING

FIRE
FLY

PUBLISHING

First published in 2002 by Firefly Publishing,

Firefly is an imprint of SAF Publishing Ltd.
in association with Helter Skelter Publishing Ltd.

SAF Publishing Ltd.
Unit 7, Shaftesbury Centre
85 Barlby Road
London W10 6BN
England

www.safpublishing.com
www.skelter.demon.co.uk

Front cover photograph: GEMS / Redferns

Cover and book design: David @ The Unit

Printed in England by Cromwell Press, Trowbridge, Wiltshire.

INTRODUCTION

In June 1976 a crisis meeting was convened at the office of Peter Grant, the guiding force behind Led Zeppelin, head of the Swansong record label and manager of The Pretty Things. The mood was serious and the meeting carried major implications for both band and their employers. Phil May, lead vocalist and perennial Pretty Thing had walked out the previous week, decamping to France and leaving them to struggle on without their main singer, figurehead and notional leader. This untimely exodus meant that he missed the prestigious gig at Wembley supporting Uriah Heep. Clearly both band and label had to consider the future.

As the meeting progressed Phil turned up unexpectedly, somewhat sheep-ish-looking and expecting to rejoin. Tensions were running high and drum animal Skip Alan, never renowned for his subtlety or patience, swivelled round and barked, 'You're always fucking off, so why don't you fuck off again?'

Phil fucked off again. The Pretty Things, as a band and an abstraction, folded.

Yet another day in the life of a group that had turned self-destruction into an artform. The band that perfected walkabout many years before Jenny Agutter. The Pretty Things had been shackled by mismanagement, scuppered by record company fecklessness, ripped off by devious associates and often demoralised by the public's constant and perverse indifference to both quality and the genuine article.

Yet still, to this day, they soldier on. The philosophically inclined might blame fate, others more cynical might blame the band themselves for failing to keep their eye on the ball or not wanting it enough. The illusion of common-sense.

Arthur Brown, the 'God of Hellfire', distilled the essence of The Pretty Things rather more succinctly than most.

'They have a proven history of violence, drug abuse and public mayhem. They've been the role-models for the generations of weak, pale imitations, the on-the-road excesses of the 70s tame rock gods, the formless pantomime of the Sex Pistols punk, and the pathetic foot-stamping of Oasis and Brit-pop pansies. They invented everything…. and were credited with nothing.'

It began for the Pretties in 1963 but it actually originated way before then when post-war American rhythm & blues infiltrated the somewhat staid post-war British psyche illustrating how music with guts, feeling and honesty could be played. When disaffected art students Dick Taylor and Phil May aped their American heroes during their lunch break, it was initially for fun and to recreate the rhythms of Chess and Excello label artists. Dick had already turned his back on the fledgling Rolling Stones and was still intending a career in graphic art. A career as a musician was never considered an option.

Nearly forty years later, older but barely wiser, these same R&B recidivists, now surely close to a kind of retirement, continue to produce outstanding music which, although it has roots in the blues, also encapsulates the musical changes that occurred throughout the 60s, 70s and 80s. Far less endearing than even the Rolling Stones they were nonetheless musically more willing to experiment and push at the boundaries, which in the early 1960s were precise, clear and relatively firm. Unlike the Stones, they never suffered the embarrassments or riches of mainstream acceptance and cannot boast sunshine retreats on Guernsey let alone Mustique.

Whilst burrowing out a decidedly turbulent career they tore away from their original R&B roots and were pushed unwillingly into pop, before wholeheartedly immersing themselves in psychedelia, mime, progressive rock, neo-heavy metal, US-style soft rock and edge-of-the-razor punk. In 1999 they returned with an album of surprising value and worth for men in their mid-fifties. It contained aspects of all previous incarnations and later that year, with a new anthem to marijuana, they again thumbed their noses at established values.

Throughout this period lead singer Phil May has remained the almost constant thread – the lynchpin holding The Pretty Things together. At times they have congregated temporarily under other names but have always returned to that poisoned Pretty Things chalice.

Consistently they have shunned the financially tempting bait of the golden-oldie tour packages and the pseudo-cabaret deals which are eagerly grasped by most of the other ageing sixties survivors. In so doing The Pretty Things have stayed resolutely on track even if sometimes it has left them both commercially and financially on the wrong side of the rails.

Tragically, today's world of the temporary musical fix thrives on the liberal indulgences of the marketing gurus. Over use of superlatives such as 'best ever', 'greatest', 'genius' and 'seminal' has blunted their effect. These grandiose terms are scattered with such frequency and careless abandon that even studied mediocrity is exulted over. One such term is cult status, but no question that the Pretties deserve such an accolade, no shoe-horning here. Bowie, the Pistols, New York Dolls, Ramones and countless bands throughout the world acknowledge The Pretty Things as inspiration for their musical stimuli and behavioural shortcomings.

Seminal R&B heroes cavorting, rocking, rolling and emblazoned in tabloid headlines alongside the Stones. Leading edge psychedelicists, pushing back the abstract and production boundaries aided and abetted by producer Norman Smith. Originators of the first rock opera and of conceptual albums before the phrase became derogated by early 70s pomposity. Harmony wizards, musically if not financially on a par with the Beach Boys, Beatles and Eagles and a clear division above the plethora of early 70s copyists. Gutripping punkers, offering more musical ability and attitude than a garage full of Johnny Rottens.

Each of these guises has been successfully subsumed into the collective, the legend known as The Pretty Things. At each phase they have excelled in every aspect other than that of widespread public acclaim and consequent financial reward. Unlike many of their fellow sixties survivors they resisted the temptation to slide into glam rock or to embarrass themselves at the altar of disco. The music, rather than success at any price.

Who are the Pretty Things? Unlike many former and current stars there is no mystique of celebrity with these guys, they are basically down-to-earth ordinary fellows. Phil May is now middle-aged but growing the remains of his hair long again after a period of trimmed normality in the early 90s. He retains an acute awareness of the Pretties place in the folklore of musicology and is anxious to protect the image, which has been cultivated and, of course, embellished over the years.

Dick Taylor is extremely congenial and it is easy to see why he is liked by everybody I have spoken to. Dick adopts no grand aspirations and appears genuinely content with his lot. A CND supporter before it was chic (although he will point out that he has never been a member of that organisation or indeed any political party) he is non-materialistic and non-mercenary. Dick has probably been too self-effacing for his own financial and commercial good but, if he had been grabbing and ludicrous then he wouldn't have been Dick.

Wally Waller comes across as cautious and somewhat reluctant to push himself to the front. He is the anchor of the group and responsible for the melody within the rock 'n' roll. His role appears to have diminished since the EMI days yet he still retains his love of music and cannot jump off the train.

Jon Povey has settled down since his wild-boy years in the 60s and 70s, when he was arrested and charged with indecency for wearing see-though trousers down the Kings Road, Chelsea. He has always occupied a peripheral role, vamping in the wings at concerts and chucking amusing asides at the audience. His falsetto and vocal skills are integral to the layered harmonies, which have proved such an important facet of the band since his arrival in 1967.

The Pretty Things

Skip Alan loves being the centre of attention and if nothing is happening he will usually make it happen. Whether destroying drum kits or mike stands or swinging from the rafters, it's all the same to Skip. Perspiring and seemingly all done in during concerts he is invariably revived by the opportunity to howl and scream the lyrics of Route 66 during the encore.

Frank Holland is still considered the new boy even though his involvement has included engineering Pretties tracks, writing and assisting on guitar or keyboards for over ten years. His more rock-veined guitar style provides a foil for the bluesier licks of Dick Taylor.

So to the story… it's pretty in name only.

Preface

Writing this book has proved an enjoyable, eye-opening and somewhat desultory experience, the more so given that I have been a committed fan since 1970 and have been able to converse regularly with Phil May and Peter Tolson, in particular, over the years. Deep down we know or suspect that our idols have feet of clay, although we hope that the blemishes and idiosyncrasies prove minor and remain concealed. This book unsurprisingly unearths some of the less salubrious aspects although it is certainly not intended to be sensationalist. Of course, occasionally this aspect rears its head, hopefully only within the context.

As I write this, The Pretty Things have existed for over thirty-eight years and during this time not a single book has been written about them and their strange and nebulous history. Somewhat naively I had imagined that all the parties concerned would be supportive towards such a chronicle and be prepared to assist in a book that should have been written many years ago. Sadly this has not happened, some members of the band and their management decided that it would be best not to assist my research. This, of course, is their legitimate right but is nonetheless unfortunate because certain aspects of the story will lack the insight that comes from personal recollection.

Over the years I have spoken with front-man Phil May on countless occasions. Phil has always been polite, friendly and willing to answer any questions and requests for information that I put to him. Previously these were in the context of a fan slavering at the altar of information, however, when that context changed to book research, he became at first diffident and then politely but decidedly non co-operative.

Originally Phil was interested in the concept of a book. He told me that their manager, Mark St John, had been pushing him to jointly write a tome detailing the band's turbulent history but that he wasn't interested. Phil's response was 'I've got better things to do. I'm not fucking Bill Wyman.' Phil explained that he had been approached by a number of writers, 'Some very well respected,' he stated, pointedly. He had refused all such requests as he felt they would not understand the ethos and nature of the band.

I make no apologies for writing this book, I have known the band since 1970 and have attended well over one hundred concerts. In researching the book I have spent many hundreds of hours interviewing or speaking to past and present members, one time managers, an ex-roadie, an ex-booking agent, four ex-producers and two of their former engineers as well as band member's ex-wives.

During the course of 1999 Phil had cause to revise his views and now entertains book-writing aspirations of his own. He believes that most rock biographies fail to tell the real story because the factuality tends to obscure the gist of it. To him, dates and chronology are for anoraks and archivists. He wants the drugs and the sex to be up front, in yer face together with the legendary on-the-road tales. What might be termed, the grim reality. Whilst this is certainly part of the story there are many other aspects and in my opinion they need to be viewed in perspective. Notwithstanding this, when Phil's book has been published I will be among the first to buy, read and enjoy it.

Somewhat bizarrely Phil seems wary of anything that might harm the band's legend. Having tried during numerous interviews to correct mis-reportings and various fabricated tales he now believes that these disparate myths need to be perpetuated. Maybe he feels they add to the band's mystique or possibly he believes that refutation will detract from the story and the aura that continues to surround them. Phil told Dick Taylor that I was a train-spotter but, as Dick said to me, 'Historical accuracy, where it's due, is not such a bad thing.' I agree with him.

Whilst undertaking research I have stumbled across numerous instances of factual inaccuracy, many of which continue to be propagated by the band and their management: glamorising the legend was always a mainstay of the music industry mavericks. Inventing the story or gilding the lily, tipping off the press about supposed indiscretions or instances of foul and loutish behaviour became *de rigeur* for certain managers and their bands and often it worked. Occasionally the hype backfired consigning accomplished and deserving bands to that musical dustbin labelled 'The Untalented Impostor'.

Unquestionably The Pretty Things do not need any further glamorising. The Pretty Things have lived the life and amazingly, unlike Led Zeppelin, The Kinks or The Small Faces, they are still around and playing, with their faculties substantially intact. They have already achieved cult status and glossy augmentations will ultimately only detract from the whole.

However I wish to offer a big thank you to Dick Taylor, Wally Waller, Jon Povey, Peter Tolson, Jack Green, Gordon Edwards and John Stax who have all proved particularly helpful and open.

By way of balance, a raspberry to Mark St. John, the band's current manager and self-styled saviour. Mark has proved a model of consistency, albeit in a negative way. This may be because of his wish to assist Phil with his mooted book or perhaps due to his lack of editorial control over this one.

'We have an agenda, which is pretty much a family affair and having anyone write a book is not, at present, a part of that agenda,' he wrote. Okay.

Drummer, Skip Alan believes that only someone within the 'family' should write the story and has not felt able to assist in this project.

Comments attributed to Phil and St John within this book are drawn from my various conversations with them, Phil in particular, and from the liner notes, articles and various interviews that both have provided over the years.

At Phil's request Pink Floyd guitarist David Gilmour and ex-booking agent Tony Howard have declined to share their memories.

A request to Bryan Morrison at Lupus Music for permission to quote from various lyrics was turned down. The band, (in this context it denotes Phil or Mark St John) asked Bryan to withhold permission.

Throughout this book's gestation I have sought neither approval nor any kind of band sanction, I wanted the editorial control that is so often lacking with these projects. There is always the suspicion that anything 'authorised' will steer clear of those areas deserving of a closer inspection. Authorised biographies are often whitewash jobs, embarrassments avoided, skeletons left secure in cupboards and a saccharine veneer applied to personalities. The Pretty Things story deserves better than this. It deserves the truth.

CHAPTER 1 – Dartford Delta Blues

Writing this tome nearly forty years down the line it is quite strange to recall that back in the early 1960s the breadth of appropriate behaviour was so finite. In this new 21st century we are used to being bamboozled by the latest marketing hype. Indeed, we come to expect it and feel almost cheated when the music charts or tabloid newspapers are not regularly invaded by legions of talent-challenged geeks.

Codes of behaviour that today are deemed acceptable or conveniently ignored were once primarily the province of a select band of English art school students. The impetus of their career was driven as much by their unwholesome image as their detonation of rhythm and blues babble.

Harold Wilson had yet to give his 'white hot technology' speech, in fact he had not even been elected when The Pretty Things first formed. Only recently had the first man been rocketed into space and the death penalty for murder was still in force. Post war privation had given way to optimism, a feeling that better things were just around the corner and that the Conservative constraints of the previous decade were about to be relaxed.

For the majority of children growing up in Britain in the late 1950s and early 1960s music tended to fall into one of three categories – the safe music of their parents, the sanitised warblings of white British wannabes with new slick hairstyles and names usually more appealing than the music itself or the new and raw imported sounds from America.

Whilst the music of Donald Peers, Glenn Miller or Joan Regan shouldn't automatically be denigrated the innocuous croonings of Mark Wynter and his ilk left a vacuum, both psychological and spiritual. Chuck Berry, Little Richard and an Elvis, who had yet to be tamed, provided the panacea for this schmaltz-sickness assisted by the occasional worthwhile home-grown talent such as Billy Fury.

The injection of skiffle had proved a relatively short-lived phenomenon although it served to galvanise many into a musical career. In good old music hall style the British 'rock & roll' stars were hurriedly pushed into the territory of the balladeer or that strange creature the 'all-round variety star', something that appeared to guarantee longevity. Cliff Richard, Tommy Steele and Adam Faith proving three examples of a would-be Elvis mutating into Dickie Henderson.

It's acknowledged that British art colleges spawned many of the country's most innovative bands and musicians of the last forty years. At college and university campuses in the early 60s small gatherings of students investigated the imported vinyl sounds of black American jazz, blues and rock 'n' roll. John Lennon and Stu Sutcliffe of the embryonic Beatles first made post-Quarrymen plans whilst at art school. Members of The Kinks, The Who, The Yardbirds and most famously The Rolling Stones also evolved and pursued their musical aspirations whilst there.

Thus it was that some thirty-eight years ago a couple of art school students and a similarly affected building site worker got together and began squeezing ragged, primeval sounds out of their basic and very primitive instruments. So began The Pretty Things. What started out as an art school diversion swiftly developed until aided by a surge of tabloid horror-speak headlines it mushroomed into an apparent level of malfeasance that tamed the Animals, buried the Zombies and kept the Stones honest.

Sidcup Art College is where Dick Taylor studied and eventually formed The Pretty Things, although today he is still remembered as much for being the guy who left and allowed Bill Wyman into the Rolling Stones. The story of how he formed a group called Little Boy Blue and the Blue Boys, with Mick Jagger, Alan Etherington and Bob Beckwith is well documented and outside the scope of this volume.

Dick was born Richard Clifford Taylor on January 28th 1943 in Dartford, Kent, although his childhood was spent in Bexleyheath. 'I lived all my youth in Bexleyheath, it's very much middling size pebble dash houses. Where Phil came from was more like a council estate.' Or as Phil suggested, 'Lower middle class'.

'Where I came from was built by my father,' explained Dick. 'If you imagine those 60s films of working class lads they really came from those sort of houses. Our house was just a fraction, if you are into the nuances of the class structure of the 60s, just a little bit better than the working classy type things'

After passing the Eleven Plus exam Dick attended Dartford Grammar School alongside fellow pupils Mick Jagger and future Pretty Thing, Brian Pendleton.

Dick's initial foray into music was behind a tiny drum kit. 'I was rattling away on my grandfather's drums. My granddad was really a fine musician he had drums, guitars, mandolins, banjos and violins and played the piano, so he played the whole caboodle. He didn't use the drums anymore which was this tiny little toy set sort of thing, well it wasn't a toy in those days it was a jazz set, very small, and I was playing those very badly. I did it with a few trad bands and things, very badly, and then switched to bass.'

Dick began playing in what became Little Boy Blue and the Blue Boys and after Tony Chapman responded to an advert for a bona-fide drummer he switched to bass guitar. Ultimately this was to prove unsatisfactory, Dick wanted to play six-string guitar, but by now they had joined up with Brian Jones which allowed a dual guitar formation with Keith Richards. So, in November 1962 Dick left, although he's at pains to point out that everything was amicable with no personality clashes. This event has allowed industry jesters their one chance to knock nice-guy Dick. After all, they chortle; someone must bear the responsibility for Bill Wyman.

'I could've ended up as Bill Wyman!' This is Dick's stock answer to the question that he has been asked so many times that it's become a real bore. 'At least I'm still alive,' he said. Dick accepts that had he stayed and tried to balance the joys and perils of success as a Rolling Stone it would have turned him into a very different person. Dick is very comfortable with who he is and has absolutely no regrets about leaving. Talking in 1999 to Ed Mabe, Dick purported to have forgotten why he left the Stones, 'Probably over nothing. It was more that I met Phil and he wanted to do the things I liked doing.'

Looking more like a trad-jazzer, with his jacket and goatee beard, Dick continued with his art studies, hoping to be accepted at the Royal College of Art, something that never materialised. Also at Sidcup Art College was Phil May. Phil had been on the periphery of the pre-Stones R&B sessions without exerting any particular influence. 'Phil was one year younger than me,' said Dick. 'Basically he was a mouthy kid who was into tennis.'

Phil had joined in various jam sessions with Dick, Keith and long time friend John Fullager and he recalled borrowing a book of R&B lyrics from Jagger who found his long hair quite amusing. There was a certain music scene happening as Dick recalled, 'All this stuff was going on and of course with me being with Little Boy Blue, and subsequently The Stones, it gave a certain 'oh, what are they up to'. We were listening to Monk, Mulligan, Miles Davis and Coleman and all that stuff as well as Howling Wolf.'

Dick remembered Phil constantly pestering him to start a band together. 'Gradually Phil and I started talking and we knew one another very well though Phil wasn't, for want of a better word, my best friend at art school. It wasn't I'm currently inseparable from Phil, far from it. It just gradually developed into this thing and then after I left the Stones it was 'come on, maybe we should start a band' and he wanted to do the singing. It was the better of two evils, him singing or playing guitar.'

Phil and Dick continued with the lunchtime music sessions which had quickly progressed from fun and noodling into more focused and realistic interpretations of American R&B. There was a nucleus, Dick playing electric guitar, Phil singing and blowing harp and John Fullagar on bass. John had been a primary school friend of Allen (Wally) Waller who had been Phil's best friend and had once lived opposite him in Sidcup. It was through the medium of Wally that at the age of fifteen John and Phil first met. John had decided to adopt the name Stax after his favourite record company, Phil later joked, 'It's lucky his favourite label wasn't Regal Zonophone.'

John hung around with Phil and Wally listening to folk music and playing with their Scalextric cars. Later they played around on John's banjo with Wally on his brother-in-law's semi-acoustic Gretsch. John remembered spending hours round Dick's house listening to his records and trying to play guitar. Eventually he accepted that he couldn't master six string and took up the relatively simpler bass. Dick had a big old French bass, an Emperor that John used at the lunchtime practice sessions.

He recalled that 'Roadrunner' was regularly played at Dick's house. It was a song they could always reliably fall back on when the sessions were not going well. Dick explained that although superficially similar to the Stones they were more primitive and tended more towards the Diddley beat. It wasn't simply a case of playing the music they liked, they couldn't hope to emulate the skills of Thelonius Monk and John Coltrane, so they turned to Chuck Berry and Bo Diddley who were easier to replicate.

Phil was born Phillip Dennis Arthur Kattner in Bexleyheath, Kent on November 11, 1944. Until the age of nine he lived in Sidcup with his uncle and aunt, Charlie and Flo May, who he believed to be his parents. Phil had never known his real mother or that he had a younger sister. His father was a sailor who had gone back to sea and disappeared. Over the next six years he suffered further family troubles. His mother entered his life wanting him back, causing a major upheaval when he was sent to live with her. Frequent house and school moves were suffered before at the age of fifteen he returned to Charlie and Flo in Erith. He once again got together with Wally Waller who was now an apprentice electrician, although by now their musical tastes had diverged. 'I was taken away from the people I lived with and had to go and live with my mother in another town,' Phil explained to Mike Stax. 'I was made a Ward of Court and wasn't allowed to communicate with those people I'd been brought up with. My childhood was spent being shunted round from house to house, school to school, due to parental fracturing, stepfathers, etc.'

The confusion of Phil's early family life exhibits a remarkable similarity to that of John Lennon whose own mother left and then returned after leaving John with her older sister Mimi.

'I used to go out with Phil's sister,' explained John Stax. 'I met his mum, she was living in Bexleyheath in a very strange little house and his sister was living there. For a few months I was going out with her, I was eighteen I suppose. Then we kind of drifted away again'. John confirmed that Phil never

The Pretty Things

talked about his family upheavals and it is only in recent years that he seems
to have come to terms with it.

Phil left secondary school aged 15 without any O levels and went directly
to Hornsey Art College before relocating to Sidcup College, something that
would prove impossible today. 'David Hockney told me he would never
have got into art school if he applied now,' Phil said, 'no A levels.'

'I spent five years at art school although nobody knew why I was there, not
even me,' Phil informed Penny Valentine some years later. Like many before
him and after, Phil found the attractions of music much more interesting
than the more restrictive regime of the art course.

When John Stax broke his arm and was unable to work, Phil and Dick
regularly smuggled him into the Sidcup Art College. He attended the art
classes and remained undetected for three months, receiving copious help
with his paintings. More importantly it enabled him to regularly join in the
lunchtime practice sessions. Talking to *Sounds*, in 1976, Phil explained how
they played in the changing rooms, next to the Principal's office. 'It all came
to a shuddering stop when half a dozen of his painting trophies fell on the
floor from the vibrations of the amplifier. He rushed in and had a nervous
collapse – suddenly realised he was spawning all these rock groups.'

The concept of a band was now becoming a reality but they decided that
another guitarist was needed to fill out the sound and to allow Dick to take
solos. An advert was placed in *Melody Maker*, which prompted one Brian
'Yeti' Pendleton to telephone the number provided. Dick answered the telephone and during the discussion it turned out that, like Dick and Mick
Jagger, Wolverhampton born Brian had also attended Dartford Grammar
School, although he had had been in the year below them and didn't know
Dick other than by sight. Brian had his own guitar, which he could play
more than competently, having been a member of various local jazz bands.
Additionally, and very importantly, he owned an amplifier. Dick recalled
with mirth that when the band first visited him at his parents house his
mother called out to Brian that a bunch of gypsies were at the door. In September 1963 he arrived to provide rhythm guitar and although at this stage
he only knew how to play jazz, Dick quickly taught him the basics of rhythm
and blues stylings.

For the band to obtain gigs they needed a name. The Stones had chosen
their name as a form of respect to blues icon Muddy Waters and one of his
most famous songs and similarly, the name The Pretty Things, was selected
in deference to Bo Diddley, their main influence at the time. The sardonic
impact of a bunch of scruffs, clearly unattractive to the general populace,
calling themselves 'pretty things', was not lost on them. Dick's memory is
slightly unclear but he believes that he and Phil sat in a pub reading though

a list of Bo Diddley titles and decided on Jerome and the Pretty Things. Jerome being Bo's friend and maraca wielding band member Jerome Green. After the first few gigs it was shortened to The Pretty Things, apparently Phil was tired of people calling him Jerome.

When Bob Dawbarn interviewed them in October 1964 for *Melody Maker* Phil told him. 'It was more or less a joke, we were laughing about some of the names on the pop scene and thinking that we would have to have one that stuck in everybody's mind. We thought of the Mojos – we hadn't heard of the group using that name – The King Bees and then Jerome and the Pretty Things.' He went on to say that the Station Hotel, Dartford advertised them as The Pretty Things and the name stuck.

Next they added another art school friend Peter Kitson on drums. John Stax's recollection is that Kitson was living in a tree on the common. They debuted at the Inferno, a club so close to the railway line that the whole building shuddered whenever a train thundered past. In fact the debut came as quite a shock to the band, they apparently had no idea that they were playing until they read a poster on the college wall advertising it. During the concert all the amps packed up apart from Brian Pendleton's so the whole band plugged into his. John Stax recalled the set being mostly Bo Diddley, Jimmy Reed and Chuck Berry stuff and for this somewhat inauspicious beginning the audience consisted mainly of students and friends.

By now it was November 1963, The Stones were lurking just outside the Top Twenty with their first single, a spikey version of Chuck Berry's 'Come On'. The Beatles 'She Loves You' was topping the charts and things were rapidly becoming fab.

Was it Dick's group? 'There wasn't really a leader,' he recalled, 'although we (Phil and Dick) were the motive power behind it.' John Stax considered otherwise suggesting that Dick thought he was the leader but acknowledged that although the three of them had started the band it was effectively Phil and Dick running things.

Dick was busy hustling gigs for the band and went to the Central School of Art to meet the President of the Student Union, Bryan Morrison who was studying furniture design. Bryan informed Dick that all future dances were booked and in the time-honoured way of dismissal asked him to leave his number for future consideration. 'I said, 'by the way what's the band's name?' 'The Pretty Things', he said, I said 'wow, what a fantastic name', gave him a fiver and booked them for the next weeks Christmas Dance.'

On the night of the gig Bryan watched in amazement. 'These guys arrived with their hair down past their shoulders, got on stage and strutted their thing, and I thought it was fantastic. I couldn't get a grant at the time and thought I might be able to make myself a tenner a week managing this lot.'

Bryan and the band talked at length and he persuaded them that he was capable of managing them. They ditched Bexley-based Neil Miller, an Art College contact who had been booking them, and teamed up with Morrison although they didn't follow the accepted route of formalising the arrangement with a proper written contract.

A week later, whilst playing at the Royal College of Art they were approached by Jimmy Duncan. Jimmy was an habitué of Denmark Street, a wannabe songwriter who turned out fairly typical Tin Pan Alley ballads. He introduced himself and spoke in a very persuasive manner, seeking to impress them with his nous and contacts. He appeared permanently frayed out on booze, but even so his powers of persuasion were such that it was agreed he should join a reluctant Bryan Morrison as co-manager. Jimmy liked a drink or ten and was full of grandiose stories and the band was concerned that he might be a joker full of big talk but, to the surprise of many, he genuinely did have contacts.

Things began to happen, the band had ten songs they could play, a manager they could leave the paperwork to and a roadie to hump and transport the gear. Lofty Riches had recently left the armed forces and after a brief period working in a holiday camp he got together with the Pretties. 'The first proper gig we did, where we all got in the van, we went up to Manchester. I remember all the old mums waving us off, thermos flask and sandwiches. Phil, it was his first big gig and he got pissed out of his head. It was a pretty horrible place, a real doss house. The room was partitioned off with this hardboard thing and the window was either side of it and someone had put a can to hold the window open to let the air in. I remember in the middle of the performance I saw this hand come through and grab the can and the window crashed down. We all came out of there scratching.'

At this stage it was inconceivable that the band was considered anything other than an addictive form of recreation as Dick explained. 'There was no thought of even the Stones making any bread. They were playing to 40 or 50 people, and it was building up, but as a minority thing, no one wanted to take over the business. They just wanted to play music.'

Although the Rolling Stones had enjoyed chart success with 'Come On', industry consensus was that the rock and beat group sounds were temporary blips like the late 50s 'Bobby' explosion in the US. That these bands and their music could be anything other than transient, mere throwaway tosh was evidenced by the post-Beatle eagerness to sign up virtually any collection of unkempt individuals who seemed capable of holding guitars and looking youthful.

Early in 1964 the Pretty Things signed a record contract with Phonogram subsidiary Fontana. Duncan had come up trumps with his industry contacts, although some in the band preferred the endeavours of Bryan Morrison. 'I wasn't totally convinced he was bullshit,' confessed Dick, 'but I knew Bryan probably better than anybody at that time and I had more confidence in Bryan's honesty than anybody else did. I would say he was at least as smart as Brian Epstein when it came to management.'

'He got us the contract with Fontana after approaching a load of various others, including EMI,' stated Pendleton. 'A drunken idiot,' was John Stax's blunt appraisal.

Morrison was distinctly unimpressed by Duncan's arrival but recalled that the band didn't want to be managed by a student – Bryan had yet to leave the Central School of Art. 'I didn't have a contract and the band felt that they needed a professional,' he chuckled. It turned out that Duncan was far from professional but this was not fully evident until some time later.

This embryonic Pretty Things had a severely limited repertoire and John Stax recounted one gig at the Royal Academy where the men were dressed in tuxedos and the girls wore long dresses. 'Typical upper-class snobs,' he sneered. The band only knew ten songs and having exhausted their set list they invited requests from the audience – but it had to be one of the ten. He remembered Phil repeatedly singing one verse, the only one he knew, of 'Too Much Monkey Business'. 'If ever there was a prima donna it was Phil, he was unbelievable.'

Dick: 'We had a guy who was playing drums who we subsequently had to say, 'Sorry, your drumming is not really up to much.' By now Viv Andrews had replaced Peter Kitson on the drum stool and within two months they had passed an audition session at Regent Sound, where they blasted a no-holds-barred version of 'Route 66'. Now fully-signed they were next told to turn up at Regent Sound studios to record their first single.

The song selected was an unlikely sounding Jimmy Duncan composition which Dick remembered as originally being a slow piano tune, a Denmark Street ballad in the style of crooner Matt Monroe. Phil recalled that it had no particular feel and that they applied a Bo Diddley beat to it. It clearly worked, it was called 'Rosalyn'.

CHAPTER 2 – Rosalyn

Within an astonishingly short period the Pretties had gone from art college enthusiasts to professional musicians with the dual thrust of a committed management team and a recording contract.

Bryan Morrison had visited the Fontana offices before the actual recording sessions to discuss the terms of the band's contract and he met with A&R boss Jack Baverstock. 'He gave me this contract to sign and I said that I would take it away to have it checked out. Baverstock responded, 'They're getting three and a half percent, and that's it.' This usurious but nonetheless common type of contract would haunt members of the band and their various managers for the next thirty-eight years. Baverstock had previously turned down The Kinks who ultimately signed to Pye on an even stingier three percent deal.

John Stax remembered the Marble Arch studios as being quite modern but housed in a huge old building built for orchestras with massive curtains draping the grey walls. It was also the studio where the Stones made many of their early records. Session drummer Bobby Graham was asked to take over for the recording session and as a result Viv Andrews left the band. The single's release was shelved until a replacement drummer could be found.

Jimmy Duncan had felt all along that an important ingredient was missing, that an experienced drummer was needed, to inject the necessary professionalism that the band so clearly lacked. He had one in mind – enter one Vivian St. John Prince. Viv Prince was a seasoned professional drummer who had played with his father's band, the Harry Prince Combo and boasted seven years experience with groups such as the Dauphin Street Trad Band and Carter Lewis and the Southerners. He had returned from Denmark, where had played jazz with The Cardinals before the small matter of a work permit had prompted an early exit. Upon returning to London he promptly joined Carter Lewis for gigs and studio work. Reputedly the very first rock star to be busted for drug possession, his frenetic style and maniacal personality provided the blueprint for drummer, Keith Moon, who spent months observing Viv at Pretties gigs before putting this accumulated lore to infernal effect in The Who.

Initially Viv needed quite a bit of persuasion to join the fold, he was busy with lots of session work and had already turned down a number of bands including The Kinks. By way of enticement Duncan offered him £40 per week and a brand new set of Ludwig drums. Viv remembered that the first week he received £8.

He also vividly recalled the band suffering the usual embarrassment of foolishly posed publicity shots where they marched along Denmark Street with bits of a Ludwig drum kit and hid in shop doorways.

Brian Pendleton stated, 'We had this guy playing for us called Viv Andrews, whose drumming was okay but he just couldn't handle being on stage.' Viv Prince most definitely could, his stage persona was manic, and so from the reticent Andrews they moved to the larger than life Prince.

Like all the groups of that era, The Pretty Things were despatched to Carnaby Street to buy 'uniforms' for their stage appearances – frilly shirts, leather waistcoats and suede jackets. Interestingly this does not seem to have given Phil any great concern, which is somewhat surprising given his often stated dislike of formality and dictat. Maybe the influence of the experienced and more conventional Duncan prevailed regarding the stage attire.

John Stax retained a vivid recollection of the 'uniforms', in particular the suede jackets, He recalled how the band used to pick on Pendleton who swiftly assumed the mantle of victim for their pranks. 'Mine got thrown in Trafalgar Square fountain… and everybody else's disappeared, but Brian always used to wear his and it was always perfect so we threw bananas at him one day. That's what it was like.' He related how Brian wanted to look smart and groomed so just before arriving at the gig they would wind down the car windows so his hair would be blown about and messed up.

'Smart', 'well groomed' and The Pretty Things have rarely been synonymous so perhaps a discriminating form of logic was at work there. In those barely post-Shadows days it was considered essential that bands take the stage wearing matching suits and preferably showcasing a snappy choreography reminiscent of the music-hall days.

It did not take long for individuality to sneak back into their stage-wear. 'You had to wear leather boots, just to be different, army greatcoats, all that kinda thing,' confirmed John Stax. 'We're wearing some pretty expensive gear now,' Viv confessed to *New Musical Express,* 'it costs a lot of bread. Some say we're scruffy, but that's only because they connect long hair with untidiness.'

Dick also recalled the tricks played on Brian Pendleton. 'If Brian would step on his guitar lead, (and accidentally unplug it) which he did regularly, Pete (Pete Watts, the roadie) would spend quite a lot of time trying to figure out what was wrong with Brian's amplifier and we all knew exactly what was going on, except Brian.' Lofty Riches cast doubt on the veracity of this story, he explained that Pete Watts was primarily the driver and the on-stage work was basically his province.

The Daily Mail provided a tremendous push with a half-page article on the band in early April. Bryan Morrison had invited journalist Robert Bickford to a gig and the write-up was the result. 'The *Mail* article was our first break,' said Bryan. 'Before that they were asking £15 or £20 an appearance. After that we were inundated with calls from clubs and agents.' Very shortly they had signed with an agent who guaranteed them £250 a week.

The Daily Mail informed its readers, 'with more humour than accuracy they call themselves The Pretty Things.' It also explained how Dick's red beard had earned him the nickname 'tufty'.

'Rosalyn' was co-written by Jimmy Duncan and Bill Farley, the engineer at Regent Sound, and was allegedly based on the late 1950s perennial 'Fortune Teller'. Released in June 1964, this two-minute eighteen-second rocker fairly belted along with a beefy descending bass line and Pendleton's wailing slide guitar directing the melody and complementing Phil's snarling vocal. This raw sound of disrespectful youth could easily have emerged during the 1976 blossoming of punk without sounding in the least dated and was clearly a source of inspiration for The Sex Pistols and their ilk.

'Dick worked out the solo and showed him what to do,' explained John Stax regarding Pendleton's distinctive slide guitar. 'Rosalyn' became one of the first chart songs to incorporate slide guitar, preceding the Stones more celebrated 'Little Red Rooster' by over five months, although Brian Jones did include some natty slidework on the Stones' first Top Twenty hit, 'I Wanna Be Your Man'. Blues artists such as Muddy Waters and Lightning Hopkins had perfected slide guitar techniques many years previously but it had yet to filter through to the popular music field.

The B-side choice was Willie Dixon's 'Big Boss Man', a powerful up-beat number, now an established blues favourite, and potentially a successful single in its own right.

In the studio and at gigs John Stax was still using Dick's old Emperor Bass. Later he moved on to a Star Bass which he hated, followed by a Rickenbacker and eventually a second-hand Fender Jazzmaster. The entire band played through Pendleton's 10 watt Vox amplifier until they bought two little blue amps from the Stones. Before Brian joined, they had been using a homemade amp and a homemade speaker. 'It had pink material across the front of it. It was horrible,' chuckled John. 'We had a 15 inch speaker inside it and we splashed out on a Miantsi echo unit. It was only a tiny thing and we were all going through it.' It has been suggested, somewhat unkindly, that Pendleton only got the gig because of his amp.

Phil still retains possession of one of the Harmony amplifiers, as Dick explained. 'They were the first real amplifiers they bought. One is still sitting around Phil's. I keep saying we should get it to the auction. We bought it after the Stones moved up to Vox. I keep saying to him retain all the original stuff in it and get it overhauled and stick it in an auction cause it's worth a fortune.'

The Granada Television pop programme *Ready Steady Go* invited the band to make their TV debut in support of the new single and they appeared, miming, as was the norm, during May. These were all day events as Viv Prince recalled. 'You had to go in the make up department… and you had to keep running through the numbers to make sure that the cameras were tracking you properly.'

The panel on television show *Juke Box Jury* disliked the record with deejay Pete Murray making typically offensive comments. They accordingly voted 'Rosalyn' a miss. 'Just what we hoped for,' sneered Phil.

Helped by this media exposure 'Rosalyn' sold 7,000 copies in its first week of release. During its third it entered the charts amidst a blitz of media condemnation that likened them to wild beasts – a hairier, more malign and infinitely more offensive version of The Rolling Stones. During a five week stay it peaked at 41, lurking some way below the first number one hits for the Stones' 'It's All Over Now' and The Animals' 'House Of The Rising Sun'.

The television appearances and frenzied newspaper reports brought an instant reaction. Longhaired, scruffy, and unapologetic they out-uglied the Stones, pounding out dark, dangerous, loud and, heaven forbid, sexual music. Phil was reported as having the longest hair of any man in Britain, a title he contested with the late Screaming Lord Sutch. The Pretties forbidding appearance served to legitimise the Rolling Stones, who by comparison were cleaner, tidier and better groomed. Those who wouldn't let their daughter marry a Rolling Stone wouldn't have risked her in the same youth club as The Pretty Things.

'You have to understand,' said Phil, 'that in those days a shot on TV of whiskey dripping down my chin on *Shindig* caused quite a stir. On TV every other group had to wear half an inch of make-up, but with us they put us on with no make-up which made us look very baggy under the eyes, as it would anybody. With The Kinks they would show a long shot with them looking very snazzy. With us it would be a close-up of us sweating.'

Shortly before the release of 'Rosalyn' *Record Mirror* had provided one of the first band interviews when Peter Jones wrote a confused introduction nominating Vic Taylor as lead guitarist. They also published an out-of-date photograph which included previous drummer Viv Andrews.

The Sunday Times ran its infamous colour magazine article in July of that year. A surprisingly in-depth three page feature by Frances Wyndham which carried a sub-heading, 'the appearance of pop groups becomes increasingly bizarre.' By way of emphasis Bryan Morrison recounted that they had received a letter from actor Kenneth More who was organising a charity event for The Variety Club of Great Britain. More innocently began his letter 'Dear Girls...'

The bands' name was again a central point of focus and Phil explained, 'we also intended it as a jest. We'll leave it for the public to agree whether we're pretty or not.'

Jimmy Duncan added, 'There are two main problems we are working on now. One is this imitation of the Rolling Stones thing. And the other, to break down the image of Phil as the leader. He gets most of the publicity but in a way Dick is the leader of the group as he plays lead guitar.'

Phil: 'The only way the national papers would write about rock then was either if someone was arrested or with a photo of you washing your hair with a caption saying, 'you won't believe it but they actually wash their hair.'

The band lived together in a leased flat at 13 Chester Street in the middle of plush upmarket Belgravia. The predictable establishment backlash brought near eviction from the flat although, paradoxically, it was an Independent Television programme that saved the day. Viv Prince recalled the residents getting together a petition to get them evicted and the band and their friends cobbling together a counter-petition. Bryan Morrison maintained that the eviction threat was another publicity stunt and that the lease simply expired. Speaking in 1998 he said. 'We did it for publicity. We were the ones that created the chucking things out of windows, the tearing hotels apart that Oasis still do today.'

Phil and Dick disagree, with Phil stating, 'I don't think those things were put in.' However he did recall a lot of hostility and hysteria from the fans. Brian Pendleton explained how audiences varied in their response. 'Down south the audiences could be really cold towards you, but up north it could be total chaos when you walked on stage.'

13 Chester Street, immortalised in a track on their debut album, was a four-storey property, owned by the Duke of Westminster, situated just around the corner from Buckingham Palace. The whole band lived there although, for a while, Viv stayed at PJ Proby's Belgravia flat where frequent visitor Phil would spend hours making expensive transatlantic calls on PJ's telephone. Phil remembered they were always having parties and suffering police raids and that the house was always full of debs and high-class women. 'We were eventually kicked out because of all the comings and goings at all hours of the day and night. When the lease came up they kind of kicked us out because they thought we were basically bringing down the tone of the neighbourhood.'

'The lot across the road messed it up for us,' explained Viv in March 1965. 'We didn't make that much noise, really. Only when we knew we had to get out did we have any real loud parties.'

The band continued to suffer for their appearance with matters exacerbated by the frenzied reporting. Phil recalled frequent hotel aggravations. 'We used to book our rooms a month in advance, but by the time we turned up they told us a mistake had been made and there were no rooms for us.'

Alan Clayson recalled that the band were invited onto a religious television programme. 'They were once hauled in to answer clerical criticism, but their verbal contributions were hastily restricted when they began upsetting the programmes intentions by using long words, talking correct and generally acting intelligent.'

During a low brow interview one music paper asked Phil the typically silly questions about his loves and hates that today's boy bands continue to endure. He told them he loved, 'Small quiet blondes, frilled shirts, prawn curry with onion sauce and reading Tennessee Williams.' His hate list was somewhat larger and included, 'Bowler hats, ties, ice cream, so-called modern art, any sport except tennis, pear drops and anyone with any kind of prejudice.'

Bryan Morrison secured the band a Tuesday night residency at The 100 Club, Oxford Street, previously the province of The Animals. Lofty remembered that at the first gig only about ten people were in the club but fairly quickly it became packed and queues were forming round the corner. John Stax recalled that one night Alexis Korner sat in with the band. 'Dick was really pissed off because he hated Alexis for some reason. Alexis was trying to keep turning his amp up, trying to cover up Dick and Dick was sort of hopping about trying to turn up his amp.' John remembered a similar incident at another residency, the Manchester Cavern. 'The Stones were playing in town one night and we were doing a late spot. Jagger and Keith sat in for a couple of numbers, I think that we did 'Don't Lie To Me', and Richards was trying to bloody take over the lead on it. Dick did not like that at all and he actually played the most brilliant lead I'd ever heard him play, really great. There was something between them. I don't know what it was.'

Talking in 1999 Dick attempted to deflate these views. 'I can't say I detested Alexis Korner, but I thought Alexis was kind of a strange character. He wasn't the great blues man that everybody... you know he's so groovy and everything but he wasn't a particularly good guitar player or particularly good singer, its just things that went on around him. A very catalytic figure. I don't think I ever hated Alexis. There was a certain element of exploitation with the Stones particularly... in hindsight I think he did a very good job of publicising all those people and also having met him a few years later I thought, 'yeah, I like Alexis really'. He was one of those characters where you never really knew whether he relied on talent or he relied on just being who he was. John Mayall and him came and sat in with us but after three notes Alexis broke a string which was very curious. I always thought that he pinged the string on purpose but wasn't quite sure. I wasn't irritated by Keith coming up at all, I was delighted that he came up I remember that distinctly because Keith and Mick came and did about three songs with us. It was in a club in Manchester and it's always stimulating to have someone come up and play with you and you always try and do extra well if they are playing the same instrument as you.'

Writing some thirty six years later in the *Latest Writs* liner notes Phil contended that Alexis tried to kill off both the Pretties and the Stones, that he considered them non-deferential and non-conformist in much the same way that the 'progressive' musicians in the 70s viewed the burgeoning punk movement.

Dick and the rest of the band were on friendlier terms with Rolling Stone Brian Jones, and on September 25, he turned up at a party held at 13 Chester Street to celebrate the group's first anniversary. Jones felt more comfortable with The Pretty Things than he did with members of his own band but was becoming increasingly touchy. Early one morning he returned to his flat with Phil having enjoyed a night out. The commissionaire remarked, 'Hi Brian, Hi Mick' and Brian went wild and reared up. 'This isn't Mick Jagger, this is Phil May!'

Record Mirror's Peter Jones interviewed Phil and Viv and the conversation turned to the media outcry over their hair and behaviour. Viv: 'This lack of TV is hard, but producers don't seem to trust us, or something. We know we're popular right now – you can prove that by checking figures wherever we play. But the whole telly scene is playing hard to get. Of course, the producers side of it isn't hard to understand – remember the Rolling Stones haven't yet had a Palladium date.' Phil complained about the reaction to their appearance. 'Our hair, our clothes, leads to trouble, you know. In pubs we get shepherded to the public bar – or right outside if we're unlucky. People do hate us. Those who are aware of us in the adult classes hate us more than the Stones. In fact, there are signs that the Stones are being more accepted by older folk.'

Although Morrison and Duncan were the managers, Phil and Dick retained distinct views regarding the songs they should record. Bryan had become very friendly with Donovan who played him his new song 'Tangerine Eyes'. Bryan sent it off to numerous publishers with the feeling that it would be picked up and become a hit. One publisher friend called and asked if he had heard of Bob Dylan – Bryan hadn't – he then proceeded to play him 'Mr Tambourine Man'. Bryan exclaimed that it was Donovan's, but the publisher countered, 'no, it's Dylan's song, Donovan's copied it.'

According to Bryan he was absolutely certain that 'Mr Tambourine Man' would be a big hit and he obtained a six-week option on it for the Pretties.

'For six weeks I kept at them, they just wouldn't listen. The publishers told me that a band called The Byrds had recorded a version but they preferred to have The Pretty Things release it and they gave me another two weeks.'

Bryan contends that Phil and Dick still refused opting instead for the Johnny Dee song 'Don't Bring Me Down'. Nine months later, in June 1965, The Byrds crashed the charts everywhere with their version.

Dick felt that Bryan might have been confusing Dylan's song with 'Tangerine Eyes'. He disclosed that Donovan had offered 'Tangerine Eyes' to The Pretty Things but shortly after, when he heard 'Mr Tambourine Man', he thought the similarity was a bit too embarrassing and the idea was dropped. Bryan, however, is categorical that his version is correct.

In her autobiography, Marianne Faithfull described the 1965 meeting between Dylan and Donovan at which 'Tangerine Eyes' was played to the astonishment and embarrassment of the assembled throng. She described it as 'Mr Tambourine Man' with different words. Donovan himself accepted the situation as he later informed *Record Mirror*, 'I didn't ever record it because I didn't want to steal it.'

Dick remains sceptical about the story, 'I think Phil would definitely have jumped at the idea of recording a Dylan song.' Lofty Riches supported Bryan Morrison's version saying, 'they turned it down flat.'

John Stax also took a different slant to Dick recalling that in 1964 Phil did not like Dylan's music because it wasn't R&B. He also recalled Morrison offering them a song but thought it was 'Tangerine Eyes' and not 'Mr Tambourine Man'.

The chronology of this period makes it difficult to be sure which if any version is correct. By the time The Byrds released their version the Pretties had released three further singles. Also, Dylan's album *Bringing It All Back Home*, from which the song was lifted was not released until March 1965, making Dick and John's scepticism seem well-founded.

The Pretty Things actual follow up single 'Don't Bring Me Down' entered the charts in October 1964. 'This was definitely recorded at Fontana with Jack Baverstock,' recollected John Stax. 'A real ancient person who was giving us bad songs to do. He was forced onto us by Fontana.' Helped by another mimed *Ready Steady Go* appearance earlier in the month it topped at number 10, during an eleven-week stay, and remains their highest and longest lasting UK chart entry. It was written by Johnny Dee and was reportedly sold by him for a pittance, £25 has been mentioned, a story Phil uses as a warning tale regarding the music business. Dee allegedly modelled himself, sartorially on PJ Proby and, although British, affected a Stateside accent and claimed to have American Indian blood, although it is suggested that the actual tribe changed with a bewildering regularity.

Record Mirror exclaimed, 'not only do The Pretty Things look like exaggerated Rolling Stones – that's what they sound like too. It's a pounding tortuous vocal with loads of R&B flavour and shouting vocal. Harmonica and jerky guitar beat with pounding drum work setting the whole item off. Quite a good tune and the performance is impeccable.'

'Don't Bring Me Down' suffered condemnation and a radio ban in the States for supposed sexual innuendo. The offending matter being the line 'I laid her on the ground.' Consequently a bowdlerised version was released by the little known Her Majesties Subjects, which made number 5 in Florida. Another band, The Jades from Forth Worth, also scored a regional hit with their version.

The single's B-side featured the first original band composition, 'We'll Be Together', credited to May/Taylor/Stax. It proved to be a basic blues performed without any great urgency and remains fairly unmemorable.

To promote the single the band were booked to join the PJ Proby headed package tour that wandered across Britain during December.

Brian Pendleton had retained his job at an insurance company but had taken so many days off for gigs and sessions that he was presented with an ultimatum – the band or the job. To the dismay of his family he chose the band.

Shortly before Christmas an appearance on *Beat Box* marked their live TV debut. The live performance was something of a rarity as most TV appearances consisted of badly performed lip-synchs with guitars often not even plugged in.

Around this time Fontana issued an EP hoping to capitalise on the Christmas rush, and their marketing guys imaginatively titled it 'The Pretty Things'. In the accepted tradition it collected the first two singles and their B-sides.

Back again at Regent Sounds they worked on the follow up and 'Get Yourself Home', another Johnny Dee Song, was recorded. As is often the case in an industry driven by profit and less interested in quality, the song bore a striking similarity to the previous single 'Don't Bring Me Down' and was disliked by all the band members. It was deemed unsuitable for the single and as nobody was really interested John Stax took the acetate home. When he emigrated to Australia in 1970 it went with him. Eventually, in 1992, it was released in Australia as a limited edition single on the Dog Meat label. Each of the singles carried a John Stax signature, a poster and a John-painted Pretty Things decal based on the original painting that Phil and Dick had emblazoned on Lofty's 'roadie van'.

John Stax suggested that the song was recorded before 'Don't Bring Me Down' and was turned down. He claimed that Johnny Dee, who was present, hurried away and came back with 'Don't Bring Me Down'. This view is at odds with those of the other group members who insist that it came after 'Don't Bring Me Down'.

Although rejected by The Pretty Things 'Get Yourself Home' was picked up by fellow Morrison act The Fairies, containing one John 'Twink' Alder, and reputedly produced by Jimmy Duncan – it wasn't a hit.

John Stax: 'I used to share a flat with Twink, who was the drummer, and we were always close, the Fairies and us, always friends. We moved in the same circles. They knew Johnny Dee and when we scrapped that song they decided to make a single out of it.' The Fairies version was released in March 1965 and *Melody Maker's* guest reviewer, Andrew Loog Oldham declared, 'This is terrible. The song's nowhere and I hate everything about it. It could be a hit, maybe – a lot of rubbish gets in the chart.'

Twink claimed that The Fairies were offered 'Don't Bring Me Down' before The Pretty Things but turned it down because of the laughable lyrics.

The song chosen for the follow-up was 'Honey I Need', attributed to May, Taylor, Smithling and Button. Dick explained the confusing writing credits. 'Well, there was a guy I went to school with called Ian Sterling, who was with Phil and I at art school, that accounts for the 'Ling.' Another guy, Peter Smith, I was at Central Art School with and that accounts for the Smith and we shared a flat at Highgate with John Warburton a friend of Pete's (Button). One day Pete said I've got a bit of an idea and we knocked it into 'Honey I Need' very swiftly. We just sat around with a guitar and wrote it between us. Because we were all there we decided to put all our names on it. Quite who wrote how much, I'm not sure.'

'I Can Never Say' continued the canny industry-wide tradition of ensuring that only self-penned numbers were used for B-sides. This allowed the writers an equal share of moneys generated by sales of the generally superior A-side. Unlike 'We'll Be Together' this one was credited to all the band members and affected an odd, almost Country & Western feel recalling the sound of Joe Brown and the Bruvvers.

'Honey I Need' entered the charts on 25th February 1965 and remained there for eleven weeks reaching number 13. *Ready Steady Go* had given the band another single showcase some weeks earlier which again involved lip-synching and another Granada programme, *Scene At 6.30*, provided further promotion. This, the first self-composed Pretty Things single competed with 'The Last Time', coincidentally the first self-penned Rolling Stones single. *Melody Maker* grudgingly commented, 'crudely commercial and it's all happening. Great aggression but it doesn't quite get off the ground. But a good seller.'

Although an up-tempo number unusually it used Dick's twelve-string Gibson acoustic, sounding sufficiently twangy that it's difficult to differentiate it from an electric, and neither did it detract from the rocky feel. Like 'The Last Time' the guitar was layered with echo and provided a counter for Stax's pounding bass. Dick recalled how the acoustic could be thrashed in the studio without having to worry about recording level tolerances.

The Pretty Things continued to receive far more column inches for their appearance than for the actual music and interviewed by Norman Jopling of *Record Mirror* Phil gave vent to his disdain. 'The fact is that most people who really stare at us in the street and make rude remarks are the same people who just dress in absolutely anything, and have their hair cut in any old style – usually short back and sides. They're just gawking, ignorant plebs. It doesn't worry us at all. But what would worry us would be if people who do take care of their appearance start looking at us and make remarks. Then we'd know something was wrong. I think that if we hadn't had success we'd still be dressing and wearing our hair in the same way. Because as we're from Art Schools we'd spend all our grant money on clothes and not be able to afford a haircut. It'd be even longer then!'

Jopling reported that the band's favourite artists were the Beach Boys, Bobby Bland, Marvin Gaye, Dionne Warwick, The Animals and of course, The Beatles. When he brought up the oft quoted subject of beat groups going out of style, Phil's response was unequivocal if slightly paranoid. 'It's all a plot by the managers who haven't got any big groups and the press who are fed up that the beat boom has been going on so long. After all, they didn't mind writing about it when it was starting but they find it a drag now so they want to finish it. Anyway, there are more group discs in the charts than ever before.'

In March, *Disc's* Penny Valentine interviewed Phil who spoke candidly, about his loves and hates: 'As Dionne Warwick and Dusty Springfield blared from the hi-fi Phil sat and talked to me about the group which has undoubtedly taken the lead as the pop rebels and the people parents hate. Phil is practically exactly the opposite of the way you'd expect a Pretty Thing to be. He is effusively polite, he continually apologised for not picking me up from the station, and extremely talkative in a charming way. 'As a group we hate pony things', their expression for things they don't like.

'I suppose I'm the great tearaway, I love night clubs and staying out all night at places like the Ad Lib. Sometimes Dick Taylor will come with me but usually we all go our different ways. We do it purposely because no matter how friendly you are you need time apart after living together in cars and hotels all the time. I like foreign films, not rubbish stuff, but films by Bergman and Antonioni. I also like books by Norman Mailer and James Baldwin. I make time to read, it's important. Viv Prince likes films but with a lot of noise otherwise he falls asleep, oh, and funny shorts, because he doesn't have time to fall asleep. It's very embarrassing going to the cinema with Viv because he snores all the time, we cover him up with a newspaper. John Stax likes films too, horror ones. He also likes horror construction kits. He has a very sick mantelpiece covered with plastic horror-men which he has made himself. Dick is more like me, and Brian Pendleton? He's very quiet and saves his money, he has the right approach I think.'

'The Dionne Warwick LP came to an end and Phil put it on again to his favourite track, 'Lord, What Are You Doing To Me'. He says that each week he has a different favourite track and he thought the words to the songs were knockout.'

'These are the only discs I can listen to now. The groups? No, only The Beatles because they're something special, and we admire them as people. They understand this business, they enjoy it and that's the right thing to do. We enjoy it and we love the feeling of being liked, it's tremendous when you are on stage and the audience is with you. I would hate to be a failure. We ad-lib tremendously because otherwise it's such a drag having a set routine night after night.

Penny informed the readers that, 'The boys have been living at home with their parents for the past few months but in a few weeks they will all be moving into a London flat.'

'We had to come back home,' confessed Phil, 'because we were all nervous wrecks after the flat in Chester Street. The washing piled up in every room and the whole thing was ridiculous. For instance, there used to be about fifty people at a time in that flat and we used to know about five of them, then I'd go to bed tired out after an evenings gig and suddenly the bedroom door would fly open and twenty people would conga over the bed and out through the door again. It was like a madhouse. Well this time it's just going to be a place to live, a home you know, and while we're away responsible people will look after it so nobody can get in.'

Pop Weekly reported that the band had been earning £1,000 per week even before 'Rosalyn' and now it was even more.

Having secured hits with their first three singles the band was ushered back into the studio to start work on their debut album. Straight away there was a problem, Viv Prince was vomiting and falling over. Fontana chief Jack Baverstock couldn't cope with what he termed 'A bunch of animals' and swiftly departed. 'He walked out after half an hour with us,' remembered Phil. Dick, as always more precise with the facts and less interested in the myth, suggested that they actually laid down four tracks with Baverstock before he withdrew. Baverstock's departure left session drummer Bobby Graham to take over the reins as producer. Bobby was more sympathetic to the band's sound preferring to catch the ferocity and raw attack rather than sacrifice feel for the sake of 'correct' production technique. Bobby also sat behind the kit on 'Baby Doll' after Viv had yet again passed out. Graham had recently released his own drum-based single 'Skin Deep', which, like most novelty releases, failed to register. He had previously played behind Mike Berry in The Outlaws and at this time was part of a session team put together by Shel Talmy which also included Jimmy Page and John Paul Jones.

John Stax recalled the sessions. 'This old grey guy in a suit didn't know what R&B was, didn't know what blues was. Anyway they dumped him on us and we never agreed with anything he ever said, nothing. So weapons were drawn straight away. We hated him and he hated us, as most of Fontana did for some reason.'

The album was pretty much a run through of The Pretty Things live set, although 'Roll Over Beethoven' and 'I Can Tell' were omitted. Also surprisingly missing was 'Route 66', the perennial live favourite and their audition song for Fontana. The band recalled that Baverstock suggested quite a few inappropriate songs for them to consider, which naturally they didn't. In typical early sixties fashion the album was pieced together in two days. On first listening it exuded a primitive turbulence, a disdain for musical niceties and frills and an emphasis firmly on percussion-heavy commitment. Even the Stones and Animals were not this rough edged.

Both Phil and Dick were extremely dissatisfied with the album. Dick recollected that he wanted to go and throw himself off a bridge whilst Phil thought it sounded like anarchy and didn't compare with the comparative technical proficiency of the Stones. 'It felt lashed together and it sounded like it,' said Dick.

Lofty the roadie agreed: 'I always thought a lot of their records sounded great in the recording studios but when they actually came out on the vinyl, and you had those crappy little radios, they sounded crap. There were some bands that had the ability to make their records sound good on the radio. The Pretty Things, and this is my own personal opinion, never seemed to sound good over the radio and on the old record players we used to have then.'

John Stax explained that the studio was designed for orchestras and they recorded in one corner of a vast room. One reason, perhaps, for the brightness and echo that filtered through to the vinyl. The cellophane, as Phil called it.

Although riotous and unlike anything that the British R&B scene had yet offered up it was not as 'lashed together' as Dick suggested. It worked admirably as a testament to the band's live act and in those days all the edges were rough, that was their raison d'être – no frills R&B.

Like many a future live performance the album opened with 'Roadrunner', not a variant on the beep-beep version cut by Bo Diddley but a raspier slide-driven affair peppered with a screeching Phil May vocal. The next track, 'Judgement Day', was credited as a group arrangement of a Bryan Morrison song. The song had actually been around for years having originated in America before Morrison or any member of the band was born and, as one band member stabbed, 'Morrison didn't have a musical bone in his body.' Years later the credits would be altered to an arrangement of a traditional song, although Morrison retained a credit as co-arranger.

Track three was '13 Chester Street', named after the legendary Belgravia residence, and was an unashamed rip-off of Slim Harpo's song 'Got Love If You Want It'. That many of Harpo's original lyrics remained unaltered only compounded the audacity. Of course, the 'transfer of ownership' of American blues songs is nothing new in the seedy and rapacious world of music. The Small Faces and Led Zeppelin were exponents of a similar filching of Willie Dixon's catalogue and even Marc Bolan managed to twist a Howling Wolf song into his T-Rex hit 'Jeepster'. 'The folk process', as Jimmy Page once described the adaptation of old blues tunes. '13 Chester Street' had an irritating quirkiness about it much of which was due to the strange, unrhythmic percussive tapping and clapping, which sounded like a cat ensnared within a cardboard box. John Stax explained that Viv tapped his sticks on a plastic chair on this one.

Bo Diddley, unsurprisingly, was heavily represented, being responsible for four of the twelve tracks. As well as 'Road Runner', he supplied 'Mama Keep Your Big Mouth Shut', 'She's Fine She's Mine' and 'Pretty Thing'.

Chuck Berry received two composition credits, 'Oh Baby Doll' and 'Don't Lie To Me', although the latter song was actually composed by Tampa Red. The album also contained two Pretty Things originals, if we ignore the stolen '13 Chester Street', 'Unknown Blues' and the single, 'Honey I Need'. The Beatles were leading the way for artists to compose their own material instead of the tradition of using the Denmark Street and Tin Pan Alley hacks, and like Jagger and Richards the Pretties were encouraged to write their own.

The band were offered a number of other songs including quite a few from P J Proby's friend Kim Fowley, as Viv explained. 'We ran through a few of Kim's songs but none of them were really suitable. Oh there were loads of songs that people used to sling at us. We would try and change them to an R&B format, but a lot of the songs were too musically intense. Too much like Glady's Knight & the Pips and stuff like that.'

Talking to Trevor Hodgett, in *Blueprint* magazine, Phil stated 'Guys like Alexis were sitting in basement clubs copying records faithfully and if you played a Jimmy Reed song double speed that was sacrilege. It was like reading the Bible backwards. And we said, 'Fuck it, we're eighteen, we're on amphetamines and it sounds better to us at this speed.'

Melody Maker offered the opinion that, 'It's easy to shrink at their appearance but when it comes to listening to an LP it's the music of The Pretty Things that's on trial. Long hair and off-beat clothes cannot permeate record grooves. In the field it explores – British R&B – it's good. Instrumentally The Pretty Things are strong, vocally they are okay but not distinctive enough. The tracks here jump along pretty well and some are good, crude and bluesey.'

Allen Evans, of *New Musical Express*, proffered a more favourable opinion. 'Here is a raver of an R&B LP, exploiting many new sound effects and some expressive, often relaxed, sometimes hysterical singing. Typical of the forward outlook of the group is 'Unknown Blues', written by themselves and featuring weirdly appealing harmonica (from John) and guitar (Dick).'

Record Mirror showed even greater enthusiasm. 'The debut album from The Pretty Things definitely comes up to expectations. Half an hour of vivid ear-blasting music. Basically blues-tinged, with some good instrumental work going on and of course a stunning powerful vocal. There's a lot of Bo Diddley influence here – after all the group took their name from a Bo disc – and several other top R&B names on some title credits. Good sleeve notes to a lively album which although it is rough at the edges proves the Things to have a great deal to offer.'

Eponymously titled, the album entered the charts in late March 1965, and remained there for 10 weeks, hitting a high of number 5 in the *New Musical Express* chart. Secure in the top slot stood the second Stones album which itself had replaced *Beatles For Sale*.

The footnotes for the US release, also on Fontana, were written in that wacky, semi-condescending style prevalent at the time. Dick, we are told, 'Doesn't care much for food, claiming he's too busy to eat.' Brian Pendleton studied 'flute, bugle and piano,' and John Stax is described as 'adept on the harmonica and violin.' When asked thirty-five years later about his prowess on the violin he just laughed.

The band was fast achieving a reputation for wild shows where anything was possible. In 1985, Phil, in correspondence with Mike Stax, the editor of *Ugly Things*, confirmed the scenes at a typical Pretties gig. Viv Prince crawling around the stage, not even playing his drums. Phil rolling around on the floor and generally going insane. Occasionally John Stax switching to harmonica and Brian Pendleton transferring to bass, usually for 'She's Fine She's Mine' and other Bo Diddley numbers. A variation on the recording sessions where Dick would occasionally switch to bass and John Stax to harp if they wanted the song in one take. Dick often devised some bass lines and for reasons of simplicity he would play these at recording sessions.

Live they were louder and more into improvisation than the early singles and albums would suggest. Viv rarely played the same way twice and Dick was moving into extended solos which meant that often songs would last for ages.

The stage mayhem was best personified by the scenes at the Blokker Festival in Holland, held in mid-April 1965. Early evening Dutch television viewers were astounded by the sight of John Stax on his knees playing bass and Phil on his knees playing harmonica then rolling around on stage and splitting his trousers, like a rabid version of PJ Proby. Phil had been asked to tone down his act, to no avail, and viewer outrage resulted in an avalanche of telephone calls to the station. The following days Dutch newspaper headlines were vintage *Sun* – 'the scum of the earth' and 'long-haired scum, not wanting to work at all.'

'It was televised live,' stated Brian Pendleton, 'and I just couldn't believe the way the crowd were having a go at the police. I remember reading that they took it off the air after four or five numbers.'

Bryan Morrison explained how for six months he had been at them to pump up their act. 'I told Staxxie to get down on his knees and Phil to roll on the floor and Viv to get out from behind his drums and drum on people's heads. 'Why?' They asked. Because I saw Bill Haley do it and the crowd went crazy. They finally did it at Liverpool or Manchester and the crowd did go wild.'

Were the Pretties yobbos and alcohol-swilling deviants? Brian Pendleton placed the behaviour into some sort of context. 'Well let's put it this way… we did do over a few hotel rooms and stuff like that but no more or less than the average rugby club. It was mainly our image that set us apart and brought us to the attention of the press.'

More than thirty years later, when bands like The Butthole Surfers, Dead Kennedys and Throbbing Gristle are accepted with barely a raised eyebrow it can be difficult to understand the reaction caused by this bunch of hairy, sneering ruffians. Calling themselves Pretty Things only fanned the flames. This was food for the media and not just the gutter press. 'They have been described as a cross between cavemen and the ugliest creatures on the scene.' reported *Pop Weekly*.

The band continued to suffer for their unprepossessing appearance, their hair in particular which attracted both amusing and offensive comments. Compared with the Beatles and even the Stones they were unruly looking. No loveable mop tops with a grinning and harmless Ringo in tow, instead a surly quintet with a menacing wild-eyed Viv. Phil in particular looked feminine with shoulder length strands and this caused abusive comments and gestures and even an attack by pensioners at a motorway café.

Frequently the band had to fend off jealous boyfriends and also girls intent on snipping off locks of hair or removing items of clothing. It was not abnormal to find the band escaping from groups of youths looking to bash the cissy longhairs. One such episode ended with roadie Philip Andronicus (Phil The Greek) being fined £25 for using a shotgun to menace a crowd of yobs who were looking to attack them.

'They were pretty raw,' recalled Lofty. 'They had crap instruments as well and played through the one amp with a few speakers in wooden boxes. I don't think they were particularly good, early. By then, the Stones were getting pretty good. But I reckon as they got on, 1965-1966 maybe, they were better than the Stones. They certainly had more vision.'

John Stax recalled with amusement that Lofty would sit on the amps shaking his head and saying, 'that's it, they're finished. They've had it now'. Apparently, Lofty announced this all the time.

The comparisons with the Stones emanated from their shared Bo Diddley/ Jimmy Reed/Chuck Berry origins and Dick's early tenure on bass. However, a careful listen to the Stones 1964-66 output shows a greater musical kinship with The Beatles than the Pretty Things. A lot of the Stones music was of the medium slow variety showing very little similarity with the Pretties uncompromising high-energy onslaught. Not until *Get The Picture* and *Emotions* did the Pretties noticeably lower the tempo and move into that typical sixties zone where quaint melody and sparse production allowed many otherwise diverse groups to temporarily tread the same musical territory.

A song like 'Roadrunner', also covered by The Animals and the Zombies, to name just two, gives support to the view that the Pretties raw sound carried a more committed and unfettered attack. An assault unsweetened by a sugary veneer or mellowed down production values – in reality the kind of description lavished on the punk uprising of the late 70s. The Animals version relied heavily on Alan Price's organ and offered a bouncy, poppy interpretation that recreated the cheerful feel of the Diddley original. The Zombies version was, superficially, the same as the Pretties yet it failed to ignite or propel and left the listener with a feeling of having missed something.

Phil turned reviewer for *Disc* and enthused about a Bob Dylan concert. 'I'd never seen Dylan live before and I was tremendously impressed, he knocked me out.' The feeling was reciprocal with Marianne Faithful confirming that Dylan had made the journey to Britain specifically to see his favourite bands, The Beatles, Stones, Pretty Things, etc.

Phil has never been short of an opinion or afraid to use a sentence when a word would do and in May he announced to *Disc* readers. 'Opening a shop is something we've been thinking about. I had a spate of doing some clothes for myself once but I took so long when I wanted some new clothes in a hurry I just rushed out and bought them, but we don't like the style of shop things much,' he said, flicking a bright pink and red tie. The only bright colour among an outfit of dark shirt and trousers and suede shoes. 'Designing for girls will be especially interesting when we get around to it. I think girls should dress to suit their personality, not the terrible fad of following fashion. I would design with a particular girl in mind, I think you've got to. Actually the most marvellous thing I ever saw was Anita Ekberg wearing a red dress.'

Phil continued to extemporise on other avenues he intended to explore. 'I'd like to open a night club. Not here, because that isn't the scene, but in Ireland or somewhere like that.' Interviewer, Penny Valentine reported that she and Phil were heavily engrossed in a discussion about foreign films, 'Phil admitted that at the moment his main ambition was to be an actor.'

In other interviews throughout the mid sixties he is variously reported to like vodka and beer (presumably not in the same glass), wearing green corduroy caps, trousers with a different coloured stripe on each leg and eating sausage, egg and chips.

Carol Ledger, then aged 15, was a frequent guest at parties that the band threw or was thrown out of. She recalled Dick sitting quietly, resistant to the alcoholic and chemical excesses and seeming slightly bemused at the antics happening around him. Phil is remembered as 'Mouthy', apparently holding opinions on everything and arguing his opposition into defeat by verbal attrition.

These were the days of the ballroom tours where assorted bands and individuals were grouped together and sent on nationwide jaunts. The combinations were often ludicrous and laughable and so it was when the Pretties were added as one of the supports for Billy Fury's UK Spring Tour during April and May. Also supporting Fury was Dave Berry, Brian Poole and the Tremeloes, and The Zephyrs.

Returning to the studio to set down their next single it was decided to record 'Cry To Me', a Solomon Burke song that Dick had uncovered and particularly liked. Explaining his version, Burke said that when he sang it slow-paced he didn't like the feel so he added horns, sped it up and made it roll and bounce, very much the Pretties method of recycling the Reed/Diddley material. On this song, though, the Pretties took it back to a more pedestrian pace, which seemed to suit it more. Phil hated the song and said that he nearly walked out of the studio, however his feelings appear to have mellowed over the years, and the Pretties even re-recorded it on 1987's *Out Of*

The Island album. To coincide with its release the band mimed a June *Thank Your Lucky Stars* date and performed a live version on *Ready Steady Go* the following month.

Released in July 1965, it made only a minor impact and during a seven week chart life scrambled up to number 36. The disappointing showing persuaded Fontana to push the punchier B-side, 'Get A Buzz', but it was too late, progress had faltered, interest had dissipated and the buzz was gone.

'Cry To Me' continued the association with the Rolling Stones who recorded their own version in May for release on the *Out Of Our Minds* album in October. Band comments that the Stones effectively killed off their version are unfounded. These were the days when the single ruled and albums were considered of lesser importance. The Stones album was released just as the Pretties single was falling from the charts and their album version had no effect on its potential.

Most mid-60s R&B bands worked with a limited repertoire and at one stage the Pretties were rehearsing Rufus Thomas's Stateside hit 'Walking The Dog', intending to incorporate it into their act. This idea was dropped when they discovered that the Stones had included a version on their debut album. Whilst walking the same musical landscape they needed to establish their own identity and not be seen as copyists.

The Pretty Things impetus was fading but Phil informed *Disc*, 'We shall never change, or I won't anyway. It's a personal thing with me I'd rather give up the business than conform. And as I won't cut my hair and I have no intention of dressing like a mod I can't see that happening. Old Dick's just had his hair cut a bit but that's not a group decision that's his own personal choice. Today, although we all live an outwardly respectable home life with our parents, we are still the same underneath. I could never start all over again, fancy going in for the Unit Four Plus 2 image, I don't think fans would accept it either. Sometimes I think we should change, certainly today we stand out in the pop scene, everyone else looks quite normal but the fans like to come and see us just because we are a change from the normal looking groups. Of course, nowadays they don't follow our style in hair or clothes but they don't with any group these days, they follow the crowd. I don't think changing would be at all beneficial to us even though our new record is much quieter than our image would suggest, we really thought we would prove it was something we could do.'

By now Viv Prince had again entered the Magistrates Court this time to answer charges of drug possession, a relative rarity in the mid-60s. He was duly fined for possession of amphetamines and cannabis, setting a trend for the existing and future group members. A further twenty six Court appearances for possession and violent behaviour would ensue in 1965 alone.

A second EP, *Rainin' In My Heart*, was released in August. As well as the title track it included 'Get A Buzz' and two previously unissued songs, 'London Town' and 'Sitting All Alone', complete with a subdued Phil vocal and a jazzy drum feel.

Less impressed was rock journalist Charles Shaar Murray. In his 1993 volume, *Blues On CD*, he waffled on about the numerous British R&B bands that covered Slim Harpo's material concluding with, 'trust me: you don't need The Kinks and Pretty Things versions.'

The follow up album was begun at Stanhope Place where they were given four days to record it. Viv Prince's excesses meant that he frequently failed to arrive for sessions and Bobby Graham, who was again producing, often had to deputise.

1965 was an opportune time to tour the United States and the band dearly wanted to. Dick: 'The only thing which with hindsight was a very dodgy one was not letting us go to America saying well the time's not right yet. It was short-termist in the sense that we should have lost a bit of money but I don't know that we had any money to lose at that point because also there was the Jimmy Duncan thing.'

Phil, however, is adamant that if the band had tasted real US success at that stage then almost certainly they would have imploded well before the 70s. This hindsight stuff cannot disguise their dismay at not touring the States. Morrison and the band concede that money would probably have been lost in the early stages but that was always the price paid to break a band in a new territory.

Bryan Morrison acknowledged that not touring the States had been a bad move. 'I was contacted by this American who told me he had The Beatles and the Dave Clark Five and he wanted The Pretty Things over there. He wanted to meet me at the Mayfair Hotel for breakfast; it was the first time I had ever seen anybody eat a steak for breakfast. He said he wanted a 25% agents cut instead of the normal 10% and I turned him down. With hindsight I should have taken it on a one year contract.'

Instead of looking to America Morrison signed them up for a package tour that would go down in the annals of rock – the infamous Summer tour of New Zealand.

CHAPTER 3 – Viv and the New Zealand Fiasco

Having dismissed the opportunity to take the Pretties to the States, Bryan Morrison signed for them to embark on a tour of New Zealand, Australia and Singapore, although they never reached the last two destinations. They were contracted to support Sandie Shaw and Eden Kane, a combination that appears preposterous now and probably did then as well. Sandie was a big star with a number of chart-topping songs. Kane, like the Pretties, was also at Fontana under the tutelage of Jack Baverstock and this, together with the Australian success of his 1964 single 'Boys Cry', was probably the relevant factor. These tours were operated on a financial shoestring and the Pretties were provided with six airline tickets, five for the band and one ticket for Bryan Morrison who chose to go along to employ his managerial skills.

As soon as the tour was announced lobby groups were formed in Australia with the firm intention of having the Pretties banned. Their reputation had preceded them and it was feared that the untainted Antipodean youth were likely to be infected by the frenzied poms. It was with the knowledge that they were being lowered into a cauldron of antiquated resentment that with some trepidation they set out in late July 1965.

Meanwhile, Viv Prince was becoming increasingly unreliable and far from adding professionalism to the group he was frequently 'unavailable' due to one or more excesses. It was during the tour of New Zealand that the problems with Viv came to a head. Numerous sprees of drunken abandon like setting fire to a hotel room culminated in the Pretties being banned for life from entering New Zealand, for corrupting the morals of the country's youth. Unsurprisingly entry to Australia was refused and a drunken Viv was escorted from the plane shortly before take off.

The tour was packed with incidents and most of them involved Viv. Indeed, by the end Bryan Morrison's ulcer was telling him 'enough' and questions were being asked in the New Zealand parliament.

Legend depicts Viv running across the concert stage with a lighted torch whilst the fire department and concert-hall staff raced after him trying to douse the flames. Other reports suggest he waved a king-sized sword and also ran amok with a plastic machine gun. These antics were blamed for the rioting that followed, which resulted in the burning and destruction of the seats by the frenzied audience. Phil blithely suggested that Viv slipped a few cogs.

John Stax told the bizarre story of Viv and the lobster in Invercargill. 'We arrived in the afternoon at this hotel and Viv stunk to high heaven. Obviously he hadn't changed his clothes for days and days and days, plus he'd had a sort of sexual reverie with these two women. Oh he was really rank! They'd sort of golden-rained all over him a couple of days previously. Plus he had a lobster that he'd bought a week before and he'd set up a little prayer mat in the lobby of this motel and he had all these groupies and stuff that were hanging around and he had them sort of praying all around him. And it smelled! He had this lobster and he wouldn't give it away – he wouldn't let go of it.

Every concert made the TV newscasts. This was the tour that inspired the classic television news announcement 'at the concert given by The Pretty Things tonight an over excited youth jumped on stage and kissed the lead singer. He was identified later as a man.' Amidst this hubbub 'Cry To Me' topped the New Zealand charts, making it the only number one they ever had.

John recalled that Sandie Shaw headlined the tour and that, 'She was a real bitch.' The Pretties, Eden Kane and various local bands were the support acts. 'Once we stopped in the middle of nowhere on this coach. The reason we stopped was because Sandie Shaw wanted a piss. So we stopped outside this farmhouse. This bloke who was the tour manager, he took her in there, and when she came back, Viv and Eden Kane got out and they pissed all over her feet. That really pissed her off!' he chuckled.

Bryan Morrison told a slightly different story claiming he was the only sober person on the coach. He maintained that Viv wasn't involved in the pissing and that Sandie was drenched, not just her feet. Dick Taylor insisted to me that he was also sober and agreed. 'Eden Kane got out and had a pee up against the side of the coach. Sandie Shaw returned and said 'what are you doing, Eden?' He turned round and said 'pissing', and lo and behold she got a little wet. I am not sure, I couldn't exactly locate where about but on her legs one presumes and she got very upset. About two hours later she hit Brian Pendleton over the head with a dinner tray for no reason that I could really fathom.' Pissed on and pissed off, one assumes.

Brian Pendleton confirmed the negative view in which Sandie Shaw was held. 'We were in a plane flying to New Zealand and Sandie Shaw was in one of her stroppy moods and I was sitting in a seat in front of where she was sitting. We started having words about something or other and she said 'I'll bloody hit you in a minute.' I said, go on then, it'll give me an excuse to throw this cup of coffee over you. She slapped my face, so I threw the coffee. She marched straight over to the promoter… and I thought, oh shit, I'm in trouble now. Anyway, about a quarter of an hour later a little note came over to me which said 'Life's too short, let's make up, love Sandie.' Oh yes, she was a complete bitch.'

Sandie was even less impressed when during one of her performances Viv appeared, several bottles of alcohol in tow, and proceeded to stroll across the stage. 'By accident I walked with some bottles in my hands across the platform. Sandie asked me to leave and I did so,' was Viv's guileless explanation.

Bryan Morrison objected to this negative view of Sandie Shaw and considered that, for eighteen-year-old Sandie, going halfway round the world with a insane mob like the Pretties and Eden Kane must have been a nightmare.

The press reported carnage on the stage. 'We have broken one chair,' Viv explained to the reporters. 'That is part of our act, we always break a chair.' The newspapers regaled readers with tales of a newly bearded Viv swigging whisky just before a concert, the golden liquid coursing down his chin as he staggered to the stage. It was also suggested that he drank whisky out of his shoe! 'We only drink whisky for our voices,' alibied the non-singing drummer. 'More artists are doing it all the time.'

One New Zealand policeman informed his local paper, 'they were drunk. You can quote me there. These Pretty Things were intoxicated. How in the world those bums are making money is more than I can believe.'

During a 1994 discussion with Terry Coates, Viv rationalised his behaviour. 'Well Skip also did it and Keith Moon copied me originally, we used to swap ideas. The Pretties did this interview one day and wore suits. They even slagged us off for that! The headlines were 'The Pretty Things borrow people's suits', etc. The press were writing complete rubbish about us, so we thought right, we'll join in with the rubbish and make it more outrageous... so we made a mess of a few hotels. All this thing about setting fire to the stage was because of Eden Kane, who at that time had a hit with a song 'Boys Cry'. I used to find all these props backstage and use them. One night, Eden was performing this particular song and I found this hosepipe on the balcony and squirted him with water right in the middle of it! Another time when he sang 'Boys Cry', I rolled out this beach mat on stage, put this palm tree behind him, set fire to it and put it out with a hosepipe.'

Viv also gave his version of the events that led to him missing the homeward flight from Auckland, countering the suggestion that he was thrown off the plane. 'A complete load of bullshit! We were on the plane going back to England and I was sitting next to Eden Kane. By then he was one of our good mates. Anyway, I had this duty-free bottle of bourbon which slid out of its brown paper bag onto the carpeted floor of the aircraft... whereby the American pilot of the plane leapt out of his cabin and said, 'I've had you pop stars on my plane before. I'm going to confiscate that till the end of the journey.' So I said, 'Look. I'm not even going to drink it. It was just an accident. It only came out of its duty-free wrapping. I'm going to have some in-flight drink.' 'Hand it over,' he said. 'Oh no, you are not going to have this one,' I said. So I just got up and walked off. I ended up staying in New Zealand for a couple more days with some friends I had made on the tour.'

Phil confirmed that Viv was really into whisky, particularly Old Granddad, and that he dropped six bottles which rolled around the plane. Unknown to them, the previous day had seen a case of air rage during which a drunken passenger had attacked a pilot with a knife. This explained the apparent over-reaction of the pilot and flight crew when they caught sight of an intoxicated Viv scrambling across the cabin floor searching for his Old Granddad.

Record Mirror's September headline exclaimed "Viv – It's All Lies!" Viv was given space to counter the stories emanating from New Zealand and to set the tone they repeated some of the more lurid press headlines. "Shocked police find long-haired drunken member of an English pop group The Pretty Things swigging whisky only minutes before their performance", "He then roamed around the stage drinking from his shoe", 'He told me he was seeing what the meths tasted like." *Record Mirror* advised "these were just a few of the reports to appear in the New Zealand press after the Pretty Things tour two weeks ago'. Viv had answers to all the accusations. 'The meths bit – well, we've got a great big bottle of water we carry around labelled "meths"! It's a private joke. We say to all the people who come into our dressing room that we're just going to try the meths'.

Viv was presented with another quote "Prince drank continually. The alcohol ran down his chin and onto the floor. He leapt onto the stage and disgorged a mouthful of the liquid. A hush settled over the theatre at this incident. Later one of them lit a newspaper and rushed around with it waving it within inches of the backdrop curtains" 'Oh no! I wouldn't have wasted alcohol by spilling it all over the place. I was drinking two bottles of coke then! And the bit about disgorging, well I was in the wings gargling as I had a bad voice. No one could have seen me doing that. Naturally there was no hushed silence, they were still screaming for us. The newspaper thing was during our act. It was at least ten feet from any curtains or the audience.'

Record Mirror quoted from a concert review in the *New Plymouth Daily News* which in its sarcastic way seemed to support some of Viv's responses. 'The Pretty Things brought the house down. They did everything but pro-vide for a lover of beautiful music – and there were none of these in the audi-ence. Theirs was R&B at its raving best. Electric excitement and an original stage style, plus good R&B drumming. Viv Prince brandishing a flaming newspaper was, in short, a very original twist to their act.'

Talking in 1998 to DJ Johnson, Dick Taylor asserted, 'I think we were truly pursued in New Zealand. I believe people wanted us to be outrageous because our press release somehow had that tone. I remember Viv also being sat on a runway in a wheelchair where he had gone to sleep…then someone thought it was a rather smart idea to push him out to middle of the runway, asleep. Then a plane came, and they realised there was something in front of them, and of course it turned out to be the drummer of The Pretty Things.' 'The promoter loved it,' said Brian Pendleton. 'The fact that we were bad for New Zealand. He actually told us to be as outrageous as possible…for obvious reasons.' Bryan Morrison agreed that the tales were massively exaggerated. 'I spent three years suing *The Truth*, the New Zealand version of the *News of the World*. I caught two of their reporters emptying two dustbins upside down, they were going to take photos and say 'look what these disgusting people have done.' Brian Pendleton explained what happened. 'We were eating fish and chips and we had a fair amount of drink. When we finished we noticed that we had made a bit of a mess so we thought, well, we can't leave it like this. So we gathered all the mess together and put it in one pile. *The Sunday Truth* newspaper took a picture of this pile of rubbish which was printed in the next issue, with the 'fact' that the Pretty Things are a load of slobs because, 'look at this mess'.' Brian Pendleton for one must have been glad to leave. His son Philip was born in August and Brian didn't see him until two weeks later.

Viv also railed at *The Truth*. 'When we were in Auckland, we set up an interview with the *New Zealand Truth*. We did one of these big 'in depth' interviews. After it was over, this reporter turned to me and said "Vivian, just show us how much you are enjoying New Zealand, leap in the air". So I leapt in the air…and that was the front-page photo they used. The caption was "IDIOT PRINCE UP TO HIS ANTICS AGAIN". I fell for it, didn't I?'

'It was amazing to see people so repressed,' commented Phil.

After the madness and stress of New Zealand the band maintained a low profile for a few months, interrupted only by their attendance at the wedding of John Stax and girlfriend Wendy. John thought he was the only band member to be married but, unknown to him or the other band members, Brian Pendleton had secretly married the previous year.

Viv's increasingly precarious position was further weakened during the October tour of Denmark. Viv stayed behind for a few extra days and his supreme ability to provoke trouble ensured a heavy beating, supposedly by the brother of former boxing champion Ingemar Johannson, although this 'fact' is in some doubt. Viv's battered face peers from the cover of the *Anthology* CD, a testament to the imbecility of rednecks everywhere.

Brian Pendleton placed Viv's battering into some kind of context. 'He had this unfortunate knack of getting pissed and starting trouble. He was okay when he was sober, nice as pie, but the drink did bring out the worst in him.' Viv was out of circulation, recovering from his injuries, for a month and for this period Mitch Mitchell deputised. This was the final straw and he had to go.

November 29th is the date given for Viv's leaving and in December *Disc* ran an article entitled 'Why Viv Prince left the Pretty Things.' 'Two beards in the group were too much' quipped Phil May, adding more seriously, 'We all liked Viv but we had a disagreement over group policy. We all still feel he is one of the best drummers in Britain but there's more to playing in a group than playing an instrument.'

Did Viv leave the band or was he sacked? Viv insisted it was a mutual decision. After missing a Manchester gig, where Les Dash, the drummer from Hedgehoppers Anonymous had to deputise, Viv was telephoned by Bryan Morrison and called to a band meeting. 'At which time it was decided that I should be leaving the band," said Viv.

Viv said 'I agree it was a policy disagreement. Among other things they seemed to think that the personal publicity I was getting was bad for the group, but I'm fed up with going on the road with conditions of playing like they are at present. I want to do more sessions but I am playing with another group a couple of nights a week. Unless working conditions on the road improve I won't go on the road again with a group.'

One of Viv's first jobs was sitting in with the Honeycombs on the new London Palladium Show, 'So that Honey Langtree could sing with Dennis,' explained Viv. In December, he deputised for an unavailable Keith Moon when The Who played Eltham Baths. This was surely a memorable event with the mad master replacing the errant apprentice.

'I want to do more things in pop than play with The Pretty Things. I also want to record groups as well as session drumming.' Although, he added, 'I'm still friends with the rest of the group.'

'He was brought in supposedly to be the professional ingredient that would hold the band together, that's the irony of it,' mused Phil, some years later. Talking to *Blueprint* magazine in 2000, Phil recalled, 'It was getting to the point where we would do only half a number and he'd have a fight with a bouncer or he'd hit some girl in the front row because she'd ripped my shirt. So I had to sack him.'

John Stax concurred, recalling that it came to a head at the Mile End Hotel in Stockport. Viv was completely out of it and couldn't play and it was agreed that the band couldn't continue like this and Phil was sent to sack him.

Bryan Morrison remembered Viv getting more and more out of hand towards the end. 'After one gig I remember him crawling around with an axe he had broken out of a fire case and smashing up tables and water systems. He'd gone completely fucking nuts.'

Bryan provided his version of why Viv was asked to leave. 'He borrowed a Revox tape recorder from me and I was living in one of those mansion flats in Kensington with the stained glass doors. One evening I heard this tremendous crash and ran out to find that Viv had thrown the tape recorder through the door. 'What did you do that for,' I shouted at him. 'It doesn't work,' he said. I just hit him, knocked him to the floor, then picked him up and bashed him against the metal doors of the lift. Then I put him in the lift took him downstairs and threw him out.'

'He was a great drummer,' Brian Pendleton recalled. 'He would start playing along the stage, on people's heads in the audience, on our guitar strings. He used to play on people's fingers which bloody hurt, especially if you were trying to play guitar at the same time.' Looking back, in 1990, Dick accepted that it was very difficult for the band to work with another drummer, 'we were spoiled, because he was so good that we didn't realise how good he was.'

Great drummer or otherwise, Viv was too much of a liability. Even for a band like the Pretties, who affected disdain for public opinion, Viv had crossed that invisible line that separated the amusing from the obnoxious and he had to go.

CHAPTER 4 – Get The Picture?

Finding a successor for Viv Prince presented the band with a major problem. Although he had finished as a liability the manic energy combined with technical prowess made it difficult to replace him. Twink and Mitch Mitchell had both tried on those all too frequent occasions when he had been unavailable (although Twink has subsequently denied this). Twink was quite content in the Fairies and the vacant slot seemed destined for Mitchell. He played with them for over a month but Dick Taylor felt that after Viv's unstructured drumming Mitchell sounded a bit tight and controlled. Mitchell himself suggested they check out Skip Alan and Dick agreed that Skip's more raucous approach was preferred. John Stax described Mitchell as a straight in a three-piece suit and expressed his amazement when, in late 1966, he joined with Hendrix and adopted his fuzzy freak persona. Typically, the band intrigued *Record Mirror* readers with the fable that they had found Skip in a dustbin, and then posed for the obligatory photo as proof!

Skip, real name Alan Ernest Skipper, had previously led his own groups The Skip Alan's and the Skip Alan Trio. Before that, aged 16, he had played for a while with the Ivy League but at that young age was not considered good enough and was asked to leave. Skip had also been a member of Donovan's band playing on early recordings such as 'Colours', 'Catch The Wind' and 'Universal Soldier'. Joining the Pretties at the age of seventeen he became the youngest member.

It was November 1965 and the new album was finished. Fontana needed a chart single to help promote the album.

Ensconced in the IBC Studio's in Portland Place the Pretties set about recording 'Midnight To Six Man' with producer Glyn Johns. Bobby Graham had fallen foul of the Fontana decision-makers and was gone, and the change to Johns was noticeable from the greater depth of the sound. This Taylor-May-Sterling autobiographical original was Skip's recording debut with the band. The production was fuller and benefited from Nicky Hopkins on piano and, according to John Stax, 'A lesbian who played Hammond organ with Goldie and the Gingerbreads.' More time and care was taken than with any previous Pretties track, over 30 takes and more than 16 hours in the studio, which was partly because the song had never been played live before. Stax, Ian Stirling and Jimmy Duncan's sister Lesley handled backing vocals. Duncan, enjoyed a modicum of success as a recording star in her own right in the early 70s and was a sought after backing singer for the likes of Dusty Springfield and the Pink Floyd.

Lofty Riches explained that, quite appropriately, the sessions actually lasted from midnight to six. Brian Pendleton recalled a slightly different time-frame as he told *New Musical Express*. 'We had a recording session one day in November, but we didn't have a song. It was panic stations. We got one written by 2 p.m. though. Then we went off to a gig in Gravesend that night, and back into London at 11 p.m. and we stayed in the recording studio until 5 a.m. But we got the number right in the end.'

'This sounds as though it could be the record to put The Pretty Things right back into the chart,' enthused *Melody Maker*. 'Written by two of the Things, Dick Taylor and singer Phil May, it's a pity the words aren't a little clearer but nevertheless a hard swinging R&B record. Might be a big one.'

Although now acknowledged as a classic of its era, 'Midnight To Six Man' spent only one week in the chart touching number 46 in January, the same week that the Spencer Davis Group hit number one with 'Keep On Running'. 'Midnight' was John Stax's personal favourite out of all the songs he recorded with the Pretties and he felt it was 'lost' amongst the many worthwhile releases that month. The excellent 'Can't Stand The Pain', another band original, was chosen for the B-side.

'Highly percussive opening', remarked *Record Mirror*. 'With piano and droning. Group vocal on a persuasive beater, with words that come over more clearly after a couple of plays. Good guitar figures… a repetitive sort of theme that has grow-on-you appeal. Stacks of excitement and chart bound. Flip is weirdly soundfilled with changes of tempo and a good lead vocal.'

Although the single failed to make the desired impact it was picked up in the States as a supreme slice of R&B action and was covered by The Jagged Edge.

New Musical Express ran a feature which author Ken Mason began with a consideration of their image problems. 'The mums and dads of The Pretty Things have been pretty worried about the publicity their boys have been getting recently and who would blame them. Some of the headlines have included 'I Was Not Drunk Says A Pretty Thing', A Pretty Thing Is Fined', Pretty Things Sue For Libel', 'Pretty Thing In A Fight.' 'Pop Group Banned' and 'Pretty Thing Robbed.' Phil explained, 'it's all dead worrying for our parents 'cos they wonder what it's all about. Some of the things happened, yeah, but there's other stories that got exaggerated.'

Mason explained that the band had 'said goodbye' to one publicist who had suggested they go around a London borough sticking posters all over the place in the hope that questions might be raised in Parliament.

The new album, *Get The Picture?* was released in December 1965 but unlike its predecessor it did not inconvenience the chart compilers. In those days only the top ten albums were listed so an album chart appearance was much harder to achieve than a hit single. Although more self assured than the debut of only eleven months previous it did not have a big hit single ('Midnight To Six Man' was not included on the album) and in those 45 rpm dominated times it was the hit single that sold the album.

Recorded mainly at Stanhope Place, the album benefited from the assistance of various guest players. Opening track, 'You Don't Believe Me', showed joint composer credits for producer Bobby Graham and Jimmy Page who in these pre-Yardbirds days was a much in demand session man. Jimmy had played on many sessions with Bobby and it was this connection that introduced him to the band.

Various sources, Phil included, have stated that Page played lead guitar on the track. Both Dick and Brian Pendleton deny this although Dick does recall playing Jimmy Page's guitar on a different track, 'We'll Play House'.

'We'll Play House' boasted the curious composing credit of Taylor/Aldo/ Gandy. Aldo was a misspelling of Alder, alias Twink, and Dick explained. 'Gandy was John Gandy whose other name was Freddy, I think cause he looked like that guy in Freddy and the Dreamers. He was the bass player in the Fairies and they were in the studio and we did 'We'll Play House'. I know Twink played the drums on that. Again we sort of cobbled it together between us, Freddy played bass.'

Twink also played drums on 'You'll Never Do It Baby' and the difference between his more subdued approach and the frenetic heavy-handed playing of Viv Prince was clearly evident.

Get The Picture? included another Johnny Dee song, 'I Want Your Love', as well as another of Slim Harpo's, 'Rainin' In My Heart', this time properly attributed to him. The Pretties version is wound down, almost waltz-like, awash with Taylor's distinctive trademark blues runs and, driven by Prince's drumming, always threatening to explode into an R&B tantrum.

'London Town' sounded strangely out of place, almost a precursor to the *Emotions* period a year further on. Described by many as folksy, the track lacked the intensity of the other eleven sounding unfinished, almost demo-like.

Five tracks were band compositions, 'Buzz The Jerk', 'You Don't Believe Me', 'We'll Play House', London Town', 'Can't Stand The Pain' and the title track. 'Can't Stand The Pain' was another track that leaped out from the pack. Not, like 'London Town' because of incompatibility, but because it pointed the way forward, beyond *Emotions*, to the future experimentations of *SF Sorrow*. It embraces surreal echo and the time changes that the band later developed to greater effect.

Dick explained to Richie Unterberger that 'Can't Stand The Pain' came together when he was just trying different chords together in the studio. Phil hummed words over it and the song appeared in half an hour. 'We'll Play House' was a variation on 'Susie Q', the old Ronnie Hawkins classic.

'The Pretty Things have built up an image of undisciplined, aggressive rebellion and it comes through in their music,' suggested *Melody Maker*. 'Much of its attraction lies in the very roughness and uncompromising attack. Wrong notes or off-key singing are just not relevant. This is a pretty typical set with the title song as one of the best tracks.'

Peter Doggett, editor of *Record Collector* later suggested that Bobby Graham had been listening to Sonny and Cher 'as the cluttered production bore the trademark of Sonny Bono's work.'

The Beatles did it, the Dave Clarke Five did it so, in January, a Pretty Things movie was filmed. *On Film* was odd and zany in the vein of *A Hard Days Night* (pre-empting the nonsensical Monkees TV style). No surprise then that they shared the same Director, Dick Clarke, who also directed the Dave Clarke Five vehicle, *Catch Us If You Can*. Phil's film star aspirations lived and died in this brief waste of good money.

'I thought he was a total wanker,' espoused Pendleton about Dick Clarke. 'One of those theatrical film 'luvvie' type people.'

On Film included four songs, The A and B-sides of the current single plus 'Me Needing You' and 'L.S.D.' Two of the songs appeared to have been filmed live at The 100 Club. 'They took scenes from that and overdubbed the sound with our studio stuff,' stated Brian Pendleton. 'Bloody terrible, I found it really embarrassing. Most of it was filmed around the Barbican and St Paul's area of London. Most of us thought it was corny even then. We actually paid for that film ourselves from our bank balance!' Phil considered it 'a lot of fun to make' and described it as the forerunner of the promo video.

The film lasted only fifteen minutes but it took a whole week to film. It was Bryan Morrison's idea and not only did he also feature in it but he is credited as producer alongside the executive producers Anthony West Associates Ltd. The script, if a film without dialogue can claim such a thing, was down to Caterina Arvat who co-directed with Anthony West. Brian Pendleton remembered that ultimately the film was only shown at one cinema in Chelsea.

Interestingly this nonsense was not Brian Pendleton's film debut. The previous year he could have been glimpsed in the D A Pennebaker documentary *Don't Look Back*, lounging around in the background while Dylan held court.

It was around this time that the band parted with Jimmy Duncan. Dick recalled the situation, which must still haunt them to this day. 'Duncan dropped out probably late '65 or early '66 because basically, I hate to speak ill of the dead, but he was milking the agency account, reasonably substantially. He was forging Bryan's signature and a load of money got drawn out from our account and from the agency itself as well. He was basically embezzling. This was also ripping off Bryan in a big way. To give Bryan his due he never actually wanted to go in with Jimmy in the first place. All the while Jimmy was there, apart from the initial contact with the record company, very little came from Jimmy Duncan. I must say I was never particularly impressed with Jimmy.'

Phil remembered, 'We didn't care about the money and we didn't know about it. We were just into playing music. Every week or so we'd come into the office and they'd give us £100 and we were happy, we had been art students living on nothing before that.'

Bryan recalled that he walked into the Charing Cross Road offices one Saturday, which was something of a rarity.' The Pretties had about £15,000 of savings at that time and I put the radio on, I distinctly recall the Righteous Bothers *You've Lost That Loving Feeling* was on. I saw some envelopes from the bank and in those days they returned the cashed cheques to you, and I opened a statement showing the band's account was minus £20. Duncan had been forging my signature over a period of about five months. In those days £15,000 was a tidy sum, you could buy a reasonable size house with it.'

Dick confronted the issue of how such an appalling financial mess could have occurred. 'The only drawback with Bryan was that he probably wasn't paying enough attention to business, and nor was his father, who funnily enough was an accountant, to spot what Jimmy was doing at that point. Because loads of money was coming in, he just didn't realise that loads of surplus money was going out. It was reasonably craftily done, I think.'

Bryan was a worried man. He had been managing the band with Duncan and was loath to sack him because he was convinced that he needed him. However Bryan's father would have none of it and told him to set the police on him and sack him or never come home again. Bryan confronted Duncan and told him to hand over his shares in the band's management or he would call in the police. Duncan agreed. 'Within six months I had signed the Pink Floyd and Elton John, all this without Duncan's assistance. I didn't need him after all.'

'They were good,' recalled Immediate's Tony Calder in 1995, 'but what they needed at the time was good management, which The Stones had, but they hadn't.' Morrison sneered at this asking who, apart from the Stones, did Calder and Oldham ever develop? Over the years Morrison has handled such chart topping acts as Wham, Elton John, and Haircut 100 as well as the Floyd. Apart from The Pretty Things Morrison failed to develop any new acts but then neither did Loog-Oldham and Calder – they snatched the Stones from Georgio Gomelsky.

Tony Calder's opinion appears outlandish and, as Ian McLagan made clear in his autobiography, even though the Small Faces achieved regular chart placings they didn't see much money from their relationship with the 'mekon' and his partner Andrew Loog Oldham.

Calder also suggested that to reduce the Pretties status as serious challengers to the Stones they used their managerial muscle to have them removed from television shows. He also related that Mick Jagger would never let The Pretty Things back on to *Ready Steady Go* after their first appearances, apparently saying of Phil 'he's just too fucking pretty…he's dangerous.'

Fanciful as it may seem some thirty-six years later, Dick believes that this did actually happen. A cryptic comment made to him whilst recording a television show indicated that they wouldn't be on any future programmes. Whilst Jagger's alleged comments appear fatuous this may disguise the reality that in 1965 The Pretty Things were noticeably muscling in on Stones territory and Phil was looking a likely contender for his R&B singing white boy title.

'The Pretty Things were never competition', Andrew Loog Oldham told me. 'They were fortunates like us who managed to not have to get a real job.'

At this stage the Pretties still did not have a written contract with Morrison. This naiveté or blind trust may appear endearing but throughout their career they have proved to be financially inept, signing deals over here, shaking hands over there, accepting the word of all sorts of devious and scheming characters and basically fucking up financially at every turn.

Interviewed by Terry Coates in 1995, Brian Pendleton sardonically recalled that period. 'When the Pretty Things turned professional none of us had a car. We just couldn't afford one. Bryan Morrison had an old Austin Seven with the window missing out of the back. Then he bought a Mini and after that a Mini Cooper… then went on to get an 'E' Type Jag and then a Ferrari.'

John Stax also harbours concerns about money earned but never received and is reconciled to the fact that the full answer will never be revealed. He suggested that in 1965 they were earning $1m and saw very little of it.

By 1967 Morrison's agency also handled acts such as the Pink Floyd, Tomorrow, The Artwoods and Herbie Goins and the Nightimers so he was no longer reliant just on the Pretties for income.

Meanwhile Phil was keeping busy by producing a single, the May-Taylor composition 'Get The Picture', for Enfield group The Moquette. The single failed dismally and Phil's production career was placed on hold for another eighteen years.

An EP, *On Film*, was issued in January containing the four songs used in the film. One track, 'L.S.D.' caused a minor sensation with further newspaper comment, complaints from the Royal Pharmaceutical Society and a ban by the BBC. The song was written quickly to fill a gap and the issued version was actually just a demo although sounding so frantic and undisciplined that it is hard to tell. Years later Phil contended that the sounds of coins being dropped on the floor had been omitted from the final mix and that this had been recorded to disassociate the song from any drug allusions. 'We thought we'd get away with it,' he reminisced. Comments lathered in guile perhaps as The Pretty Things both then and today do not care who they might have offended.

The lyrics clearly relate to financial concerns (L.S.D being pounds, shillings and pence in pre-decimal Britain) but the double entendre was obviously not lost on them or the label. LSD was not a widely known indulgence and in January 1966 it had yet to be banned and had not taken on the hippie drug-taking connotation that would apply throughout the following years.

Tabloid newspapers, quick with the story but slow with the facts, would scarcely have heard about LSD at this time. Consider the *News Of The World's* later concerns about druggies 'injecting reefers'. This represented a further example of the Pretties being ahead of their time in the context of both drugs and social outrage. Eighteen months later The Beatles would be rebuked because of the symbolistic initials and lyrics of 'Lucy In The Sky With Diamonds' and the vague 'smoke' and 'dream' references in 'Day In The Life'.

In May of 1966 The Pretty Things new single, 'Come See Me' showed a slight chart improvement managing a high of 43 during a five week stay. This classic was deserving of top ten status and like its predecessor was a supreme slice of resentment seething with menace and boasting an impressive thumping bass line. This really was a hit gone missing, Stax's steam-hammer bass, Dick Taylor's fuzz-tone accompaniment, his urgent yet controlled solo and Phil May's confident, powerful vocals complete with lip curl and sneer. Unrecognisable from JJ Jackson & Sid Barnes' original it is now seen as a stomping mid-sixties classic. Punk, before its time.

Dick's guitar pyrotechnics are amongst the first to be unveiled on vinyl. Jimmy Page claims to have had the first fuzz box and told Ritchie Yorke that The Pretty Things then got one followed by Beck, Hendrix and the rest of the industry. Six months previously Paul McCartney had used fuzz bass on 'Think For Yourself' from The Beatles' *Rubber Soul* album.

Like its predecessor the single boasted a Glyn Johns production that uncovered the brutish element but managed to retain excellent production values and, like its predecessor, it featured a Nicky Hopkins piano accompaniment.

Melody Maker's guest singles reviewer that week was Keith Moon. 'It's Entwistle! 'My Generation' type beginning. I like the backing…kind of new wave as far as pop music is concerned. The song is very ordinary. I recognise that voice but can't think who it is. I've noticed the backing on a lot of these records has been better than the singers. Oh, The Pretty Things. Viv Prince R.I.P.'

'Grunty guitar sounds early on,' informed *Record Mirror*. 'Then Phil May takes over at a brisk mid tempo and the whole thing fairly raves later on. A natural hit, we'd say, for the fury of the attack as much as anything. Flip has a controversial title but turns out to be harmless enough. Not so strong either.' *Record Mirror* was clearly not phased by the chemical connotations of 'L.S.D.'

Later that month Phil told *Disc* readers that, 'I should think we are the only group that's still using harmonica as the basic instrument on stage. We don't jump on the bandwagon when new sounds come along it seems our fans like us the way we are. At present the chart is full of Bacharach and melodic sounds and every group that goes on stage is doing the same numbers. As far as records are concerned we keep to our sound because it's ours. People have come to us with some lovely stuff which is obviously a hit, in fact other people have done it and it has been a hit. It is too pretty for us, we couldn't afford to do it. Music is getting too pretty these days that's why The Troggs have had such a huge hit. 'Wild Thing' had to happen because in a chart full of sweetness it was gassy and happening, it knocked us out.'

Phil then touched on the band's philosophy. 'Yes, it does surprise us that we're still popular, that we still get chart success, but we won't conform. I suppose you could say we do what we want and to hell with everyone else but that's a bit strong, the way I put it is like this, we play what we want to play every single number. We won't conform with trends, that way we're happy and it looks like our fans are too.'

The Pretty Things still attracted the wrong kind of attention. Phil raged to the *New Musical Express* that they experienced prejudice at a club up north. 'They seemed to have a big mod craze on. There was us up on the stage – but the attendants wouldn't let anyone with long hair come in to hear us. I was furious. It's racialism, that's what it is. Colour prejudice – only with the hair.'

At this point in mid-1966 The Pretty Things had reached the end of phase one of their career, the R&B/garage/punk years. Despite Phil's condemnation of the Bacharach type melodies the 'new' Pretties sound would resemble that far more than the established stomping R&B sound. Looking back at the fuss and the crass media condemnation a musical innocent could easily conclude that here stood a sorry bunch of degenerates without musical competence or a single socially redeeming feature. Image over substance, a media creation. The reality is that like the Sex Pistols, over ten years later, there was indeed a substance, a primitive energy combined with worthwhile and lasting compositions. Like many other UK bands they took to established blues material but, unlike their peers who applied gloss and a sanitised veneer they vandalised it. They upped the tempo, applied a jungle beat laced with exaggerated percussion and a frenzied drum attack. This musical corruption went much further than the likes of the Rolling Stones who appeared quite pleasant and homely by comparison.

The change could be garnered from Phil's July interview with Norman Jopling in *Record Mirror*. "REFORMED" ran the headline. 'Things reached a terrible state,' explained Phil, 'TV producers just didn't want to know and they're only just beginning to change their minds now they've heard our new record. We couldn't get any TV plugs, which are a necessity to sell records. And after all, that's basically what we are in the business for. Our aim is not to alienate our R&B type fans but to try to make new fans with a new style as well as keeping the old ones.'

The interview turned to stage performances and Phil couldn't resist a dig at the opposition. 'We try to give a good stage act. I think we do because we're always busy and we always play to big audiences. I think that when you go to see a group you expect to see something visual. Otherwise you might just as well go home and play the record. Now, it isn't many groups that can duplicate their record sound, so then it's even worse when the group doesn't move or give a show. Take Spencer Davis. They're the best group I've heard on stage. They duplicate their record sound perfectly – can even improve on it. But they stand there looking miserable when they play. As though they're not enjoying it.'

Phil then sniped at the music press for failing to report how well they went down when supporting the Walker Brothers. He also touched on the subject of 'new' drummer Skip. 'I'm glad we've got Skip, because he's the only drummer who could have filled Viv's place,' although he added, 'I still think that Viv is the best drummer in the country.'

Another single release was required during the Summer to create a momentum and for this they had a new producer, Steve Rowland, who was foisted on them by Fontana. After the relative failures of the two Glyn Johns-produced singles the label turned to Rowland the one time Hollywood actor. Rowland decided on 'House In The Country', a tune by Ray Davies of the Kinks. The Kinks were riding high with 'Dedicated Follower of Fashion' and 'Sunny Afternoon' and despite the band's misgivings Davies's song was recorded and released with the more memorable 'Me Needing You' as the B-side. Phil said that the band had been given four Ray Davies songs and that he actually preferred the others. He thought that politically it was considered preferable for the better Kinks songs to be retained for their own album, although 'House In The Country' was itself included on the Kinks own *Face To Face* album four months later.

Corporate opinion prevailed and the band's views were, not for the first or the last time, discounted. Their own compositions weren't considered strong enough and in time honoured fashion the unit-movers turned to the established song-writers.

Melody Maker noted: 'Most commercial record ever recorded by the Pretties and written for them (sic) by master pop craftsman Ray Davies. It's a bright bounce-a-long tale about a country house, played with the Things usual gutty drive. Nice – and a hit.'

'House In The Country' spent two separate weeks, each at number 50 in late July and early August 1966. When the Kinks album *Face To Face* was released in October of that year it amply demonstrated how only Ray himself could extract the maximum from his curious, whimsical songs. On this particular song the band sounded ill-at-ease and frankly their version was unconvincing and remains one of their lowest moments. 'I always felt it was a dumb song,' said Phil. 'Not even a good Kinks song.'

Revealingly, Phil maintains that around this time he was contacted by The Kinks management and asked to join them as vocalist. He declined and it seems that The Kinks were oblivious to this approach.

Fontana was pushing for a big hit and the band even made a live recording of the single at Twickenham Studios for the *Ed Sullivan Show* – unfortunately, or perhaps fortunately for all the Pretties US garage fans, it was never shown.

This was the first 'pop song' that The Pretty Things had recorded. Its lack of danger and lightweight status being emphasised by Cliff Richard's decision to sing it on his 1968 BBC television show.

'House In The Country' marked the last appearance of The Pretty Things in the UK singles charts.

In an August interview with *Disc*, Phil rounded on The Beatles with a startling condemnation that revealed a bizarre political outlook and a worrying lack of prescience. 'The Beatles have reached their peak and now they're on the slide. They're out of touch and should give it up now instead of just clinging on. When The Beatles got their MBE's it was a clear sign of The Treasury using initiative and realising that interest had to be maintained in such a moneymaking outfit for the British economy. But you can't go on giving out MBE's forever, The Beatles trouble is that they are living in a house with the windows shut, they're cut off by security from the scene outside and they can't feel the pulse of the business. They stick to visiting places like The Scotch and Sybilla's where they meet a tight little circle instead of being able to go out and play gigs every night and know what the fans really want.'

Later that month saw the release of *Revolver*, the album which over the years has overtaken *Sergeant Pepper* as the most lauded recordings of their career.

Phil went on to explain the change in musical stance that began with 'House In The Country' and continued throughout the remainder of their Fontana days. 'We were mad ravers but that scene is over. Pop used to be a good time for everybody but now everything has become so serious. People want to analyse pop songs in the same way that they analyse jazz. We're not reforming or anything like that, fans still want to see a good act after all, it's just that we've reviewed our record making and realised that raving's out.'

Phil's comments would be confirmed over the following six months. The Pretty Things output would change dramatically. Unfortunately it would also serve as a reminder that a change of image is itself useless without the assistance of a supportive record company, a sympathetic producer and a clutch of worthwhile tunes.

Twink took over from an indisposed Skip Alan and played on the new single 'Progress' released in December 1966. Like 'House In The Country' this was pop, not R&B, and again it failed to seriously interest the record buyers, although according to *Disc* it reached #30. Like 'House In The Country', it was produced by Steve Rowland and was another non-Pretties original. It was a worrying harbinger of the style soon to be unveiled on the *Emotions* album where mediocre pop songs would receive the illusory enhancement of intrusive brass and string orchestration. The song, unremarkable and typically 1966 pop, is memorable only for the strange tortured-puppy yelps that dominate the final choruses.

Melody Maker's review was understandably gloomy. 'Since Viv Prince left the Pretties seem to have lost some of their impetus and their new 'clean, short-hair' image doesn't seem to have had much effect. But this is a competent, catchy performance and a good production, while not particularly original. Let's hope the Pretties make some progress and all the shouting at the end could be the main sales point.'

The Pretties embarked on a tour of Denmark with a temporary guitarist. Dick had been taken ill at the last minute fortunately Billy Harrison from their friends and fellow R&B band Them deputised and the six-date tour proceeded.

The band's contract with Fontana required a third album and through to early 1967 the group worked on what eventually became *Emotions*. The recording schedule precisely mirrored that of the Beatles who were entrenched at Abbey Road recording *Sgt Peppers Lonely Hearts Club Band*. The new Pretties album proved a major departure from the Bo Diddley and swamp-beat rhythms of the first two releases. Soul music was going through a boom and the band's R&B numbers did not go down well with the mods. 'That was a very difficult time,' Phil told *Sounds*. 'We didn't really know what we wanted to do. We just knew we didn't want to do soul.'

Dick, of course, loved soul and was responsible for finding 'Cry To Me' and 'Come See Me'. As he explained to Richie Unterberger, Ppeople who actually lived in London would probably much prefer to go and see Wilson Pickett, go see some American bands, 'cause all the English groups, we could go and see them anytime.'

The Mods, short haired, well groomed and sporting expensive clothes, favoured imported soul music and select home-grown bands such as The Small Faces, The Who and Geno Washington's Ram Jam Band.

Interestingly John Stax recalled touring France with the Spencer Davis Group and Bill Haley. After one Pretties rehearsal the Spencer Davis Group started tuning up and ran through their new song 'Gimme Some Loving'. 'We rushed up afterwards and said, 'Could we record that song?' And they said 'no, we've just recorded it.' 'Gimme Some Loving' was very much in the soul vein although by this time, such musical genres were becoming blurred.

By late 1966, mounting pressures began to take their toll on some band members. The continuing lack of success, lack of gigs and the gradual change from R&B to a poppier sound was increasing the tension. Firstly, Brian Pendleton departed. The band had been blissfully unaware that Brian had married two years earlier. 'That was a strange situation,' says John Stax, 'There were these three mousy birds that used to hang around, and he married one of them.'

Dick Taylor elaborated, 'Pendleton just disappeared. I can remember the event of him not turning up to a rehearsal. We were rehearsing in some place in North London, which was unusual for us 'cause rehearsing was reasonably unusual. Then he didn't turn up and that's when alarm bells went. Then, when we went to do a gig and he didn't turn up for that, I think that's when we thought right, he's really gone. Then Pete Watts and I went round his flat, figured out which one was his flat and found the broken acoustic guitar and a list of things, including the wedding ring, which was stuck on the dressing table. It had a broken mirror and 'oh my god, they've had some big fight or what have you.' I don't think they did, they were just moving out or whatever but from our point of view that's what happened, he just buggered off and never contacted us.' The band didn't see him again until they had a meeting with the Inland Revenue for the winding up of The Pretty Things company in 1968.

Brian refuted most of these claims. 'On Christmas Eve I phoned the band and told them I was leaving. I'd just got married and my wife had just had a baby… and I was financially broke.' Apparently it was not just the financial side, Brian was psychologically shattered. 'Shot out. Three years on the road is a hard life.'

Talk of missing a December gig in Leeds is rubbished as is the suggestion that he had smashed up his guitar and just disappeared. Brian conceded that he suffered some kind of breakdown. 'I suppose I did in a way. Everything took its toll… as with John Stax who left the band three months after I did.'

'We were pretty horrible to Pendleton at times but no-one really disliked Brian I must say,' confessed Dick. 'Brian used to spend quite a lot of time around my flat so we couldn't have been at war with one another. Not like some bands where after a few years the band members won't talk to one another. We never approached that sort of level, like Pete Quaife and the Kinks and The Who had their moments as well didn't they, you know, terrible.'

Later, Brian would regret his departure but at the time he was so emotionally and physically drained that he could see no other route forward. After the Pretties he moved his wife and son back to his parents' place in Beckenham and began working as an insurance underwriter. Although no longer in the big league he continued playing and gigged with various jazz bands and the Kent Jazz Orchestra.

His son Philip revealed that Brian was drinking very heavily whilst in the band, often a bottle of whiskey a day towards the end. He was also under severe family pressure, his father disliked his son being a musician and pressed him to change his surname so they would avoid the rock 'n' roll taint. The pressure was something of an embarrassment to him and he didn't mention it to the band.

John Stax was also becoming disillusioned with the band's non-R&B direction and disliked the new style songs written for the album, only playing on two of them. He preferred the garage band sound of previous years. He told an Australian radio station in 1996, 'Those two albums are the real Pretty Things. The rest is just dross. We weren't playing my favourite 12 bars anymore. Phil and Dick were always the leaders of the band… I wasn't too fast whichever way we went, as long as we were enjoying ourselves and playing music that I liked. But they did the songwriting. They were always looking for the latest thing to do, that would give us a head. Same as a lot of bands. Dick and Phil were always jumping on the latest bandwagon and I wasn't interested. It's either a twelve bar or nothing, forget it. That's what I play, that's what I like playing.'

However, Stax's differences with his fellow band members were not all musical. It is clear that personality clashes were coming to the fore. 'I was getting sort of eased out for some reason. I don't know why. I was really pissed off, and I remember ringing up the papers to let them know I wasn't sacked, I'd left. Yeah, that was pretty bad that.' This was early in the New Year.

'It wasn't the only reason,' he told me. 'I was married and had a child and we were only working once or twice a month. It's not enough money and I was driving a cab trying to make ends meet.'

John went on to a spell with Denny Laine's Electric String Band where he was joined by the itinerant Viv Prince. The band was a precursor to the Electric Light Orchestra with two cellos and two violins. 'We were doing all originals, Denny's stuff.' They played just the one gig, which John vaguely recalled being in Nottingham then, for various reasons, it disintegrated. John continued driving cabs for a while, 'then I moved down to Hertford and had to get a regular job. It was a bit of a shock.'

The Pretty Things future looked uncertain. With a new album underway and Fontana pressing for its completion they had lost two original members. Many bands in this position would have folded and gone their separate ways but Phil had ideas which projected beyond the new album and would involve a former childhood friend.

CHAPTER 5 – A Transfusion of Fenmen

The birth of the *Emotions* album mirrored the first real fracturing of The Pretty Things. Although the band was already on its fourth drummer the other four members had been together since November 1963 and had established a clear identity.

The loss of Pendleton and John Stax was inevitable given Phil and Dick's desire to push forward into new musical territories. Manager Bryan Morrison and Fontana, in the form of Steve Rowland, also seemed happy to replace them with 'real musicians'.

Brian Pendleton recalled the early days of the *Emotions* sessions which again took place in Philips Stanhope Street Studio. 'I was still actually with the band when those sessions started. I got the feeling that the others thought I wasn't good news anymore... the same goes for John. They brought in loads of session musicians for that one. I think Mike Carr the jazz pianist played some piano on that album.'

Brian then recalled the next time he met members of the band. 'We actually saw each other at the Board of Trade enquiry into The Pretty Things Ltd. We were a Limited Company and the Board of Trade issued the band with a writ. We didn't pay any income tax because, the first year of our career, Bryan Morrison did not disclose any of our company accounts. We were all directors and we had to answer the allegations. That was down to the management. Bryan Morrison set us up with his father as the accountant, who did not disclose them.'

The vexatious secrecy agreement that now surrounds much of the band's dealings with Fontana allows little light to be shed on the outcome of the tax issue. It seems that a relatively small amount of money was owed in the form of unpaid income tax and after The Pretty Things Ltd went into liquidation the Inland Revenue placed a garnishee order on the Fontana royalties, thereby ensuring that these were paid directly to them. Some years later, just before the re-issue boom brought about by the cassette tape revolution, Fontana purchased the royalties from the Inland Revenue for a modest capital sum and presumably made a pot of money out of the band for a second time. The 1980's CD explosion allowed them a third bite of the cake.

As with the later EMI shenanigans this corporate mugging would be challenged in the 1990's when the band and their management realised the extent of the financial abuse suffered and were mature enough and desperate enough to mount a legal offensive.

Assistance in completing *Emotions* came in the form of keyboard player

Jon Povey and bass player Wally Waller, both ex-Bern Elliot & The Fenmen. Wally, in the days when he was plain Alan Waller, had lived opposite Phil in Erith and was his oldest friend, having known him since the age of four. Their harmony skills helped embellish and flesh out an album that most Pretty Things fans, and even the band themselves, consider an artistic low point. Although their status was always that of band members they didn't join officially until after the Fontana contract had expired.

Opinions vary on whether Wally Waller & Jon Povey were introduced before or after the departure of Stax. Liner notes and reference books imply that he left and a replacement was brought in as an emergency measure, John avows that he was pushed. 'I was a bit pissed off really, I was sort of torn when I left. I really didn't want to leave then, at the same time we weren't getting any work and I didn't want to do *Emotions*, I didn't like that either. I remember going along to one of the sessions and they had another bass player there. I thought, oh yeah? I'm fucking pissed off here and I thought, fuck it I'm out of here. I rang up Morri and told him, I explained everything and said I'm leaving he said 'oh, we was gonna get rid of you anyway."

Talking in 1999 Dick Taylor conceded John Stax's version as basically factual. 'It's not like Pendleton who just went whoosh. I think he thought long and hard about it, did John. I don't know why we didn't use him, it seemed pointless not using him but the general thing was we have to have real musicians who can really play properly on the album and this was from Steve Rowland. It was all crap basically, it was all nonsense, you know. I think that's what alienated him and we would have been happy to use him, I certainly would have been happy to use him. Wally and Jon weren't brought in. I think there might have been a band which consisted of Wally playing one guitar, me playing lead guitar, Povey on keyboards and Staxie on bass I think that would have been a reasonably happy arrangement but Staxie was gone, he made up his mind he was going. John's version is pretty true really.'

John is adamant that he was never in a band with Wally or Jon Povey. Although he has regrets, particularly about the way he was eased out, he still considers the *Emotions* album to be 'crap' and is glad he didn't stagger down that particular musical avenue.

Alan 'Wally' Waller was born on April 9th 1945 in Barnhurst, Kent, close to Erith where Jon Povey was living. Wally had been turned on to music at an early age, often playing his brother-in-law's semi-acoustic Gretsch. Originally a jazz fan it was the shock of hearing Little Richard and the new rock 'n' roll that prodded him towards a musical career. He played rhythm guitar in a number of bands including instrumental outfit The Martials, who played mainly Shadows and Ventures covers. This was where he first met drummer Jon Povey, three years his senior.

Around 1962 Wally and Jon joined another local band Bern Elliott & The Fenmen, whose lead singer Bern was Phil May's cousin. 'They're related but Phil doesn't like to talk about it,' explained Bryan Morrison.

Wally had replaced guitarist David Allen and opted to retain the surname for professional use. 'We became very popular very quickly in our area,' confirmed Wally, 'then we had a chance to go to Germany for a couple of months.' Jon Povey recalled the trip to Hamburg as a very dodgy deal. 'We were playing instrumentals plus a few Bernie songs and a lot of R&B and black artist music.' The visit opened their eyes to the Liverpool sound, which consisted of scouse interpretations of American music imported through Liverpool docks. 'I heard music I'd never even thought existed before,' said Wally. 'Hearing these guys singing three part harmonies was a real revelation to us,' agreed Jon.

They arrived back in England, broke, having had problems extracting their money from the promoter. However the influence of that period ensured they now took a completely different musical course and they started to learn the new American R&B sounds. The band played a concert at The Scala, a big ballroom in Dartford, and amongst the thousand strong audience was Peter Sullivan of Decca Records, who later expressed an interest in auditioning them in the Decca studios.

One of the songs they recorded was 'Money', which The Beatles had included on their *With The Beatles* album. Wally recalled that when the guy at the recording test read the titles on the Beatles album and he saw this song called 'Money', he quickly dug out the Bern Elliott tape mixed it up and slapped it out. Within a week it was charting. The song climbed to number 14 in November 1963 and remained there for 13 weeks.

Success introduced the fledgling group to the world of package tours. Jon Povey: 'We were asked to do a Rolling Stones tour. In those days you played the Gaumont or Odeon Theatres and instead of showing a film they would pull up the screen and you would have bands playing and the whole thing would be packed out with screaming girls. You would have John Leyton, The Swinging Blue Jeans, Mike Sarne, The Rolling Stones, Jet Harris and the whole package would go out and play – you would play for ten minutes, do three or four numbers and then the next band would be on. Then we did *Ready Steady Go* and it put us on the map very quickly.'

John Stax was rather less impressed with The Fenmen, he recalled that they wore shiny green suits and used to play Beatles covers. 'They were sort of a local band makes good, but not real good.'

Their follow up, 'New Orleans', was not such a success stalling at 24 over three months before the Pretties released 'Rosalyn'. The band suffered internal strife when Bern Elliott, who increasingly saw himself as the star, decided that the other band members should be on a wage. He then set out on what proved to be a spectacularly unsuccessful solo career leaving The Fenmen to carry on without him – as a harmony band. Their version of 'Rag Doll' failed to chart and they left Decca for CBS where they recorded a version of The Mamas and Papas 'California Dreamin'. Their final single was 'Rejected', which it was. An inauspicious and ominous portent as it was one of the first Wally Waller originals. 'Rejected' had a very Mamas and Papas feel with Beach Boys harmonies and an altogether West Coast vibe and deserved a chart placing. Notably, the B-side was entitled 'Girl Don't Bring Me Down'.

During this period Wally started getting together with Phil again. On those rare occasions when they were both back at home they used to meet and piece together bits of music. To Wally's surprise some of these ideas were used on *Emotions* and Phil then asked him and Jon to add harmonies and play on some of the recordings.

Jon Povey: 'We did three or four tracks on that and Phil said would Wally and I like to join the band because he liked the harmony stuff and wanted a keyboard. I switched from drums to keyboard and Wally came and played guitars and bass.' Jon had received classical piano training so the move from drums was not quite as bold as it may have seemed to some.

By now 'Tufty' Taylor had dispensed with the beard and in its place affected a thin drooping moustache, as did Skipper. By contrast the Fenmen, Wally and Jon Povey, looked positively smooth and well-groomed, although time would resolve this dichotomy.

In April 1967 Fontana issued a single, 'Children' b/w 'My Time', as a precursor to the album and, as the album would, it disappeared fast into bargain basement sales. 'Children' employed a kazoo riff sounding more like a comb and paper job and included military drum fills and the recorded sounds of school children at play. The song's one saving grace being the lovely harmonies courtesy of the newcomers. 'My Time' again featured ethereal harmonies as well as intrusive brass and an intermittent harp. The song itself was quite ordinary with the lyrics stretched and pushed to fit the melody. Released around the same period that 'Strawberry Fields' and 'Purple Haze' were charting it is difficult to imagine how the single could possibly have been considered a potential radio play let alone a hit.

Released in May 1967, just weeks before *Sgt Pepper*, *Emotions* revealed a band attempting a difficult change of direction. This was the first album where the group had written all the songs and whilst many of the lyrics displayed hints of the imagery and psychedelia captured in their later EMI period, the production and arrangements were decidedly lightweight. Skip's drum sound lacked both the depth and weight of live performances and Dick Taylor's guitar often sounded tinny like an unamplified electric. Dick:

'It's very funny, because Steve Rowland who produced it, who was always going on about getting really big guitar sounds, Who-type sounds, didn't actually bloody do it. It was very frustrating to work with him.'

Rowland, also produced chart regulars Dave Dee, Dozy, Beaky, Mick and Tich as well as future chart entrants The Herd. Fontana believed he would add a commercial gloss and come up with a hit single. 'This was the guy who was a real producer, who was going to get us in the charts with real commercial stuff' chuckled Dick, 'in fact I think we did better before.' Dick was right, the tracks produced by Rowland lack the attack and fire of the previous two years as well as the depth, fullness and inspiration of the coming Norman Smith era. More pointedly there wasn't the imagination and clarity of the previous Glyn Johns produced singles which had retained the fury and drive of the live band allied to a greater musical sophistication.

Three of the *Emotions* songs carried a co-writing credit for Ian Sterling who had also assisted on previous compositions. Ian was an art school friend of Dick and Phil and at one stage shared a flat with Dick and roadie Pete Watts. As well as the *Emotions* tracks he had co-written 'Honey I Need' and often provided backing vocals. After marrying another art school friend, Maggie, he formed a company called Downtown Darkroom, specialising in photographic services and never again interacted with the band. John Stax recounted, 'He was always pissed. He was always getting into fights, he was a wild man.'

Emotions was recorded with three bass guitarists. As well as John Stax and Wally it benefited from the assistance of Gary Taylor from The Herd. The Pretties recorded twelve tracks – mostly unmemorable. According to current band manager Mark St John, the opening track, 'Death Of A Socialite' retains the curiosity value of being the only song written by The Pretty Things to be played by Bo Diddley. David Blakey, controller of Bo Diddley – The Originator website has been unable to corroborate this and one cannot imagine how such a thing might sound.

This album has suffered much castigation over the years because of the brass and string adornments of Reg Tilsley. It has been reported that the 'tampering' was a final embellishment by Fontana with Phil contending that the album was 'hi-jacked by the record company'. With the band effectively disowning the album it has further been suggested that they were concentrating on songs for their new EMI contract. Allusions to it being a contractual obligation album have also gained credence. However Dick Taylor was quick to pour water on these suggestions. 'No, we were quite heavily involved in it. Phil was obviously very heavily involved in the writing of it and I think a lot of it was stuff which Phil really wanted to do, in terms of the songs. I think the treatment of the songs was not what he really wanted and not what I would have wanted, but it wasn't done merely to fulfil a contract.'

'It was all down as basic song ideas and backing tracks, and suddenly out of the blue they pull in Reg Tilsley', asserted Phil.

Tilsley, has a different recollection of events. He described the album as 'a perfect marriage between The Pretty Things and The Not So Pretty Things' and called it a 'betrothal of The Pretty Things kind of music and my kind of backing.' At the suggestion of Fontana chief Jack Baverstock he met with the Pretties and producer Steve Rowland, they told him that their old sound 'had become yesterday' and that 'four part harmonies, orchestral backing and imaginative arrangements was the order of the day.'

Tilsley said he realised the exciting possibilities of such an album. He recalled how the band's demo recordings landed on his doormat allowing him to set the music and chords onto a manuscript and he saw that the songs all related to one theme, 'The emotions of a human being under different conditions.' He decided against using a large orchestra on the basis that it would prove unwieldy, electing instead to use three distinct musical groups comprising woodwind, strings and brass. He submitted that the resulting orchestration was sympathetic to the music, a view with which hardly anybody concurs. He asserted that 'a feeling of intimacy' was created and that the arrangements 'seemed to create themselves.' This sounds a somewhat desperate alibi given that much of the orchestration is brash, discordant and unsympathetic.

In an article in the *SF Sorrow* fanzine he explained that with 'Growing In My Mind' there was 'an obvious empty sound at the beginning growing into a deep swelling tutti figure for the centre passage evolving into a repetitive pulse from the celli and harp.' The over-elaborate descriptions explain much about the over-elaborate arrangements and serve to confirm yet again how less can be more. This particular song, a favourite of Phil's, was one of the few worthwhile creations on the album being lyrically excellent as well as providing a haunting melody. The orchestration was less obtrusive and on this occasion did not detract from the recording.

Describing one track, 'The Sun', Tilsley waxed lyrical about 'wistful chord sequences' and, ignoring the hyperbole, this is clearly one song to have benefited from the orchestration. He went on to explain that 'Death Of A Socialite' had a 'crazy-type rhythm pattern' and that he 'just had to put shock chords in that one both with high celli and taken on with the brass.'

Interestingly he claimed that the orchestrations were recorded with the band in the studio, whereas Phil has always sought to imply that they were welded on at some later stage when beyond the band's influence. Interviewed in the summer of 1999, by Mark Andrews for *Progression* magazine, Phil still claimed, 'The *Emotions* album was hijacked halfway through recording. We could have said, 'fuck it, it's not coming out like this, but they would have told us to make another album for them. Reg Tilsley thought he was doing the right thing by having orchestrations on there, but it's got fuck all to do with us.'

'It was a bit of a mistake,' agreed Dick by way of understatement. 'It wasn't done 'oh my god, you know, now they're doing that'. We had meetings, we was there when lots of it was done. We did have doubts about the way it was turning out but we certainly didn't walk in and find there were strings and things on it when they weren't before. We knew extremely well that there were going to be.'

In a Peter Innes interview for *Rock 'n' Reel* magazine Phil adopted a more circumspect outlook and agreed that it was a joint effort. 'I've never actually said it was all bad, I agree that some of it worked well, but it was the way the whole thing was railroaded through that got to us. In different circumstances, as with *SF Sorrow* later, we developed our own enhancements but using instruments and techniques that were ours, within our vision, our range. Certainly we would never have used an MOR backing to coat the material in sugar and shit. Tilsley would come up with an orchestrated score for cellos and violins to play over our music. It was more or less, 'what do you think of that?' Seeking our tacit approval.'

Reg Tilsley's final thoughts were, 'I'm sure you will agree with me that, in a short period of time, the music of the Pretties has progressed from their earlier image to a more balanced diet of sound. Their young wild music is still there, but it is blended with that extra something that comes from playing for wider and more discerning audiences in this country and abroad.'

Sorry Reg, I am afraid that hardly anybody agreed.

Jon Povey took a defensive tack: 'We weren't very happy with *Emotions*. The songs were fairly good but it wasn't produced particularly well and all this brass and stuff all over it ballsed it up.' Wally, similarly cautious, opined, 'I don't think it's one of the better albums. I think the band was going through a strange time, and I think some of the orchestration, in retrospect, seemed to be, well, not really quite what was needed. It was an experiment that maybe wasn't entirely successful.' Skip in his inimitable way cut through the circumlocution saying, 'We had some crap producer who produced a crap album called *Emotions*, which is the only thing I wish the band wasn't associated with.' Skip's view is understandable given the puny and hollow production treatment of his drum sound.

Years later, *Closed Restaurant Blues* on the Bam Caruso label, and the re-mastered *Emotions* on Snapper Records, showcased a number of tracks from which the orchestrations had been removed – although a faint trace of them remained. The bootleg release *Pure and Pretty* also contained seven tracks, allegedly the original demo recordings which were delivered to Tilsley. The *Emotions* recordings were fairly faithful to these 'demo' tracks although they were overlaid with harmonies and lead guitar and occasionally new vocals. These tracks serve to confirm Dick's story. The band, having constructed the demo recordings, then met with Tilsley and this resulted in the demo's being given to him to interpret and to weld his arrangements onto. Having written the musical scores he and the band and his various ensemble's entered the studio and recorded the album together.

Listening to these bare tracks is an unsettling experience. Without the orchestrations they sound sparse and barren although if Tilsley had not been involved they would have been fleshed out and subjected to the band's own arrangements. The austere non-orchestrated versions are unpalatable leaving the listener whistling or humming the missing orchestral accompaniment. 'It's almost charming because it's got that 60s British film sound,' suggested Dick, almost apologetically.

The album was an abject failure commercially as well as musically and Fontana themselves recognised this and issued the album as a budget priced product with an ugly, badly photographed cover. Even the inclusion of a song titled 'Tripping' failed to excite public comment. This recording, one of only two uninfected by orchestration, was about the band's friend Donovan and contained a reference to his alleged use of methedrine. Unlike the diffident 'L.S.D' this song embraced the drug culture with specific references, but such was its lack of quality and Fontana's lack of interest that it was never picked up.

Quite simply, the songs are not very strong or melodic and this, in combination with the dreadful production and bizarre orchestration identifies it as the only duff album the band ever recorded.

Tilsley and the Pretty Things really were chalk and cheese. Whereas the band was known for loutish behaviour and unrelenting wildness, whether in the studio or on stage, Tilsley operated in a different universe, having his own orchestra at the BBC in Birmingham during the fifties. He hosted numerous radio shows such as *Melody Hour* and *Mourning Music* and had worked with Ruby Murray, Shirley Bassey and other easy listening luminaries. In the sixties he advanced to working with Tom Jones, Lulu, Engelbert Humperdinck and PJ Proby. Whilst this was progression from big band scores to the newer hit parade artists the warp jump to the Pretties was far too ambitious and it rebounded on all parties.

Tilsley, like the Pretties, forged a long-term relationship with De Wolfe Music, working primarily on film scores. He also added his orchestral touch to the Pretties first sessions for De Wolfe. These came after those for *Emo-*

tions indicating that the band's resentment was not fully formed at this stage.

A comparison with Love's classic album *Forever Changes*, released nine months later is instrumental in seeing where the band and producer went wrong. Like Phil, Love's Arthur Lee was also unhappy with the brass and string embellishments, but, unlike the *Emotions* latherings, they worked wonderfully. The secret, perhaps, is that on *Forever Changes* the adornments were sympathetic and added to the structure, encouraging the full extent of the melody and often adding an attractive counterpoint. Of course, it also helped that the songs were stronger and more fully evolved, containing better melodies and lyrically more confident.

Another comparison, with the majestic *Sgt Pepper*, which was recorded at the same time, does the Pretties few favours. *Emotions* showed a band in stumbling transition, saddled with unsympathetic production and still trying to assimilate the skills of the Waller/Povey duo. By contrast, *Sgt Pepper* highlighted a band at the heights of artistic endeavour, aided and abetted by a skilful and supportive producer in George Martin. Never again did The Beatles seek to thrust so firmly at the frontiers of rock or experiment in such a committed manner and never again did the Pretties dive so unspectacularly into the trough of 'progression'. Phil's 1966 comments to *Disc* came home to roost at this point. The Beatles had not lost touch, they did know what the public wanted, another excellent album crammed with strong songs gilded by George Martin's exemplary production techniques. *Sgt Pepper* was strong enough to pull public taste along with it, pushing aside barriers and extending pop music further into those barren arenas of respect and artistic esteem. The Pretty Things offering was not even to their own liking, let alone that of the record buying public.

One area where the album did compete with *Sgt Pepper* was through the track 'Death Of A Socialite'. By purest coincidence both May and John Lennon wrote about the death of Guinness heir Tara Browne, although the Beatles track 'Day In The Life' merely touched on it on one verse. Dick recalled that Browne 'fried' on the road where he lived.

Emotions also compared unfavourably with albums made by other Pretties contemporaries during the same period. Hendrix was burning up the fretboard and extending the boundaries assisted by Chas Chandler and Eddie Kramer. His debut album, *Are You Experienced?* sounded mature by comparison as did the efforts of The Small Faces and The Who. 'Itchycoo Park', 'Here Comes The Nice', and 'I'm A Boy' all displayed the polish and direction that *Emotions* strove for but singularly failed to achieve.

Unlike previous band compositions *Emotions* softer songs were lyric-led as opposed to musical ideas with words grafted on. Phil explained that the songs were borne of personal incidents and observations and likened the methodology to the old blues artists where the words were as important as the musical content. Phil didn't feel it appropriate to write lyrics about a cottonpickers woes or downhome Tennessee moonshine and English place names rarely inspired memorable song titles, 'By The Time I Get To Uttoxeter', anyone?

'Growing In My Mind', was the only song written in the old music-first style. Perhaps revealingly it was the only song from *Emotions* to be retained in the Pretties live set thirty years later. The best track on the album and Phil's favourite. 'It really is a nice song and great to play live.'

Dylan's influence inspired many artists, including The Beatles, to begin composing songs with meaningful or obscure lyrics. Back in 1963, even The Beatles were part of the 'moon in June' brigade with such lyrically forgettable songs like 'Thank You Girl' and 'Tip Of My Tongue'. Throughout the 1964-66 period The Pretty Things compositions had been firmly in the blues tradition telling of woeful relationships, 'We'll Be Together', or Diddley-laced pop such as 'Honey I Need'.

As well as The Beatles other bands had pushed songwriting ahead. 'My Generation' showed Pete Townshend writing about his own age group and the impact of the post war youth explosion. The Pretties had used a similar theme on 'Midnight To Six Man'.

Townshend continued with insightful lyrics on 'Substitute' and 'I'm A Boy' and the Rolling Stones also traversed similar ground with songs like 'Mother's Little Helper'. Phil May clearly felt compelled to progress likewise and on *Get The Picture?*' he had taken tentative steps with 'Can't Stand The Pain'. Fontana's insistence on finding the hit song meant that gems such as 'L.S.D.' and 'Me Needing You' were consigned to the B-side. The lyrical progress stalled on *Emotions*. Perhaps Phil was trying too hard to be meaningful and not being himself, whatever the reason the songs didn't stand on their own merit lyrically. This brief hiatus would end once he had escaped the clutches of Fontana and the restrictive Rowland/Baverstock regime.

After *Emotions* had been completed Jon & Wally played their first gig as Pretty Things at Les Sable D'olonne in France where future Pink Floyd manager Steve O'Rourke chaperoned them on behalf of the Bryan Morrison Agency. Wally reported that the resulting mayhem was an unnerving baptism into the disorder that embraced a typical Pretties gig. As he explained in the *Freeway Madness* sleeve notes, 'We had left behind forever the orderly musical discipline that ruled supreme at The Fenmen. Nothing that bland could ever again satisfy taste buds that had now been exposed to the most outlandish and exotic cocktails.'

CHAPTER 6 – The Psychedelic Underground Beckons

As 1967 unfolded the creative forces within the music world were pushing harder at the barriers. As well as the acclaimed *Sgt Pepper*, Jimi Hendrix had propelled himself into the spotlight with singles 'Hey Joe', 'Purple Haze' and 'The Wind Cries Mary' and his seminal guitar extravaganza, *Are You Experienced?* Cream, with their *Fresh Cream* album and 'Strange Brew' single, paralleled Hendrix's rocky style leading the way toward the 'progressive' hard rock format of the early 70s. On the poppier side, The Monkees were dominating the charts with their albums, vying with the seemingly irrepressible *Sound of Music* soundtrack for the top spot.

For The Pretty Things the shift to the next phase would be swift, a quantum jump, a startling metamorphosis. Indeed, a seasoned listener would probably have failed to identify the new sounds as the work of the R&B wretches. Free of the Fontana channelling and the blinkered production they would create rather than simply record. Songs would not be written but unfold and evolve. Instruments would be chosen for their sound and vibe rather than the purist values of guitar, bass and drums or the old-school patina of orchestration.

The band members immersed themselves in the burgeoning London underground scene. The sense of musical freedom multiplied by the experimentation of The Beatles fed through to the wider scene and new bands appeared, intent on exploring the new genre. Many existing R&B bands also chose to adopt the new underground ethos. The Spencer Davis Group lost the Winwood Brothers with Stevie forming Traffic to move beyond the R&B/soul boundaries of his previous music. The Paramounts cast off their R&B clothes and emerged as Procol Harum with a new dual organ/piano based approach and the added factor of Keith Reid's avant garde lyrics which, like Phil May's, often touched on his favoured maritime themes. Even poppier bands like the Spectres reinvented themselves as Status Quo to perform cod-psychedelia.

Phil recalled the sensation of being pigeonholed by Fontana, maintaining that no dialogue existed. At this point memories differ, Phil contends that they had their contract with EMI and were just looking to leave whilst Dick is adamant that the period between recording *Emotions* and signing to EMI was quite extensive.

As usual Dick's recollection is more correct as confirmed by extensive archive delving. 'There was a gap in between. We weren't signed with anybody for a short period and that was when we started doing all the stuff like

'Defecting Grey' and all that. By that time Jon and Wally were in the band and psychedelia was up and coming both from other people and from us and we did 'Walking Through My Dreams', 'Turn My Head', 'Mr Evasion' and all those things. We recorded a load of demos at Denmark Street, in Southern Sound and we weren't contracted to anybody and included in that lot was 'Defecting Grey'.'

Jon Povey: 'We began to get into a style of things where the new line up would be very much a band thing rather than an augmented, orchestrated set up where it would be strictly organ based, drums and guitar. The Pretty Things, never having had an organist before, we tended to experiment with the organ and with effects and sounds and all that kind of stuff. I was a big fan of musique concrete, which was all sort of French sounds of pianos being chucked out of buildings and all that kind of stuff, backwards tapes. We went into that era, if you like, where we were experimenting with them kinds of things. So out of that came things like 'Mr Evasion' and 'Defecting Grey' which was three or four songs pieced together made into one song, which was quite interesting as nobody had ever done anything that went into 3/4, into 4/4, back into 3/4. It took a long time to do and was never released in that format.'

Jon thought that it was at this stage that EMI became curious. 'EMI got interested through those things. That was a very interesting period and we were experimenting with all that stuff musically and graphically with Phil's cover drawings of *SF Sorrow*.' The addition of Povey's Farfisa organ created possibilities that the previous incarnations could not have contemplated.

Dick was also a fan of avante garde sounds as he told Alan Clayson. 'We were listening to some pretty weird stuff – Sun Ra, musique concrete, John Cage, Pierre Henri. Phil and I were also both mad on modern jazz.'

In the midst of this The Pretty Things were booked to play at the 14 Hour Technicolour Dream, a benefit gig for *International Times*, an underground magazine that had been busted back in March. Held on April 29th 1967 in Alexandra Palace it attracted 10,000 fans who turned up to see the impressive line up of Pink Floyd, The Move, The Soft Machine, Savoy Brown and many others. Although the Pretties played in their new psychedelic style it is strange to consider that the disappointing *Emotions* had not yet been released. A fan impressed by their performance would have been bemused and horribly disappointed upon buying it.

On September 28 1967 The Pretty Things signed a contract with The Gramophone Company Ltd (trading as EMI Records) and their signatures were witnessed by Steve O'Rourke of the Bryan Morrison Agency. Skip's father, Matthew Skipper, had to be a signatory as Skip was still under the legal age to sign a contract.

'The Agreement', as it would later be referred to in various Court hearings, was made official on October 2. It was a one-year rolling contract, which allowed EMI the option to extend it annually for up to five years. The Pretty Things obligation for the first year was two double-sided singles – four recordings in all.

For each single the band would receive three old pence – about one-and-a-quarter pence in today's revised currency. An album would net them 42 old pence – seventeen-and-a-half pence today. Both would be paid on 85% of UK sales. If sales exceeded 250,000 the royalty would rise to three-and-a-half old pence. Strangely the contract was for a fixed sum whereas the Fontana deal had specified a percentage, an omission that spelled financial disaster as inflation quickly eroded historic values and served to underline how pop was seen as a short-term fad.

In respect of the contract EMI paid the sum of £3,500 to the Bryan Morrison Agency as an advance payment of future royalties. The band would have to sell 330,000 singles or 23,500 albums before they received another penny. This advance was relatively modest compared to the £5,000 that Bryan Morrison had secured for the Pink Floyd some months earlier.

EMI placed them on the Columbia label, into the capable hands of staff producer Norman Smith. Then aged 44, Smith, or 'Golden Bollocks' as he was nicknamed, had begun working as a tape engineer at Abbey Road Studios in 1959 and had served as engineer on all the Beatles recordings from their first ever session in 1962, that spawned 'Besame Mucho', up until the final recordings for *Rubber Soul*. Effectively he had been George Martin's right hand man.

Smith was formerly a saxophonist and big band leader during the fifties but gave it up to work at EMI. In February 1966 Norman became Recording Manager in EMI's A&R department and had produced a number of artists without achieving chart success. Smith recalls that his main act was, 'Herbie Goins, an ex American Air Force chap. He was the closest I heard to a jazz singer. He did impress me, we had a go, we sold quite a lot. That's in the days of the pirate ships.' Shortly after this he was handed the Pink Floyd who had just enjoyed success with their Joe Boyd produced debut single, 'Arnold Layne'.

Norman's first contact with The Pretty Things came through Bryan Morrison, whose agency also handled Goins and the Floyd. 'Bryan Morrison actually sounded me out on The Pretty Things. Up to that time they had not got a very good name, particularly because of the drummer. So I said to Brian, this was after Floyd had made a success, yes I **would** be interested but I wanted to make it clear also that I wouldn't put up with any of those antics that I've heard about. He said 'well I can assure you they are completely changed' so he brought them in to my office, we had a chat, we got on very well. I was, I must admit, rather apprehensive of course, as one would be, perhaps they were as well. A fairly nervous kind of initial meeting but after that we got on like a house on fire.'

The first EMI recording session with Norman Smith took place on October 3 when they ensconced themselves in Sound Techniques Studio in South West London and produced the classic psychedelic single 'Defecting Grey'. This collage of various recurring themes lasted for over 8 minutes, an inordinate time for a single in those pre-'Hey Jude' and 'McArthur Park' days. Traditionalist thinking and the pirate radio stations airplay considerations demanded editing it down to around three minutes and label bosses instructed Smith to do exactly this. Norman edited it down to four and a half minutes but then dug his heels in. The freshness and inventiveness of the band appealed to him and was in keeping with the surge in studio exploration techniques pioneered by The Beatles and Pink Floyd. Vocal distortions abounded with helpings of pub piano, sculpted harmonies and frequent time changes.

Before signing with EMI they had recorded a version of 'Defecting Grey' at Southern Sound. Although this studio was technically inferior to Sound Techniques the demo version had a vibe that they failed to recapture. Norman and the band preferred the demo version but EMI rules disallowed them the luxury of a choice – non EMI recordings and non-EMI producers were proscribed.

Dick: 'He was interested in doing 'Defecting Grey' and when we did it he was actually the first one to say that he didn't think it had the same atmosphere as the demo. That certainly made me think that this guy was not too bad because he's saying I've done this production but I still don't quite think I've captured, or you lot maybe haven't done it as well. Even with the whole of EMI's recording expertise it didn't have the same atmosphere.'

Wally concurred: 'We never recreated that original feel. It's very hard to recreate things. It was done in a small demo studio in London under very trying circumstances. But things happen, there's no way to explain it. You can go into a really beautiful studio with every gadget in the world, and you can't find that magic thing.'

Thirty-two years later, in an interview for *Progression* magazine, Phil explained the song's storyline. 'It was the first gay song. We used to call everybody who did a normal job 'greys' – people who wore grey suits and ties, and so on. The character in the song was a defecting grey; i.e. he had found something in his life, which took him out of what was perceived as normal. He was making that transition. There were no words like 'outing' or whatever, but no one ever asked me what it was about.'

The flip side was the crafted 'Mr Evasion', which was another song about establishment figures looking to break away from their metaphorical chains. Both recordings epitomised the explorative ethos and the quest for new sounds that permeated much of the music scene in England in 1967. 'Mr Evasion' was completed during the same sessions as 'Defecting Grey' on October 11 and 12.

This 'sad Mr Ordinary' theme was fast becoming a trend. Ray Davies may have started it with 'Well Respected Man' and other songs, and Jimi Hendrix added his contemptuous comments on 'If Six Was Nine', where he sneered at 'white collar conservatives flashing down the street, point their plastic fingers at me'.

Chris Welch, reviewing 'Defecting Grey' for *Melody Maker*, was sceptical of the band's new direction. 'Good old Pretty Things. Right in the middle of the sitar, backwards guitar, electronics and bits of tape sellotaped together, you can hear a rocking group bashing away. You have to put up with a bit in three four time and some coy singing, then comes the blast. It's all a terrible mess but quite fun. It's a pity groups ever discovered that word "progress".'

Rather acerbic, although the last comment was almost right – it was a pity they ever discovered the *song* 'Progress'.

Not surprisingly this strange, extended single failed to feature on the coveted playlists of the new and hip BBC Radio One. Did EMI push it? No way. Quite simply, it was not heard and with the pirate stations finished, the single stood little chance of charting. On November 27th 1967, a month after its release, the band recorded a *Top Gear* session at Piccadilly. As well as 'Defecting Grey', they performed versions of the next single, 'Talking About The Good Times' and 'Walking Through My Dreams' as well as a great song that was never recorded – 'Turn My Head'. At the same time The Beatles were recording and releasing 'I Am The Walrus'. The Pretties had caught up with The Beatles in just seven months!

On November 1, they had paid their first visit to the Abbey Road Studios. In Studio 2 the band, Norman Smith and engineers Ken Scott and Mike Sheedy started work on 'Bracelets Of Fingers', a song that would eventually form part of the *SF Sorrow* album. Undeterred by the disinterest in 'Defecting Grey' they continued recording and from November through to January 1968 crafted a glorious pairing for release – 'Talking About The Good Times' – complete with the dull thud of a Tibetan drum and much use of the Fairchild Limitors – and 'Walking Through My Dreams'. Both songs featured the layered harmonies, which were becoming an increasingly prominent feature of their work. January also saw the first sessions for the song 'Private Sorrow'.

In November, EMI issued a press release highlighting the Pretties transition from R&B insurgents to boundary-pushing artists. Dick explained the band's philosophy, 'We want to start from scratch again and introduce our audiences to our new sounds. Our main problem in the old days was that we were more popular on the Continent than over here, playing R&B, so now we want to concentrate again on the British market and take the risk of losing out on our success abroad.'

This typically prosaic release informed that 'Phil likes peace and hates violence'. Dick, we are told, 'dislikes routine and says his hobby is trying to make a huge hit record'.

The band's lifestyle had moved in line with the burgeoning counter culture and for the two new band members the changes were dramatic. Jon Povey: 'We started taking more and more drugs and we went from the clean squeaky image, which I had anyway with The Fenmen, into a fairly decadent lifestyle which was taking LSD and cruising around meeting those kind of people in that lifestyle.'

Talking in 1998 to *Noise*, Phil explained, 'Experimenting with drugs ran parallel with our musical experimentation. When we were in art school there were all these 'don't do's – you can't grow your hair long, you can't do this, you can't do that. The minute someone would put a fence around something we were very interested to find out what was on the other side.'

During this period they showed a noticeable leaning toward US style harmony rock. The absorption of Povey and Waller had introduced Fenmen-style harmonies as displayed on 'Talking About The Good Times'. Their fascination with The Byrds – harmony vocals as well as 12-string guitar – led to the Pretties performing 'Why', 'Renaissance Fair' and 'Eight Miles High' as well as new self-penned numbers 'Turn My Head 'and 'Spring'.

Jon Povey: 'We used to do 'Eight Miles High' and 'Why'. We were very influenced by the Byrds at one stage because we loved that 12-string guitar, that Rickenbacker. We had the originality of the R&B stuff and it was like R&B with harmonies then it developed into complicated songs and tunes because we were very much into *Sgt Pepper's* as an album, very much into Crosby Stills and Nash, that harmony thing.'

CHAPTER 7 – The First Rock Opera Is Born

The concept of popular music and the idea of what constituted 'the song' expanded as the 60s continued to unfold. The Beatles had destroyed the traditional view that an album should consist of an accumulation of previous hits or a series of cover versions. *Rubber Soul* had contained fourteen original compositions with no filler and *Revolver* ploughed ahead with equally superb melodies and the special production effects that Abbey Road was soon to become renowned for. *Sgt Pepper* had pushed on even further with its story thread of an imaginary band playing a concert.

It was in this age of radical thinking, with the opening of previously locked musical-doors and with the boost of acid and a whole cocktail of groovy drugs that The Pretty Things found themselves as 1967 proceeded. The jump from *Emotions* to *SF Sorrow* was one of massive proportions, equivalent perhaps to The Beatles vaulting straight from the lightweight bitter-sweet pop of *A Hard Day's Night* to the mind-expanding grooves of *Revolver*.

The first Rock Opera, a psychedelic masterpiece, the ultimate missed opportunity – how best to describe *SF Sorrow*? Sadly, whilst the unknowing public are still likely to consider The Who's *Tommy* as the first rock opera, assuming this derogated term retains any real meaning, discerning music fans will be aware that this accolade actually belongs to *SF Sorrow*. *Record Collector* magazine tentatively suggested that *The Adventures of Simon Simopath* by Nirvana (UK 60s version) might be the first. It is indeed a fact that *SF Sorrow* was preceded by *The Adventures of Simon Simopath*, Nirvana's science fiction pantomime. This commercially unsuccessful album (familiar story, right) carried a central theme that like *SF Sorrow* revolved around the life of the title character. Unlike *Sorrow* the album lacked a cohesive story, which implied a plot structured around song titles. Also, running for less than 26 minutes, it barely qualified as an operetta.

A Rock Opera is, by definition, a concept album but a concept album is not necessarily a rock opera. A concept can be nebulous, for example a dream sequence or the day in the life of a sparrow, whilst a rock opera must retain a story thread and involve one or more characters promoting the narrative through their songs.

SF Sorrow was recorded through Winter 1967 to late Summer 1968 whereas the *Tommy* sessions extended from October 1968 to March 1969. Sorrow's birth passage preceded *Tommy* and was clearly the template for many future concept albums. Was *Tommy* one of them? Opinions differ regarding this and Pete Townshend has become increasingly defensive and defiant in recent years. Talking to DJ Johnson some thirty years later Dick said, 'I always thought what a good guy because he always said 'yeah, we listened to it', but now he's going 'you know, I never heard it.'

SF Sorrow was released in the UK three months before The Who completed the *Tommy* recording sessions so there was plenty of time for Townshend to have heard the tracks and incorporated themes or snippets. For a fact there are significant storyline parallels between *SF Sorrow* and *Tommy* and these are deserving of a closer inspection.

SF Sorrow starts with the main character's birth and Tommy starts similarly. Sorrow witnesses the tragic death of his girlfriend and becomes traumatised whereas Tommy witnesses the murder of his mother's lover and becomes traumatised. Sorrow meets a mysterious character, Baron Saturday and Tommy meets a mysterious character, the Acid Queen. Sorrow is taken on an amazing journey and, guess what? Tommy goes on an amazing journey. Sorrow confronts his own reflection and Tommy confronts himself in the mirror.

Arthur Brown put these parallels in perspective advising that in post World War II Britain the twin subjects of trauma and isolation were not uncommon. Arthur explained that Townshend was already working on his Rael project, which, he says, was originally intended for him. He said that Kit Lambert advised Townshend to keep the concept approach but turn it into something for The Who.

Twink is in no doubt that The Who listened to *S. F. Sorrow* extensively, as he told Ivor Trueman in 1985. 'They phoned Phil May up and said, 'Hey Phil, we think it's great and we're working on something very similar.'

Other than 'Pinball Wizard', where the intro reeked of 'Old Man Going', the songs themselves bore little similarity to *SF Sorrow*, certainly no psychedelia, but the storyline and the concept did appear remarkably similar. Another group, Rainbow Ffolly, suffered a similar loss of credibility because of The Who. Their album *Sallies Fforth* included jingles as links between the tracks but any perception of innovation was destroyed when *The Who Sell Out*, containing similar links, was released more speedily. Like The Pretty Things, Rainbow Fforth had recorded their album before The Who.

Tommy was released in the UK just five months after *SF Sorrow* and due to *Sorrow's* relative failure the significant similarities went unnoticed. The Who's label, Track, did a good job of marketing the 'new' concept whereas Columbia simply released *SF Sorrow* and let it drift on the winds. Either they failed to recognise it as different or they weren't sure what to do.

The original Columbia release of *Sorrow* included a gatefold sleeve complete with lyrics and narrative which related the life story – birth to senility

– of Sebastian F Sorrow. The album's roots can be traced back to the experimentation evident on the 'Defecting Grey' single which Phil described as 'A maquette for the album.' The band wished to break from the then typical notion of an album being five A-sides and five B-sides which they found both boring and restrictive, effectively a accumulation of their previous twelve months achievements.

Two songs that would eventually appear on the album, 'Bracelets of Fingers' and 'I See You' had already been recorded before the idea of a rock opera had been rationalised. These were carefully worked into the storyline although band members concede that the story was often adjusted to fit around the songs. Neither 'Walking Through My Dreams' nor 'Talking About The Good Times' could be fitted into the story and they were issued as a single.

Dick recalled how it was Wally who came up with the idea of an album with a story thread. 'Now Phil always says he wrote the story and then we hung all the songs on it, I think that the story also developed with the recording of the album. I think that the story kind of got modified and pushed along by the writing of the songs. He didn't have the words as they are on the cover until quite late because I remember typing it all out, laying it all out, actually I think I got my sister to type it all out if I remember rightly. Wally and I would both agree that that is how it appeared.' The band was taken with the idea of a connected storyline and Phil, who had written a short story about a Sgt Sorrow, then shaped it into the album concept.

Wally: 'I heard people tell me about *Sgt Pepper* before I heard it, it sounded like they done a story, I mean the words rock opera never occurred to me but I thought they did a story with music. I thought what a brilliant idea, why on earth didn't somebody else think of that, trust The Beatles to do that. When I got *Sgt Pepper* it wasn't that. It was a bloody brilliant idea and I thought why don't we do it? Why don't we go for it? Well we did, eventually, with a story of Phil's which grew and grew as we got into it, it kind of evolved, the basic story was Phil's but every song almost wrote itself really.'

Dick had discussed this with Wally. 'Wally said, "it cheeses me off because Phil always says it was his idea and actually it was my idea." Wally was saying how gradually over the years it has become Phil's big idea when the actual idea of doing a story, that came from him listening to *Sgt Pepper*. I can remember listening to *Sgt Pepper* with him and we can remember both being in the same place and listening to it on the car radio on the dock. In France I believe, or waiting to go to France. I've rather made a point of saying in interviews and things it was Wally's idea. I think that's fair enough really. Historical accuracy, where it's due, is not such a bad thing. I'm not gonna counter some of the things that have gone into myth but it doesn't fit together as well as the truth does.'

Wally: 'The story of *SF Sorrow* wasn't my idea, the idea of doing that format for an album was my idea. Phil was already writing a story, I mean I didn't know and when I suggested it it didn't go down too well, but it just came to pass that we did. It was me who brought it up during a tour of Denmark. I remember saying it in the car.'

Jon remembered the main idea being Phil's and that the band then developed the character, 'It was almost like writing a script for a particular character.' Wally explained it was 'a case of songs inspiring words and vice versa.'

Phil's standard response is that he wrote a short story, Sergeant Sorrow, which he suggested to the band who approved it. From there he developed characters and expanded the story, demoting Sorrow to Private in the process. 'Sebastian Sorrow is a timeless sad story', Phil told *Melody Maker*. 'But it's not about anybody in particular. There are bits of all of us in it. Each track is about a phase in his life ending up with the loneliest person in the world.'

Dick discussed the problem that arises when each band member retains a different recollection of the same event. 'That's absolutely true of any historical situation, it's one thing I really figured out. I must say, as usual, as everybody does, my memory of events is more accurate.'

Norman Smith explained that he also harboured the notion of making a concept album. 'I did then say to Phil that I wasn't interested in recording nine to ten tracks or songs. I was very interested in, and had thought about it in the past, of a concept album and he thoroughly agreed. He said, 'well you know that's strange really cause I've also thought about that' and of course then he came up with the idea of the story of *SF Sorrow* which I thought was terrific and we thoroughly enjoyed making it.' With a wealth of studio trickery, *SF Sorrow* is truly the first rock opera. Most definitely an inspiration for *Tommy*, regardless of Pete Townshend's recent protestations.

'Fourteen months on acid' – Phil's description of the recording process. By his own admission he was out of it much of the time and there are many segments he cannot recall. 'I had a fantastic time on acid', he confessed to Trevor Hodgett. So fantastic that he had quite forgotten that the album sessions extended from November 1967 through to September 1968, a ten month period.

Jon Povey remembered those days for affording the freedom and creativity to work. 'Very much a free time with no cares and, apart from the odd shilling, being able to do virtually what you wanted to. In many cases unlimited studio time because one wanted to record, one wanted to play one's songs. It allowed you to let your creativity come forward, out of that came

SF Sorrow which was written in an entirely different way, a story first then a track here and a track there. Then, as time went on, trying to fill up what was left with a meaningful track, which was quite difficult. That was all written in Phil's house in Erith, in the front room. I was living there as well, in the spare room.'

The band members were constantly together under the same roof and Povey recalled that it was very much a family thing. 'We were all in the same house virtually and we would come and start whenever we felt like it and we would influence it either from a percussional, rhythm, harmony or chord change point of view.'

The R&B days were now distant memories and Phil confirmed that in 1967 EMI was the place to be if you wanted to experiment. He compared it favourably with Fontana where they were 'so close-minded it was like working for the Ministry of Defence.'

The album was a long time in the making in order to accommodate studio bookings and gigs, which provided much needed income. Between recording sessions the band continued to gig hard. Wally: 'We'd dash off to Germany for a month, and then come back and we'd have a couple of days to sort things out with what we'd do in the studio. Then we'd do maybe a week in the studio and then we'd have to go somewhere else.'

The main engineer on *SF Sorrow* was Peter Mew who was a regular from April 1968. Prior to April he had assisted Ken Scott on the sessions for 'Talking About The Good Times' and 'Walking Through My Dreams', as had Mike Sheedy. Peter had only joined EMI two years earlier and recalled how very fortunate he was in landing the job. 'I was an assistant engineer and I turned up one morning to be an assistant and the engineer (Ken Scott) didn't turn up. So it was 'can you take over'? I did a day with them and Norman said they'd like you to carry on and do the rest of the album.'

Peter remembered the period 1967 to 1975 as the single most exciting and adventurous period in record production, a period, coincidentally, that exactly parallels Norman Smith's production career with the Pretty Things. Peter recalled that that Norman Smith was a 'new cutting edge producer. People like me were new engineers, up till then it had been people kind of in a rut, if you know what I mean. Just about the late 60s period there were several new engineers coming on, Geoff Emerick and Tony Clarke after me, who were very much into the new technology, much more prepared to be experimental and try different things.'

With just four tracks recorded the band was rocked by the unexpected departure of Skip Alan. Skip had fallen in love with a girl from Biarritz and abruptly left sending the band a brief telegram.

Skip brought his girlfriend back to England intent on leading a 'normal life', quite some objective given that neither could speak the other's language. 'I just left them deep in the shit,' reminisced Skip. They married and then Skip moved to France where he worked as a DJ in a bar. 'I had OD'd on the scene and had to get away.' The relationship soon foundered and they divorced with Skip returning to the UK.

Skip's departure left the band with a big problem, only four tracks had been recorded and they were behind a schedule that had already been extended twice. In desperation the band approached old friend and previous stand-in Twink. Phil recalled Twink wanting some financial reward for assisting them, which posed a significant problem as they were virtually broke. The only option was to offer him a share of the publishing on the album even though the songs had mostly been written. Twink himself remembered Phil asking him to 'help us for a month' – in the event he lasted almost eighteen months.

Twink was already well travelled. He had replaced Viv Prince on numerous occasions including a couple of tracks on *Get The Picture*? After the Fairies, Twink joined The In-Crowd which then metamorphosed into Tomorrow. With the failure of the classic psychedelic release 'My White Bicycle' and the album *Revolution* as well as singer Keith West's preoccupation with his 'teenage opera', Tomorrow had imploded leaving Twink without a gig.

Twink was not party to the band's contract with EMI although he was already signed to EMI through his contract with Tomorrow. This apparently insignificant matter would later cause Twink much financial grief and provide a major headache for all concerned.

During 1967 they had used Abbey Road Studio 2 but after this they were switched to Studio 3 so that Beatles sessions could continue in their favoured Studio. The band utilised the 4-track equipment and experimented with backwards tapes, ADT, out of phase microphones, varispeed, ring modulators and various new gadgets pieced together by EMI's Chief Engineer Ken Townsend. Dick Taylor recalled them bouncing down all these sounds from one machine to the next, sometimes hundreds of overdubs and tracks. As well as the flavour of the month sitar they started using the mellotron, a keyboard instrument that used pre-recorded tapes. A favourite of The Moody Blues it suffered from being relatively immobile, due to its size and its unerring capacity to quickly become out of tune through loss of calibration.

Povey was making use of a Lowrey Organ, which was often fed through a Leslie Speaker as well as sometimes using George Harrison's sitar when it was conveniently left around the studio.

Wally recalled the actual process of recording. 'Everything was four track, and we'd record probably bass, drums and maybe a keyboard on one side and a rhythm instrument on the other side. That would be the original four-track. Then we'd mix those four tracks down to two on another four-track machine, so the centre tracks would be the stereo of what we'd just done, leaving us two spare tracks either side. We went through four or five generations sometimes, just doing that. Every time we went to another generation we'd put on some backing vocals or something then we'd have to mix down again, leaving us two spare for the stereo. Sometimes when we came to the final mix we'd be adding things live because we couldn't get them onto the tape.'

Dick explained how one key track came about. 'With 'Balloon Burning' there was quite a lot of plagiarism in there, some of it unconscious. With the da-da-da-da-da riff I unconsciously plagiarised Love's *Forever Changes*. The second song on one side has got that little riff, but briefly as part of the guitar solo. I probably heard it and completely forgot that it existed and that became the riff but the da-da-da (descending riff prior to chorus) was an album by The Fifth Dimension, and I had that album and there's a track on there which has got that little bit, a phrase like that done by the backing on there and I kind of took that and twiddled it around. Now that was something Wally didn't realise, he said when we were writing 'Balloon Burning' 'I did this blah, blah, blah' I thought, I know where I ripped that off from. So I know exactly how that appeared because I did lift and change something and then Wally figured out the chords to go behind it.'

A careful listen to 'A House Is Not A Motel' on *Forever Changes* confirms Dick's story. At the tail-end of the track John Echols hammers out the staccato riff that Dick then borrowed.

SF Sorrow contains the first and so far only Pretty Things number to be 'sung' by Dick Taylor – 'Baron Saturday', which was recorded between April and May 1968. Dick's vocal skills barely exceed Skip's and, presumably aware of this, he was reluctant to do it. Phil explained that in the studio he had to be faced away from the band to keep his nerve.

'I was doing it one way and it didn't work,' explained Dick, 'I went into ham-actor mode and did it. My Richard Harris voice,' he chuckled.

With 'Bracelets of Fingers', the album also contained one of the first songs about wanking, Self abuse is common within the music industry but wanking was not a conventional theme. Phil expressed amazement that nobody grasped it at the time, he expected to hear from EMI but they never realised. In this instance Phil was following Townshend whose 'Pictures of Lily' had charted in 1966. The final track, the plaintive 'Loneliest Person', was written by Phil in a French garret when he was alone and perhaps because of this it is often singled out as an autobiographical track. Phil assures that it wasn't, that it was written especially for the album. With only Phil and Dick on the track it proved relatively easy to put down being dealt with on two separate sessions in June and August of 1968.

Peter Mew recalled how Abbey Road offered the perfect environment for serious artistes. 'There wasn't pressure on Abbey Road producers because Abbey Road was a facility for the record company. Now it's not, the whole accountant thing has taken over. We didn't have to make a profit, we were a tax loss. There wasn't the pressure there is now. I never got the impression at all, throughout that period, that there was any pressure on anybody to keep the cost down of the recordings. There was always enough time to get things right.'

During this period they took a four-week late Summer break to appear in their second film *What's Good For The Goose*. Foolishly and incorrectly labelled a soft-core sex film – it was actually a hotchpotch of old-style British slap-stick humour, cod-psychedelia and slight nudity – it starred Sir Norman Wisdom as a starch-shirted bank manager who falls for flower child Sally Geeson. The film originally included a scene where a topless Geeson is pictured with Wisdom in his hotel bedroom. This prurience proved too much for the powers that be and for video and television screenings the scene was excised.

It was very much a film of its time, something that could only have been made during that very short period when flower power was relevant and had been assimilated into the national consciousness. It could even be described as quaint although most reviewers would probably favour the word 'crap'. Even Wisdom, in his autobiography, allowed it a mere chronological mention as if embarrassed by its very existence.

Although Phil had previously spoken of his ambition to become an actor the band's involvement was for one reason only – the money. It was originally intended that they would write two songs for the film and they expected their stay on the film set in Southport to be two weeks. Gradually they were written more and more into the script because, as Phil recalled, 'The script wasn't working. In fact, it was a piece of shit.'

The film deal was arranged through Phil's connection with De Wolfe, a music library company which supplied background music for films, television and radio. What was originally intended to be a cameo part eventually turned into a fairly major film role. The band was seen playing, as the Happy Apple Band, at a discotheque surrounded by 'hippies' and flower children, all of whom are revealed as poseurs and free-loaders. Later, the band featured at a party that teetered on the edge of implied orgy. Wally could be seen canoodling under a blanket with a 'flower-child' although word is he actually entertained more than a passing fancy for elfin co-star Sally Geeson.

During the long delays between filming, plenty of acid was dropped and they continued writing for *SF Sorrow*. They had plenty of time, eight weeks altogether. Phil listed some of the excellent imported dope that they smoked. 'Every week there was Nepalese, Temple Bliss, South African Gold and lots of different stuff coming through. Some days they called us for shooting and we didn't know where we were. Christ knows what they thought.' To obtain their dope they involved Wisdom's seventeen year old understudy to score for them in nearby Liverpool, something that Wisdom was less than impressed with when, rather mischievously, the band told him.

'We did have a lot of fun,' Twink recounted to Nick Saloman. 'We went up for two weeks in Southport and it was like a big family living in a hotel together'.

Complete versions of five songs were included in the film although sound levels were reduced when the preposterous dialogue intruded. Apart from the rather uninspiring title track the four remaining songs 'Alexander', 'Eagle's Son', 'Blow Your Mind' and 'It'll Never Be Me', were excellent. Another De Wolfe issued song, 'Rave Up, sounded as if it came from the same sessions although it was not included in the film. The songs formed part of *Even More Electric Banana*, the third in a series of recordings made for De Wolfe, who specialised in providing background music for film, TV and radio. One presupposes that the Electric Banana name was inspired by the lyrics to Donovan's 1967 hit single 'Mellow Yellow'.

Ulf Marquardt in the liner notes to the *Electric Banana* CDs suggested that the De Wolfe recordings were intended to 'offer an avant-gardistic alternative'. Band members recall otherwise. Jon Povey sounded disgusted saying, 'Yeah, don't really want to talk about that too much. It was just purely to get some money.'

Wally considered the material lightweight, 'It was of that time, it was all kind of flower-power stuff, I don't think they really stand up today to too close a scrutiny, that's my opinion. I'm not a fan and I can't see why people find that exceptional. To my mind we've done lots of good stuff but to my way of thinking that doesn't get anywhere near the real cream. Most of that stuff is second rate,' he explained. 'Some of it is all rightish but most is stuff we didn't think was good enough to put on an album of our own and we wouldn't put our proper name to it.'

Wally recalled that Phil had arranged the De Wolfe connection before he and Jon Povey joined. On the initial *Electric Banana* album, De Wolfe had insisted they record four songs by a fellow named Peter Reno, 'Free Love', 'Cause I'm A Man', 'Love Dance And Sing' and 'Street Girl'. Phil refused to sing them and Wally and Jon took the mike for these unexceptional recordings. One of the best songs, the band written 'Grey Skies', eventually surfaced as background music in the film *The Haunted House of Horror*.

Phil's dislike of singing lyrics other than his own has become notorious within the band. It has been suggested that many a good song was 'lost' because it arrived fully formed and lyrically complete, although nobody would argue that any of the four Reno compositions fell into the 'good' category.

Dick recalled that De Wolfe issued albums where one entire side consisted of instrumental versions, the backing tracks without vocals or choruses. 'When it was first issued they put out all the vocals on one side of the album, they were on 10 inch vinyl with quite plain covers with a drawn banana and diagonal writing. They weren't meant for public release but it was in the music library and it was really breaking the rules at the time because we weren't paid musicians union rates because we were getting money for the writing and stuff, so it was very unofficial. So if a film producer wanted something to go on his film he could either choose something vocal or something instrumental and you may have noticed there were some that weren't written by us, and the guy was a TV producer and he wanted his songs on these albums. So in some of his shows he could use his own stuff and he saw it as a way of making a little bit of money on the side so that other producers would think, oh Peter does this. I presume that's how it works. Anyway, that's how it started, with Peter Reno.'

"Street Girl', yeah Wally sang that. It was a bit like when we got 'Rosalyn' it was Denmark Street with a bloke pounding it out on a piano. These were similar, they sounded a bit sub-Matt Monroe. It was like "Oh, what the fucking hell are we gonna do with these things?' We just put whatever riffs we could muster up against it, changed the chords around a bit and turned it into what they then became.'

Wally, who enjoyed a productive long-term relationship with De Wolfe in his own right, remembered how they recorded an album in a day for a flat fee. 'And then, of course, you get the royalties coming in for them throughout the years from the Performing Rights Society, our equivalent of BMI and ASCAP over there. Everything was done in a small eight-track demo studio just big enough to swing a cat around. If we had a De Wolfe session coming up we'd sit down and in an afternoon we'd thrash out the whole thing and we'd walk into the studio still fixing a few lyrics and in an afternoon the whole thing's down. That's the way it works, It's almost like a telephone box the bloody thing was so small, that little studio we used. In the early days it was only four-track it was like a demo studio down Wardour Street.'

Jon Povey agreed, 'In those days it was very much four-track recording where you bumped over vocals and everything while you were doing something. So you put bass on and did vocals on the same track, fairly dated in this day and age but then you didn't have any choice.'

Dick posed an alternative view of their musical worth. 'Funny thing is the things like 'Alexander' and all the stuff around then is actually some of the best stuff we did, a lot of people have said to me you should go back to it, it's really good stuff. It's a bit like the way we're so rigid in our condemnation of *Emotions*, you listen to it again and think hang on, we've missed the point here. Here we are slagging it off but there's some good songs, some good stuff on there. I find one of the most interesting times for The Pretty Things was just after *Emotions* was finished and we were off Fontana and we weren't on EMI. All these bubbling up ideas and the demo's and I think it was a time when we were doing stuff just because we wanted to, we didn't really care if it sold or not because there was no one to sell it to. At that point there wasn't a record company. By the time it got to *SF Sorrow* and *Parachute* it was almost too... formed.'

Nonetheless, Dick excepted, the band members do not view the results with any fondness, although many fans consider the best of the material on a par with their official output. Jon Povey gave his grudging assent to this view, 'There was some good stuff there. It wasn't really meant for anything, there was some material around and we went in there just to play it and we got paid for doing it – we needed the bread.'

The first De Wolfe issue was *Electric Banana* with Tilsley Orchestral, in 1967. Less avante garde than *Emotions* the orchestration sounded bland. The following year came *More Electric Banana* and in 1969 *Even More Electric Banana* containing the five film songs. After a four-year hiatus the band recorded *Hot Licks*, subtitled (Progressive Rock Music) then, in 1978, *The Return of the Electric Banana* (Vocal and Instrumental Group Sounds) which also included tracks by various members of later Pretty Things spin-off the Fallen Angels.

'I See You' had been recorded prior to the idea of an opera and a version, complete with Phil May lead vocal as opposed to the Jon Povey version, had been one of the songs recorded at a De Wolfe session earlier in 1967. The song was conveniently integrated into the storyline.

During the *SF Sorrow* sessions producer Norman Smith effectively became a sixth member, as Phil explained. 'He was so creative. He actually encouraged us to go further and we were all writing and giving input.' Smith's inspiration was such that he became part of the creation process in the same way that George Martin influenced The Beatles. Smith also received a co-writing credit on 'Well of Destiny', a melange containing snippets of previous songs interwoven with tape loops, mellotron and guitar riffs and the typical Pretty Things percussion wash. It is Smith whose voice can be heard intoning the names of the dead and missing at the tail-end of 'Private Sorrow'.

How did the Pretties compare with their friends and rivals the Pink Floyd?

In terms of record sales, no contest. The Floyd had caught the imagination of the underground movement and helped by their two psychedelic hit singles 'Arnold Layne' and 'See Emily Play' they had achieved a loftier perch than the Pretties who were still tarred with the 'just an R&B band' brush. In terms of musical proficiency it was a different matter.

The Pink Floyd didn't possess great skill as Norman Smith explained. 'I think they would be the first to agree with me that their instrumental skills during the time of Syd Barrett were not exactly top session standard. They (The Pretty Things) knew their instruments, they knew how to play them. Well I wouldn't say they were superior, perhaps I wouldn't use those sorts of words, more capable, more able. They obviously had their weaknesses too but they knew it.'

The final song, 'Death', was laid down in September and they now turned their attention toward the album artwork and layout.

Although EMI had allowed unlimited studio and production time somewhat perversely they balked at the idea of a gate-fold sleeve and Phil received a telephone call asking if it was really necessary to print the story and lyrics inside. The upshot being that the band had to pay £500 toward the cost of the sleeve in £100 instalments. *Sgt Pepper* had been the first album to print the lyrics inside a gatefold and it was a great success but the Pretties were not the same cash cow, in fact they weren't even in the same herd as The Beatles, and self sufficiency was the only answer.

To save on costs they decided to do much of the work themselves. Phil painted the menacing cover art, which also adorned the inside of the gatefold, and Dick took the photographs on the back cover.

Looking back, in 1999, Phil admitted nostalgia in respect of the EMI period. 'They gave us the best studio in the world to experiment in. We had unlimited studio time. We used to take acid and lock ourselves in the studio... it was a great creative environment.' The tripping was carried out without the knowledge of Norman Smith or Peter Mew. It was an unspoken rule that chemical ingestion was not carried out in any noticeable or flagrant manner.

Norman Smith: 'I wouldn't allow anything like that in the studio. The nearest they would come to that they would smoke a joint, I didn't mind that so much, but that's where it stopped.'

Thematically, *SF Sorrow* was just somebody's life story. *Sorrow* is born on the first track and on the last, 'The Loneliest Person', he is old, senile and isolated. 'It's a theme that's been used hundreds and hundreds of times, but it hadn't ever been used on a record,' explained Phil.

Peter Mew engineered for quite some time before it became apparent to him that the album was conceptual. 'I think it became obvious fairly early on but not right at the beginning. All I'd heard were the rhythm tracks that had already been started and it only became obvious later, because you don't necessarily record things in the order they are on the album. As soon as you started recording a track that was designed to link two tracks together then you heard 'I've written this story and he's done this and then she gets on the Hindenburg'. Quite often songs appeared to be written in the studio.'

Twink was now getting into the music, which at first he had found difficult. His fondness of mime and love of prancing about in hats and bizarre clothing was to find an outlet within the *SF Sorrow* theme.

The rock opera concept was a major step forward and was ahead of its time. Phil: 'When we emerged from the studio and played the radio in the car on the way home what you heard was nothing like what we were doing. That's when I thought Jesus, maybe this isn't going to be a commercial success.' During the lengthy recording of *SF Sorrow* the charts and the airwaves were filled with songs like The Love Affair's 'Everlasting Love' and 'Rainbow Valley' and Steve Rowland's production of DDDBMT's 'Zabadak' as well as contributions from Lulu, Cilla Black, Engelbert and many other MOR artists. The Beatles kept themselves in the frame with their *Magical Mystery Tour* and the *White Album* whereas the Stones disappeared for quite a lengthy period until 'Jumping Jack Flash' emerged.

TV and radio broadcaster John Peel put it most succinctly. 'The Beatles were cute, The Stones were students, but The Pretty Things were plain frightening and much better at psychedelia than The Stones.'

To his eternal credit at no time did Phil May succumb to the late 60s early 70s trend of trawling through Tolkien and concocting whimsical, frivolous lyrics akin to nursery rhymes. Psychedelia proved a double-edged sword, because although it offered scope for countless expansions of both music and the imagination it also opened the portals to a tremendous gush of nonsensical claptrap served up as a contemporary lyrical tract. This embarrassing trend caught out many of the Pretties psychedelic contemporaries. Fortunately for them their cupboard is empty of ill-considered balderdash such as 'Three Jolly Little Dwarfs' (Tomorrow), 'Good Wizzard Meets Naughty Wizzard' (Aquarian Age), 'Mr Small The Watch Repairer Man' (Kaleidoscope) and 'Just Above My Hobby Horse's Head' (Blossom Toes).

Phil May's facility as a songwriter has been woefully ignored and it is his ability to fashion adult themes without introducing facile rhyming couplets that keeps the lyrics as fresh and enjoyable today as when they were originally penned. The ability to inform using understandable yet crafted language is a trait missing from most contemporary compositions. Avoiding embarrassment is not enough, the ability to say something worthwhile and memorable is missing from many songs including those on million-selling albums such as the Electric Light Orchestra's *Out Of The Blue* and T-Rex's *Electric Warrior*. Many respected writers have lyrical skeletons in their cupboards as a trawl through the Paul McCartney songbook will attest.

As a taster for the album, Columbia issued 'Private Sorrow' b/w 'Balloon Burning' as a November 68 single. Having lampooned them twelve months earlier, *Melody Maker's* Chris Welch now took a different stance. 'A vastly improved group who deserve more attention than they are getting. Both their live and recorded performances are a far cry from the rough old days. This is meaningful and inventive and should appeal to all *Top Gear* fans, which includes me. P.S make this a hit folks.' The folks didn't, apparently they preferred Marmalade's 'Ob-La-Di-Ob-La-Da' and the funtastic 'Quick Joey Small' by the Kasenatz Katz Singing Orchestral Circus.

EMI's archives show that the two previous singles had not been big sellers. By the end of April 1968 'Defecting Grey' had sold 6,860 copies in the UK and a mere 480 abroad. 'Talking About The Good Times' had sold 4,880 and 330 in the respective territories.

SF Sorrow was finally released in December 1968, ten weeks after the final mixing sessions, thirteen months after the recordings began and fully five months before The Who unleashed *Tommy*. The album failed to gain widespread acclaim and was never a contender for chart success. The Pretties sat and watched as some months later *Tommy* reached number 2 in the UK album charts.

Perhaps it was a mistake to release it in December, with the Christmas frenzy on all things printed and sold. The album was accorded scant review space by *Melody Maker* who advised their readers, 'A much improved group, exciting on stage and experimental on record with a Phil May story set to music of the life of *SF Sorrow*.' A review so short and to the point was never likely to persuade the uninformed reader to investigate further. However, Allen Evans at the *NME* was impressed. 'As soon as I heard the opening track, 'SF Sorrow Is Born', I had to have a quick look at the cover to convince myself that this group was the old Pretty Things. Yes, there they all were (sic). They have improved out of all recognition and have produced an album which should rate as one of the best of 1968. So, if you're tired of hearing how good the latest Beatles and Stones LP's are, this could be for you.'

As Evans suggested the December album charts were dominated by The Beatles *White Album* and the Stones *Beggars Banquet*. The *NME* apart, critical acclaim was muted and it is only with the passage of time that the album has received due recognition from the critics.

Years later, in September 1999, *Record Collector* championed the album in their series on British psychedelic groups. 'The LP has a justifiable claim to be the ultimate British psychedelic long-player (alongside the Floyd's *Piper*

At The Gates Of Dawn, of course) *SF Sorrow* differs in its mono and stereo formats and is legendary as Pete Townshend's inspiration for *Tommy*.'

Alwyn Turner writing in the excellent *Rough Guide To Rock*, lamented, 'Regrettably it provided the inspiration for Pete Townshend to write *Tommy*, but it far excelled that work and remains one of the few concept albums worth hearing.'

Talking to *Melody Maker's* Alan Jones in 1975 Phil conceded that *SF Sorrow* was a suicidal project. 'The record company tried to promote it but weren't at all convinced of its commercial appeal and were very dubious that there were even enough people in the so-called underground to make it, or the band, a viable product.'

Phil acknowledged that EMI simply didn't realise that they had a unique product. The phrases 'Rock Opera' and 'Concept Album' were yet to be bandied about let alone understood and it was released as though a normal product.

The album's appeal was not enhanced by live performances. The complexity of the production and reliance on mellotron made it impossible to play all but three or four tracks. During 1969 the Roundhouse at Chalk Farm provided the venue for two mimed performances of *SF Sorrow*. Phil read the story and each band member portrayed a character to backing tapes accompanied by a psychedelic light show. Twink played Sorrow, whilst Dick and girlfriend Melissa took the parts of Sorrow's parents. Wally played a worker and Twink's girlfriend portrayed 'the girl next door'.

Phil explained how the visual aspect of their concerts had changed from the early years. 'We started using more visual things, visual props – like models of the band made out of hardboard and plywood, cut out and painted, pianos filled with flowers which Skip would then smash up with a pick-axe. Jon was quite into his sitar things; he wanted to play that on stage. In retrospect it seems slightly pretentious and affected, but it wasn't really at the time done for that reason, not consciously.'

Skip had of course left them over a year earlier – the axe mayhem dated back to late 1967 – and replacement Twink was the guiding force behind the mime sequences.

Twink informed *Melody Maker* that he was studying ballet, and 'using mime and movement in a pop concept. We are very pleased with *SF Sorrow* we have already started doing a mime play to the story of the album. It's very expensive to put on but when we did it at the Roundhouse it went down very well. We have screens and people working lights while I play SF Sorrow wearing a black leotard and a white face.' Phil added, 'We've never enjoyed ourselves as much as we are now. I feel we have got something to say and something to offer. We do all our own material.'

Years later Twink expressed dismay that Phil and Dick appeared to play down the success of the mime shows.

Derek Boltwood wrote an underground column in *Record Mirror*, and spoke with Phil about their changed ethos. 'Even the most brilliant music isn't enough – you have to entertain, put on a good act. We've rehearsed the basis of our show but obviously we put different things in each night. It's very much a 'show-business' scene now – we use make-up on stage sometimes, and Twink does his sword swallowing routine or his mime, and we try to establish a contact with the audience on top of our music.'

During April 1968, *NME* announced that The Pretty Things had signed with Tamla Motown. 'First non-American act to join the label. Tamla vice-president, Barney Ales, concluded negotiations with the Thing's manager Bryan Morrison during his London visit last week. Tamla will represent the Things in the US, Canada and Hawaii.' It would have repercussions for all concerned.

'This could be a big move for us,' Phil postulated. Twink was similarly impassioned 'People'll take notice of us here now that Tamla have signed us. Berry Gordy has told everyone that they've got to get their fingers out and get us away, and the label. They're spending a fortune and it's got to work'.

Certain articles and Phil himself have suggested that both band and management fought against the Motown connection but this doesn't quite fit in with the facts. Bryan Morrison signed the band to Motown and presumably nobody held a gun to his head and Phil and Twink's upbeat comments made clear their enthusiasm.

EMI's normal US outlet was Capitol, but for whatever reason they turned their corporate back on The Pretty Things and Pink Floyd. It has been suggested that EMI was determined to deal with Tamla-Motown, which would allow them to issue the successful Motown catalogue in the UK. In return Motown would receive rights to certain EMI artists in the States.

During this period the band recorded a session for Sunday evening's *Top Gear* radio programme and the tracks chosen showed the group already moving on from *SF Sorrow*. Although 'The Loneliest Person' was in evidence to support the album they unveiled four new songs. 'Send You With Lovin', 'Spring', and 'Marilyn', none of which were ever put on vinyl and, revealingly, 'Alexander', the song recorded for *What's Good For The Goose*. 'Alexander' formed a regular part of the band's live act and must have been adjudged worthwhile although Wally and Jon today consider it of little consequence.

On June 13th 1969, founding member Dick Taylor left The Pretty Things. Dick remembers the date precisely because the following day he got married. 'I was basically bored. There are many factors that lead you to make these decisions. The whole music business was going in a direction I wasn't hugely enamoured with.'

Dick elaborated to George Evers in 1990. 'The music business had got into a sort of period that I didn't find so much fun. It was just starting to go to seed, and starting to go a bit rotten. Because I had been in the same job for five years it's like having a job for five years, exactly the same. A lot of people connected my leaving to my first marriage. In actual fact the two things were not as connected as it might have seemed to some people, including possibly Phil, but I really wanted a change.'

By way of goodbye Phil drew a cartoon of Dick with a pipe and slippers.

'I announced the date that I was leaving,' said Dick. 'Not all that long before, but a bit before. It wasn't an acrimonious thing, basically I said I've had enough… at the moment or whatever. There weren't all that many gigs going on at that time which was one of my reasons for leaving because it was starting to look a non-job. We were doing stuff but strangely we weren't working much at that point.'

Phil revealed that Dick was getting less and less involved in the music and the band. His leaving 'wasn't such a great rend in that sense. He just wasn't putting it into it (the music), so only his presence was missing… his contribution at that time had gone down to pretty much zero. He admits he was just going along because he didn't know how to stop.'

Dick: 'Several people have asked whether it because I was disillusioned because I thought *SF Sorrow* was gonna do really well and it didn't. Obviously you're cheesed off if something doesn't sell as well as you think it would, having gone through the stuff we went through to produce it. It not doing well meant that was one obstacle to my leaving removed. So I thought well, we're not exactly financially hitting the high spots and I was quite interested in doing other things, producing and stuff. My whole working life up to that point had been occupied by The Pretty Things and so there was a reasonable amount of internal pressure from within myself saying what else is going on out there.'

Dick did make a temporary return when he played a set with the band at the Isle of Wight Festival two months later. This was the year that Dylan flew over. 'I wasn't officially with them but I did do it which Brian Hinton in his book says was an unusually uninspired set from us. I like to think that, well, I wasn't there for the whole of that set. I can remember it being a bit flat and thinking, Oh Gawd, I'm glad I'm out of this.'

Replacing Dick with a single new member was an impossibility. As founder, arranger, composer and guitarist he occupied a pivotal position. Wally came more to the fore and took control of the writing and arranging tasks, something he had done in the latter days of the Fenmen and had

assisted with on the *Sorrow* sessions. To replace Dick the guitarist they turned
to fellow EMI signings the Edgar Broughton Band and 'borrowed' Victor
Unitt. Twink related that Phil sent him to check Vic out and if Twink liked
him then he was okay.

Meanwhile, Twink had started work on his solo album, titled *Think Pink*,
Mick Farren had arranged the deal with Sire records the previous year and he
also occupied the producer's chair. Ensconced in London's Recorded Sound
Studios, Twink called upon a cavalcade of friends and colleagues including
Jon Povey, Wally and Phil. Jon played mellotron on three numbers and sitar
on a fourth, whilst Wally contributed piano to one number and Phil added
handclaps. Wally's memory of the event is somewhat nebulous, 'I have a
vague recollection of going along to a studio once, and playing a bit of piano
on something, it was at Decca Recording Studios in Broadhurst Gardens.'
Jon is equally unspecific, 'I don't remember them very well only that the
studio was crowded full of freaky people floating about with joss-sticks.' In
other interviews Twink has suggested that Stanhope Place studio at Marble
Arch was the recording venue.

To add to the 'family' atmosphere Viv Prince turned up and drummed on
'Mexican Grass War' and, just prior to joining the Pretties, Vic Unitt, added
lead guitar to two tracks. The theme was complete when Hipgnosis designed
the cover as they would the next four Pretty Things albums.

In spite of the family image Twink was not too popular with the band and
Wally in particular. 'He and Wally absolutely hated each other', confirmed
Phil. 'Cause he's full of shit, basically, in a nutshell,' said Wally. 'A band is a
good band with good musicians in it. A, he's not a good musician and B, he's
terribly false. He's a poseur, we didn't hit it off at all I'm afraid. We had a little
altercation on stage somewhere.' Matters came to a head at a Roundhouse
concert when Wally punched him and a brawl ensued with Twink ending up
flat on his back.

Jon Povey felt it was just chemistry. 'I don't think there was any particular
reason, I just don't think that Wally sort of really thought that Twink was
any good. I liked Twink as a drummer, I liked his simplicity. He was a bit of
a show-off guy, a bit of a showman therefore he would kind of dominate. I
think he put his efforts into showing rather than playing and this band has
always been a playing type of band rather than a showing type of band and I
think that's where the kind of abrasion occurred. He would sacrifice the playing sometimes so he could prance around on stage in a funny hat. I think
that's what really got up Wally's nose. Wally's very much the musician's man,
very much the controller of music.'

Melody Maker described Twink as, 'A strange and violent drummer noted
for his anarchistic solos often consisting of simply bashing the snare drum as

loudly as possible without any particular rhythmic pattern.' 'I do it because I can't play drum solos,' explained Twink.

This behaviour and other weirdness, such as playing the drums without any shoes on, was a particular feature of Twink's makeup as Keith West pointed out when recalling the 'My White Bicycle' sessions. 'We went out into the street in front of Abbey Road and got a policeman to come in and blow it (a police whistle) on mike. Twink was running around the studio with his hat on and we were smoking dope so we had to be careful.'

Writing in *Ugly Things* magazine, Mick Farren described how a typical Pretty Things/Deviants double bill would end in chaos with Twink screeching in the microphone or stripping whilst the rest of the band performed a marathon version of The Byrds 'Why'. Interestingly, given the disdain directed towards the *Emotions* album, 'There'll Never Be Another Day' formed a regular part of their play-list throughout the late 60s.

'I think in the end we fired him,' recounted Wally. 'We did a gig I think it was the Isle of Wight. It wasn't the big festival but he was incapable of playing, he fell of the back of his chair, he was absolutely ga-ga so we finished the set with Povey on drums and bye bye Twink and hello Skipper again. He's a weird guy he's just full of crap, me and him just couldn't see eye to eye. He's not like a real person.'

Speaking to Nick Saloman for *The Ptolemaic Terrascope* magazine, Twink explained his reason for leaving was to concentrate his efforts on his Pink Fairies Motor Cycle Club and All Star Rock and Roll Band. He was also becoming more interested in the things that Mick Farren and Steve Took were doing.

As Wally stated, Twink left and Skip Alan returned to the stool for another stint as drummer, continuing the strange game of musical drum-chairs that the Pretties played more enthusiastically than any other major band.

Also in August, *SF Sorrow* was finally released in the States. It appeared on Rare Earth, a new offshoot of Tamla-Motown, set up to target the 'progressive/psychedelic/whiteboy' market.

Dick's recollection is that Rare Earth didn't want the Pretties but EMI forced the band on them. Whatever the truth, this unsavoury horse-trading served to delay the US release of *SF Sorrow*. Rare Earth was only finally able to get off the ground in August, eight months after the UK release. *Sorrow* became one of five albums issued simultaneously to christen the label. All the releases were initially sold in die cut round top covers, which was another reason given for the delay.

'They really messed up the sound too, at Motown, I was most disappointed with that,' complained Norman Smith. 'They sent me over an acetate or something like that, it sounded absolutely dreadful compared to what we had put on. I think at that time I did complain very heavily and it might well be that they withdrew the original one.'

Dick recalled The Who urging them to get their album out before *Tommy* in the US, which disastrously for the Pretties didn't happen. *Tommy* came out three months earlier and attained number 4 in the *Billboard* charts. The success of *Tommy* meant that when *SF Sorrow* did receive its belated release it was seen as ripping off The Who's rock opera concept with *Billboard* even suggesting that they were trying to jump on the *Tommy* bandwagon!

Talking to Jon Kirkman for *Rock Ahead* in 1998, Phil explained the problems. 'To be fair to Kit Lambert and The Who they tried very hard for us to put pressure on Tamla, they gave us their release schedule, and we told Tamla. Tamla, for some reason, didn't think it was very important, and of course it screwed not only that album but *Parachute*. It was the wrong label. Really, you couldn't think of a worse label for The Pretty Things to be with.'

Another problem with the Motown deal was money. Dick told Ed Mabe that Rare Earth's accounting methods caused the band much consternation. 'They never reported how many they sold or accounted to us. It was very difficult to know how many copies were sold.' This particular concern eventually formed the basis of the band's civil action against EMI.

CHAPTER 8 –The Parachute That Failed To Open

With the abysmal failure of *SF Sorrow* in the commercial arena there was a buzz that EMI were not intending on exercising the third of their six annual options. Label mates Pink Floyd had enjoyed top ten albums with *Piper At The Gates Of Dawn* and *Saucerful Of Secrets* and in comparison The Pretty Things were losers. Bryan Morrison was sufficiently unnerved to write to EMI:

'You may have heard during the past few months of our attempts to get your company to record another LP with the Pretty Things. Please try not to keel over with shock.

I realise of course that as a business venture it does not appear to be a financial proposition to spend more money on this group, and believe me, I do see your point on this. However, over the past month or so I have been making some enquiries myself, and I have come up with some revealing bits of information. For instance, the French L.P. sales for "S.F. SORROW" has just gone over the 6,000 mark, the Benelux countries and German sales are about 5/6,000 and our own United Kingdom sales are now around 7,000. At the moment I do not have any sales figures for Scandinavia, but just on the territories mentioned, you'll notice that the L.P. achieved a sale of 18/20,000 records. This of course is excluding America, which I am sure at the very least, will show a sale of around 10,000, which means that within a few months, the total world sales of "S.F. SORROW" will be between 26,000 and 40,000. I think you will agree with me that the sale of 40,000 is not beyond the realms of possibility.

To sum up, I would have thought that an L.P. with sales of between 30/40,000 would have been considered in most circles as being a good seller, and therefore well worth producing another.

I eagerly await your comment and hope that you are keeping well.'

EMI were undecided and it was only after EMI boss Ken East had discussions with Norman Smith that Bryan Morrison received an August reply confirming that a further 12 months option would be taken up.

Whilst these contractual options were in the balance Phil and Wally were approached by an affluent Frenchman, Phillipe DeBarge, who wanted them to produce an album for him. 'He wanted to do something Pretty Things-esque and maybe get it off the ground in France,' remembered Wally. As always the band needed money so they readily agreed. The album was cut at the Nova Studio in Marble Arch on eight-track using the Pretties as the backing musicians. Wally recollected that both Skip and Twink played on various tracks. The sessions extended throughout late Summer and Autumn of 1969 and recent addition Vic Unitt also contributed guitar, something that became obvious when the *Parachute*-like solos unfolded. Interviewed for *Ugly Things* in 1985, Wally was asked, by an incredulous Mike Stax, about the great songs the band had given DeBarge. 'Well, I don't know how great they are, but obviously if we would have felt they were that wonderful we wouldn't have given them away.'

The DeBarge album was never officially released, although bootlegged versions are in existence, complete with original acetate scratch. The eleven tracks included three of the *What's Good For The Goose* soundtrack, 'Alexander', 'Eagles Son' and 'It'll Never Be Me' plus the concert regular 'Send You With Lovin''. The DeBarge version of 'Eagles Son' incorporated a repetitive descending guitar riff that later formed the basis of 'Scene One', the opening track on *Parachute*.

The album, later known as *Phillipe DeBarge*, was recorded midway between *SF Sorrow* and *Parachute* and contained the only recordings the band made with both Twink and Vic Unitt. Wally also supplied some lead guitar on the album showcasing his diverse musical talents and pointing the way towards the *Parachute* sessions.

As Mike Stax had suggested it was quite extraordinary that a band of such renown should gift high quality songs merely to gratify a rich mans eccentricity. Apart from Dick they will disagree with this view, considering the songs to be B-grade. Overly harsh assessments of songs that stand the test of time a lot better than the majority of the *Emotions* tracks and many from the later *Freeway Madness*. The fact that a number of them formed part of their concert repertoire verifies that this lowly opinion did not have universal appeal back then.

With Dick gone it left Phil and Wally as the main song-writers as Phil explained. (*Parachute* was) 'all really Wally and myself. Wally really filled in a lot of Dick's previous role in the band as far as his contribution in songwriting and arranging.'

Unlike Dick's song-writing approach, which was built primarily around guitar riffs, Wally brought chord structures and melodies allowing Phil free reign with the lyrical tracts. Jon Povey recalled how Wally went through an extremely prolific creative period. '*Parachute* wasn't like *SF Sorrow*, it wasn't even intended to be a rock opera writing thing at all. Wally hit on a rich vein of material and we let him go and he basically had to do it because it was good stuff. At that time very much a Beatley influenced thing.' Wally recalled the period vividly, 'I did quite a lot of preparatory work because I had just got a Revox (four track reel-to-reel tape recorder) and I was using and loving it. It was a very creative time I was living at Westbourne Terrace in a room on the same floor as Phil and I'd rush next door and say listen to this, listen to that. We put it together very quickly.'

Whereas *SF Sorrow* was a group concept, based around a Wally idea and a Phil story, *Parachute* was purely Phil and Wally, as Jon Povey confirmed. 'Wally did an amazing job on that because he wrote most of that, recorded it on a Revox, came and played it to us.' It has been said that *Parachute* was virtually a Wally Waller solo album, with melodies and arrangements nailed down and even some of Vic's solo's being choreographed by him. 'A slight exaggeration, I think,' suggested Povey. 'Certainly the ideas for the songs that he wrote – he didn't write all of them – he had down basically. He would come in with that thing completely recorded and we would learn it or we would add to it or subtract from it. The band's always been a band where everybody puts an input into it. There's never been one guy that's dominated it.'

'Sometimes Wally and I would get back at three or four in the morning, stoned out of our brains,' Phil recounted to Mike Stax. '(We would) start writing and write till 12 o'clock the next day and then go out to a gig. The party was part of the writing. It wasn't something you stopped working for to do, it just fused into it. It was all of one – the life was all about the music, and in the middle of a party somebody would pick up a guitar and a song would be written. There wasn't any barriers or demarcation lines.'

Wally: 'Despite what we felt after *SF Sorrow*, and we felt despondent, as soon as we started working seriously together, we started getting very pleased with the songs that we wrote. It was kind of the healing of the wounds, and also I think we were finding different places again – new musical places to explore.'

Parachute followed the *SF Sorrow* trail of thematic song-writing however it differed inasmuch as *Sorrow* was the poignant narrative of a sad little man's life story whereas *Parachute* dealt with the then topical theme of the city and the country, an abstraction conceived by Phil. They wanted an album with some kind of thread going through it. Phil recalled, 'It was one side 'country'' and one side 'city.' It was various episodes, which related to city living, which a lot of people were thinking about at that time – dropping out and going to the country. It was just really giving both sides, not particularly making a personal decision on it, just reflections on both environments. Basically the songs are just little cameos of various things that happen in either of those two different environments.'

Wally explained the concept to Mike Stax. 'The way we rationalised the title, *Parachute*, is it's a last form of escape, but it's not necessarily the answer. It doesn't mean you're safe just because you use a parachute. There's a lot of things that can happen on the way down.'

'I never thought I could write,' Phil admitted to *Melody Maker*. 'But I had to for the album. The point was we couldn't do what we wanted to do with other people's songs. I don't think anybody can take us apart musically so now we can get into a lot of things which we want to. We can really be cruder and get into some straight rock things. 'We also want to do some harmony trips,' added Jon Povey. Phil's confessional response indicated that on previous albums he had taken a lesser role being primarily the wordsmith.

The new album was recorded over the course of six months although the actual studio time was only around two hundred hours – about a month. 'It was much quicker than *SF Sorrow*, we did it all in one or two stints,' explained Wally.

At the tail end of September they entered the Abbey Road studios and started work on 'The Good Mr Square', followed a few days later by 'Scene One'. Two weeks later they worked on 'In The Square' and 'Cries From The Midnight Circus'. A single December date produced 'Grass' although January was heavily utilised in recording 'She's A Lover', 'Miss Fay Regrets' which had a working title of 'Jam', 'Sickle Clowns' provisionally titled 'Stick of Rock' and 'Parachute', which is shown on the recording schedules as 'Norman's Piece'. Phil recalled that often they worked on songs that had yet to be fleshed out with lyrics or a title. 'We'd finish a session and they'd ask what it was called. And we'd say, oh... call it a stick of rock.'

February and March concluded the sessions, which also included non-album track 'Blue Serge Blues' and an initial attempt at future single 'October 26ᵗʰ'.

The band was extremely pleased with the resulting album. Even Wally who usually had reservations was very happy. Unlike *SF Sorrow* or *Emotions*, Wally took lead vocal on a number of tracks such as 'Sickle Clowns', 'The Good Mr Square' and 'Rain'. Described in some volumes as the bands heavy metal indulgence the reality was not nearly so simplistic. Norman Smith obtained a fuller, more bass-heavy sound than on previous recordings. Less frantic than *SF Sorrow* it displayed a melodic approach allied to soaring harmonies, sympathetic guitar solos from Vic Unitt and a crisp production, reminiscent to many of The Beatles *Abbey Road* album.

Heavy metal? Not in the Led Zeppelin or Deep Purple sense. Where those bands would usually structure songs around guitar riffs the *Parachute* material was formed mainly around the melody with the heavy ambience crafted on.

Although *SF Sorrow* is generally considered as the jewel in the Pretties crown, not least by Phil, this assessment is based as much on Sorrow's preeminence as the first rock opera as on the musical content. *Parachute* by comparison is a much more assured and mature affair, this is a band come of age, secure in the knowledge that the content is up there with The Beatles, and that Norman Smith's production is up there with George Martin's.

The album's opening track 'Scene One', awash with reverberating piano swells then joined by a fat acoustic sound which is quickly set upon by Skip's cascading drums before, finally, launching into a descending riff powered by guitar and bass. Harmony and counterpoint harmony informs of the city in suitably vivid terminology – 'iron-laced populations' and 'molten fields'

'The Good Mr Square/She Was Tall She Was High' could have been lifted from The Beatles *Abbey Road* and who could have told the difference? Indeed the harmonies are reminiscent of 'Because'. Wally takes lead vocal using his 'high voice' with the song mutating as Povey leads on the second section. According to Phil, Mr Square was a dysfunctional individual who inhabited a sad and unreal world of newspaper clippings.

Track three introduced a glorious trilogy. 'In The Square/The Letter/Rain' set out sedately with a combination guitar and harpsichord intro followed by the three-part harmony tale of a girl leaving both the city and her boy-friend for the 'freedom' of the fields. 'The Letter' explained how she wrote to him rationalising her actions and is lifted by the buoyant cadence as Phil plaintively evokes the loss and despair – city life that's too heavy, so she runs for the hills. The third section, 'Rain', crackled with energy as Wally's trebly rhythm guitar hacked out a descending chord structure which was swiftly augmented by an intruding rhythmic bass and Skip's measured drum pat-terns. These cascade into a pulsing crescendo as Wally howled the misery of standing alone, in the rain, at their meeting place. Unitt's guitarwork spar-kled as it fused with the rhythm and added to the general air of disquiet which itself was exaggerated by the gloomy sounds of rain and thunder.

'Miss Fay Regrets' recounted the story of an over-the-hill film star and her descent into a nightmare of failure and an inability to come to terms with her physical decay. Wally's guitar riff announces the beginning before the rhythm cuts in and Phil's guttural vocal informs that she's corrugated steel platinum to feel. The song was a quick write in the studio whilst Norman Smith took the night off. Norman had suggested they do a bit of rock 'n' roll as the rest of the album was less frantic. Wonderfully evocative lyrics that tell the story not merely through the narrative but via the injection of intense, troubling images.

'Cries From The Midnight Circus' opened with Wally's quintessential 'real sneaky little' bass riff, quickly battered aside by Skip's cymbal heavy rolling drum attack. Phil's compressed vocal, rasping, vicious and ominous, informs of the denizens of the night. The hookers, pimps, models, hoodlums and rock stars all of whom frequented sordid alleys, arenas and London late night drinking clubs. Povey's organ solo processed through a Leslie Cabinet adds the perfect disturbing touch of fear and edge to the one track that could justifiably be described as heavy metal.

Phil's personal favourite track is 'Grass'. It opened side 2 with a chiming rhythm guitar, cymbal intense drumming and fluttering, tremolo-heavy guitar solos gliding over an ocean of mellotron. Phil's double-tracked vocal drifts across the soundscape embellished by exquisite harmonies, Wally in best 'John Lennon mode' on the chorus, strumming his battered Framus acoustic. A great song with a faultless stop-start arrangement.

'Sickle Clowns', Phil's *Easy Rider* song with hoarse vocals by Wally and another cymbal bender from Skip. Jon Povey described the story of Vic Unitt's guitar solo. 'An intuitive sort of guy, one of the best solos he did was on 'Sickle Clowns'. That was done on Edgar Broughton's guitar which for some reason he'd brought in with him. In his slightly unbalanced mental state he said, 'It's got Edgar's vibes on it,' and he went out and did a rocket. He did a quite good solo on it, for him.' EMI's session sheets show that this song was completed in one session on March 20th 1970.

Track eleven, the live favourite 'She's A Lover', offered up three and a half minutes of beautifully crafted pomp. Congas, tambourines, mellotron and Leslie-gorged organ feeding the time changes and a magical stereophonic guitar dual in the middle. Skip's drumming shone particularly on this track. Phil's voice seems to be double-tracked and slightly speeded up, presumably to enable a higher range.

The penultimate song, 'What's The Use', had been written by Phil some time before and was introduced into the concept. It was a simple and plaintive lament to the fading ideals of the flower power era. 'I just had it hanging around,' he explained. Wally strummed a 12-string guitar alongside a strange ringing chime on the beat. Engineer Tony Clarke who had previously worked on The Beatles version of 'Kansas City' and would later assist Paul McCartney as well as producing Camel and Stephan Grappelli, explained. 'There's a track on it with a very high frequency, lovely note like a cymbal. It's Norman, a couple of two-bob bits or half-a-crowns, balancing them, hitting one against the other. It's not like any percussion instrument.'

The album concluded with the title track, 'Parachute', which was a writing collaboration between Phil and Norman Smith. Jon Povey supplied the vocals, which were multi-layered in a Brian Wilson harmonic way and which took ages to get right. Jon often jokes about Norman poking him with a stick or grabbing his bollocks to help him to reach those very high notes.

The song, and the album, finished with a sequence of bass-heavy descending notes melding into the whine of an oscillator being wound up and sounding, initially, like an air-raid alarm before it stretched out into the distance where only canine listeners could notice. Tony Clarke described the methodology. 'There were two oscillators. If you actually listen to it you can hear a bit of a glitch halfway through where we changed from one oscillator to another. It's not a lovely curve because you couldn't get that sweep on one oscillator.'

Tony recounted the time and effort that Norman took on that last track. 'It was really hard work, it was eight track. It was four or five-part harmony layered four or five times. We had to keep bouncing backwards and backwards and forwards. The writing of the song did take some time, there was a lot of discussion between Norman and Jon. On the eight-track I think all the harmonies finished up on one track and there's automatic double tracking to give it a wider spread. That block harmony would have been seven or eight generation. I remember it being incredibly hard, perfectionally. Hard work for him, 'right do that again, we'll have another one of those'.'

Norman Smith's role in the construction of the album cannot be overstated, his touch and firm hand is apparent on every track as Tony Clarke explained. 'As a producer he was unique, the way he would look at the song and always move it to where it might go, the melodic structure. He definitely stretched them.'

Norman Smith's production was evocative of The Beatles *Abbey Road* album, which on reflection is perhaps not so surprising. The entire album is melody-based but relentlessly driven by the rhythm section of Wally and Skip and augmented by Povey's keyboards. Guitar is an occasional adornment with fat acoustic and 12-string featured as much as electric lead.

Wally: 'We used to go out to the clubs right after the sessions at Abbey Road and get really messed up, but you wouldn't have to be at the studio until 2:30 the next afternoon, so it was all right. We'd never get wrecked when we'd be doing something serious – getting our act together as it were – but when you're out of school it's alright.'

Parachute positively oozed mellotron and, like all previous and future Pretties albums, it would have more than its fair share of percussion. The electric guitar playing is uniformly excellent although, unusually, Wally played many of the riffs that would normally fall to the guitar player. Songs mutated as they were played and as the other band members and Norman interpreted them.

Vic Unitt's guitarwork caused problems as Wally recollected. 'Apart from a few lead bits he didn't do much at all on *Parachute*. I did most of the rhythm parts and most of the figurative parts. Apart from a few real solo licks he didn't do much at all.' During his short stay Unitt always came across as temporary. Wally: 'He was a nice enough guy, but you've got to be quite a strong personality in the band because you've got to make your point. He had nothing to punch out about, he didn't punch his weight at all. That's what you want in a rock 'n' roll band you need somebody who can lay some down, especially from the guitar department it's like a centre forward in a football team, you've got to have somebody who can do something a bit special now and then, put the ball in the net.'

Norman Smith agreed with Wally. 'From recollection he was a bit of a temperamental boy or moody boy, never showed a great deal of enthusiasm so it might be it contributes to the difficulty in getting exactly what you're after.' Norman spent a great amount of time ensuring that the guitar overlays blended with the rhythm and vocal tracks although Wally's pre-production on the Revox meant that less time needed to be spent on the arrangements and harmonies.

Parachute stands supreme. The epitome of superbly crafted adult rock music. Unlike Beatles, Stones and Beach Boys albums not one track can be faulted, not one song is weak. Check out *Abbey Road* or *Sgt Pepper*, neither 'Maxwell's Silver Hammer' nor 'When I'm Sixty Four' can be considered notable constituents of these otherwise outstanding albums.

Much of the experimentation and freshness of *SF Sorrow* had been retained but had also been enhanced by the seasoning of confidence and experience. The result, a body of recorded music that bridged the chasm between the melodic sounds of The Beatles and the brash underground progression that serious listeners were rapidly unearthing.

Whilst the band was consumed by *Parachute*, Dick Taylor was settling into a new role as a record producer for various United Artists bands. Doug Smith and Richard Thomas operated a management company, Clearwater Productions, which represented Hawkwind, Skin Alley and Cochise. After United Artists had asked Dick to produce Hawkwind, Clearwater consequently asked him to produce Cochise and Skin Alley on a freelance basis. He also did some sessions with a group called High Tide, which never saw the light of day. Dick was more involved with Hawkwind, a band he described as, 'technically incompetent'. Some less affable souls might go further.

Dick contributed guitar on the Hawkwind album, and on the single 'Hurry On Sundown'. Additionally he played a number of gigs with them, enjoying the spontaneity and spirit of the band.

1972 found Dick reassessing his musical life and he ceased producing altogether. 'I was finding it hard to find bands that I really liked,' he explained. The experimental and exciting Sixties had been replaced by a corporate ethos, which he found restrictive and boring. He left the industry and worked for Jean Machine for some years, eventually becoming their Transport Manager. He found the time for occasional returns such as playing with Auntie and the Men From Uncle, a band fronted by Julian Isaacs who originally played under the stomach-churning name of Auntie Pus. From this period came a one-off single 'Halfway To Venezuela', which also featured future Damned member Rat Scabies on drums.

During the *Parachute* sessions they continued to fit in gigs and October 1969 saw them playing major festivals in Europe. An appearance at the First German Blues Festival at Esseen supporting headliners Fleetwood Mac was followed later that month by the Amougies Pop and Jazz Festival in France alongside Yes and Chicken Shack.

As 1970 unfolded a further upheaval occurred when Vic Unitt departed, 'medically retired', as one band member ingenuously put it. Chemical over-indulgence and the struggle to complete the *Parachute* solos had taken a toll. Vic's tenure was brief but during this period he contributed to an album destined to be regarded as a classic.

Jon Povey considered him an acid-head who got damaged. 'He went a bit off the rails. We liked him, we liked his kind of guitar approach.' Phil disagreed, describing him as a nice bloke who didn't contribute much musically. 'He was like a journeyman guitarist and he didn't really fit in with the band basically. He didn't stamp his mark on things, he didn't make the fate of the band his own.' 'He was a nice guy,' agreed Wally, 'but he was also a pretty strange guy. He was always there. Many mornings I'd wake up in my bed and he'd be sitting there beside me, he'd appear very early in the morning and we had to explain to him that in this flat nothing happens at that time of day.'

Jon Povey: 'We had to teach him because he was suffering from a bit of electrical damage you know, he burnt a few fuses out in the brain and it was hard for him to concentrate. He was a very emotional man and sometimes Skip and him would reach a fairly heated point and then we would have to kick Skip out the studio, calm Vic down.'

'I think Vic just didn't feel comfortable, he didn't feel it was his place,' said Phil.

With *Parachute* soon to be released the band urgently needed a guitarist. Tony Howard the band's booking agent knew that Eire Apparent, another NEMS band that he booked, were planning to split up. This would leave their eighteen-year-old lead guitarist, Peter Tolson, out of a job. Howard booked them into The Speakeasy. Tony alerted The Pretties and they came down to check him out. The next day he got the call to join them.

The invitation presented the young guitarist with a dilemma, he had already agreed to join Black Cat Bones where his friend Kenny Felton was the drummer. He felt the pull of loyalty, but there again he had always been a fan of the Pretties. 'I just couldn't turn it down,' said Tolson.

'I went down to Phil's, they played me *Parachute,*' he remembered. 'I really wanted to join them, I didn't care what the material was (but) it wasn't what I expected, it was more of a progression from *SF Sorrow* than a transition.'

Phil remembered the event slightly differently. He explained that Eire Apparent's rhythm section, Chrissie Stuart and Davey Lutton, played in the same football team as Wally and himself. 'They said to us that they had the most brilliant young guitarist. That we should give him a try cause he's absolutely brilliant and it'd be a real drag if he doesn't play anymore. So I arranged a meeting and Pete came round with his guitar to Westbourne Terrace and we took some drugs and we played all afternoon. We just jammed, and it was like instant. I couldn't believe it. It was love at first sight.'

Tolson's arrival, during May 1970, heralded a new era for the band. His intense playing not only injected menace and a hard-rock edge into the music but propelled it right to the front. 'I was a million notes a minute man, I played over everything. I was trying to impress the guys.'

Jon Povey recalled his early experiences of the Tolson guitar technique. 'Well he's a good player,' he said in a rare moment of understatement. 'When we first saw him we thought he'd be great and when we got him into the studio and he started doing 'Summertime' it sounded like a violin… that and 'October 26th'. The guitar work on that is just sensational. He was very much a technician in many ways because although he would have a lot of frills in his playing he was technically quick, very adept, a very fast little player.'

Peter recollected going into Abbey Road studios with the Pretties to do some 'ghosting stuff'. 'We did a song called 'Check Out, Check, Check, Check Out', one of Wally's B-Movie things. It was the first time I'd ever been in a proper studio, the first time I met Smithy and the first time I actually got paid.' The song was originally intended as a single to be released under the name King Checker and The Checkouts, although for reasons lost in the mists of time it never happened. A different version of the song was recorded for the Phillipe DeBarge album and the Tolson assisted version has never been released.

Peter was born in Bishops Stortford in Hertfordshire, in September 1951. He was a late-in-life baby for his devoted parents who had despaired of ever starting a family. The story would be lovingly told in the song 'Peter', on the *Freeway Madness* album.

He first picked up a guitar as a youngster and very quickly learned the riff to 'Walk Don't Run'. When he grew older he acquired a Rapier 33 and began playing things like 'The Rise And Fall Of Flingel Bunt', the Shadows bluesey hit from 1963. Although a keen sportsman he quickly became disinterested in the school regime, which he remembered as being full of fascist teachers, and dropped out at age 15 to play guitar. However, unlike the majority of aspiring British guitarists he wasn't part of the 'Clapton is God' brigade being more impressed by the technique of Yardbird, Jeff Beck. Years later he remains in awe of that technique. 'Beck! Have you heard the Honeydrippers' album? There's a version of 'Rockin' At Midnight', Beck soloed on that, he played slide with his fingers! Beck has got to be the surviving hero out of all of them. He just blew me away, he blew everyone away and I just had to sound like that.'

Through 1966-68 he played in local bands until a friend went to see Eire Apparent at Rambling Jacks Blues Club in Bishops Stortford and discovered that they needed a guitarist to replace Mick Cox. He arranged for Peter to audition and, after hearing him play he was asked to join. It was May 1969, ten months later he was a Pretty Thing.

The managerial agreement with Bryan Morrison ended when Bryan sold his company to NEMS, although he retained a connection via his music publishing company Lupus Music. Various Morrison personnel transferred across to NEMS including Steve O'Rourke, who with Tony Howard had been the band's regular contact with the agency. O'Rourke later became manager of Pink Floyd. Wally Waller felt that Morrison had lost interest in the band as he had so many other pies for his fingers.

Phil believed that NEMS bought Morrison's agency to reduce the competition. 'When the NEMS boss saw all these long-haired guys loitering around his foyer he said who are this lot? 'You've just bought them,' he was told. 'Well unbuy them then.'

For a while Phil tried to balance management and band duties and received great assistance from Howard and O'Rourke but it was not working to anyone's satisfaction, a full-time manager was needed. Help was at hand from the departed Morrison who suggested his friend, journalist, freelance writer and domino opponent Derek Boltwood. Derek already knew the band having penned a number of supporting pieces in his 'From The Underworld' column in *Record Mirror*. 'I had been writing about a number of underground bands and within the business I was known and had a reputation and The Pretty Things were a band's band and I was attracted to the idea of managing them. I don't think there was anything formal, they didn't come along to me and say 'we need a manager, here sign a contract', or anything. Bryan was very helpful in providing know-how, I guess he recognised there might have been a bit of synergy between the Pretties and myself.'

Derek somehow contrived to manage the band in tandem with his writing career. 'I wasn't making an income out of The Pretty Things I was making an income out of writing and putting the effort into managing The Pretty Things.'

In June 1969 EMI had introduced a new label, Harvest. The idea was to place their roster of 'progressive' acts on the one label, a label that was dedicated to catering for the underground market that had developed from the embers of the psychedelic explosion. A reflection of the Motown approach with the Rare Earth label, perhaps.

Rare Earth had been formulating plans for the Pretties to visit the States to promote *SF Sorrow* and the forthcoming *Parachute*. Quite what happened is unknown, it seems that arrangements were made by Rare Earth but the band failed to turn up at Heathrow Airport for their flight. Motown Vice President Barney Ales was most aggrieved as shown by his March 1970 letter to EMI's Ken East.

'As you may know we had embarked upon extensive plans relating to this act even to the extent of providing airplane tickets for the group to come to the United States for engagements, promotional activities, and other matters. As you know these tickets were not picked up, nor were we advised that they were not going to be picked up, nor were we advised that the group was not coming.'

Ken East had written to Motown in February enquiring whether Rare Earth would release the Pretties from their contract and in reference to this Ales stated. 'As far as releasing the group against the money we have spent on them or for any other sum of money, frankly, Ken we are not interested in doing this. We do by this letter, exercise our option under the agreement for the period of September 1 1970, to August 31 1971.'

During April, Harvest released a single as a taster for the album, 'The Good Mr Square', it was backed by 'Blue Serge Blues'. Jon Povey co-wrote this particular song with Phil and Wally and it recounted the story of him loping through West London in outrageous attire and being stopped on suspicion and consequently busted for possession of dope. 'We looked fairly outrageous in those days. Even for those days we still looked hairy and colourful – bright yellow trousers and red boots, lots of hair. Walking across the road in Chelsea, one should be more sensible, and one isn't, so one gets busted. Basically, I thought 'Blue Serge Blues was quite a good title for it really, We called it 'Navy Serge Blues' originally.'

When they visited Jon's house the police found more dope in a Christmas present that Phil had bought him. 'I was really pissed off, so we got together and wrote this song.'

Harvest seemed to have been paying scant attention to the Pretties, a reflection, perhaps, of their less than adequate marketing skills. The new single's picture sleeve showed a photo that included previous band members Dick and Twink. Peter Tolson who had already been in the band for a month and Vic Unitt, who had actually played on the record, were both absent.

Hipgnosis were again contracted to design the cover, as they did for many a Harvest artist, and their interpretation of the City/Country theme was an atomic child standing with right arm outstretched in the centre of an elevated three-lane highway. A City skyscraper loomed on one side and a giant tulip on the other. Disconcertingly, what appeared to be a massive grey boulder loomed threateningly in the distance. The whole scene was imbued with a burnt orange tint, which added to the menacing aspect. Tony Clarke did not care for the cover one bit. 'I didn't like it. I always said I did but I thought it was a bit psychedelic.'

Record Mirror was unimpressed with the single and editor Peter Jones, postulated, 'Still changing direction as far as I can make out. In fact, a rather so-so opening, heavy behind lightness. Doesn't really make it.'

Harvest also included 'The Good Mr Square' on the double album sampler *Picnic: A Breath of Fresh Air* which appeared later that year.

Parachute obtained a UK release in June of 1970 and encouragingly *Melody Maker* was most impressed. 'Hands up all those who think the Pretty Things are a bunch of uglys playing an old Bo Diddley riff masquerading as an original called 'Rosalyn'. Seriously though, it's good to see musicians who came up in the mid sixties R&B boom and who have presumably been through some hard times coming back with something as freshly inventive as *Parachute*.'

Record Mirror also applauded. 'Brilliant instrumental blending acoustic instruments with thundering beat and wild spacious harmonies. After six years with the group Phil May is still in fine form on lead vocals and this is definitely the best they've ever done.'

Fighting it out at the top of the album charts was *Bridge Over Troubled Water*, the Simon & Garfunkel classic, Dylan's disappointing *Self Portrait* and The Beatles *Let It Be*. *Parachute* did manage to sneak into the chart at number 50 for one week but that was it. Years later Phil rationalised the disappointment. 'The critical reception was a buzz but you either sell or you don't, that's what it's all about really. It's pointless making a good album if no one's going to hear it. You can't exist forever on critical acclaim.'

Despite being a superbly crafted album containing memorable songs, sales of *Parachute* were a massive disappointment. Tony Clarke reflected on the matter. '*Parachute* was a very, very enjoyable time musically within the realms of the tensions you get when you make music but the overall effect was really very, very good and at the end very positive about where this could take the Pretty Things. I felt they were very happy with it and it was more melodic structured.'

To promote the album The Pretty Things recorded a show at the Paris Cinema for John Peel's Sunday radio programme and in July did a session for Dave Symonds at the Playhouse Theatre where they recorded 'In The

Square/The Letter/Rain', 'She's A Lover' and 'Sickle Clowns'. During this period the band was being booked out for less than £100 a gig and with only Peter and Skip owning their own equipment it meant that Phil's mike and the P.A. had to be hired as did Povey's organ plus various amps and speakers. Because of this they often lost money. Peter wryly recalled that Phil's bar bill was often more than the booking fee.

The state of their finances had not changed since the *SF Sorrow* days. Gigs were somewhat haphazard and profit margins low, sometimes non-existent. EMI had not provided any money since October 1967 and apart from the De Wolfe diversions their only funds came from touring.

Morale had reached such a low level that a change of name was considered. Speaking to *Sounds* in 1972 Phil highlighted Tolson's indignation at the possibility. 'We'd been his heroes. It was The Pretty Things he wanted to play for, not anybody else.' Two years later Phil told the *NME* 'If six new people had all walked in at once then there would be a case for it, but in some ways it'd be more snide to call yourselves something else and have all those Used-To-Be Pretty Things tags.'

August 13 saw them at London's Lyceum Theatre for a performance filmed by the BBC. In September they recorded yet another *Sounds Of The Seventies* session, this time for Allan Black. All four songs came from *Parachute*, 'Sickle Clowns', 'Grass', 'Cries From The Midnight Circus' and 'She's A Lover'.

Interviewed by *Sounds*, in 1974, Phil looked back on the difficulty of playing *Parachute* material. '*Parachute* had lots of different segments and tracks that made it fucking impossible to play on stage without being schizophrenic.'

September saw the US release of *Parachute*. Like *SF Sorrow* it appeared on the Rare Earth label and like *SF Sorrow* it died a horrible suffocating death from lack of real promotion. Astounding really that a label desperate to gain recognition as an underground outlet could fail to see the profit centre that *Parachute* potentially represented. Four months later *Rolling Stone* magazine would proclaim it Album of the Year and the resultant neglect is tantamount to criminal. Wally examined the matter with Mike Stax: 'As I understand it, all the *Rolling Stone* Albums of the Year before or after have all been platinum albums but because of all the stuff that went down we didn't ever actually get any figures on it. Business-wise we were just completely screwed by EMI and Tamla-Motown.'

Rare Earth had no idea how to promote white UK rock bands. Dave Edmunds, whose version of 'I Hear You Knocking' had topped the UK single charts that year, also suffered from the label's marketing deficiencies.

Billboard's January 1971 review was also enthusiastic and it is hard to comprehend how Rare Earth failed to take advantage of such top-drawer recognition. That the Pretties were not being paid for US sales served to compound their misery.

Life went on and Peter Tolson took part in his first official Pretties recording session when, on October 27th and 28th, sessions for 'October 26th' took place at Abbey Road. Written by Phil and Wally as part of the *Parachute* sessions its working title was 'Revolution' and it featured Wally singing lead with the band adding tight ethereal harmonies to the chorus. Tolson supplied an exquisite guitar solo and, at the very beginning, some pedal steel. Peter recalled arguing with his German girl friend and then playing the beautiful yet forlorn mid-song solo as she stood watching the session from the gallery above. The recording highlighted his extensive use of the wah-wah pedal, which was such a feature of the Pretties stage shows. A year or so later Tolson stopped using wah-wah when his pedal broke and financial constraints ensured that it would not be replaced for some time.

Wally recalled these sessions in discussion with Mike Stax. 'The first time we went into the studio we did 'Summertime' and 'October 26th' all that wah-wah stuff – and 'Cold Stone', and that was basically his main riff. He was very instrumental in writing 'Cold Stone' and also 'Summertime'. And that was his first time in the studio with us, and he would just come up with some breathtaking stuff.'

Chris Welch, reviewing for *Melody Maker* considered. 'A good Norman Smith production and most unusual for the Things. Not that one infers a good production is something of a rarity from this quarter of the globe, but they have come up with some uncharacteristic vocal harmonies almost of Beach Boys calibre. The song deals with revolution, all students will be aware that October 26th was the day of the Penge uprising, and it is my bet that this lazy and attractive sound will be a huge hit. A huge hit.' He was wrong, hugely wrong.

John Peel, writing for *Disc* was less impressed. 'Waspish guitar opening and then, curiously, the Pretties sound like CSNY with pimples and moles. This lacks the basic drama of the Pretty's LP tracks and something of a disappointment. 'Cold Stone' is on the other side and we all prefer it. The playing and singing on 'Cold Stone' seems much stronger and much more convincing – this is the side you're likely to hear on *Top Gear* and the record is worth acquiring on the strength of it.'

Released in November 1970 'October 26th' received scant radio play although Stuart Henry did feature it on BBC Radio One's new releases programme. As Peel suggested, the flip-side, 'Cold Stone', showed the band at its upbeat best, a pulsing riff, tumbling unpredictable drums and Phil May's growling vocals punctuating whenever a gap appeared and singing about a 'weasel that might just be a stoat'. Tolson's guitar swarms all over the song, wah-wah, slide and thundering chords. The song quickly became a staple of the Pretties live act and during 1971 was the opener at concerts. 'Cold Stone' boasted the innovative percussive sounds of Phil's ashtray. Phil recalled that the high-hat sound wasn't right so they sent a taxi to collect his ashtray and it is this that you can hear alongside the opening riffs. 'It's the ashtray we used on *Parachute*,' he remembered. Phil told Mike Stax that, 'it had been given by the famous Phillipe Debarge, and it was the most funny, quite good, well constructed French silver ashtray which had that thing where you pressed the thing down and all the cigarettes spun into the bottom of the thing and it popped up leaving a clean ashtray. We were using it as a high-hat and banging it with a drumstick.'

'Cold Stone' became the first song co-credited to Peter Tolson. Peter remembered the descending riff being written by Chrissie Stuart, Eire Apparent's bass player, who should also have received a writing credit. Peter recalled Chrissie being invited to Westbourne Terrace to pick up his share – £4 or so – he didn't bother. Tolson's shift into the song-writing chair mirrored the withdrawal of Wally as a creative force. The lack of recognition was hurting and an increasing interest in production techniques was leading Wally to question his place in the band. Tolson's arrival offered new musical avenues that Phil was intent on exploring. Wally's music was more in the Beatles and Beach Boys arena and pushed against the increasingly rocky path.

Peter recalled an initial difficulty in forcing issues on songs and arrangements. 'It was a struggle cause, coming from where I was coming from, I was very quiet, very shy, wouldn't say boo to a goose, and I'd only just started. These guys were the professionals, been around for a long time, done a lot of stuff, worked with the Beatles, Floyd and that shit. It was a learning exercise and a lot of things were gotten away with.'

Joining the Pretties was not merely a musical decision but a lifestyle shift. It introduced Peter to the essential rockers fuel, alcohol. Previously he had not bothered with beer or spirits and although the Eire Apparent boys had puffed on the weed they were not great drinkers either. The Pretties however had a history of heavy drinking and in their company Peter soon found himself on lager and whiskey.

The band's live act was now predominantly *Parachute* material with 'Old Man Going' from *SF Sorrow* and a few R&B standards such as 'Mona', 'King Bee' and of course, 'Route 66'. For a period the show included a drum solo from Skip which would last between 5 and 10 minutes and allowed the rest of the guys to relax with a beer behind the amps. Tolson would then emerge and launch into a solo improvisation that included scat-singing and yards of feedback. After five or ten minutes of virtuosity a revived Skip, together with the rest of the band, would then wander back on and chug into the remainder of the concert. With hindsight Tolson has concluded that Dick Taylor was always better at playing the *SF Sorrow* material, Peter confessed he couldn't really get into it.

The band was often out of it with drugs and alcohol fuelling their motors and sometimes blowing the engine. Tolson recalled one gig where they were the support band to Tyrannosaurus Rex. Peter and Marc Bolan were alone in the dressing room playing similar white Strat's when two spaced-out guys wandered in uninvited and in their drugged haze sat on the carpet, grooving to the sounds. Peter was tuning his Strat whilst Bolan was strumming his. 'Just then Jon Povey and Wally came in and upon seeing the uninvited guests they launched into them, beating them up and then throwing them out. Bolan and me just looked at each other. Then Jon came back in and asked who they could beat up next. I'd never seen Wally that way before, or since.'

It was around this time that Phil split with his long-time girlfriend, the model Gayla Mitchell. This was a blow and for a while he went to pieces. Another, far greater disaster struck when returning from a Reading gig Derek Boltwood was involved in a near fatal car smash.

Plans had been afoot for an inaugural US tour in September, with promised support from Rare Earth. These plans foundered without Boltwood's steady hands on the wheel. His assistant Steve Woolley battled on manfully with support from Tony Howard and the band themselves. 'I had this crash that laid me out, knocked me back and I was in hospital for a long, long while. Came out and wasn't a hundred percent for a long, long time. It screwed up the American tour and I suppose that's when... I wouldn't say it was my commitment disappeared, but the whole thing didn't go forward any more.'

The accident could not have come at a worse time for the band. With Tolson's blazing guitar adding an extra combustious ingredient to the *Parachute* material they were arguably at the peak of their powers. Phil himself suggested as much to Caroline Boucher in a July 1970 interview for *Disc*. 'After all this time I finally think we've got a group of people together who are really into the music and are good musicians. The Pretty Things have always had their fair share of good musicians – it was just that people like Dick Taylor didn't feel the way we were writing and it was hardly fair on him or us.'

The university circuit still continued to provide the bulk of the bread and butter gigs, March proving typical with bookings at Twickenham College and Westfield College. The latter, an all-nighter, with Caravan, Gracious and a number of local bands again emphasised the extent of their commitment to good causes and also their lack of financial nous. As it was a charity event they gladly gave their services as they had numerous times in the past but, after the gig, they were dismayed to find that all the other name bands had received generous expenses. The Pretties, as ever, took it financially on the chin.

In April they played another all-nighter at a wretched dive called The Temple. This underground venue boasted shiny, sticky carpets and an entrance that it shared with The Pink Flamingo Club where patrons ran the gauntlet of pushers, drunks and other disturbed and unsavoury characters of the night. Midnight circus indeed.

A visit to the rank toilet facilities involved antics such as side-stepping the drunk, trotting across the piss-covered floor, watching the low-life shooting-up in doorless cubicles and avoiding the occasional vomit lake.

This particular concert featured possibly the most professional performance of Skip Alan's career. Severely under the weather because of food poisoning from an early evening meal he perched on his drum stool for the 3.00 a.m. performance and midway through the gig puked copiously over his right shoulder whilst simultaneously keeping perfect time and not once missing a beat. Needless to say the show went on although it's not known whether he managed *Route 66* that night.

The band's financial position was worsening and in desperation Phil telephoned EMI. He asked for news of *Parachute*'s sales in the States pointing out the good reviews it had received in *Billboard* and *Cashbox*. Phil complained about the outdated royalty agreement and suggested that the US deal be renegotiated with another record company. He felt that a different label could buy out Motown's interest and also provide cash to buy the band new instruments. Other than noting Phil's comments no action was taken.

Desperate for chart recognition to go with the critical acclaim the band and Norman Smith took to the studio during March and April to record 'Stone Hearted Mama' a jaunty rocker with an infectious keyboard groove. With the engineering support of John Kelly and Nick Webb they recorded thirteen takes of which take four emerged as the single. For the third consecutive single release Wally took the microphone and gave a controlled husky rendition. The instrumental middle eight showcased Tolson's facility for a memorable quick solo as he competed with Skip's perfect drum fills. The song was a rare but blatant attempt to penetrate the singles charts and Wally in particular retains no real affection for it. Jon Povey recalled that Norman Smith liked it a lot but confessed, 'We've never been any good at singles apart from the early stuff. We're hopeless at trying to write a single, it doesn't come naturally, we're an album band.' Wally disclosed that originally 'Stone Hearted Mama' didn't sound anything like the end result. He felt that

Norman was under pressure at EMI because of the money invested in the band and he was trying for a hit sound and Norman agreed hat this was indeed the case. Kudos counted for nothing when the sales remained low.

Released in May 1971 it traversed the usual Pretty Thing route of little airplay and fewer buyers and added to the general air of rejection felt by the band and Wally in particular.

The single boasted a double B-Side, 'Summertime' and 'Circus Mind'. Along with 'Cold Stone', 'Summertime' which was completed in one take on April 5 represented the only writing collaborations between Phil, Wally and Peter Tolson. A gloriously happy song it was a testament to their continued ability to produce great music from the pit of despondency. Bouncy and awash with lush harmonies the song is remembered by Jon Povey for the quality of Tolson's guitarwork. 'It sounded like a violin, like Stephan Grappelli playing violin on it, it's just the most amazing guitar solo.'

Chris Welch told *Melody Maker* readers that 'Phil May (sic) leads the Things into a solid boogie beat. The voice is somewhat buried in the track but backing guitars have a nice T-Rex echo and the chords are interestingly moody. Some of the music appears to be playing backwards.' Certainly the song did recall the feel of recent hit 'Ride A White Swan' with its bouncy beat and it may well have been the template used by Norman Smith.

'Circus Mind', the working title of which was 'Unknown Blues', was unusual, effectively a duet between Phil's plaintive vocal and Tolson's guitar fed through a Leslie Cabinet. The lyrics, possibly reflecting Phil's fractured love-life, again highlighted his facility with words. Future bass player Jack Green, talking in 1999, concurred. 'Phil was such a gifted lyricist, I still think he must be one of the best lyricists in the world and he's never had credit for it. He's really very creative and exciting... a very artistic guy. I mean, I was in T. Rex before that and Marc Bolan was supposed to be artistic whereas he wasn't really. He was cool, but next to Phil he was a bit of a barrow-boy.'

The imperatives and the influences on this band have always been wide and varied. Although originally inspired by Bo Diddley, Chuck Berry and various Chicago and New Orleans swamp sounds they have remained aware of the contemporary sounds and have always sought to integrate these and update their own music. Back in 1960, when Phil studied at Hornsey College of Art, his teacher, John Sturgess warmed him to the classical composers, particularly Stravinsky and this willingness to listen, learn and experiment has permeated his and the band's music to this day.

During the summer of 1971 Phil had an obsession with the T. Rex number one, 'Get It On', playing it virtually non-stop apart from a brief interlude of Rod Stewart's 'I'm Losing You'. He has always kept in touch with the current climate as evidenced some years later when Phil absorbed the new 'punk' sounds through his friend, Wreckless Eric, and artists such as Graham Parker and Squeeze. He has always been supportive of those acts that push at the barriers and refuse to stand still musically.

During the Spring of 1971 the band began to falter. The euphoria of *Parachute's Rolling Stone* accolade soon dissipated in the aftermath of Rare Earth's failure to capitalise on it. Derek Boltwood's car smash meant that plans to tour the States were ruptured and the band continued to ply its trade at the treadmill gigs of university campuses with occasional forays to the Roundhouse and the Lyceum.

'Wally was getting more into writing at that stage,' proffered Boltwood, 'My feeling is it all petered out at about the same time. We were hoping to dispel the image of being a band's band. It just didn't happen, what happened was *Parachute* cemented the image that the Pretties had of being a band's band. At the time I think it was a hugely influential album. As far as the Pretties were concerned it was a significant step. We just didn't', for a whole load of reasons that might have been chemistry between the band members. It was because there was an awful lot of baggage there, they were carrying a lot of baggage from the past, we were just not able to take that huge step forward.'

Boltwood's accident also played a major part in the wind-down. 'After my accident I guess I wasn't as committed as I had been. Looking at it from the chaps point of view maybe they thought of it as yet another blow. We'd done the UK tour and had some really downer gigs and the chaps used to come off stage and I think at the time all of them were feeling fairly suicidal, it probable affected Wally more than most. My girlfriend had been in the car with me and injured her leg and was hospitalised for a while. She came out before I did and she started going out with Wally which was not necessarily part of the split but, in retrospect, it was all part of the falling apart.'

The crash and the transfer of his girlfriends loyalties to Wally was a watershed in the bands life as EMI artists. Wally's relationship with Derek was never the same and they hardly spoke to each other again.

May saw an appearance on Mike Harding's early evening radio show which highlighted the single, 'Stone Hearted Mama', 'Circus Mind' and a never to be recorded potential classic 'Slow Beginnings'.

'Slow Beginnings' continued The Pretty Things exasperating and, from a fans viewpoint, irritating habit of composing songs of astonishing quality which, for reasons best known to the band, were never recorded and have since fallen into the misty slipstream of their history. 'Turn My Head' and 'Spring' from 1968, 'Spider Woman' and 'Schoolgirl' from 1972 and 'Living Without You' from 1974 are superior to much of the De Wolfe catalogue and, in the opinion of many, to some of their official recordings. Nevertheless they remain officially unavailable, even in a BBC Special format. The reason for this failure was explained to Mike Stax by Wally. 'I think that when you've made an album, you've got a lot of songs lying around, and songs are things that don't have a long life in your brain, because when you're writing them, after a month or two you've got other songs you want to put on your next album. So you've got a certain amount of natural wastage, or what would be natural wastage.'

Neither Peter Tolson nor Jon Povey could remember 'Slow Beginnings' but reminiscing in January 2000 Wally recalled, 'They were good songs... I can't remember 'Spring' but I remember 'Slow Beginnings', I thought that was quite a good song. I can just about remember it. Maybe we should dig it out and do something with it.'

The following month the band recorded a set for Dave Symonds *Sounds of the Seventies*, a BBC Radio One show. Like the previous radio session it was recorded at Maida Vale and 'Slow Beginnings' again featured. This song, now a regular concert highlight, showcased the collective strengths of the band. A memorable introductory riff ablaze with Skip's ricocheting drum fills leading to one of Phil's best vocals and evocative lyrics. At the tail end of the chorus Wally charges in with his inimitable John Lennon growl paving the way for Tolson's fantastic solo complete with scorching slide.

'Summertime' also received an airing and completing the set was a mighty rendition of 'Cries From The Midnight Circus'. This tempestuous version really ripped with Tolson's guitar shredding the central riff that on *Parachute* was driven by Wally's bass. This is the recording that was included on the 1991 *'On Air'* album of BBC sessions although, for reasons unknown, and it was certainly not time constraints, Tolson's second wailing solo was perversely and unnecessarily removed. Talking in 1998 Peter explained the cranking up of the song. 'The riff on the album wasn't played by a guitarist but by a bass player. It didn't seem to work for me so I thought if it's gonna work let's kick it up the arse.'

The band had visited Abbey Road and recorded a similar arse-kicking version during August 1970, which was intended as a Rare Earth single release in support of the planned US tour. Phil had a white copy, but insanely he and the band appear to have forgotten about the recording, with Phil even suggesting it never happened. The acetate, like most of Phil's vinyl collection, has been lost or thieved and the masters presumably mislaid. A hell of a shame as it captured the essence of the full throttle live version.

The release of 'Stone Hearted Mama' was timed to coincide with a UK Tour primarily encompassing town halls. Starting at Bournemouth it progressed through the South West to the North West, back down South, back up North, in fact all over the place. The itinerary appeared to have been chosen by a sight impaired epileptic throwing warped darts at a map of England.

The tour ended on July 9th, when they played the Silvergate Ballroom, Lincoln. It was also the end of the road for Wally. He chucked it in to join Norman Smith as a house producer at EMI, as Jon Povey recalled. 'Wally saw a future for himself at EMI as a producer, he liked the job and he was made a house producer. Wally was really into his music, into his technicalities. He was an electrician by trade he knew all about where the cables went where they plugged in and where they came out.'

Wally: 'It's very difficult to leave a band like The Pretty Things but in the end, the frustration was so deep. It was terribly difficult because The Pretty Things are like a family really.' Wally was still upset about the lack of support that the label had given *SF Sorrow* and *Parachute*. He felt that the people at EMI didn't have a clue about the albums, didn't know what they had got. Perhaps worst of all the commercial failure of *Parachute* and the later singles had dented his faith in his own ability to construct songs that were both musically relevant and commercial. 'It was deeply disturbing,' he told Mike Stax, 'I was so disappointed with how we'd come unstuck really. I felt good about the music, and that was worrying that what I felt good about wasn't publicly acceptable. It was deeply disturbing. It's hard when you get knocked like that. Now, I still feel good about the music and I feel a lot better, because I realise a lot of other people like it too, but at the time I didn't really know that. I thought, I'm so completely wrong here, I've gotta change tracks and do something else.'

Although Wally did not allude to the tension between himself and Phil it was plain that their failure to agree a concerted musical policy was another important factor in his decision to leave. Peter Tolson explained that when he joined it focused Phil's attention toward a more retro R&B approach. Wally was pushing in a different direction and although Phil had gone with him on *Parachute* he was now intent on exploring different musical ideas. Wally denied this, but revealed, 'A lot of our music has come about through tension.'

Wally had planned his departure for some time, although manager Derek Boltwood was totally unaware of this. A mere nine days after the last gig he began production duties with Barclay James Harvest. As an EMI house producer Wally was taken under Norman Smith's wing and because of Norman's own touring commitments as pop star Hurricane Smith, he took over with BJH.'

Peter Tolson was also unaware of Wally's imminent departure but it didn't come as a great shock because he had noticed Wally's falling interest.

'You could see it, towards the end, falling apart,' insisted Boltwood. 'Fewer and fewer people were turning up and you get into that downward spiral and you see the aggression being contained between individuals. I think the personality difference between Wally and Phil was quite evident, because Wally was wanting to take more and more of the writing and wanting to push more and Phil, he's a pretty cool guy, you never know what he's thinking. Maybe he was feeling, without showing it, that he was being usurped.' Derek remains emphatic that 'Phil was and is the soul of The Pretty Things. One of the great things about the Pretties and one of the great things about Phil is that Phil is a hell of a nice guy and for all their individual personalities they are all nice blokes. Great ideas, great music and great energy. Absolutely lived the life to the full and they were genuinely in it for the love of it. They were in advance of their time, they did a lot of things because, intuitively, they knew it was right.'

Whilst Wally was embroiled with Barclay James Harvest, EMI wrote to Motown advising that the band had broken up and that they were releasing The Pretty Things from the contract which would otherwise have expired on 31st August. They confirmed, 'There will not be any further product to make available to you.' Motown Vice President Ralph Seltzer replied some six months later informing that they would be exercising all remaining options under the June 1969 EMI-Motown agreement.

CHAPTER 9 – Warner Brothers First Time Around

Wally Waller's departure in July 1971 marked the close of an era, the end of the golden EMI period. The Pretty Things went through a period of introspection and inactivity. They gigged sporadically although such appearances were fairly sparse. Skip wasn't prepared to hang around so he went off and joined the band Sunshine, whose members included Jack Green and Gordon Edwards who would later join The Pretty Things. Peter was living low off the hog and remembered those times as very lean. Years later Phil explained that EMI had lost faith in them and showed no interest in persevering with what was clearly a non-mainstream act. Critical acclaim couldn't be banked and as ever the faceless minions in the accounting department over-rode any musical considerations.

It was Skip's involvement with Sunshine which acted as the catalyst that brought about the reformation of the band, a new management deal and a new recording contract. Sunshine was handled by Circle, a management company controlled by Bill Shepherd who also represented Home and Quintessence. Whilst out driving Skip played Bill Shepherd a tape of *Parachute* and Bill was knocked out by the music. Skip told him that it was The Pretty Things, the band that he had previously been with and that they had split up. Shepherd was astounded that a band of such obvious quality had splintered, and seeing potential he decided to try to piece them together again.

Shortly after this, whilst holidaying in Greece, Phil received a telegram from Bill Shepherd urging him to reform the band. Upon his return Shepherd persuaded him that the Pretties should be resurrected and that under his management they would prosper. He would negotiate a new record deal and they would finally tour the States. Shepherd's enthusiasm and relative youth (he was in his early thirties) was impressive, and it galvanised Phil into reforming the Pretties in a serious manner, not just as an occasional gigging entity.

Wally's defection meant that the band had lost not only a bass player and a proven composer but also a tremendous lead and harmony singer. To fill the bass spot they called on Peter's long time friend Stuart Brooks who had previously played in Leafhound and Black Cat Bones. In Peter's mind this redressed an imbalance. When he had turned down the opportunity to join Black Cat Bones two years earlier the band had folded leaving Stuart out of work.

Replacing Wally the vocalist was another matter, Stuart didn't sing so, very much against his will, Peter Tolson was press-ganged into stepping up to the mike for harmony duty. He was obviously uncomfortable with this and with hindsight wishes he had never started, 'I can't sing,' he reflected with regret, 'it was just persuasion.' Peter's voice fleshed out the harmonies but it didn't really work.

Phil and Peter were left as the main song-writing focus with occasional assistance from Jon Povey. They wrote most of what was to become *Freeway Madness* at Phil's retreat in Norfolk, complete with obligatory bag of weed. They also did a lot of work with the Revox at Westbourne Terrace and also spent a couple of weeks at an old vicarage in Bicester where many of the songs were conceived. One stand out track, 'Havana Bound', was written in the studio where the band had left Tolson to find something whilst they scarpered. Once he had the main riff nailed down Pete scarpered as well and with hindsight feels that the late 90s version, which is played with descending chords instead of single notes, works a lot better.

Up to 1971 The Pretty Things had limited their drug intake to hash, speed and acid but it was whilst at Bicester that the double-edged joy of heroin first surfaced. Peter Tolson was suffering from a raging toothache, which was bringing him down, and needed some kind of pain-killer. A dealer friend was with him and suggested that Peter rub his gum with some heroin. Peter instantly felt better, in fact he felt great, and thought, 'Maybe this stuff isn't too bad.'

This initial dalliance led both Peter and Phil to try speedballs, a potentially lethal heroin/cocaine cocktail. During the *Freeway Madness* recording sessions cocaine was much in evidence and Jon Povey soon made it another obsession to add to his lust for surfing.

The album took shape through late 1971 to mid 1972 with the songs mutating as they became staples of the live act. For a while, the early gigs included a departure, an acoustic spot where Phil would also strum a guitar for the song 'Country Road'. This mellow California-style approach proved unsuccessful, and it was dropped fairly quickly.

By now, due to the infusion of funds by Shepherd, the band had their own P.A. and instruments making gigs easier and more profitable. Unfortunately this still did not make for lucrative gigging, Ed Bicknell, who in 1972 was booking them for Bill Shepherd, confirmed that the band went out for between £100 and £175 a night. 'At mid-day we'd get a call from some venue saying that that night's act had cried off and did we have anybody. We'd get on the phone and the Pretties would all pile into a minivan and head out to Watford or somewhere.'

June 1972 saw the band playing a double-header with the fleetingly popular East Of Eden jigging their jig at London's Lyceum. Memorably this high profile afternoon gig included a string quartet and the return of Wally for a one off special. An acoustic version of 'Summertime', a fabulous 'The Good Mr Square' and the *Parachute* trilogy 'In The Square/Letter/Rain' were the string assisted highlights of the set. The set included Wally's new song 'Over The Moon' which had been recorded for the new album with added orchestration. Peter recollected that this was the catalyst for Wally's reappearance.

Yet again the band plied their trade on the university circuit and town halls together with regular BBC radio sessions. August 1972 found them again laying down tracks for BBC's John Peel radio show. 'Love Is Good', 'Spider Woman' and 'Onion Soup' were the new songs offered. The session highlighted Phil's thankfully temporary mannerism of punctuating every song with shouted asides of 'Allright'. 'Spider Woman' contained eight such exclamations! It also showcased the turbo-charged rock version of 'Don't Bring Me Down' that launched with a feedback molested chord progression before charging into a decidedly up tempo heavy rock performance that worked surprisingly well. Phil's vocals belted along apace adding more to the tune than in previous and future lower key performances.

A week later they returned for another Peel session recording 'Love Is Good', 'Onion Soup', 'All Night Sailor' and 'Rosalyn'. This latter recording was particularly memorable with Dick Taylor returning after some three years absence to add his brand of authenticity to the song. Although this event would appear to be noteworthy, it transpires that Dick has completely forgotten about it and assures that it never happened. The comprehensive *BBC In Session* book served to confirm his appearance.

Sadly, for a band of such repute, they found themselves playing gigs as the support for inferior bands. Sheffield City Hall saw them supporting Stray, and later they would endure a series of gigs at the new Sundown Theatres opening for the temporarily popular but barely capable Hawkwind.

During the previous year David Bowie had risen to superstar status through his 'Ziggy' incarnation and had reversed the fortunes of Mott The Hoople. By producing their version of his song, 'All The Young Dudes', Bowie transformed Mott from progressive also-rans, on the verge of splitting up, into big gigging, *Top of the Pops* regulars. Through his intervention Mott The Hoople were reinvented as a main stream act, inhabiting that nebulous region between the glam-rock and progressive-rock camps.

Bowie's reverence of the Pretties was ultimately highlighted on his June 1973 *Pin Ups* album, which included not one but two of their hits, 'Rosalyn' and 'Don't Bring Me Down'. Dick recalled Bowie following them around from concert to concert in the early days. 'He admired Phil particularly. I think to a certain extent we contributed to the birth and development of his career.' In the mid sixties, when he played with The Lower Third and the

King Bees, Bowie's repertoire was very R&B oriented and the inclusion of two Pretties numbers paid due homage to their early influence.

During autumn 1972, Phil revealed that plans were afoot for Bowie to produce a single for them, to see if he could do a similar revival job as achieved with Mott. The song chosen was Lou Reed's 'Sweet Jane', a live act staple of both Reed and the Velvet Underground. For reasons long forgotten this venture never progressed and the Bowie connection appears to have withered. Phil dismissed it as just talk down at the club, although he did suggest that it would have been a Phil May solo single, not a Pretty Things deal. Peter Tolson recalled that another Reed song, 'Vicious' was also under consideration.

October found the band again in the BBC studios, this time for 'Whispering' Bob Harris. They recorded three songs from the forthcoming album, 'Religion's Dead', 'Peter/Rip Off Train' and 'Havana Bound' plus an old favourite, 'Roadrunner'.

By this time producer Norman Smith had finally received a return on his years of musical endeavour and rather improbably had metamorphosed into pop star Hurricane Smith. He scored three UK hits between June 1971 and September 1972 one of which, 'Oh Babe What Would You Say', hit number one in the States. Wally Waller played bass and guitar on Norman's two main hits, 'Babe' and the excellent 'Don't Let It Die'.

Smith's chart success involved touring and promotional obligations and he became unavailable for production duties so, for the new album, *Freeway Madness*, they turned to Norman's protégé – Wally Waller.

Bill Shepherd had secured them a contract with Warner Brothers and whilst this allowed an album to be funded, and hopefully supported, it also presented a problem, because Wally was a house producer contracted to EMI. Wally's answer was to use a pseudonym – Asa Jones, a name he also adopted when producing Sunshine's eponymous album that same year which also came out on Warner's. Engineer Tony Clarke was also brought in although he was also contracted to EMI and playing a cautious hand he declined any kind of album credit. Tony remembered how it began. 'I got a phone call from the manager at the time. He drove up to Abbey Road in a big limo and said they were doing this album and were trying to put the original *Parachute* team back together again. But they never paid. I remember half way through the sessions they asked me how I wanted to be paid? I said by the hourly rate, and I'm sure everything will be fine. We finished the album and it was a really worrying time. They had an office and I remember going there on numerous occasions and there being no one there and then putting letters through the door. (Eventually) someone was there one day and I got paid.'

Wally also got stiffed, he had negotiated a fee and a small percentage and to this day has not been paid his producer's fee. He insists that he would have produced the album for free but nonetheless it left a nasty taste. It seems that only Bill Shepherd profited financially from The Pretty Things endeavours during this period, a view also held by Gordon Edwards regarding Sunshine and other Circle bands. Nonetheless, Jack Green entertains fonder memories of Shepherd, he remembers Bill's youth and vigour and how everything was impressive from the Aston Martin to the expensive suits.

Ed Bicknell agreed that Shepherd didn't have much idea as a manager but that he liked the trappings of success. 'Flashy limousines filled with totty. He had the only Mercedes with curtains that I've ever seen.'

Perhaps revealingly, EMI chose not to exercise the option built into the original 1967 contract, which allowed them to re-sign the band if they negotiated another recording contract before August 31, 1973.

With Wally and Tony Clarke moonlighting, the sessions for *Freeway Madness* had to take place during the late evening and often extended into the night. The Pretty Things located themselves at Willesden's Morgan Studios with insufficient material for a complete album but buttressed by the dual stimuli of coke and heroin.

Phil contended that the album was required to coincide with a planned tour of America. A tour was not possible without product and the support of the label, and this was what Shepherd had promised them.

Tolson was now the Pretties' main songwriter although, without any rancour, he considers that Wally's production technique involved him trying to make the songs sound a bit like his own material. 'Some he did, some he didn't,' said Peter matter of factly. Tolson felt that a number of his songs were non-Pretties material which got twisted and pulled until it fitted the 'Pretties sound.' *Freeway Madness* contained nine tracks, seven of these were May-Tolson joint compositions with the other two being Phil collaborations with Wally and Jon Povey.

Freeway Madness was released in December 1972, never a good time for non-mainstream artists as established 'stars' and Greatest Hit compilations fight it out for the big Christmas sales. This particular year witnessed a deluge of K-Tel packages as well as albums by Rod Stewart and Slade. The latter artists proved that hit singles still propelled albums into the charts and Warners naturally required a single to push the Pretties album.

Although no longer in the group Wally offered up his song 'Over The Moon', which recounted the story of a doomed romance with a female rock star. Very much in the *Parachute* camp of melody based composition it was virtually complete apart from requiring a few lyrical additions from Phil. Wally took the vocals, aided by a lush and sympathetic orchestration courtesy of Don Harper. This made it the fourth consecutive Pretty Things single to feature Wally on vocals. Predictably it failed to receive airplay and did not even sniff the lower regions of the chart.

Flipside, 'Havana Bound', again epitomised Phil May's facility with droll and meaningful lyrics. Amongst the rock fraternity perhaps only Richard Thompson and Chris Difford can stand comparison with Phil for consistent lyrical ability over such an extended period.

The tale of a plane hi-jacked to Cuba, a common episode in the early seventies, it featured sterling guitar-work by Tolson and excellent interplay between bass, drums and guitar. The song, a favourite of Phil's, has remained part of The Pretty Things live set throughout their career.

Skip coined the album title, *Freeway Madness* because, as Phil said, 'this was obviously an album about being on the road.' Opening track, 'Love Is Good', painted the picture of a typical stateside groupie whilst 'Country Road' touched on the loneliness of touring. 'Peter/Rip Off Train' combined two songs about Peter Tolson. The first section, 'Peter', was autobiographical, and related his birth to parents who had waited ages to have a child. It neatly segued into 'Rip Off Train', a valediction of the music business which recounted Tolson's audition for the band before it wandered off into a fictional account of showbiz manipulation. Wally's distinctive growling voice could be heard to good effect on the chorus harmonies. Peter Tolson felt that segueing these two songs together wasn't a good idea musically. He suspected it was done because it had happened on *Parachute* and that they wanted to do it again.

Hipgnosis again designed the cover, this time in collaboration with Phil. It featured a hand-tinted photomontage of current and past band members inside Dave Gilmour's car. Lazily, when the album was released as an American CD, on The Medicine Label, the artwork was mirrored so that it showed only the right half of the photo, the then current band members. For the third consecutive album the lyrics, very sensibly, were printed inside the gatefold over a photo of the band and Skip's dog Sasha.

Although not a big seller *Freeway Madness* did garner another excellent review from *Rolling Stone* magazine. Reviewer, Stephen Holden, described it as, 'A carefully conceived studio album, its near perfect combination of seemingly disparate elements: neo-classic English white blues, alternating with a Crosby, Stills and Nash derived acoustic style wonderfully reworked in bracing off-harmonies. The end result is a mixture of visceral raunch and harmonic sophistication that sounds consistently fresh.'

Discussing the album in 1998 Dick Taylor felt that it lacked something. 'I had slight reservations about it.' He is right, the album definitely lacked something and coming after *Parachute* and the brace of Harvest singles it has to be viewed as something of a disappointment. This relative failure is most evident on 'Country Road', which is an unconvincing attempt at California soft rock complete with grammatically corrupt lyrics, melded to fit the rhyme. Peter Tolson believes that the song was used because there was a gap on the album. 'Spider Woman', a much better contemporary song was not used as it was written too late for the sessions. 'Allnight Sailor' offered uncomfortable listening with obtuse lyrics and a strange Rolf Harris warp-style sound made by Jon Povey and a piece of hardboard. This track also includes the rarity of Skip 'singing' on the chorus! It is saved from abject failure by Tolson's jangly, yet melodic guitar work. Bridging this track and the final song, 'Onion Soup', was a strange buzzing noise. Peter chuckled recounting that it was a furry toy which buzzed when turned upside down! 'Onion Soup', which was always Phil's favourite track, suffered from lyrics that were contrived or overly subtle, depending on your viewpoint. The coda, 'Another Bowl' also seemed to be a last minute studio creation that was omitted from live performances.

There are high points, 'Havana Bound' provided a classic riff highlighting the combined strengths of Tolson's guitar and May's singing. Stuart Brooks excellent bass technique offered a solid counterpoint to Tolson's unsettling licks in the instrumental middle eight. Stuart can also be heard to good effect on 'Love Is Good' and 'Come Home Mama'. Peter Tolson recalled that this last track was conceived from the tail end of 'Onion Soup', a comment which is authenticated by a close listen to the later live versions where chord and time change similarities abound.

Tony Clarke's later comments betrayed a sense of disappointment with the outcome. 'Away from the focus of Abbey Road, the focus and professionalism that we had on *Parachute* was not on *Freeway Madness*. It was very loose. It is very difficult to keep up that attention to detail. If you don't then this is what happens, you don't get a progression from *Parachute* into another album, into where the band should have gone.'

Although *Parachute* had enjoyed minor chart success the release of *Freeway Madness* was some thirty months later and what little momentum *Parachute* had built up had long since dissipated. Times had changed, psychedelia was history and the 'serious musicians' played progressive music. Heavy metal, US styled country-tinged AOR or overly long instrumental pieces were the name of the game.

Freeway Madness sounded nothing like *Parachute*, which was a shame. With Wally still involved producing as well as writing and singing, and with Tolson's guitar adding another dimension to the attack, there was potential for a tremendous follow up, which sadly didn't happen. The songs weren't as strong and the overwhelming and cascading sounds that energised *SF Sorrow* and *Parachute* were also missing.

Many critics and fans consider *Freeway Madness* as the album where the band trod water. Warner Brothers failed to provide any worthwhile support, a real downer and a sad harbinger of the second Warner's experience eight years later.

Freeway Madness proved that the band had not managed to fill Wally's shoes. Stuart Brooks might have played excellent bass but that was it. Songwriting, vocals and additional instrumental skills were the key elements that Wally brought to the band. Therefore, early in 1973 Gordon Edwards was invited to join. Sunshine had recently imploded and Shepherd had gone missing, as had a sizeable sum of record company advance money intended for another Circle band, which to this day has remains untraced.

Gordon's song-writing skills, vocals and all round musical ability made him the perfect choice to flesh out the sound. He's slightly unsure but believes that it was through the Skip Alan/Sunshine/Bill Shepherd connection that he was invited to join. Certainly Skip was the only current band member that Gordon knew at that time.

Born in Southport on Boxing Day 1946 Gordon confessed that he had never heard 'Rosalyn' or 'Don't Bring Me Down' until he joined. Although a multi-instrumentalist, he was primarily a keyboard maestro utilising his classical training which supplied the dexterity, speed and precision that was so pronounced on later songs like 'Singapore Silk Torpedo'. Gordon's prowess on guitar also allowed the band to feature dual lead guitarists when the occasion demanded.

'They asked me to come along and audition and I knew I could get the part because none of them were fantastic musicians,' he scoffed.

1973 also marked The Pretty Things inaugural tour of the States. Nine years after they first burst on the scene and raised the pulses of hundreds of future US garage bands and nearly three years since *Parachute* had been lauded by *Rolling Stone* magazine. The Pretties ought to have been headlining and selling out arenas. As cult status demi gods, with a history of proto-garage band mayhem and rule breaking, their first US tour should have been big news, but it wasn't. Peter Tolson says they played small dives and, frankly admits, 'I was out of it most of the time in the States. Can't remember much.' And, by way of explanation, 'Groupies used to bring their own stash of dope as an in with the band.' The tour was brief, as in two weeks brief, and apart from one gig supporting Rory Gallagher the remainder were low key.

For touring a certain focus was required and cocaine was the favoured method for Tolson and many of the band. Peter used the drug to centre himself on the music without distractions but was always careful to cut down when back in the UK.

August 1973 saw them at the Hippodrome, Golders Green recording an *In Concert* for a future Radio One broadcast. Compere Pete Drummond announced that the band would be recording a new album in America, 'in downtown Burbank and I hear that Jimmy Miller will be producing it.' It never happened, the Bill Shepherd contract was up for renewal and Phil had other irons in the fire. The BBC recording found its way onto *The Forgotten Beebs*, a bootleg on the Tendolar label and in June 2000 four of the songs would be included as bonus tracks on the re-issued *Freeway Madness* CD.

The Radio One broadcast highlighted a different version of 'Onion Soup', much improved and radically different to the version on *Freeway Madness*. It revealed how many of the Pretties songs twisted and evolved over the course of numerous performances, never for them the safe but mundane option of replicating the recorded version. As always, the show closed with 'Route 66', or 'A41' as Phil introduced it. Povey jumped onto the drum stool allowing Skip and Phil to share rasping vocals on a song they have all but made their own.

Throughout this period 'Babbling' Brooks was feeling increasingly discontented. Unlike the others he was quiet and workmanlike exuding neither flash nor spontaneity. He didn't seem like 'family' and Skip appeared to despise him, much as he did Twink. At gigs he was often seen hurling drumsticks, mid-song, at the taciturn Brooks back. 'Amazing bass player,' confessed Jon Povey. 'Very quiet boy, a very straight quiet guy, friend of Peter's. Skip hated Vic Unitt as well, but Skip doesn't really hate anybody Skip is just Skip and he didn't like me when he first met me.' Stories of Jon Povey and Skip thumping each other at gigs have done the rounds. 'It was loaded handbags at twelve paces stuff,' scoffed Peter Tolson.

It was at this stage that Stuart Brooks finally baled out, disappearing for a while before emerging some time later to play bass in Silverhead, the Michael des Barres vehicle. Peter says that Stuart was pushed. Like Vic Unitt he never really fitted the Pretties style. Silent and solid he epitomised the honest working musician ignoring stage presence and concentrating on his music and such has never been the Pretties bag. Stuart remains the best and only true bass guitar player the Pretties ever had. Wally and future incumbent Jack Green were both converted and, in Jack's case, frustrated rhythm guitarists and John Stax, in those early maniac days, was a relative novice.

During 1973 The Pretty Things recorded their final sessions for De Wolfe, issued as *Hot Licks*. All of the songs were strong, 'Good Times', 'Sweet Orphan Lady', 'I Could Not Believe My Eyes', 'Walk Away', 'The Loser' and 'Easily Done'.

Perversely, although Gordon Edwards is correctly credited as co-writer of 'Good Times' he is omitted from the list of musicians. This is palpably false as his distinctive vocals are clearly heard on several tracks. The thorny issue of royalties, or the lack of them, is exposed by Peter Tolson's assertion that he has earned more from co-writing 'Good Times' than any song from a 'proper' Pretty Things album, 'Good Times' was used as aural wallpaper on numerous television programmes and films. Like most previous De Wolfe recordings Skip was noticeable by his absence and Jon Povey took over the drum stall performing more than competently.

Gordon Edwards recalled, 'We went to the De Wolfe studio and we just, literally, wrote songs in the studio, because we realised they didn't have to be that good, but by the time we finished them they didn't sound too bad. Povey was the one who suggested we do this thing in the studio don't worry about writing great songs. The only money I've ever had in royalties was from De Wolfe.'

CHAPTER 10 – The Pretty Things Swansong

The Bill Shepherd period had failed to produce the desired push forward. *Freeway Madness* was not as strong as *Parachute* and sales were relatively low. Additionally, the band was dissatisfied and frustrated at Warners inability to promote them in a meaningful way.

'We were on the verge of splitting up. In fact we had virtually split up, a depressing time.' explained Phil. 'MainMan approached us, Bowie wanted to produce a band and they asked if we could wait two months. But we weren't prepared to wait. We didn't know if we'd be together in two months. It looked like we might just have to stop. We were sitting around feeling really pissed off and suddenly I remembered Robert Plant telling me that we could get on Swansong. We weren't sure at the time what they were going to do with the label, but it seemed to be working and they sounded quite serious about having a proper outlet for music. We needed a manager to put it all together, somebody we could trust. We needed somebody who could break this cult thing, 'cause in America, especially, we're thought of as a cult band.'

The previous summer, whilst at The Speakeasy, Jimmy Page had approached Phil and explained that Zeppelin were planning to start their own record company, maybe six months down the line, and they wanted The Pretty Things on board. As with many such approaches Phil felt it was just talk and didn't consider it a serious proposition but months later, spurred by dissatisfaction with Bill Shepherd and Warners, Phil made contact with Swansong.

The contract with Bill Shepherd was close to expiring so, on behalf of the band, Phil agreed a deal with Swansong, but with a condition – Peter Grant would also have to manage them. Phil was very impressed with the way that Grant had manoeuvred Zeppelin, particularly in the States and he knew him personally from the days when Grant assisted Don Arden's acts on the mid sixties package tours.

The Pretty Things became the second act to be signed by Swansong, Bad Company being the first. 'I had always idolised the Pretty Things,' admitted Robert Plant, 'and I still can't get over the idea that they're on a label that I partially own.' The band didn't just sign with Swansong they acquired the complete works – record deal, management, publishing and bookings. It is said that Grant insisted that the publishing rights form part of the deal and this apparently trivial matter would later prove responsible for disruptions and bad feeling within the band and writing credit imbalances that exist to this day.

Melody Maker questioned Phil about the Swansong deal and the forthcoming album. 'One's wish to play may have persevered in the face of common sense, but it did seem a bit silly to make another album that wouldn't be properly promoted. At least with Peter Grant he's someone who cares about the people, he doesn't care about all the record company executives he's interested in the people who are going to do something. He set up everything for the album and spent a fortune on us before we'd even signed a piece of paper.'

August saw the introduction of a new 'Thing' when Jack Green was brought in on bass to take over from the departed Brooks, although his vocals, song-writing and acoustic skills were of even greater worth. Jack's musical history was littered with Pretty Things associations and the 'keep it in the family' ethos was proving strong. Jack was born in Glasgow in March 1951 and began writing songs at an early age. During the early 1970s he was introduced to Gordon Edwards by Len Black, a publisher who each had been using. They got together, it clicked, and they became firm friends and musical associates, eventually sharing a flat and writing songs together. It was a natural consequence to form a band and Jack, who for two years had played 'Woof' in the pit cast of the musical *Hair*, persuaded a number of fellow cast members to join them. Thus was Sunshine formed with an extravagant Warner Brothers launch amid marquees in Holland Park. Jack considered their original drummer awful so they acquired the temporarily out of work Skip Alan. An album was recorded with Asa Jones aka Wally Waller overseeing the production. By this time Skip had left to rejoin The Pretty Things and Terry Slade sat behind the drum kit. Their manager was Bill Shepherd and their publisher was Bryan Morrison, thereby completing a quartet of 'Pretty' connections.

Sunshine and Shepherd parted in 1972 and Jack recalled that Bryan Morrison took hold of the reins for a while until two new guys came along with a management deal that seemed worth pursuing. The band failed to move forward and split fairly quickly after. Morrison contended that Sunshine was one of the more talented bands he had dealings with 'great songwriters but they didn't want it enough.' Bryan considered that when things got tough they backed away from the struggle.

Sunshine broke up at the end of 1972 and during the following months Gordon was introduced into the Pretties and Jack Green joined T. Rex, primarily for the money, as he explained. 'It was a bread thing mainly, the members of the band hardly talked to each other.'

Being in a band centred on elfin star Marc Bolan could have been a problem for a songwriter but Jack remains phlegmatic about it. 'That was okay. Marc was a big star at that time and he wrote all the songs and they were bloody good and they were huge hits so that was fine with me. He used to listen, he would ask me to play him something I'd just written then and I would play him something and in those days my stuff was so totally different from his or what it is now. There certainly wasn't any rivalry or anything, I wasn't jealous of his writing I thought he was good, he was a good writer, and looking back on it now he's better than we thought then.'

Jack joined the Pretties only days after leaving T Rex and a short while after Stuart had left. Just in time for the end of the *Silk Torpedo* sessions, the band's first Swansong album. Jack added his vocal support to the harmonies but did not play bass on every track, as he recalled. 'I was never a dedicated bass player. I'm a guitarist, I can play bass but I've got no ideas on bass. I think I was on every track but some of the bass was played by Pete Tolson. I probably wasn't that good so Tolson covered some of the bass, not all of it but some of it. What they wanted me for was the writing.'

Certainly Jack was not as adept or technically proficient as Stuart Brooks. Peter Tolson confirmed this adding, immodestly, that he himself was a better bass player than Jack. 'I wrote all the bass lines for *Silk Torpedo* and *Savage Eye*.'

Silk Torpedo, the first ever UK release on Swansong Records, was recorded during the summer of 1974 and released in October of that year. The Hipgnosis cover painting, in best 60s pop art style, depicted a sultry maiden balanced precariously on a torpedo, which hurtled over the waves rather than under them. A sailor waved her off from a distant submarine.

The album release was celebrated with a Halloween bash at Chislehurst Caves in Sussex, an event that remains vivid in the minds of those who attended. A phalanx of magicians amused as did the naked women writhing in tubs of jelly. The entertainment also included a fire-eater, strippers dressed as nuns as well as food and drink aplenty. Gordon Edwards tried to recall the hedonistic scene. 'I think they hired George Melly and the Feetwarmers. We basically went along just to get drunk and a bit stoned and really enjoy the evening. That's all I remember really… I must have got very pissed that night.' The event was a suitably hedonistic opening for the Pretties thirty month Swansong soiree.

Recording the album appears to have been a bizarre experience. Doing things the Swansong way meant doing things the Zeppelin way and the Pretties assembled at Headley Grange in Hampshire where over the previous 12 months both Zeppelin and Bad Company had successfully recorded albums and, even more successfully, had partially destroyed the building and its contents. Using the Rolling Stones' mobile studio and reunited with the production skills of Norman Smith, they set to work armed with a varied collection of songs. Norman, displaying the trappings of his 'Hurricane' Smith fame, swept into Headley Grange in a black Rolls Royce complete with a double-breasted suit, silk shirt and tie which he had twirled into a fist-sized knot.

Norman and Phil very quickly fell out over some lyrics Phil had penned for the song, 'Psycho-Symatic Boy'. Norman stormed off, and drove back to London after shouting Phil out for taking the piss out of the mentally ill. Three days later Norman returned and by then Phil had transformed the lyrics into one of his favourite maritime themes and renamed the song 'Singapore Silk Torpedo'.

Twenty-five years on Norman could recall the incident only vaguely. 'We did have a few words. It's such a stressful occupation at times that any fuse is likely to blow. It's also the type of business where even a few hours later you've forgotten it and you carry on.'

The ballroom had been turned into a recording studio where Smith and engineer Keith Harwood could operate. Whilst still in the first few days the session suffered another calamity when the 18-foot Bosendorfer Imperial Concert Grand piano arrived from Harrods. As it was being unloaded, the delivery lorry's tailgate failed and the piano, the most expensive in the world, thundered down onto the gravel drive – and was totally destroyed. Surprisingly Peter Tolson couldn't recall any of this commotion, 'I'm a heavy sleeper,' he explained mysteriously.

Also living amongst the Zeppelined debris of the Grange was a goat and the temporary intruders had to endure the presence of this beast which haunted the kitchen region. The creature possessed a vile and disconcerting habit of mounting the old oak dining table, its rank reproductive organs dangling, whilst it stared at the hapless diners and their Chinese takeaway.

Phil recalled that both Zeppelin and Bad Company had lived and recorded there during the previous twelve months and that hardly anything was left in one piece, not one bed had four legs! Some time later he was quite irritated at receiving a missive from Peter Grant who was concerned at the numerous valuables which had gone AWOL from Headley Grange over the previous 12 months. 'There was this great list of stuff, some of it really valuable, a Canaletto or something, and I particularly remember he mentioned a priceless pair of antique Chinese duelling pistols. Well there had been God knows how many people down there over the year. So I wrote him this note… Dear Peter, how dare you suggest that any of us could possibly be capable of being a thief. I suggest that you apologise, or I'll come down the office and blow your fucking head off with my priceless antique duelling pistols.' Phil related that, fortunately, Peter Grant was most amused and showed no inclination to reprise his Count Massimo professional wrestler persona.

As always these tales tend to be embellished over the years and the reality is slightly different. In September 1974 Superhype, the Grant/Zeppelin Management Company that hired the Grange, received a letter from Willard Morel of Organisation Unlimited complaining about missing and damaged items. Morel asserted that Superhype was responsible for the cost. Peter Grant's secretary, Carole Brown, sent a memo to all the members of Led Zeppelin, Bad Company and The Pretty Things requesting that the miscreants own up. She copied them Morel's letter which listed the items, and painted a vivid tale of the madness and mayhem caused by 12 months of rock animal excess.

List of items missing from Headley Grange
6 pillows £15.00
4 blankets £8.00
1 eiderdown.. £10.00
Quilt cover (checked gingham) £10.00
11 sheets £22.00
10 pillowcases.. £10.00
13 towels £26.00
1 nylon sheet £1.00
2 bedspreads.. £7.00
2 double sized bedspreads (blue and white)
2 single bedspreads (candy striped) £15.00
1 red sleeping bag £5.00
Set of sheets... £10.00
2 carved hall chairs (missing).. £105.00
2 kitchen chairs (broken)... £25.00
2 dining room chairs (missing) £15.00
Plain Japanese chest.. £20.00
4 rugs missing (3 6' x 4' and 1 9' x 6') £100.00
1 saddle bag... £8.00
Out of a 60 piece set of matching blue and white china,
7 pieces remain. Replacements if obtainable will cost £25.00
        Total £437.00
        Less... £157.50
Taken from remaining deposit £279.50

Page two provided a list of additional missing items:
Missing from the locked attic, padlock was changed,
Japanese antique flintlock gun, finely inlaid
North West frontier rifles

Set of Stuart crystal, approx 6 goblets, 10 wine glasses. 8 port glasses, 11 liquer glasses, 2 decanters
Dressing table stool (mahogany)
Deal kitchen table about 6' x 3'
2 over mantle mirrors, one 4' x 3', the other smaller with ornately carved wooden frame
Kidney shaped dressing table
1 upholstered armchair
1 radiogram
1 black and white television set
Oval lacquered mirror (from hall)
3 table lamps – 1 copper, 1 brass, 1 silvered circa 1910
Coffee set, cups and saucers, coffee pot, sugar bowl and jug
Thai wicker chair, half burnt (remains found)
2 curtains, each of an original set of four
Also the original curtain rail, one brass one wood with knobs
Awaiting an estimate for repair to smashed wooden banisters, damaged pan-elled doors and new panels for serving hatch. Also repairs to light fittings and paintings.

Whether Superhype ever recovered the missing items or extracted dam-ages from the people involved is not known but, upon expiry of the Swan-song contract, each Pretty Thing received a bill alleging that individually and jointly they owed $750,000. It is more than likely that this outlandish figure included the cost of the missing and damaged items.

The Pretty Things went into the sessions with songs written by Phil and Peter Tolson as well as a number by Gordon Edwards and Jack Green. *Silk Torpedo's* songs were markedly different from those on *Freeway Madness*, they exuded a rockier feel and were enhanced by a fuller production.

One particular session, for 'Is It Only Love', retained great memories for Gordon Edwards. 'I was playing the piano part on it, which I knew backwards. Norman Smith, the producer, decided to get someone to write some string parts for it and suddenly there were twenty to thirty professional string musicians from the London Philharmonic Orchestra, and I was as nervous as fuck.' Norman Smith had arranged for Graham Preskett to score the orchestration and also brought in the Silver Band, a Welsh colliery band who arrived with cases of beer in tow.

Peter recalled, 'We really tried to make 'Is It Only Love' a hit single. It was only Gordon who was allowed to play on that – that was Smithy's idea.' 'Eve-ryone else was in the booth' said Gordon. 'They had a brass band over there and some of the London Philharmonic over there and I'd only gone up to grade seven on piano. Although I was fairly good I still felt a bit intimidated by these really professional musicians. I liked the song the way it came out, I like the difference between having that brass band right at the end.'

The London Philharmonic did not want anything to do with the Silver Band so the studio had to be partitioned off to segregate them. Phil reported the hassle caused by endeavouring to record the orchestra and the beer swilling colliery band together. 'The London Philharmonic didn't get any beer because they were such a snotty bunch of bastards. They said to Norman Smith, 'Look, we are going to knock this off in one go. Can't we just do our bit and finish? The Silver Band are going to be playing this for hours to get it together.' Norman said, 'No, you stay where you are, we are paying you for a full session. We want you recording together'. The Silver Band took ages to get in tune. They were all over the fucking place. Not because they were pissed but because they were only semi-professional, I guess.'

The orchestration on this track presented an about-turn for Phil as only four years earlier in an interview with Andrew Means of *Melody Maker* he revealed, 'I'm not very fond of brass, I must admit. I'm not into Colosseum at all and I think Chicago have lost their rock feeling.'

Jack confirmed that he and Gordon had written 'Is It Only Love', while Gordon had penned 'Joey' and 'Singapore Silk Torpedo'. The album credits however show the respective writers as May, May/Povey and May/Tolson. 'Me and Gordon wrote 'Is It Only Love' a couple of years before we joined The Pretty Things. It wasn't really a Pretty Things track but they seemed to want to do it, Norman Smith wanted to put brass and that on it. Originally it was very much an acoustic guitar, bass and drums song with vocal harmonies between me and Gordon and it did come across much lighter that way.'

Although Jack and Gordon actually wrote the songs both the label and the album sleeve credited other band members. How could it come about that both Jack Green and Gordon Edwards would give away their songs to other band members? Jack Green, who to this day remains aggrieved, explained that both of them were tied to a publishing contract with Bryan Morrison and that Peter Grant insisted they give their songs to other band members. This ensured that Grant's company, Sole Survivors Music, would obtain the publishing on all of the album tracks. 'Peter Grant said when the rest of the band get the cheques in they'll give you the royalties… yeah, right' said Jack. 'I am honestly not bitter about it because I don't think it earned all that much money. They spent a lot on promotion, these people, and I think it all went on that. I'd love to have my name back on the tracks for sure. I think they might have mentioned it, they said if I joined the band (in 1995) they'd put my name on the tracks.' Jack didn't rejoin and they didn't credit him when the albums were eventually re-issued.

Gordon Edwards continues to be disturbed by the loss of song-writing credits and associated royalties. 'I just think it's detestable to steal from us because if it wasn't for me and Jack they would never have had that chance to join Swansong. When we joined they gained two extra songwriters, two extra instrumentalists and two extra singers. They just wouldn't have sounded the same, in fact half the songs they were singing were ours! When anyone asked about a single most people turned to me, because they weren't any good at writing singles.'

Gordon recalled that in 1972 he and Jack signed a three year publishing contract with Bryan Morrison which allowed Bryan the option of an additional year, effectively tying them up until early 1976. 'We basically said when we were over at Swansong, well let's just not tell him. As far as he's concerned Jack and I haven't signed anything at all and by the time we do start making money our contract with him will have run out. What I've been told recently is Bryan Morrison wouldn't have given a shit at the time anyway.'

John Povey however insists that Jack and Gordon were being greedy, 'They tried to fiddle it. It's their fault. If they had said that's what they were doing and been straight with everybody then it wouldn't have happened. But they didn't want to tell anybody that they were signed to somebody else, depriving that person of his income anyway, so it was their decision really. Their decision not to spill the beans and tell Peter Grant. They were quite happy at the time to do it, you can't really cry over spilt royalties. Nobody's sitting around in a penthouse on Sunset Boulevard going 'ha, ha, ha poor old Jack', it's not like that.'

Regardless of whether Jack and Gordon were fiddling Bryan Morrison or whether Peter Grant was involved in duplicity it is fact that songs which they composed were credited to other band members. 'Dream' (Povey) and 'Joey', 'Is It Only Love' and 'Bridge of God' (May) were all Gordon Edwards tunes as was 'Singapore Silk Torpedo', credited to May/Tolson. Phil supplied the lyrics, most notably on 'Singapore Silk Torpedo'.

Ironically, Phil has expressed irritation at having to gift a share of the *SF Sorrow* publishing to Twink. 'It still really hurts me that those songs, which were all written before he even arrived, bear his name.' The Green/Edwards position is more serious and demeaning. At least Phil and the band continue to have their names on the *SF Sorrow* material and receive royalties.

Gordon described his song 'Joey'. 'That is very Beatlely, I must say, the number of chords in that song, incredible, I didn't think Pete would get them, it's very difficult playing chords with five notes in them. He was following the chords, he was playing three triads, three notes in the chord instead of trying to use all the strings. The chords were going up in semitones, which none of them had seen before and luckily it worked and it was the favourite track of John Bonham. With 'Joey' I wrote the whole thing, the lyrics, the music. It was a long song and they just played it the way I had written it and luckily they all liked it. I used to say to them, 'any bit you don't like, just say." He also recalled that Led Zeppelin actually played 'Joey' as part of an encore one night in the States.

Peter Tolson recollected Gordon and Jack playing a demo of 'Joey', which had originally been cut by Sunshine. It was a piano song, with a honky tonk bounce. Peter believed that Sunshine's version was much better, that Norman Smith overdid the production by adding unnecessary guitars and numerous overdubs which ultimately detracted from the end result.

In a quite astonishing eye-off-the-ball review the *Dutch Progressive Rock Page* suggested that 'Singapore Silk Torpedo' had been inspired by The Who's 'Pinball Wizard', and likened the brass band on 'Is It Only Love' to *Sgt Pepper's*.

To coincide with *Silk Torpedo's* release Swansong placed full-page advertisements in the music press to help push the album. During November Swansong organised a rare television appearance on *The Old Grey Whistle Test*, where the Pretties performed two numbers, 'Singapore Silk Torpedo' and 'Dream/Joey'. This level of promotion exceeded anything that previous management or labels had achieved and served to enhance the band's name and credibility enormously. It provided a structure and a base from which a calculated assault on first the UK and then the US markets could take place. For the first time in many years The Pretty Things really felt that this was it. With this kind of thrust from Swansong they would definitely make it.

Talking to *Sounds* about the new album provided an opportunity for Phil to mix his metaphors and sound rather fatalistic about the whole business. 'I tend to take things as they come. I don't feel that much different this time than any other time a record is released. It's just that I feel a lot more confident about the people behind us this time. Still, I'm very aware of the Russian roulette quality of the music business. You know, land on a red or black number and win a prize.'

Allan Jones review in *Melody Maker* was positive and complimentary. 'On stage Phil May might still shake his ass and jive about as if it were still 1965 but this album, like *Parachute*, confirms that The Pretty Things not only survived but have virtually transcended that period. It's somehow reassuring to think that after almost ten years on the road May can still muster enough energy and force to bring off an album like this. Phil May is singing as well as I've ever heard him.'

But the two tracks that really affirm the consistent faith that many people have placed in The Pretty Things are 'Belfast Cowboys', which overcomes one or two lines that could have buckled the song and 'Is It Only Love', which is the album's real high spot. There are more moments to value in this record than in a dozen albums by some of the bands that didn't even exist when 'Rosalyn' was first released.'

Silk Torpedo contained a mix of slow medium tracks and hard rockers. Some of these didn't really work, like the percussion heavy 'L.A.N.T.A." which seemed like a last minute studio creation to flesh out the album. 'Belfast Cowboys' also suffered, in this instance from lyrics which targeted the Catholic/Protestant troubles in Northern Ireland but wound up sounding trite and overly sincere.

Lyrically the album found Phil at his lowest ebb since *Emotions*, scratching around for inspiration and only finding the occasional piece of gold on 'Atlanta' and 'Maybe You Tried'. The production also seemed a trifle cluttered with many songs begging for a quiet moment or a lessening of the tempo.

November saw the band return to the Golders Green Hippodrome for another BBC Radio One *In Concert* set. The concert was bootlegged as *London Live Torpedo* and issued on the Oh Boy label. The set list is worthy of scrutiny as it highlighted the typical gig song order of that period. Beginning with 'Old Man Going', from *SF Sorrow*, they then launched into 'Living Without You', a Gordon Edwards song that the band never recorded. The rest of the short set was made up by tracks off *Silk Torpedo*, 'Joey', 'Belfast Cowboys', 'Bridge of God', 'Come Homa Momma' and 'Singapore Silk Torpedo'. In addition to this they played 'It's Been So Long' from the yet to be recorded *Savage Eye* album.

With focus on the band because of the albums' release, Phil took the opportunity to complain vehemently to *Sounds* about the current music scene. '*Top of the Pops* is so incestuous now. Ya don't get on unless you've had a hit, ya don't get a hit unless you get on. Good singles by Lennon and Clapton didn't make it here. I mean, how can you compare 'Whatever Gets You Through The Night' to Mud? Both records are commercial but one is (he makes an unpleasant face) and the other is music. The one good thing is that none of these glitter bands have actually made it in America, which shows there is some sanity left. God, I mean if the top of the bill at the next Woodstock was Mud, Sweet and all those hit bands you'd just have to walk away quietly.'

The beginning of 1975 and 'Is It Only Love', backed with 'Joey' is released with high hopes of denting the single's chart which showed Mud's Christmas hit still placed at number one. Radio Luxembourg made it their Record of the Week and it received heavy airplay although again it failed to make the Radio One playlist – the kiss of death for virtually any single. John Peel reviewed it for *Sounds* and admitted that after initially being unimpressed it emerged as a fine piece of work.

January was also the month that Phil married Electra Stuart. They had had met some years previously at the local tennis club and had lived together in Electra's Talbot Road house for some years. Electra's father was noted sculptor Oscar Nemon-Stuart who worked out of a studio in St James Palace. As a child Electra was one of a select band of children allowed to play with the young Prince Charles.

'Joey' managed to receive Radio One airplay when a John Peel session was broadcast in early January. Recorded at Maida Vale Studios the short set also comprised 'Belfast Cowboy/Bruise In The Sky', 'Big City' and a very strange choice – the theme from the television comedy, 'Not Only But Also'.

Shortly before the album's US release Phil and Electra took a break in Rhodes where they rented Roger Waters villa. Robert Plant and family were en route to pay a visit when the car crashed injuring Robert, his wife Maureen and their two children, Jimmy Page's daughter Scarlet was fortunate to be unhurt.

Silk Torpedo received its US release during May, timed to coincide with another States-wide tour. *Rolling Stone* magazine, that bastion of knowledge and font of rock opinion, combined its review of *Silk Torpedo* with one of Queen's *Sheer Heart Attack*. Scribe, Rod Scoppa, submitted that in the recordings, 'There exists clear evidence of intelligent minds at work; there's even the suggestion of taste here and there.' He contended that the bands early recordings, including *SF Sorrow*, sound dated. However *Parachute*, *Freeway Madness* and *Silk Torpedo* are 'tightly packed, delightful albums that tend to improve dramatically with repetition'. He further suggested that 'this trio of albums resembles the work of Mott The Hoople at its peak'. His insights went further, in 'Come Home Momma', he saw 'unresolved oedipal conflicts', in 'Singapore Silk Torpedo' 'sex role confusion' whilst in 'Joey', he unravelled 'the meaning of dreams'. Fortunately after this Freudian clap-trap came the admission, 'The Pretty Things are a marvellous rock and roll band. I don't know how May and his band have managed to escape the attention of the American rock audience for so long, but *Silk Torpedo* should change that.'

Silk Torpedo eventually reached 121 on the *Billboard* chart, a placing that sounds relatively modest but implies sales in excess of many UK Top 40 entrants.

In a spirit of hope rather than expectation, Swansong tentatively pushed another single at the record buyer when 'I'm Keeping'/ 'Atlanta' was released in June. It received scant airplay proving another in a long line of disappointments. To make matters worse the Camden label decided to cash in on the publicity generated by the Swansong push. Under licence from EMI they released *Parachute* and *SF Sorrow* as a gatefold sleeve double album as part of the Harvest Heritage series. Not only was this confusing to buyers in the UK but it also irritated the band members who had still not received a penny from EMI since signing in October 1967.

The band was spending a lot of time on the road in America and unlike the low key 1973 tour they were supporting major acts at large stadiums. Jack Green recalled one successful gig that turned into a classic rock group event. 'I remember some pretty good gigs in the States. We'd been playing a long time in the road and the more you play the better you get. I remember a gig in Houston and we did play a fabulous gig. We came off the stage and we completely trashed the dressing room, very badly but hilariously. It was one of the best nights I ever had. Normally I can't do that type of thing but it was more custard pie stuff than anything. I remember, back stage in American gigs they are full of food, and Peter was walking about with this huge cream cake in the palm of his hand, making out he was going to throw it and Phil walked past him and just tipped it straight into his own face.'

Jack also recalled an amusing incident regarding Phil's habit of just disappearing after gigs, the dreaded walkabout. 'One day for a laugh we thought we'd follow him. So, after the gig we got changed and waited, we watched cause we thought he was going to be sitting by the river, having a drink, writing some lyrics. We eventually tracked him down to a café in front of a huge plate of chips. We thought he was being artistic (but) he was just eating chips.'

Peter recalled that on tour the band members grouped together to share hotel rooms. Usually Peter was with Phil, Jack with Gordon and Skip shared with John. Touring was made easier by the fact that the band now owned their instruments. Those who pay attention to such matters, Peter Tolson played a cut-down Fender Strat with a Rickenbacker single pick up through a Dez Fisher effects pedal board and an MXN phase shifter. Gordon Edwards used a Fender Stratocaster modified with built-in fuzz and effects through a Vox AC30 and also a Grand Piano fitted with a Countryman pick-up. Jack Green used his Fender Precision Bass through two Ampeg bass stacks and Skip belaboured the Ludwig kit complete with obligatory cowbell.

In February Swansong decided to release a single to promote the forthcoming album. The plaintive ballad 'Sad Eye' was chosen with 'Remember That Boy' as B-side. By way of promotion the band appeared on Janet Street-Porter's television show which, because it was aired on a Sunday afternoon, achieved relatively low viewing figures.

Sounds reviewer Alan Lewis found the song appealing, voting it single of the week. 'So slow and woeful and quiet that only the most adventurous stations will play it… but just possibly a surprise hit, all the same. A gentle shimmering acoustic guitar that to me recalls some early Love track and a beautifully modulated vocal which recalls Crosby, Stills and Nash at their best. Two comparisons which may surprise you but then the Pretties long ago moved out of that 'poor mans Rolling Stones' bag, a fact which hopefully will now, at last, be recognised.'

Touring America became a regular feature for the Pretties with the promotional might of Swansong pushing hard. A stateside slot supporting The Kinks on their January/February 'School Boys In Disgrace tour' was arranged affording the band worthwhile exposure, however the relationship between The Pretties and The Kinks, and specifically Phil May and Ray Davies, was very strained. Phil recalled the constant aggravations put on them. 'There was a lot of animosity, cause we blew them off the stage every night. They were doing this schoolboys thing and Davies would come on in this straw hat and blazer, like Max Bygraves, and it was embarrassing. They insisted that we couldn't have the grand piano on stage, only the keyboards. Another night they said The Pretty Things can only have half-lights. Davies would get his manager to do the dirty work, he had the job of telling us all this and he hated it – stabbing us in the back. Davies was a horrible geezer, a cunt.'

Phil May and Ray Davies appear to be of a similar make with each seeming to believe his view to be the right one. Having two such characters in regular close proximity was perhaps asking for trouble.

Jack Green and Peter Tolson vaguely recalled some of the back stage unpleasantness and Jack agreed how embarrassing it was to see Davies in his schoolmaster attire and the rest of the band in short trousers. 'However, at the end, when they played 'Waterloo Sunset', all was forgiven.'

Gig reviews fail to support Phil's notion that the Pretties went down better than The Kinks. The *San Diego Union* stated, 'The Pretty Things, another English group of long-standing was second on the bill but proved unable to arouse any excitement.'

The Oregonian was also unimpressed. 'The music on record may be fine but the live act Saturday was little different than any other rock group. The band, six pieces, had little fire during most of its set, but finally shook the doldrums in the final 15 minutes with two new songs 'Volcano' and something with the words Rock & Roll in the title. Flashy music with a gutsy manner.'

However, Mikal Gilmore of local music paper the *Ragmag* also reviewed the Portland concert. He pointed out that Bowie, ELO and Little Feat were also in town, 'Predictably the Kinks/Pretty Things show draws the smallest house, a meagre 500 patrons. Equally predictable the show totally smokes, dwarfing by comparison any other show in Portland since Springsteen. Another English band of no small stature, Pretty Things opened the Kinks show… (they have) in one form or another been kicking around for about a decade… but one thing the PTs are not is pretty. Onstage they are about as motley as Lynyrd Skynyrd and just as strong. Where on their albums the Pretties rely on the keyboards to carry home the sophisticated melodicism, on stage they forego some of the complexity for dynamism… they are a cohesive and driving band reminiscent of Mott The Hoople in their prime. In contrast with what was to follow the Pretties are devoid of theatrics, something of a study in minimalism. It's hard to say if the crowd was familiar with their material (doubtful considering almost all of it was from *Savage Eye*) but they responded favourably to the band's fervour and professionalism. The PTs may have to live out their career regarded as some sort of rock curio relegated to footnote status in a pedant's history of English rock but they deserve better.'

A Swansong sponsored press party was held for the band at Jayne Mansfield's Beverly Hills mansion on February 12 where the usual plethora of celebrity guests sidled along, including Mick Ronson, Michael Desbarres and the disliked Ray Davies.

One of the final gigs was the Municipal Auditorium, Atlanta. Kelly Hidge, for the *Austin American-Statesman* applauded their longevity and felt that they were still 'blossoming'. 'The band's punctuality was laudable but the right-on-time appearance may have gotten their portion of the show off to a bad start. It seemed as if the modest crowd response reflected this. Nevertheless the band drove undaunted through 'Remember That Boy', 'It Isn't Rock & Roll', 'Under The Volcano' and 'Drowned Man'. The band reached both its high and low points in vocals. Most impressive was guitarist-pianist-vocalist Gordon Edwards. His voice strong and controlled even in higher ranges provided for emotional leads as well as tight harmonies. But lead vocalist Phil May didn't fare as well. He wasn't in top form and would have fit more comfortably had the band dropped the songs down a pitch or two.'

The chemical influx and associated pressures from these lengthy American tours was increasing. Success on the Swansong scale was proving a double-edged sword and a concerted blood-letting was not too far round the next corner.

CHAPTER 11 – The Break Up

In May 1976, Swansong released their second Pretty Things album, *Savage Eye*. Recorded at Olympic Studios in Barnes, it carried on from *Silk Torpedo* by incorporating hard rock songs, soft melodic tracks and some typical mixed-tempo numbers. This was the album that propelled a youngish Mark St John along the slippery gangplank that led ultimately to stewardship of the good ship Pretty Things. Not a revered album in the fashion of *SF Sorrow* or *Parachute* it already sounds dated, very 70s, and it sold nothing like its predecessor *Silk Torpedo*. Peter Tolson conceded its frailties, feeling that they had a weak collection of songs and this filtered through to the sales.

'The band went into the studio with only one musical idea,' he lamented. 'I'd written some songs and they took the ones they wanted and turned them into Pretty Things songs, not how they'd been written.' Disillusion was settling on Tolson by this point. 'I thought should I get out and do my own thing? But the musicians I wanted to play with were either dead or playing in other bands… I couldn't play with a bunch of semi-pros.'

Peter had been approached by one legendary band who asked if he would join them on bass. Whilst this change appealed to him he would also have been required to play keyboards and this would have proved a weak area. Years later he concluded that the excesses of this particular adventure would almost certainly have killed him as it eventually did their drummer.

Norman Smith was again in the producer's chair and the late and much lamented Keith Harwood again the engineer. Gordon Edwards: 'he was one of those guys who would listen to what you wanna say and try and get that sound that you wanted, He didn't have any ego at all he was just a very good engineer.'

Hipgnosis once again provided the cover art, their fourth consecutive Pretty Things album, and they came up with a painted fingernail pulling at an eye. Inside the gatefold the lyrics were printed together with individual photographs of the band members and credits. To continue this 'savage eye' theme the cardboard dust cover was decorated with a gigantic iris.

Savage Eye, is described by Mark St John as an album recorded with cynical confidence and amid a certain degree of mounting tension. Many fans consider this the album where Phil May was consigned to the chorus and there is a certain degree of truth to this, but the position, unknown perhaps to many fans, was that the direction of the band was now influenced by input from five songwriters. The compositions from Jack Green and Gordon

Edwards couldn't be described as typical Pretty Things fare. Often more melodic and catchy they sometimes made uncomfortable bed-partners for the more strident creations of May and Tolson. Norman Smith's busy production also served to mask May's vocals as well as some of Tolson's guitar and on occasions both were completely lost in the mix.

The inclusion of the Jack Green and Gordon Edwards songs took the band into a much poppier area and the Swansong band cannot readily be identified with either the R&B years or the EMI period. Whilst not *The Pretty Things* the direction and music proved worthwhile in its own right as anyone fortunate enough to have seen or heard the Pretties spin-off Metropolis will vouch.

The transferring of song writing credits that started with the *Silk Torpedo* album gained momentum on *Savage Eye*. That gorgeous ballad 'Sad Eye', although credited to Peter Tolson, was entirely the work of Jack Green, as confirmed by Peter himself and by Mark St John in the *Anthology* liner-notes. Phil May's 'I'm Keeping' was also a Jack Green tune with lyrics by Phil. Gordon Edwards was solely responsible for the 'Jon Povey compositions' 'It Isn't Rock n Roll', and 'Theme For Michelle', a paean to Gordon's first girlfriend, and also 'My Song', which carried a Phil May credit. Gordon also supplied the melodies for 'It's Been So Long' and 'Remember That Boy' which on the album were again credited solely to Phil May.

''It's Been So Long' is mine, because I also sold it to Maggie Bell. Phil wrote some of the lyrics to it, I put down some rough lyrics and I gave it to Phil and he liked the song, and I said if you want to, change some of the lyrics. It's been so long, which is the chorus, I wrote, so I took him a song that had the chorus and the rest of the lyrics he could put what he liked. So, he wrote between a third and a quarter of the song I suppose.'

'Remember That Boy': 'I remember that song because I wrote this really heavy riff right at the beginning and they were so pleased with the riff they said, 'yeah, carry on and write the rest of it'. Pete put in just two or three seconds of guitar because we had a riff going and he would say instead of playing the riff four times all the same let's put one in the middle and change it and do it like this.'

Gordon's songwriting style was to pick out the melody and perfect the music and arrangements whilst retaining a 'working lyric'. He saw little point in expending effort when there was a chance that the song might be rejected by the band. This also allowed Phil to completely change or vary the lyrics as he saw fit.

Gordon rationalised the matter of his songs being sung by Phil. 'I used to let him sing some of my songs because I didn't want him to feel left out, otherwise he might have started thinking that me and Jack were trying to take over the band. So I would go to him sometimes and suggest that the song's all worked out, I'll sing the first verse you sing the second? I was quite happy to let him do it. But if anyone ever asks me I'll always say Jack was the best singer then maybe me then maybe Phil. Because Phil always sang the same way every time whereas I could vary it, I could sing low and I could sing very high.'

Gordon also extemporised on what he saw as Phil's songwriting limitations. 'Phil only knows just a few chords and he just manages to make something from that and luckily someone else would come in and maybe put something in the middle which would jazz it up a bit, make it a bit more interesting. But he's very unsure of his own playing. He'd play stuff to us and Jack and I would listen to it and we'd know that the only way this is going to sound really good is to put in a fuck of a lot of work on it. It was just the barest idea there, maybe the verse would be good but we'd have absolutely no chorus so there'd be no hook line. You've got to have a good hook line, that's what it builds up to.'

Jack Green offered his own recollection of The Pretty Things songs that he and Gordon had written. 'Gordon wrote all of 'Joey'. 'Atlanta' was written mostly by Phil, I think I might have written a middle eight for it. I wrote 'I'm Keeping' which was also, in my view, totally ruined by Norman Smith. 'Bridge of God' was Gordon and Phil, I wrote a middle eight, 'Ave Maria'. 'My Song' was Gordon, totally, one hundred percent. 'Theme For Michelle' was Gordon, written about one of his girlfriends years ago. 'Tonight' was Gordon. Again, I think the way they recorded it was so totally wrong. Those tracks could have had so much more integrity. Norman Smith was a bit of a jazzer, which none of us was into and he tended to get all these inky, dinky, dinky type rhythms and I just sat there with my mouth open. But we couldn't say anything. I was the newest member with the least clout.

Tony Clarke, not surprisingly offered a different view and expounded his opinion of Norman Smith's production skills. 'The great art of the producer is that you sit and its not your painting, it's the artists painting. You're there to develop that and if there was a tendency for it to go towards a more melodic or smoother style, which inherently is Norman himself, he wouldn't be completely open to someone for the most powerful part of that music to be stated to him.'

Peter Tolson told the story of the day Jack Green came into the studio with a new song – 'Sad Eye'. 'You should have heard it. There was Jack, me, Phil, Jon and Gordon one summer afternoon at Filbert Road. Jack said I've got this song, what do you think? He played it so well, it should have been recorded there and then.'

''Sad Eye' was just me and an acoustic guitar,' agreed Jack. 'I recorded it and sang it at the same time and added another acoustic guitar. I remember I did that because we actually had a gap on the album and they thought has anybody got any other songs and I said well I've got this, it doesn't sound exactly Pretty Things material, more like Cat Stevens. Norman Smith said he thought it was quite good.'

The album kicked off with Phil's favourite track 'Under The Volcano' which he wrote after reading Malcolm Lowry's novel of the same name. The song is retained even today in the band's repertoire. 'My Song' and 'Sad Eye' lower the tempo, providing a soft interlude before 'Remember That Boy' explodes into a riffing frenzy accompanied by a Skip drum extravaganza, described by Mark St John as the best he'd ever recorded.

Side two opened with 'It Isn't Rock 'n' Roll' combining a melodic keyboard led intro with a fierce rocking chorus that somehow fails to quite seam, sounding exactly what it is – two different and fairly average songs welded together. 'I'm Keeping' proved a different mix from the version previously issued as a single and led into 'It's Been So Long' which was given to Maggie Bell and appeared on her Swansong album *Suicide Sal* where Phil assisted on the background vocals. Boasting a full production this rich ballad was boosted by close harmony work and a repetitious chorus which carried on a tad too long. 'Drowned Man' switched into a mid tempo recollection of a dead ex-roadie, moodily enriched by a tinkling piano. The 'drowned man' was roadie Howard Parker, 'H' who is said to have been holidaying on a Greek island and was last seen rowing out to sea and is presumed drowned.. As 'Drowned Man' finished it segued into 'Theme For Michelle', an hypnotic piano solo piece courtesy of Gordon Edwards which served to end the album on a wistful note.

In its review, *Billboard* described it as 'a more mature music, sounding at times like a funky Moody Blues with the MOR feeling that the Moodies often had. Vocals even resemble Paul Simon at times.' This, perhaps a reference to Gordon's vocal on 'My Song'.

In the States, Sire rleased a best of entitled *Pretty Things Vintage Years*, which resurrected the Fontana recordings. Greg Shaw's liner notes painted vivid pictures of the band, the era and the mayhem, and clearly he is a fan. Unfortunately the tract was spoiled by the occasional factual inaccuracy such as informing that Jon Povey joined the band and then Wally followed later.

Peter Tolson waxed lyrical concerning Gordon Edwards' musical proficiency, about how he could come up with a complete composition overnight. He also recalled that Phil and Jon Povey considered Gordon strange, 'They called him an oddball and used to take the piss out of him.'

Throughout this period Jack Green and Gordon Edwards, and to some extent Peter Tolson, continued to feel unhappy with the production technique of Norman Smith. Gordon remembered thinking that Norman was getting on a bit, 'Even then he was in his mid-fifties.'

Jack Green agreed, 'Well that's true. Him and I had completely conflicting ideas about the ways things should be produced. The trouble was I was about the youngest in the band, probably. These guys were real seasoned vets and it was very hard for me to lay down any law at all because I was so young. They got away with things. They were adding strings and horns and making it sort of middle of the road whereas it could have been quite an aggressive track, a track with a bit of integrity. Unfortunately I found that Norman Smith really took the integrity away. Whereas Phil would just tend to go along with everything Norman said, which also annoyed me. Like I say I was young, I couldn't really say much about it.'

Jon Povey did not accept this. 'Those two guys were in a kind of different place. Where Phil, Skip, Wally, Dick and myself were into natural music, I think Gordon and Jack were much more into commercial music. Therefore, the blend of Norman and using our natural way and the blend of Gordon & Jack in a commercial way didn't always work out. If you listen to the 70s stuff they were on there's some great stuff on there, no doubt about it, but it is a bit dated. It's dated more than anything else, that particular period even though musically it was very strong, vocally it was very strong. I think it was due to the way the songs were approached, possibly. I don't think Norman ever did anything we didn't wanna do he was very much a sixth/seventh member of the band. He would never say you've got to play that he would just listen very carefully. I was a great fan of Norman's I think he did an amazing job and he was great to work with. He always kept the rudder firmly in place when we were waltzing off somewhere and bring us back.'

Norman Smith recalled disagreements with Jack in particular. 'Well, you see, Jack Green came in after what I consider the peak of our career together, The Pretty Things and myself. I didn't want anybody sort of taking over leadership or whatever, it becomes very touchy. I think at times Jack gave me the impression he was a bigger influence than even Phil May. Or he tried to be.'

Jack: 'I really didn't like Norman Smith's productions at all, anything we even did ourselves was better than that. He would put such horrible little bits in, I knew as soon as you record these things it's gonna affect you every time you hear it. If you make a mistake at a gig you can probably live with it because it's a flying moment but if it's on record you hear it over and over and over again you've got to be very careful what you put down.'

Wally Waller, who had returned from working in France, briefly popped his head into some of the *Savage Eye* sessions. He sympathised, feeling that Norman's production on *Silk Torpedo* and *Savage Eye* was 'overgilding the lily.' Wally considered Norman's best days were on *Parachute* and *SF Sorrow* and that the Swansong era was less productive. A view that most people, including Norman, would agree with.

Although a hard-line rock 'n' roll animal Jon Povey made time to engage Norman Smith in that most riotous of rock and roll pastimes, golf, as did Wally Waller. Derek Boltwood also remembered that, 'For all the talk of sex, drugs and rock 'n' roll, the number of gigs we went to where, if it was a nice day, we'd get a cricket bat and ball out and have a knock up on the nearest green. Phil still found plenty of opportunities for the best of three sets, Jon Povey continued to pursue his love of surfing and Skip was fast developing a lust for cruising on the open seas. The band was beginning to move on to the next phase of their development as individuals and as a group.

Jack Green recalled that one time in the States they were due to play a high profile gig where Jimmy Page, Robert Plant and various Swansong executives were in the audience. Meanwhile, Jon Povey had slipped away to Hawaii with a girlfriend for some extra-marital and a bout of surfing and in his obsessive way had become so engrossed that he forgot the gig completely. The band winged it as best they could and a contrite Povey had to make suitably apologetic noises when he eventually surfaced.

'We said well, we can do without Jon, no-one's gonna miss Jon when you've got all that noise on stage', stabbed Gordon Edwards. 'Sometimes we were both playing piano and Povey's piano was turned down very low… because he wasn't a very good piano player.'

Ed Bicknell recalled Jon's appetite for the opposite sex and sardonically called him 'a life support system for a penis.' Gordon agreed, 'That's what it was down to when we were touring the States, he seemed more interested in pulling birds and shagging than doing anything else.'

The band returned to Abbey Road's studio 3 on three occasions during April to record 'Tonight'. The song was chosen purposely as a likely hit single because Swansong was still looking for the band to achieve a chart placing and, like the album, it appeared in May. 'Tonight' was a Gordon Edwards song that Phil hated and still detests. The record label stated that Gordon wrote it and publishing credits were split between Sole Survivors and Leeds Music.

By now the Bryan Morrison contract had expired and Gordon was finally allowed a composition credit. Issued with another of his songs 'It Isn't Rock n' Roll' as the flip side it performed in the great tradition of post 1966 Pretty Things singles and sank with barely a ripple.

Years later Phil vowed his hatred of the song yet Peter Tolson recalled that at the time they were all very happy with it.

'Tonight' was not the hit single that the Swansong brass wanted. One review described it as 'fast-moving and reasonably bomping exercise with a chorus reminiscent of an early 60s song called 'Party Lights'. Phil May's vocals are always a pleasure, but this is disappointingly lacking in muscle. The B-side, 'It Isn't Rock and Roll' is far more interesting'

Caroline Coon, reviewing singles for *Melody Maker* took an entirely different tack. "Tonight', which was recorded two weeks ago, could be a breakthrough single, a huge hit for the Pretties. Phil May and Gordon Edwards, who wrote the song, share the vocals and, without selling out or playing to the lowest common denominator, they've pulled off a fine commercial coup based on a consistently solid chugging rhythm track. The single moves lightly though various unfussy and lyrically direct changes. It builds with laid-back confidence, stays right to the end and there's not an indulgent word or note on the track. This was obviously conceived as a single and a single classic it is. The record of the week.'

Jack Green recalled how, during the recording sessions, Norman Smith asked him whether he liked the version of 'Tonight' that they had just finished. 'I told Norman that I thought it was just totally the wrong direction from where I thought this song would go. He replied that he would do one copy for me and he'd do the rest for everybody else and he'd see me in the charts. I always remember that.' The band's enthusiasm for their own ideas can be gleaned from the credits which stated, 'Produced by Norman Smith and The Pretty Things'.

Peter recalled his own disenchantment with Norman's production. 'A number of times I'd gone in with a song that I'd written for The Pretty Things, sometimes I'd go in with a song that was good but I hadn't written for the band and this other material I wanted to go like they were written. But it was taken away from me, I wasn't allowed to do that, never allowed to do that. Not by Norman, (or) by the band. It'd come out sounding like the Pretties, but not what I'd written. It was very frustrating.'

July found them playing an all-nighter at the Lyceum. Bottom of the bill was an unknown band just beginning to make a name for itself – The Sex Pistols. John Povey recalled their energy but considered, 'The thing that sticks in my mind is that they were the most chronically out-of-tune band I'd ever heard.' Peter Tolson remembered them as poseurs. 'They said, 'we don't do your drugs, we've got our own… sniffing glue'.' Then they proceeded to smoke all my dope.'

The Sex Pistols unprepossessing demeanour and brand of irreverence can be traced back to The Pretty Things and the Stones who both burst onto the scene harangued by similar verbal onslaughts from the media. By the 70s the Pretties had cast off many of the rough edges, mainly due to the relative sophistication of the Edwards/Green input. The R&B essence remained but had been sugared by harmonies, catchy melodies and, on vinyl, the Norman Smith wall of sound. Live they were a different proposition. The limitations inherent in concert performances meant that many of the production niceties were missing and a heavy almost metallic ambience turned the clock back to the 60s on numbers like 'Under The Volcano' and 'Onion Soup'.

Twenty-four years later, Phil May confided to *Uncut* magazine. '(The Pistols were) a breath of fresh air because rock had retired to its farms in Esher and been writing very navel-studying cerebral songs, wondering whether to be into Swiss Zen or German Deutschmarks, or moor a yacht in St Tropez or Monaco.' A prod at The Pink Floyd, perhaps.

The Pistols attitude of defiance was very Pretty Things-ish and Phil considered 'If you had come to the first Pretty Things gig, you'd probably think about us then what you think about the Pistols now.' Continuing the theme he said, 'We'd started on the streets, and I loved seeing the Pistols and the anarchy coming through again. We'd always been targeted as rubbing the establishment up the wrong way and I think that's one of rock's main jobs.'

The Pretty Things rock'n'roll circus continued and they embarked on a tour that was intended to finally break the States but ultimately succeeded in breaking them. Jon Povey considered the matter one of duality. 'We had it, we blew it, we had it in our hands and Phil wasn't happy and decided to go. If we'd had coast-to-coast success in America we'd probably be in the Betty Ford clinic or dead or living in Los Angeles somewhere in another time. It's very hard playing. One tends to fall into a lifestyle, which other people are doing as well, so you tend to feed off each other. Very much an unusual lifestyle, not recommended really... it's a bubble.'

Stories abound of massive drug use and an increasing dependency. 'We were all quite into it, but not over the top,' explained Jack Green somewhat defensively. 'They spent all their advance on coke, within three months,' Peter Grant recalled. 'It was more than $100,000, a lot of money in 1974.'

In the States, Peter Tolson had discovered mescaline and on one occasion played for days on automatic with no lasting memory of where, when or why. The band continued to enjoy cocaine and still gambled with the temporary delights of heroin.

Although dragged along by the Zeppelin machine they quickly discovered how easy it was for even that leviathan to veer off course. Jack Green recalled 'You'd go into Swansong offices and Richard Cole (Led Zeppelin's road manager) would just be lying absolutely prone over a table smacked out of his brain. That seemed to be the way they carried on doing business.' Looking back Pete Tolson evinced, 'You couldn't say the management was inept when we was with Swansong, but you could say the management wasn't focused.'

Jon Povey continued the theme, 'There was a lack of communication, promises made that weren't fulfilled. I think we thought that because we were Led Zeppelin (sic) we were gonna make it, and we did to a degree. I think we thought we were gonna make it more, we did our bit I think we produced, at the time, two very good albums – very interesting music – and there were problems of communication with the record company and distributors, all sorts of things. Led Zeppelin were throwing money into things which just goes to show you can throw lots of money in but it doesn't necessarily mean you'll get lots of money out.'

Although Swansong had provided tremendous financial support and had projected them in a more focused, PR oriented way the commitment seemed to be petering out. Jack Green remains unsure about the effect that the Zeppelin backing had. 'I don't know whether it helped or not. I don't know what the album sales were. Like I said, I never got any royalties from The Pretty Things. You know, you go out you promote an album you never see any money, you're on a wage and that's all you get. Any money that's being made is going straight into production.'

In a 1996 *Rock Online* interview Phil conceded that the States was too large a country for the band. Swansong had wanted the band to base themselves in the US but Phil affirmed, 'There were far too many drugs circulating, imagine the environment for a young English group?' He felt that settling there would have turned them into a bunch of junkie delinquents. Additionally, the band missed home – Europe more so than England – and the way of life.

During 1976 a power struggle was raging within Swansong. Steven Davis in his book *Hammer of the Gods* recounted that Peter Grant fired Swansong Vice President Danny Goldberg and it was shortly after this that the Pretties folded. 'Led Zeppelin knew how to produce only instant success. There was no desire to spend the long plodding years usually necessary to build, nurture and develop an artists career.' Goldberg later became publicist for ELO and at one time managed Nirvana. At the time of writing he is chief of two-time Pretties record company Warner Brothers. Phil was unequivocal that the second half of that last tour was sabotaged, that the contracts for the later tour dates were never completed, that they were found gathering dust in some Swansong office drawer. Phil lamented that the band sat in Penascola or Lafayette and watched the album fall from the charts.

In his later years Peter Grant stated that starting Swansong was a mistake. He wasn't able to give the label the effort and care that it and its artists deserved. Led Zeppelin was the main focus and artists such as Maggie Bell found it difficult to make suitable contact with Grant. Richard Cole was never sure why The Pretty Things were signed and like Grant his main task was the nursing of Led Zeppelin with all other matters secondary.

The disintegration of that last US tour didn't seem too momentous at the time. Jack Green: 'What I remember is having a week off in a hotel with a semi-tropical atmosphere and glass wall. We could watch the rain pouring and gales blowing while swimming and lying around the pool. There was even an indoor putting green and a sauna. I had a great time. I don't think any of us were too worried.'

Phil however was becoming increasingly disenchanted and strung out. During the tour he had been talking of leaving and Gordon Edwards recalled one particular episode. 'Phil was in his hotel room on an American tour. Somebody came to me – I think it was Skip – and said to me that Phil was really pissed off and talking about going home... we ended up locking him in his hotel room.' Prima donna lead singer stuff? 'I'm sure at times he was putting it on. He wanted us all to get down on our hands and knees, please Phil don't go... pathetic when you see it.'

For whatever reason Phil's neuroses took control during early summer. The precise reasons will probably never be known. Drink and drugs certainly played a part, altering perceptions and untwining normal social restraints. Disillusion with Swansong's ability to convert the earlier *Silk Torpedo* success into a real career push must have had an impact as well as perhaps the knowledge that with Jack Green and Gordon Edwards' writing and singing skills, his own position as figurehead had been diminished. The relationship with Electra was also under pressure and was not helped by her discovery of his penchant for wearing her clothing. Additionally, he was wrestling with competing sexual preferences, attempting to come to terms with the bi-sexuality that had continued to resurface over the years.

Late April through May involved an extended UK tour. An extremely lightweight affair compared to the major US arenas it took in such premier venues as the Leas Cliffe Hall in Folkestone and the Floral Hall, Southport. Success seemed to be eluding them yet again. Then in early June, after further conversations with a bottle of Jack Daniels, Phil chose a 'stop the bus I want to get off' career suicide move, apparently decamping to France for a few days. 'I was getting very much out of order,' he confessed to Mark Andrews. 'Drugs were causing me lots of problems. Everyone else in the band was freaked out by my behaviour, but then again they were all freaked out too.'

The other band members were not overly perturbed at this excursion, Phil had walked out before and the threat was always peeking out from behind a bottle or a line. Days later they waited in the dressing room at Wembley fully expecting a repentant Phil to arrive muttering some apology or other. It gradually dawned on them that this time he was not turning up, this time it was not local walkabout or a bluff.

Supporting Uriah Heep in a high profile gig at Wembley is not the best way to introduce a new vocal line up and Jack Green and Gordon Edwards did well to cover for the absent singer as John Ingham confirmed in a *Sounds* review. 'The major surprise was the absence of Phil May, now a member emeritus. The strange thing was that he wasn't really missed. Oh, there was the odd moment when a flying mane of hair and a joyous smile would have fitted in well, but Gordon Edwards and Jack Green filled the vacancy admirably.'

As if the pressure of playing without the lead vocalist was not enough the panic of the gig was compounded when the power was abruptly turned off by somebody in the Uriah Heep camp. It seems they had been playing a bit too well.

After the fiasco of the Wembley concert it was decided that a meeting had to be held at Swansong's office. To the band's great surprise Phil turned up and announced that he was back in the band. This was the last straw for Skip who told him to fuck off.

Jack Green: 'I was pushing for Phil to get back in the band I just didn't think the Pretties were anything without him. I think it was really me and Peter who were saying we should really try and get him back. They suggested I do it, but I knew how this would go down with Swansong, it would look as if I was trying to jump into Phil's shoes. That's exactly what happened, we started taking over all the vocals, me and Gordon, and he (Peter Grant) thought we'd pushed Phil out. Cause we were quite good, we were quite capable of singing, they thought we must have been trying to get him out and they never liked us after that. Basically it was Jon Povey and Skip who decided that Phil had walked out enough times.'

Gordon recalled that their argument was, 'You've done it once, how do we know you won't do it again?' Swansong tried to place a positive spin on the split with a press release. 'Phil wants to move in a different direction and the band wish to continue as The Pretties. Swansong will stay right behind both Phil and the band to help them achieve their aims.'

The band continued to gig, but decided that without May they could not realistically continue as The Pretty Things and for their remaining contracted gigs they billed themselves as 'The Pretties'.

Speaking to Terry Coates in 1996, Gordon Edwards was defiant. 'Look, I didn't want Phil to leave but I felt we had to change the name because Phil wasn't there, cause how can you call it The Pretty Things without Phil May, for fucksake? That would have been insulting him and he wouldn't have liked that.'

Jack Green painted a similar picture. 'We didn't know what else to do, Phil left, so we thought we either split up or we carry on. We are still signed to Swansong, I think that was the way we looked at it. It was a bit of a shock when Phil left. He didn't turn round and tell anyone he was going to do it, it just happened one day. Why he did this I'm still not sure, but he did. So we had a record company and Led Zeppelin behind us, so we thought let's keep going, let's try and see what we can do. So we did put together some things but obviously they weren't that interested because Phil May was The Pretty Things and that's who they were really interested in. It's only understandable really.'

Peter Tolson contended that Phil's problems were not so much drug-induced as alcohol related and, 'Prima donna lead singer stuff.'

Although Phil has never explained his walkout, comments made twenty years later provide a clue to his disenchantment. The two Swansong albums were designed to appeal to American markets and whilst neither bland nor plod-rock they veered towards safety. Safe rock has never been on Phil's agenda and the more commercial leanings of Jack and Gordon were leading the Pretties towards less dangerous musical statements. The fact that Jack and Gordon's songs encompassed a vocal range which Phil found difficulty in reaching must also have been a factor.

CHAPTER 12 – Deliberation, Disappointment & Duplicity

Following Phil May's defection, the remaining Pretty Things went through a period of reflection. They decided to carry on but to change the band name. 'The Pretties' was too similar to The Pretty Things and would forever be indelibly linked with Phil May, so it was changed to Metropolis. However, before Metropolis was up and running there was a further rupture when Jon Povey departed. The truth surrounding his departure from The Pretties/Metropolis illustrates how difficult it is to piece together any history when the people concerned retain sharply conflicting memories. Povey is adamant that the other band members wanted him out, 'They had all the aspects of what they wanted, they had Gordon and Jack. It was a Gordon and Jack commercial venture, they had their own way of doing it, it was very much centred around them, those two singing.'

The event occurred at the beginning of 1977 and Peter Tolson proffered his version. 'Jon didn't get sacked, he fucking walked out. Jon was never in Metropolis. The way I remember it, I'd heard a rumour that the plug was going to be pulled on Metropolis. I got wind from one of the roadies who'd heard something from the office. That night we went to the premiere of *The Song Remains The Same* and Jon was there and I said don't bank on a retainer showing up. Four retainers showed up, Jon didn't get paid, he walked. We didn't have knowledge of this, it was a surprise to all of us.'

Without Phil around to hold the family concept together the previously submerged aggravations and irritations surfaced. Jack Green had long been unimpressed at Povey's musical abilities, the phrase, 'Untalented, directionless hanger-on' being used. 'Anyway, we already had a keyboard player called Gordon, who could actually play.' Gordon agreed, 'He found a band, years ago, that he could hang on to and he would throw in his bit every now and then which would be ideas for arrangements, but that was all. He never put anything musically in, he couldn't play very well.'

Jon Povey decided to look down other non-musical avenues. 'I went off and built surfboards and buggered around, tried to do a bit of music on my own but I wasn't into it all that much. 'Six months after that (Metropolis) I wasn't doing anything and a guy who ran the Pink Floyd was running a skateboard business and asked if I would like to do something. I needed the money and I went to join them and helped them out. Phil, at that time, was forming another Pretty Things which he got together with Wally and I wasn't included in that either so I was the guy out of that whole thing at that particular time. Then we came back together again to do the *Cross Talk* album.'

Metropolis carried on as a quartet accepting bookings on the university circuit and regular band haunts like Islington's Hope & Anchor. All previous Pretty Things songs were dropped except for the Gordon Edwards song 'Living Without You'. Excellent fresh material such as 'Yangtse River', 'Shame Shame Shame' and 'Love Me A Little' was introduced and the band seemed on the cusp of a successful career. Their playing retained the crispness of sound which had always been an essential component of The Pretty Things.

'Metropolis was the best band I ever played in,' confirmed Peter. Was it the music, the camaraderie, the spontaneity? 'The lot,' he replied reflectively. Jack Green recalled, 'Towards the end, when we were in Metropolis he (Peter Tolson) was probably at his height. He was playing the best guitar he'd ever played.'

Metropolis recorded demos of various songs and legendary producer Jimmy Miller took the helm for some of these sessions but insufficient material was cut for an album. Years later Phil revealed that Peter Grant never entertained the slightest notion of promoting Metropolis. Grant had told him, 'if you want to record Phil, be my guest, but if they're going to try and work without you, they can record for a hundred years, and I won't release a fucking note of it.' Moreover, he fucking didn't.

Gordon Edwards suspected this when he told Terry Coates, 'Maybe it was that Peter Grant didn't see Metropolis as a viable thing… and after awhile pulled the plug on it.' Regardless of the actual reason it is patently obvious that Grant wasted Metropolis. Instead of supporting them and building on the goodwill and reputation engendered by The Pretty Things, he sacrificed them possibly out of his allegiance to Phil and his mistaken belief that they were responsible for Phil leaving the band. Given the extent of Jack Green's later solo success, it may also have been a foolhardy decision commercially. To be fair to Grant he had already started his drug phase, possibly this and having to deal with Zeppelin's enforced sabbatical meant that a relatively low-profile act like Metropolis was too far down his schedule of important matters. Nonetheless, Swansong certainly appeared supportive at the beginning and booked them as support to Bad Company at their prestigious Earls Court gig.

Additionally, Peter Tolson began to discern a degree of ill-feeling from Jimmy Page. Possibly, he sensed that barely contained suspicion that an ageing gunfighter feels when in the presence of the new quick-draw rival. Peter felt that this might also have contributed to Swansong's lack of long-term support.

Jack Green explained that they had problems trying to communicate with

Grant. 'We did a bit of recording and spent ages trying to find out if Peter Grant had heard it. He seemed to be avoiding Gordon and I like the plague. We eventually got called in for a meeting to be told that Jimmy has had this great idea… that we play in pubs.'

The final nail in the Metropolis coffin was Grant's belief, possibly a genuine misunderstanding, that Jack and Gordon were double-crossing him regarding publishing rights. Swansong's publishing arm Sole Survivors had previously benefited from the Green/Edwards songs that should have been published by Bryan Morrison's Lupus Music. This showed how paranoid Grant could be.

'Grant got some peculiar story that Jack and I had gone to a publisher to do a deal behind his back. In fact what we'd actually done was gone to the publisher that he'd gotten for us. We just said we've got these songs which our band will not do, they just don't suit the band, so will you get them to other artists. A few days later somebody told him, I think it was a roadie called Graham, I'm not sure, that we were doing something behind his back. I sat in his office all one afternoon and he refused to speak to me, I went home. Came back the next day did the same thing. I was getting all the excuses like 'he's on the phone to the States'. I sat there for several hours, when the door opened I walked through and asked him what's up, why wouldn't he talk to me? All he said to me, with three big guys around him and at least an ounce of coke on the table, 'If you don't leave this second I'm gonna throw you out the window.' So I left. He was just acting like a complete thug.'

Although it all ended in tears, both Jack and Gordon retain fond memories of their stay in The Pretty Things. Jack emphasised that they all got on as individuals as well as musicians. 'I loved working with everybody we were also very good friends we used to hang out socially and Phil was a bit of an icon. The thing I was most proud of was actually being in The Pretty Things. I learned such a lot, it was a good training ground for me. As I say, I was young.'

Gordon: 'I enjoyed every tour. I enjoyed every second that I was with them.'

When Metropolis folded the members went in different directions. Gordon Edwards had already added swirling organ to a track by The Only Ones called 'Creature Of Doom' for old friend and former flatmate Peter Perrett. He then auditioned and joined The Kinks, replacing John Gosling, touring the States with them along with his Marks & Spencer heiress girlfriend Maudie. He lasted fourteen months before departing and in 1996 he explained his reasons to Terry Coates. 'It was driving me crazy. Some nights I had to have half a glass of whiskey to be able to go on and do the gig, because we never changed the numbers round on the bill.' After three tours of America he had had enough and left in July 1979.

Former Kinks drummer Mick Avory explained that Gordon was trying to introduce changes and that was not the thing to do in The Kinks. Jack Green explained that he and others thought very highly of Gordon's musical ability, but then so did Gordon. 'Ray Davies is a genius,' stated Jack, with the implication that Gordon should have contented himself with a lesser role.

Gordon was still suffering from the chemical indulgence that began in The Pretty Things and although he could obtain the dope he couldn't afford the expensive detoxification clinics that his girlfriend was able to fund. Shortly after The Kinks episode, Gordon split from Maudie and has remained in virtual hibernation apart from a slight resurgence in 1996, of which more later.

Jack Green quickly discovered he was unable to work properly due to the terms of his Swansong contract. 'Peter Grant was a pretty hard guy to manoeuvre. It was very hard for me to get around Peter Grant, he was an aggressive looking guy and he had a way about him that was... heavy. When The Pretty Things split up Peter Grant was still sitting on our contracts and we had about nine months to run on this contract. Consequently they just sat on the contracts which they were entitled to do. I had to wait nine months before I could actually sign anything else or go into anything else in the music business. So I had to get myself a job outside of the music business. I went into theatre again, for nine months I did bloody *Superstar*. I had to, you know, it was all I could do, I was seriously getting poor and I didn't know what to do. It was Skip who suggested it. And it honestly hadn't dawned on me to do it. I thought bloody hell I'll try, and I did, I got it and I was in there for about nine months much as I hated it but I had to. I waited till the contract had run out and eventually I went into Rainbow.'

Jack took the part of Simon Zealotes in *Jesus Christ Superstar* in London's West End and then jumped ship joining Richie Blackmore's Rainbow. Jack stayed with Rainbow for three months, which included recording the *Down To Earth* album at a castle in Geneva.

'Then I signed up with RCA, I got my own record deal. While I was signed up I was in New York I had just finished the album, signed the deal and I suddenly got word from Peter Grant's lawyer or something that I, personally, owed Swansong $750,000. Now we could have paid this as a group or individually but before we could do anything they wanted that money paid back.

'I'd just signed to RCA so not only would I've been sued by Swansong I was gonna be sued by RCA too. So I was in a right state. My manager at the time took this letter to every music business lawyer in New York but they all said, 'well, we're very sorry Mr Green, but it's legal.' They went into it eventually and said, 'When did you use a helicopter?' I said, 'I've never used a helicopter!' So, somehow Led Zeppelin were using our account for some of their stuff.

'My manager found a guy called Harold Ornstein in New York, At the time he was about 70 years old and he wrote the music business statutes. He said, 'Well, you've got to write to Peter Grant saying thanks for all your help but you'd dearly like to be let out of this contract.' Then he spoke to him said, basically, 'why is anybody as big as you standing on somebody as small as that? Why don't you let them go'? And he did! Setting a precedent for the rest of the band who were also let out of the deal.'

Since leaving The Pretty Things, Wally Waller travelled many different musical paths. He had vacated his position as staff producer at EMI and involved himself in another project with Frenchman Phillipe Debarge. 'We wrote the songs and he would go away and write a French lyric and sing. Then he asked me to get some English musicians and go to France and do it. I lived there for eighteen months, had a lovely time, but it wasn't very satisfactory in the end. That's when I came back and Phil was having ructions with The Pretty Things and that's when we both went off and did something, did some odd tracks down in Rockfield. Pete and Ed Deane came and we did things like 'Space Between Worlds' and a few other odd songs. Then eventually that drifted apart and Phil and I got involved in the Fallen Angels.'

After departing the Pretties Phil had taken Electra and daughter Sorrel to live for a while on a barge on the River Seine. This spell of calm ended when Peter Grant called suggesting he make a solo album. Against his instincts he journeyed to Rockfield in the winter of 1976 to try and put it together. Gradually various ex-Pretties joined him, first Wally Waller then Peter Tolson and Skip Alan who were still involved in forming Metropolis. Also in attendance was guitarist Ed Deane, who for a while stayed with Phil and Electra at their Talbot Road place. Wally suggested that Peter didn't seem to get on with Ed although Peter doesn't remember this and confirmed Ed as an excellent guitarist. Ed advised that he and Peter formed a mutual admiration society. Some years later Deane fronted the 'East European band' in the film *Stormy Monday* and played regularly with the Dana Gillespie Band. Ed recalled that working in the studio with Phil was arduous work, because he kept wanting to redo various bits.

The project was to go out under the name Dogs of War but ultimately the sessions were unproductive in terms of an album's worth and Phil decided to sever links completely and leave Swansong. 'First Skip came down then Peter and it was getting to be a Pretty Things album, but it wasn't the time to do one. So after a few tracks I stopped and I asked Peter Grant to give me my contract back, and I left Swansong.'

Why was it inappropriate to cut another Pretty Things album? Phil's concern may have been the return of the pressures, the weight of expectation and the alcohol and chemical intemperance that had caused the *Savage Eye* band to implode. Equally he was weary from leading a band and the demons that occasioned the 1976 hiatus continued to plague him.

Four or five tracks were half completed and the tapes handed over to the company. When Swansong recognised that Phil wouldn't be recording and that The Pretty Things wouldn't be reforming they also lost interest. Like Wally, Peter Tolson remembered 'Space Between Worlds' as being a very good song. Phil explained that it was about the limbo world that exists between life and death. Presumably today it festers somewhere in a dark and dusty tape cupboard. The song 'Dogs Of War' was also recorded and would later resurface at the Fallen Angels sessions. Another song 'Take Me Home', a Wally composition, would appear on the *Return of the Electric Banana* album on De Wolfe. These and the other completed numbers should have been made available perhaps as bonus tracks on the later Snapper label reissues. After all, Swansong did provide two far less appropriate Metropolis tracks.

At this point Phil was encouraged by Wally to join a project called The Fallen Angels. This doomed venture started with a nucleus of Mickey Finn (not to be confused with Jack Green's old T-Rex colleague), Greg Ridley and Twink. Twink was the first to go, being sacked after crashing his car and failing to make a session. Numerous personnel changes brought the planned album to a halt until Phil and Wally signed up in the Spring of 1977. By this stage only Finn remained from the original incarnation.

Phil claimed he was tired of leading a band and having to write material for them. He wanted to turn up as just the singer. Perversely, this was exactly the situation he turned his back on when baling out of The Pretty Things nine months earlier.

Phil had been assured that all the songs were ready and it was on this basis that he agreed to join, as the vocalist, but when he arrived they only had the one song, Mickey Finn's 'Fallen Angel'. 'I ended up writing the rest of the songs, running the band, and it was almost like being in The Pretty Things again,' he griped.

Fortified by £100,000 of private backing from Godfrey Bilton, a City of London financier who almost certainly viewed his investment as venture capital, the Fallen Angels, descended on the Aquarius Studios at Rue Thalberg in Geneva in July 1977. They comprised Phil, Wally, Mickey Finn, Chico Greenwood, Brian Johnstone and Bill Lovelady.

As an exercise in stress management it was an unmitigated disaster. Massive alcohol consumption, rowdiness and recurrent intervention from the police blighted the six weeks stay. 'It's all a bit of an alcoholic haze', confessed Wally. The Swiss police took a very close interest in Mickey Finn whose wasted features caused them to mistake him for Keith Richards. They promptly administered an appropriate scrutiny.

Only ten days had been gainfully employed. 'The Fallen Angels wasted nearly £500,000 and nearly killed me,' remembered Phil. During the stay he managed to crash three cars. 'I was really out of it. I rolled off a mountain and woke up the next morning in a field of cows, hanging upside down in my seat belt.' Hertz refused to give him a fourth car, 'I don't blame them,' says Phil. 'I wouldn't give me another car either.' A further chemically prompted activity involved the theft of a train!

It's been said that Mickey Finn adopted a very laid back approach to the sessions – apparently he laid back on the floor of the studio whilst recording his guitar parts. This may have been because of tiredness or alcohol abuse or possibly due to an alleged incident involving his wife and a bottle that was somehow smashed over his head.

'I don't remember a lot about it,' said Wally. 'We didn't get a lot done. I don't think the results justified the money spent, that's for sure. It wasn't our finest hour.'

These and subsequent UK sessions produced fifteen songs. Apart from 'Fallen Angels', Phil composed the remaining songs, individually or with Wally and the other band members. Some years later a ten-track album secured a limited release courtesy of Butt Records.

The album isn't anywhere near as bad as the protagonists make out. Sure it could have been better and with less alcohol and a better mix it could have been an exceptional album but nonetheless it isn't a dog. It improves with repeated listening and many of the songs recorded were very strong. In fact, it has dated better than either of the two Swansong albums. It is not too much of a stretch to imagine 'Dance Again' and 'Girl Like You' gracing any 70s Pretty Things album and '13½ Floor Suicide' hinted at the menace which permeated the *Cross Talk* recordings two years down the road. Peter Tolson recalled '13½ Floor Suicide' being around at the Rockfield sessions. Wally recalled the Fallen Angels period as 'terribly unreal' and doesn't consider the songs themselves as very memorable although he can't really recall them too well and until recently didn't even have a copy.

Another five tracks mysteriously turned up on another De Wolfe issue, *The Return of the Electric Banana*, where they were combined with 'Pretty Things' tracks from the 1973 De Wolfe sessions. All of the Fallen Angels songs, although De Wolfe avoids mentioning the name, were May/Waller

Above: The Pretty Things circa 1966
Photo: © Jørgen Angel - www.angel.dk

Left: 13 Chester Street, London. The
legendary Pretty Things residence
during the late sixties, until the
mayhem got all too much.
Photo: Alan Lakey

Above: Early Swansong promotional photo.
(l-r) Jack Green, Phil May, John Povey, Gordon Edwards, Skip Alan, Pete Tolson.

Top left: The Pretty Things at Niagara Falls during the Swansong era.
(l-r) Phil May, Pete Tolson, John Povey, Jack Green, Gordon Edwards, Skip Alan.

Bottom left: Poster hoarding for the *Silk Torpedo* album in Los Angeles.
Peter Grant arranged for it to be put up overnight opposite the band's hotel as a surprise.
Photos: courtesy of Jack Green.

Above: The Led Zeppelin days.
(l-r) Gordon Edwards, Pete Tolson, Phil May, John Povey, Skip Alan, Jack Green.

Left: Viv Prince at home in Portugal, 1994. **Right:** Pretty Things manager, Mark St. John.
Photos: courtesy of Terry Coates

Promotional photos of "The Pretty Things Project", the 1987 European line-up.
Photos: courtesy of Terry Coates

Top left: The Pretty Things after the Marriot Hotel comeback gig in 1995. (l-r) Skip Alan, DickTaylor, John Povey, Wally Waller, Frank Holland, Phil May and manager Mark St. John.

Bottom left: Post-gig party, December 1995 at The Borderline. (l-r) Gordon Edwards, John Povey, Dick Taylor, Skip Alan, Wally Waller, Frank Holland and at the front Phil May.

This page: The launch of the *Anthology* album at London's 100 Club.

Right: Wally Waller.
Below: Skip Alan (left) and John Povey (right).

Photos: courtesy Terry Coates.

Above: Perennial Pretty Thing, Phil May, onstage at the launch of the *Anthology* album, at the 100 Club, London, 1995. *Photo: courtesy Terry Coates*

tunes but strangely, and perhaps for tax mitigation purposes, they were cred-ited as Stuart/Waller. Stuart, of course, being the maiden name of Phil's wife Electra.

Upon returning to the UK the band fractured and Phil attempted to finish the album by bringing in new players to complete the recording. Out of a gig ex-Pretty Thing Jon Povey was called up for organ and vocal duty, as was drummer Fran Byrne and guitarist Ed Deane, both recently of Frankie Millers' band. The album was completed after a fashion at Trident Studios, with assistance from producer John Porter and engineer Bob Potter, although to nobody's real satisfaction. Phil considered the album unfinished because the issued product comprised rough mixes and guide guitar parts. He felt the tracks needed remixing and was unimpressed with John Porter's contribu-tion. In his and Wally's minds the album is considered unworthy of much comment and has been consigned to history.

Phil had clearly taken control of the band and when the album appeared it was released as by Phil May and the Fallen Angels on a limited basis in Hol-land and Germany where The Pretty Things name has always commanded greater respect and acclaim than elsewhere.

The inclusion of Jon Povey made it a pseudo-Pretty Things album although UK fans had to wait four years for a low profile release by which time both the Fallen Angels and The Pretty Things had ceased to exist.

After the disappointment of Metropolis and the Dogs Of War sessions Peter Tolson was scratching around for work. Also having problems at this time was German heavy rock band The Scorpions. Ulrich Roth had left and they were busy looking for a replacement lead guitarist. Amongst those considered and asked to audition was Peter who seemed unsettled from the outset. 'They flew me over to Hanover, full of fascists. They wanted me to play loud and I didn't feel like it, so I played some melodic stuff and they weren't happy. They showed me these songs written in English – English lyrics by Germans! They had no real meaning and I told them. They said, 'It is good enough.' I said to them you play in C and I'll play in E, and they said, 'But we won't be in tune,' and I said, 'It is good enough', and flew home.'

Unbeknownst to Peter, the Scorpions had discussed the matter with Phil and he told of their disbelief and their astonishment that Peter would choose to walk away from them. He said Peter told them their music was shit. Hind-sight is a wonderful thing and Peter occasionally wonders what might have happened if he had fallen in with their methods and made a go of it. The money would have been healthy, but would he? After all they were massive in Japan, but then again the lure of the cash jackpot has never featured in the Prettie's history, which is why they are so poor yet so bloody relevant.

Jack Green also had a close encounter of a megadollar kind. He recalled a mid 70s gig at the Marquee and being approached by two Australians. They asked whether he would be interested in joining a group that they were basing in the UK. Jack thought it was a bit of a joke and politely declined. It was not too long before AC/DC became one of the biggest bands in the world.

Some time after the Scorpions episode, Peter was asked by Edgar Broughton to join The Broughtons, a spin off from the Edgar Broughton Band. 'In 1979 I had a day job and had just started a family. I had been brought in with the promise that there would be the opportunity to have my material rehearsed, recorded, whatever. When it came to it, Edgar had written all the stuff, he gave his brother Steve a chance on one track and nobody else got a look in. Then they asked me to go trekking round Europe, five or six months doing coastal resorts, and I said no.'

Unlike Skip, Peter only likes water in his whisky and the thought of bobbing round Scandinavia's provincial resorts was anathema to him. The subsequent Broughton's album, *Parlez Vouz English*, was a desultory affair with Tolson battling heroically against the mediocre tunes. Fortunately, the album has not received a CD release and has conveniently slipped into the wastebin of musical history.

Talking in 1999 Peter accepted that he had made some dodgy career moves. 'I made a few mistakes. Unbeknownst to a lot of people I was made quite a few offers from other bands. Maybe if I had taken them... I don't know. It's water under the bridge now, in some cases the people that were involved will deny it, it is probably best left where it is. It shouldn't go on the record because it never came to anything. Sometimes it is a matter of regret to me. Because working for a living ain't what you'd call fun.'

Dick Taylor had turned away from the music scene some years earlier, and had been working in the clothing business apart from the occasional gig or session. This changed dramatically during the initial excitement and upheaval of punk when he was reinvigorated while attending a Clash concert. It seemed fun with a fresh, non-corporate approach and he decided to return to what he did best, playing music. At the same time, around December 1977, a friend, Pete Dello, contacted Phil and asked him and Dick to reform The Pretty Things for a one off concert in Holland. They were up for it, as they say. All costs paid. No problem. Right?

None of The Pretty Things were involved in any meaningful music projects and this one-off seemed a harmless enough means of enjoying a brief continental break. It sounded too good to be true and of course, in time-honoured Pretty Things fashion, it was. Dello explained that he was opening a Pretty Things workshop at the Midas Club in Amsterdam and had asked Phil and Dick to perform at it. To his probable astonishment Phil and

Dick agreed as did Wally, Skip and Jon Povey. They all turned up on July 8th 1978 to play to over 600 fans. Peter Tolson had not been invited to join them, though with hindsight he will probably feel this a worthwhile omission from his CV.

The show was secretly recorded and, some time later, Dello was found to be touting the tapes around as the latest Pretty Things album. Eventually a CD surfaced in the States on the Jade label.

Phil was particularly disturbed by what he saw as a rip-off by a friend. 'The only reason we did that gig was as a favour. We actually did it for nothing. We only got expenses; he just put us up in a hotel. He fetched the tape over and played it to us and said can he put it out? We said, 'No, it's a piece of shit.' It was a disgusting recording. The next thing I knew, I was in Los Angeles in Greg Shaw's office and he showed me this letter written by this guy where he had actually put himself up as the official Pretty Thing representative and said that he had Phil and Dick's permission to licence this record and he was asking Greg Shaw for something like $10,000. I should have kept the letter really. That would have been good evidence legally.'

'The guy conned us, but we've been conned so many times,' added Wally. 'It was a very ill-rehearsed, good fun gig.' 'It was awful,' Phil continued. 'Basically it's like having your wallet stolen.' Augmenting the reformed Pretties line up, according to the bootleg's sleevenotes, were Dutch musicians William Van Houten on second guitar and Leen Kok on drums although Wally could not recall either of them and believed them to be two local musicians who jumped up on stage and jammed a bit. The concert featured traditional Pretties R&B fare with 'Big City', 'Big Boss Man', 'Roadrunner', 'Rosalyn' and 'Route 66'. 'Old Man Going' provided the only post '66 song although 'Ealing Blues' and 'Paddington Jam' represented two knockabout additions which the band cannot now remember. Presumably they were 12-bar throwaways.

During September and October 1978 Phil did some gigs as Phil May and the Fallen Angels with Wally, Chico Greenwood and, returning from a stint with Whitesnake, Brian Johnstone. It indicated that he didn't see any future in the reformed Pretties and was still looking for that elusive missing element as well as a few quid. Ed Deane who played guitar in the band remembered this and their one other gig as great fun but disappointedly recalled Phil being adamant that Ed couldn't play 'Don't Bring Me Down'. 'He said only Dick Taylor should play that.'

Meanwhile Wally had started work on an album for De Wolfe entitled *Do It*. Issued as by The Wally Waller Band it was effectively a Wally solo album augmented by some of the Fallen Angels. 'I virtually did everything myself, got Ed Deane in to put some licks on. I may have got Chico Greenwood in to lay some drums on. I think I probably worked to a rhythm track and then had to put drums on top of that, it never really works that way around that's why I didn't do it again on the next one. Like all De Wolfe issues it had vocal tracks one side and the instrumental versions on the other. As a means of finding an outlet for his songs it was a worthwhile project however it hardly paid the mortgage.

The perilous state of their finances drew Phil and Dick to again consider the non-receipt of royalties from EMI. They had also been concerned at the complete lack of accounting, from Motown subsidiary Rare Earth, and decided to look into the matter. Apart from the initial advance and the funding of the various sessions the band had not received any money from EMI or Rare Earth. EMI responded citing a six-year time bar which, they suggested, put an end to the matter. It did, for a while.

CHAPTER 13 – Cross Talk and Angry Words

The Monster Club – a horror film starring Vincent Price. Trust the Pretties to appear in two films, one a sex-comedy that was neither sexy nor funny, the other a horror movie that wasn't scary. Nevertheless *The Monster Club* boasted a halfway decent soundtrack including the Pretties and the Ramones, so no problem there, but the film... the film consisted of four short stories recounted by supposedly hideous creatures, all fully paid members of *The Monster Club.*

The film attempted to straddle the twin walls of humour and horror and in the process fell heavily, damaging both itself and the poor innocent viewer. Those who managed to stave off the tranquillising effects of the script will have watched the film limping to a welcome conclusion with Vincent Price turning to the house-band, The Pretty Things, and beseeching them to 'play our song'.

Wally's bass intro joined by a Skip drum fill followed by Tolson's quintessential riff. The mimed performance is effectively the highlight of the entire film. Dick Taylor confirmed that he had never managed to stay awake long enough to watch himself and the rest of the band.

The Pretties somewhat surprising involvement in *The Monster Club* was arranged through a dope dealer friend of Jon Povey's. As a result of this introduction Jon asked for and received one third of the publishing on Phil and Peter's title song.

Peter recalled that the song took a while to come together, 'we sat around and talked and talked and talked. I got up, went upstairs and took a line and came down and said, 'This is it.' I had no idea what I was going to do and just winged it.'

This celluloid embarrassment was filmed at Elstree Studios where Phil was approached to try a solo acting piece. The end product was left on the cutting room floor, forgotten and never to be seen. A fitting result if it was of similar quality to the rest of the film.

The one worthwhile result of the 1978 Dutch reunion fiasco was the regathering of the faithful. Povey, having been sidelined by Metropolis and the Dogs of War project was back behind the keyboards. Dick was gradually regaining his touch after his years in the non-musical wilderness and Phil had exorcised some of the demons. Wally was back in the fold after his Fallen Angels and other European exploits and Skip was still Skip. Peter Tolson had been keeping afloat with the Broughton's album and sessions with Jack Green.

Peter had found working in a factory no fun and the opportunity to play guitar on Jack's solo album *Humanesque* was a great boost. Peter played on nine of the tracks, with Jack's former employer Richie Blackmore playing on the other. Jack made very clear the high esteem in which he holds Tolson's guitar playing. 'I thought he was absolutely brilliant, he was probably one of the best guitarists in Britain, he had real style. The thing that I used to like about Pete, we were so close musically, whatever I did he knew how to interpret it. He could interpret, musically, exactly what I meant. I could play three notes and I knew he would know what I meant by that. You only get that when you play with somebody for a long time.'

Gordon Edwards felt similarly: 'When we used to do rehearsals, Skip used to record them on his portable ghetto blaster and I used to bring a copy of these tapes home and listen to them and Pete's lead guitar playing really used to send a shiver down my back. Pete was very melodic and he wouldn't play fast just for the sake of it, whereas in these heavy metal bands every guitarist tends to play fast. That's why you can't really tell one guitarist from the next.'

Jack Green, Phil May, Gordon Edwards and Dick Taylor all rate Tolson's guitar capability in the highest league. All the more astounding then that Hugh Gregory, in his 1994 opus *1000 Great Guitarists* should omit Tolson from his list. Dick Taylor makes the thousand as do those famed fretboard wizards Chris Difford, P J Harvey and Marc Bolan.

'To me he ranks easily as good as Clapton,' voiced Gordon Edwards. 'He was as good as Hendrix, but a completely different style. To me he was one of the best guitarists about.'

Phil remembered that after the Dutch reunion gig he met up with Pete Tolson and they started writing some stuff together at Dave Gilmour's home studio. Phil got in touch with Dick and then everybody started drifting back together again. 'I think Gilmour actually played on the first thing we did for the *Cross Talk* album.' Peter recalled these sessions but couldn't remember Gilmour actually playing on them. 'Dave produced one or more tracks and I followed most of his advice when completing the second solo on 'Falling Again'.

Phil had spent much of 1979 living in Hollywood where, in his own words, he was, 'Doing drugs and tennis – tennis and drugs.' Phil was fortunate in having a wife who was sufficiently well off to allow such luxuries. He had secured himself a management deal with Judy Knight and had formed his own Phil May Publishing company. With around £4,000 he funded demos of the songs that he and Peter Tolson had written and these were hawked around before Warner Brothers took the bait and agreed a one-off album deal.

Peter, out of economic necessity had taken work at the Co-op biscuit factory and had been fitting in the writing and recording between work and commitments to his family. Despite the years apart it all fell into place easily. The bleak and forbidding 'No Future' being a prime example. 'I'd got the riff and I knew what I wanted and he just looked at me and by then we'd got sufficient rapport that he knew what I wanted so he came back with the tune,' explained Peter. Was it easy to fit back into The Pretty Things? 'Yeah, some of these things will never go.'

Writing in the booklet to the 1995 *Anthology*, Phil recalled, 'it was one of the most impressive bits of guitar riffing that's been presented to me to come up with lyrics on. I found it incredibly easy to write this because it was such an extraordinary piece of guitar playing. Peter turned up at the house and plugged in and started playing this riff, and it was easy.'

The power structure within the band was noticeably different to the previous Pretty Things' incarnations. Musically it was Phil and Peter controlling things with Dick, Wally and Jon adding pieces, but consigned pretty much to the background. Wally had spent years producing albums, but as a musician he remembered how hard it was for him when other musicians argued over production niceties. Phil contributed the lyrics with Peter composing the bulk of the music and being responsible for most of the arrangements. 'It was the first album where I had all the equipment I wanted, Marshall stacks, etc,' recalled Peter. He also felt it was the first album where he had been able to influence and direct the music. The guitar intro on 'It's So Hard' being cited as an example of something that Norman Smith would not have allowed. Peter also wrote a number of the bass lines that Wally would then learn for the sessions.

Within the *Anthology* sleevenotes, Mark St John observed that the tension between Tolson and Taylor was palpable. Both Peter and Dick scoff at this view. Of course, St John was not around at this time.

'The only problem I had with Dick was that he could never play like I could play, so when he was supposed to do the rhythm part on a song, say *No Future,* he didn't play it that way so it didn't sound… Dick couldn't play it that way and it wasn't what I had written. If you're gonna do a version of the song fine, but if you're gonna do 'The Song' then play 'The Bloody Song' and don't fuck around with it… I've got no problem with the chap at all.'

Dick: 'We managed to get on as well as anybody could under the circumstances, shall we say. I mean, Pete's a bloody awkward bastard. I'm not saying I dislike him at all but he can be… he's not the easiest of people. I never had any rows with Peter at all, ever, so I don't think it was a major problem.'

Tolson also derided St John's *Anthology* comment that on 'No Future', 'you can hear the man falling apart.' 'I wasn't falling apart at that point, (but) a lot of things were.' A comment on the band's financial situation, drug dependency and overall despondency.

The album came together fairly quickly. In the EMI days studio time was virtually unlimited and with Swansong no expense was spared but financial constraints, and Phil's preferences, involved a cheap studio, quick nightime sessions and a sparse production. The production duo of Phil Chapman and Jon Astley oversaw the proceedings although their role was more restricted than Norman Smith's in that the songs and arrangements were already pretty much in place. Peter Tolson felt that the production benefited from their minimalist approach: 'No Smithy wall-of-sound ideas.'

Unlike *Savage Eye*, where much of the album was written or finished in the studio, the band had mapped out most of the music with only final touches and arrangement alterations needed.

Apart from Phil the remainder of the band had day jobs and the sessions placed them under tremendous strain. 'When they arrived they were exhausted,' said Jon Astley. Jon Povey was making surfboards whilst Dick was driving a van. Peter continued at the biscuit factory whilst Skip worked a twelve hour day trying to keep his father's business afloat. Such was the pressure on Skip that he had to miss certain sessions, so on 'I'm Calling' and 'Falling Again' they turned to Dave Gilmour's long time friend Willie Wilson.

Wilson is another musician who has crossed numerous paths with the band and their associates over the years. In the mid-sixties he drummed in Jokers Wild with school friend Gilmour and in 1970 he played in Cochise whose United Artists album was produced by one Richard Clifford Taylor. Wilson also played with the Sutherland Brothers & Quiver and as supplementary Pink Floyd drummer around the time of *The Wall* album.

Warner Brothers reputedly paid Phil around £100,000 for the album and, not unnaturally, he pulled in the other Pretty Things for the recordings as Jon Povey explained. 'We were paid to be on the album so we were paid by Judy Knights management company cause she took on Phil as a solo artist and we came along and made a Pretty Things album. She didn't want to sign the rest of us, I suppose it's cheaper to sign one guy and get the band anyway than it is to sign the band. We just got paid for it, we got a certain amount of money for doing it which we agreed to do but it was Phil's own project with Judy.'

'Phil definitely didn't get stitched up,' acknowledged Dick Taylor. 'Actually he did rather well there, we all made a little bit of money out of it.' Peter Tolson remembered being paid £1,250 and assumed that the other band members received the same 'little bit of money'.

In real terms *Cross Talk* was a Phil May solo album where he co-wrote the bulk of the songs with Peter Tolson and used him and the other Pretty

Things almost as session players. Astley recalled, that Tolson apart, the others didn't seem to know quite what was going on, although he recollected Dick having some input. He vividly recalled Phil's continual moodiness and the occasion he was confronted with, 'Last night you nearly drove me to suicide.'

The sessions stretched from the end of February until the middle of March with a regular schedule of four evenings a week commencing at 6.00 through to midnight.

The recording sessions were swift compared to EMI/Swansong days. Wally: 'We often laid down two rhythm tracks a night, which is good for us.' Crammed into the converted dairy that was the Matrix Studio in Covent Garden, they hurriedly laid down the tracks. 'The equipment seemed to be hanging off the walls, held together by gaffer tape,' recalled Phil. Nothing like the sixteen-track sophistication of Olympic Studios.

By all accounts the atmosphere was highly charged and the sessions were punctuated by numerous ill-tempered flare-ups and flights of caprice. 'Cocaine fuelled', was Phil's description of the late evening sessions. Certain things hadn't changed since the Swansong days and coke ingestion was one of them. Phil, Peter and Jon Povey were habitual users, which influenced their playing, behaviour and songwriting. Phil took charge of the sessions telling Jon Astley to make certain songs sound like this or like that. Astley is adamant that they were intended to produce some very commercial material and added that it was during this period that *The Monster Club* soundtrack song was cut.

Whilst Phil Chapman took care of the engineering and knob twiddling and kept out of the firing line, Jon Astley was taking a more creative role trying to add to the songs or assist in the arrangements. A coked up, paranoid Phil soon fell out with Astley and took to calling the duo Acidly & Cheapman.

Astley remembered Phil bringing in compilation tapes for the other band members containing songs he wanted them to listen to, like 'Brass In Pocket' by The Pretenders. Apparently, he was looking for a new wave vibe. At the time Phil was listening to a lot of new wave material, such as The Police and Squeeze.

Karen Berg was the Warner Brothers A&R person who signed Phil to the contract. One evening she turned up, and upon seeing the fiasco of a studio was appalled. She asked Astley why, given the size of the budget, the sessions were being conducted at Matrix. Astley himself was dismayed when he was told the figure. He explained that Phil was responsible for choosing Matrix, which he had managed to obtain cheaply because of its night-time availability.

Late March through to mid April saw the album mixed and the tapes were sent to New York to be cut by Bob Ludwig at Masterdisc. Although the Pretties were pleased with the album there was a definite disappointment with the eventual sound. The band had been very happy with the Astley/Chapman mix and the sound carried an edge and roughness that they liked, it slotted nicely into the post-punk scene. During the mastering process the rough edges were smoothed and the menace reduced for a more palatable sound. Probably for American consumption, guessed Phil.

Buttressed by the excellent supporting single 'I'm Calling', *Cross Talk* was released in August 1980. The record was credited to The Pretty Things, which it was entitled to be, but the album sleeve gave the game away by emboldening the Phil May name and enlarging the font to indicate his enhanced status. Perversely, given the studio, the chemicals and the lack of cohesion the resulting album was superb. *Cross Talk* was, in Peter Tolson's opinion, the best work he ever did in or out of The Pretty Things. He also considers it the best album the band ever recorded. Imagine then the disenchantment that he and the band experienced when the curse of The Pretty Things reappeared on the release date.

'I loved the album', confirmed Jon Povey. 'I thought it was very well played, a cracking album, but it died a death because it only ever had two copies printed of it, or five and half.'

Dick Taylor explained. 'We put it on the turntable and it sounded great, we turned it over and it sounded great again. Only trouble was it was exactly the same as the first side. We had the first ever one sided record.'

Tolson recalled, "'I'm Calling' got to 41 in the charts and Warner Brothers stopped promoting it. The first 100,000 copies of the album, they released with two 'A' sides. Another 100,000 had the 'A' and the 'B' sides but with the labels on the wrong sides, so DJs who would've played it couldn't be screwing around with this so they took it off the play list.'

An additional negative element involved BBC Television's current affairs flagship, *Panorama*. Shortly before the album's release it exposed an industry-wide payola scandal and named Warner Brothers as one of the guilty parties.

After the Jimmy Duncan theft episode, the non-promotion of *SF Sorrow* in the UK, its delayed post-*Tommy* US release on an unsympathetic Motown subsidiary, the inability to capitalise on *Rolling Stone* magazine's *Parachute* accolade, EMI's failure to acknowledge or pay royalties on US sales, the unfulfilled promise of the Bill Shepherd period and the chemical/stress induced failure of the Swansong era this latest calamity confirmed their status as the unluckiest band of all – Badfinger excepted.

Peter Tolson expressed some misgivings about his solo on 'No Future' and the chorus, which he felt didn't quite mesh with the main song idea. 'The only gripe I've got about that was the mix of the solo, I had a better mix.' That apart he felt the music was the most pertinent of his career. The track 'She Don't' illustrated this better than most. A moody, edgy song, punctuated by a choppy, melodic yet almost tortured Tolson solo, with May's anguished vocal providing the perfect injection of despair. The song was written around the time that Peter's son Jesse was born and generously Phil gave his share of the song-writing credits to Jesse. Did Jesse receive much money from the song? Peter replied dryly, 'Oh yes, a couple of pounds. As he was a minor the money came to me and I made sure he got a toy.'

Tolson took all of the solos on *Cross Talk* apart from Dick's solo on 'Lost That Girl'. Introduced by Phil's wailing double-entendre, 'help me find her, Dick' the solo is more straightforward, less off-the-wall than anything Tolson created and to Pretties fans is instantly recognisable as a brother to the short and urgent mid 60s solos at which he excelled.

Dick has always been honest and humble about his contributions to the record. When an interviewer asked him to confirm that he had played lead guitar on *Cross Talk*, Dick responded 'No I didn't, I only played lead on 'Lost That Girl', Peter Tolson played the other solos. Many musicians would have remained silent, acquiescing to boost their own egos, not Dick, he doesn't need that false acclaim.

'I'm Calling', the initial single release was also the first track on the album. Featuring a catchy intro complete with violin-like synth the central riff buzzed and pulsed with a waspish demeanour. Amazingly it was chosen as Single of the Week on *Radio One's* Simon Bates show. This mid-morning programme catered to the sugary and terminally sad, particularly with its schmaltzy 'true story' slot, and was the last place one could have imagined hearing The Pretty Things. Of course, the sugary and terminally sad have never comprised The Pretty Things fan base and they didn't buy the single in any great numbers. This is assuming that Warners had managed to stock the major outlets in the first place.

Throughout the previous thirteen years they had struggled to receive any major radio coverage. Were The Pretty Things now considered safe enough for Radio One listeners? Were they tame by comparison with The Sex Pistols and The Damned?

Two months later the May/Waller song, 'Falling Again' b/w 'She Don't' was issued in a final attempt at singles chart glory. Once again Radio One picked up on the song and it received worthwhile airplay but never made even the lower echelons of the charts.

'Neat and controlled, music to run a bath with. Its melody disappears as rapidly as it arrived', sneered the *Melody Maker* reviewer.

'Falling Again' constituted yet another example of May's blatant captivation by seafaring themes. This fascination can be recognised in various songs on Pretty Things albums – 'Allnight Sailor', 'Singapore Silk Torpedo' and 'Sea Of Blue' being the more obvious examples, although 'Falling Again' and 'It's So Hard' also contain maritime references and 'Sea About Me', from a later 1981 session, makes nautical play with the spelling.

Phil's affinity with dockland life in various countries is vividly described in the liner notes to the 1995 *Anthology*. Mark St John wrote about accompanying Phil on a drinking tour of the dockland haunts whilst amused band members suppressed smirks at knowledge of the hard night ahead.

This maritime attraction probably originates with Phil's father, a sailor who left the family and returned to the sea when Phil was a child. The lyrical allure may represent a subconscious desire to be reunited with his lost parent. Equally this may all be Freudian claptrap and simply that Phil likes sailors.

In the States *Good Times* reviewed both *Cross Talk* and Jack Green's debut solo album *Humanesque*, which was released at the same time. Reviewer, Victor Chirei, considered that *Edge Of The Night* displayed the influence of Elvis Costello and that 'I'm Calling' showed touches of Rick Derringer, he also suggested that 'No Future' owed a debt to The Police. He commended the freshness, which he put down to Phil May's vocals and the airtight rhythm section. 'Never anything less than their own music, animated and magnetic. It satisfies the ear and the mind equally.' Nonetheless, Chirei considered Green's *Humanesque* more interesting than *Cross Talk* because of its distinctive sound. 'Green's voice is clean and young, his expression spirited. He is also the album's producer making full use of the production room to establish any number of nuances.'

Billboard suggested that although *Cross Talk* offered quality cuts in the progressive rock vein, 'The LP is weighed down with too much filler rock. Still, it's saved by clever story-telling lyrics and faultless musicianship.'

Year's later Phil considered the *Cross Talk* band one of the best he'd worked with. 'I also think that a good line up means volatility and therefore that's when a band is more likely to blow up. A good band is more likely to have problems than a band which has one or two members who completely rule everything else and the other people are just sidemen. Take the Davies Brothers for instance, they rule The Kinks and you are either in or out on their say so. When you have five or six members who are equal in talent and potential with an incredible lot of writing going on together, that's when it's like a kind of neutron bomb capable of blowing itself apart.'

Jack Green confirmed that in the Swansong era things were the same. 'The trouble with The Pretty Things was there was all chiefs and no indians, everybody had their ideas. The way I've realised things subsequently is the best bands, people that have got their own sound, always have the same end product in mind. When they're trying to record, if everybody in the band can see, visualise the end product together you've got a really good band, and probably an original band. The Pretties were always 'I wanna do this' and some of the others 'well, I wanna do this' and it was always a bit push and pull you know. I always felt that everybody in the Pretties knew that. I think they're still like it as far as I know.'

Jack also explained why he thought they were like this. 'The one thing about the Pretties is that most of the guys are pretty creative. They weren't just in it for the job they were always trying to create, which made it fun, interesting. They did play together quite a while but they had so many different ideas. Maybe Phil would say, 'No I don't wanna do that type of stuff I wanna go and do more progressive stuff.' I was never quite happy with that, what happened was the tracks bouncing from track to track on the album were so diverse. You would never be able to put on a Pretty Things album and know what you were getting. You got a ballad then you got some weird rhythmic thing then you got another strange sort then eventually you maybe got a rock song then you'd get something else.'

Peter Tolson totally disagreed with Jack's view citing The Beatles *Revolver* as an example of how such a musical melange could work.

Cross Talk has been described as The Pretty Things tip of the hat to the burgeoning new wave movement. Released well into the punk era its moodiness and bite jump out at the seasoned let alone the casual listener. The overall feel is at odds with previous Pretty Things releases. Two obvious areas are the sparse production, pared down and crisp with plenty of space between the notes and Tolson's guitar work. On previous recordings he had crafted sympathetic solos and smooth runs up and down the scales, often sounding like a violin as Jon Povey suggested. On *Cross Talk* Tolson preferred to parade rougher textures and to replace the melodic runs with choppy chords, snarling staccato bursts and brief, almost violent, solos sounding like a guitar in torment. His playing added a threatening quality exuding despair and despondency, a perfect fit for the uneasy ambience that enveloped the majority of the songs.

Over the years Peter had formed the view that his earlier guitarwork was 'too melodic' and this album demonstrates how a feral style of playing altered the atmosphere of what might otherwise have been a softer, less interesting album. He remarked that on joining the band in 1970 he introduced menace and never has that been more pronounced than on *Cross Talk,* where it stalks several of the tracks particularly the ironically and almost autobiographically titled 'No Future' and 'Bitter End'.

The band gigged in support of the album and they were supported by Warner Brothers who subsidised gigs by up to £600 a time to cover equipment rental costs. This lasted for only a short period before they balked at the expense. The shows were disappointing and Peter Tolson remembered that the band played terribly. 'Simon Fox and Wally forgot a lot of the arrangements and Phil mixed up the verses and choruses.'

Peter Tolson was fitting in tour commitments with the Jack Green Band and this duality caused a degree of ill-feeling with Phil and the others. Peter recalled that Phil advised him about various gigs that had been booked. Peter told him that he couldn't do them because of a promise he'd made to Jack Green. 'But you're in The Pretty Things,' he was told. 'Yeah', Peter replied, 'but I'm getting five times as much for the Green tour and, anyway, I'll be bringing back ideas for the band'.

Given the circumstances it was decided that a cover guitarist was needed and Peter was asked to teach a young replacement the parts, note for note. In the event the gigs never went ahead and on the day of his return from the States, Peter had to get ready for a Pretty Things gig at Dingwalls the same night.

Using boxing parlance the band was groggy, on the ropes and being urged by well-wishers to retire. Personal troubles began intruding on projects and the future looked increasingly shitty. Peter Tolson and partner Gilly had started a family and financial pressures were mounting, exacerbating the usual argumentative sides of their natures. The band members were drinking heavily and using all manner of substances. Jon and Peter were continually strung out on coke and Skip, who never was a dope fiend, was consuming vast quantities of his favourite tipple Pernod. Wally was in the throes of a new relationship with Sarah, who was later to become his wife, and Jon was going through a divorce from Valerie which came between him and his two sons, Aaron and Christian. Additionally, like Wally, he was at the start of a new liaison with girlfriend 'Rogie.'

The band was at a low, no-future ebb, thinking that things could not possibly get worse. It was at this stage that they encountered Mark St John.

CHAPTER 14 – The Revelation of St John

By the end of 1980 The Pretty Things were going through the motions. The *Cross Talk* fiasco had drained them, Peter Tolson recalled they put everything they had into the album and the letdown was enormous.

Now, like Sebastian Sorrow at his lowest ebb, they met a mysterious stranger who through persistent persuasion, took them on what would be an amazing journey. Enter Mark St John, unsuccessful rock drummer and experienced tape-operator then engaged as an engineer at Freerange, a small independent studio nestling in London's Covent Garden.

Interviews, articles and liner notes are littered with references to St John's moment of revelation. That instant when he first heard 'It's Been So Long' at Surrey Sound Studios. When Norman Smith's son Nick played the tape after a late session on the Police's debut album. In the initial throes of born-again Pretty Things idolatry he sought out first their records, tee-shirts, and then the band themselves. St John had somehow persuaded Freerange owner Nick Abson to fund production of a Pretty Things album. Now all he needed was The Pretty Things.

Their apparent inability to say no to a record deal combined with St John's exhortations led to them entering Freerange in the Spring of 1981 to start work on a new album. Engineer Marc Francs was enlisted to support the rookie producer, Mark St John.

St John considered it 'unprecedented' for an established band to associate with a relative nonentity such as himself, and suggested that it defined their characters. More likely, with no contract, no management and no future. St John offered a doorway, which they chose to walk through oblivious of what awaited on the other side.

Skip however didn't come along for the ride. He was trying to sustain his father's business, which required his full time attention. His non-availability meant that Simon Fox was retained for the sessions. Simon had previously drummed in Be Bop Deluxe and had also played alongside Peter Tolson on the second Jack Green solo album. Peter recalled that he drummed in a more methodical manner compared with Skip's jazzy flourishes.

Mark St John has emerged as a truly enigmatic fellow, a form of dual personality. This is best exemplified by a desire to be seen and noticed at concerts, including a preference for skin-tight trousers and earrings. These sartorial lapses are balanced by an obsession concerning personal privacy that extends to masking his past and refusing virtually all requests for interviews, including one for this book.

His past is veiled in secrecy. Particularly those undocumented years between his purported work on the first New York Dolls album in 1973, assisting producer Todd Rundgren and engineer Ed Sprigg, and the first Police album in 1978. By his own account the previous year his permanent accommodation included a Chevrolet Impala parked in London's Soho Square. Some have confused him with Mark Norton, the sometime Kiss guitarist who has also used that same impressive surname.

During the 70s he drummed with the rock group England, a progressive band which included Frank Holland on guitar and keyboards and had a smattering of success in Europe. 'Complicated riffs and on-another-planet stuff. Extremely technically good', stated Dick Taylor. England rehearsed for years and apparently even signed a recording contract, but for some reason it all fell apart.

Years later he and Frank Holland would become partners in a Soho recording studio, which was purportedly financed to a greater degree by Holland who had been left a considerable sum by his father, a successful Brighton caravan park owner.

According to Tolson, St John asked the band how many hours it had taken them to record *Parachute*. Two hundred he was told, so on studio owner Nick Absom's behalf he contracted Freerange to fund the same number of hours for the intended new album. The sessions went very slowly with only five songs being finished. 'Goodbye Goodbye', 'Goin' Downhill', 'Wish Fulfilment', 'The Young Pretenders' and 'Sea About Me'.

The 1981 versions of 'Goodbye Goodbye' and 'Goin' Downhill' are markedly different from the end product which eventually received a release on the *Rage Before Beauty* CD in 1999. These two songs were remixed, overdubbed and Tolson's distinctive guitar was all but obliterated. Peter recalled that he laid down some of the keyboards on 'Goodbye Goodbye' because Jon Povey couldn't get the right feel. St John later observed that Povey was angry at Tolson's 'quiet asides' (guitar embellishments) on the track 'The Young Pretenders'. Clearly the mood was anything but amicable.

The relationship between Peter Tolson and Mark St John appears to have been mutual distrust from the outset. Peter, who maintains a great affinity with those he considers friends, is not the sort to warm instantly to any individual. St John, being a forceful character, is the antithesis of all that Peter holds dear. St John, for his part, also found Peter difficult to get close to although this did not detract from his appreciation of Tolson the musician. In the sleeve notes to the 1995 *Anthology* he described him thus. 'Tolson was arguably always the best electric guitar player of his time. Too difficult to ever be really accessible to the mainstream, he was a bolshie, hunted, violent, but sensitive man who pretty much reflected his personality in his playing.

When he was on form he was unstoppable, and when he was off form, he was still better than the opposition.'

The Freerange sessions were unorganised and ill-tempered. Tolson recounted that Phil was hitting the bottle with a worrying regularity and this is borne out by his strained vocals on the original session tapes.

Jon Povey recalled the strangeness of those days. 'We were very much into drugs and cocaine in particular and that's very personality changing. I was also going through a divorce and Wally had just met his girl, there were all sorts of things going on like that and it was all very highly charged. Really, there wasn't any foreseeable future at that point. It was just another recording session and we weren't rehearsing that much so it was kind of into the studio and see what comes out and I don't particularly like working like that. I'd rather rehearse first and then go in the studio but that's how it was, that's the reality of it. A couple of them worked nicely, I mean 'Going Downhill', 'Goodbye Goodbye', but some of the numbers didn't work well.'

During a short tour of Spain the tensions within the band began to bubble up. Peter and Gilly were going through a difficult period that eventually led to them parting. Wally was consumed by his relationship with Sarah whilst Phil kept very much to himself. Jon centred his attention on new love Rogie and became engaged in a violent confrontation with a waiter who he felt had disrespected her.

Jon's cocaine habit had started around the time of the *Freeway Madness* sessions when Phil and Peter introduced him to a particularly affecting brand. Jon is described by those who know him as having an obsessive personality and after this introduction he centred much of his attention on coke. Like Peter Tolson he was regularly spending £1,500 a week to fuel the habit.

Towards the end of summer it became unhinged. Peter and Gilly had another raging argument and he disappeared. Jon was busy in the studio laying down some Hammond organ overdubs and Rogie, as usual, was sitting in the control room watching and waiting. Phil who was also superfluous suggested that they pop out for a drink.

Rogie's absence was soon noticed and upon hearing that she had just left with Phil, an enraged Povey sped round the corner raced into the bar and proceeded to drag Phil out by his hair. During the mayhem windowpanes were broken and both were bleeding and somewhat beaten up. St John who had followed and attempted to break up the melee received a knee in the face and ended up with the protagonists down in the cells where they were kept until the morning. St John confirmed that everyone was 'Very pissed off'.

St John didn't see Phil again for well over two years, Peter for six years and Jon and Wally for nearly fourteen years.

Dick explained the aftermath. 'I was a bit puzzled as to what was going on because we went to this little studio in Twickenham and I was unaware that Phil and Jon had had such a major punch-up. We did this stuff just mixing and mastering or whatever, in this funny little place and we went and did some tape copies I was chatting to Mark and he said Phil just went, just disappeared, and really I was just waiting for the next thing to happen.'

This was not quite the end for the band. Not yet. Dick: 'The next thing to happen was Phil called me and we did a German tour and I think that really made Pete feel very disillusioned because we did quite well. We did some dates in Joe's Bierhaus in Berlin and some other places. We were working somewhere in the South of Germany when the promoter heard over the telephone that his child who was very, very sick with cerebral palsy, had died. Povey and Pete went to the airport with him, he had a big bag of money and all the receipts for the tour. They said 'Sort the money out later, you're in no position to do it now', and that was it. He disappeared, he went off with his bag of money never to be seen again. He surfaced again marrying some rich woman in England and now lives being an artist or something. I remember Pete being really pissed off, I mean we were all pissed off about this money disappearing and that also had quite a bit to do with the thing folding up.

This unsavoury experience caused Wally to rethink his position. 'I thought, I don't want to be in this business.' This, rather than the Freerange fisticuffs, is where it all fell apart. Wally and Peter drifted away and it just petered out. The German tour still haunts Tolson who expressed a desire to find Richard the promoter and 'Rip him apart'. Dick believes that Phil eventually got some money out of the fellow but the episode left a vile taste in everybody's mouth.

Phil's memory of the band fraying is distinctly different. 'Dick, our producer Mark St John and I sat down soon after we began working in the studio and we all agreed that we were facing too many business problems to carry on as we were.' St John's assertion that he sat for days waiting for them to turn up, and that they never did, has a more realistic ring to it.

Talking to Terry Coates in March 1993, Phil placed the split into context. 'Everybody just had a mental breakdown. Peter snapped, Povey went completely divvy and walked out of the studio.'

Whilst these escapades were unfolding *The Monster Club* film was released as was the soundtrack on the Chips label.

Wally kept alert by making another album for De Wolfe whilst Peter Tolson rejoined Jack Green for album and touring duties. Jon Povey turned his back on music, retreating to his Battersea home with Rogie. Phil and Dick also kept their heads below the parapets for a while. Shortly after this Freerange Studios went bust and St John joined the 3 million unemployed.

CHAPTER 15 – The Bleak Years

The years 1982 through to 1994 saw an end to the band in all but name. The legacy was kept alive with intermittent activities using the Phil, Dick plus extras format. The Pretty Things name still counted for something in Europe and this is where they were forced to concentrate.

The 1980s proved a graveyard for musical expression and ideas. Strange tangential varieties of the punk explosion gained a foothold, such as the dreary new romantic brigade. Whilst the public suffered under the quadruple onslaught of rising inflation, rising unemployment, volatile interest rates and a consistent right-wing monetarist economic policy the individual Pretty Things took refuge in whatever shelters they could locate.

Wally busied himself with another album project for De Wolfe, entitled, *I Don't Feel Well*. The album was credited to the Charlie Flake Band and Wally confided that Peter Tolson had suggested the name, a by-word for coke. For this recording Wally opted for a rhythm section of himself on bass and Chico Greenwood on drums. Tolson supplied the classy guitarwork that he and Wally believe ranks with his best ever work.

In a positively bizarre move De Wolfe determined that Wally's vocals weren't groovy or hip enough and elected to replace them with those of a younger sounding vocalist. 'They wanted somebody who sounded more like Gary Numan or someone like that. There was a young kid there and the actual tracks on the album are not me singing.'

The album recalled *Parachute* with its evocative Beatle-like melodies and again illustrated the formidable strength of Wally the songsmith. Like Jack Green, Wally is not a committed bass player and his occasional forays on the acoustic, twelve string or rhythm guitar betray his real preferences.

By now Jon Povey had settled into a more normal family life. Married to Rogie and living in Battersea he found work as a Showroom Manager in the bathroom industry, a position he still holds today.

Peter Tolson toured North America on a couple of occasions with Jack Green's Band and contributed typically superb guitar to Jack's next two albums, *Reverse Logic* and *Mystique*. 'Well, I got a gold album for *Humanesque*,' explained Jack. 'I think *Reverse Logic* also went gold and then I did another one, *Mystique* and then another one, *Latest Game*. They were all big hits in Canada. That's where my main market was so that was where we really concentrated. In the UK, *Mystique* got to number one in the import charts, *Humanesque* got to number two in the import charts and they did really well considering what they sounded like.'

Late in 1983, Peter's disaffection with the music business finally curdled. Jack Green explained the circumstances. 'I don't know the reason why but I do know how it happened. I had written a couple of songs for Roger Daltrey and he wanted them done the way I did them so he wanted to use the same musicians that were on my tracks. I got Pete in to play guitar and we were in the control booth waiting for him to set up and get a sound. We were all talking and we looked out there and he's packing his guitar away… and this is a Daltrey session! I said what are you doing? And he said, 'Oh that's it man, I'm finished,' and I said, 'Wait, hold on a second what do you mean?' He said, 'Well I'm fed up, I don't want to do it anymore.' I said 'What don't you want to do?' He replied, 'I just don't want to be in it anymore.' That was it, he stopped. This was unbelievable. He was a cracking guitarist, he was one of the best. It broke my heart when he stopped playing. To me he really was the best, he was better than any of them.'

Peter recalled the demo session clearly. 'That was the day I decided I'd had enough. I was seeing things that should have gone one way go another way again. I was pleased for Jack that Daltrey was covering his material. But I was getting really close to the edge there, there's much more to life than this. I'm all or nothing, and if I can't get myself right in there… that's what I said when I went back (to the Pretties in 1994). I'm not part of the Phil and Dick show.' Peter also expressed a sincere dislike for Daltrey and this may well have been the final straw.

Jack's song, 'Walking In My Sleep', written by him and poet friend Les Adey, was eventually issued by Daltrey as a single in February 1984 and from the *Parting Should Be Painless* album.

Jack went on to make a fourth album, which he described to me amidst much self-deprecating laughter. 'The last one was quite good, *The Latest Game* it was called, I brought together Simon Kirke and Boz Burrell who hadn't played together for ten years. I used them on drums and bass. I got every star I could muster. Snowy White on guitar, Jim Capaldi on percussion, Kelly Groucutt from ELO on bass on some tracks and it sounded like… shit.'

After this Jack decided to retire from the business and with wife Jackie moved to Ibiza to a large and impressive property where he worked as an RCA house writer, collaborating with others such as Nicky Chinn and Jim Diamond. 'It wasn't I had had enough, I was writing. I was doing quite a lot for a publisher, I was writing my songs every year and picking up quite a large advance. Basically, everyone I knew was in the music business and it was just getting so unbelievably boring. I'd never met anybody from any other form of work and when I went out to Spain I met other people who were interesting and I learnt to relax.'

By the early 1990's the Green's were running out of money so they put the house on the market. Jack took to solo gigging in pubs and clubs in Ibiza and Tenerife. When the house was finally sold they returned to the UK focusing on the South Coast because Jackie came from Portsmouth. A trip to the Isle of Wight persuaded them to settle there where by chance both Dick Taylor and Marc Bolan's ex-personal manager, Mick O'Halloran, were also living.

1981 witnessed the media circus event that passed as the wedding of Prince Charles Windsor and Lady Diana Spencer. In attendance at Westminster Abbey was Charles' childhood friend Electra and her husband Phillip May. Who could have imagined, back in 1964, that the 'mouthy kid who loved tennis' and sneered at his Belgravia neighbours would turn up as a guest at a Royal Wedding?

Apart from Jack Green, all of the ex-Pretty Things kept low profiles through the early 1980s although December 1982 saw a rare Phil May outing when he guested on 'Big Boss Man' on the Blues Band's 'farewell' concert recorded for the *Bye Bye Blues* album.

Rock journalist Alan Clayson reported that 'On any Tuesday evening throughout 1984, you could have seen The Pretty Things for 50p in the function rooms of a Little Venice hostelry.' Of course, this was only Phil and Dick fronting a loose ensemble of friends.

Dick: '(They started) most definitely before that. I think it was '82 or '83. By that time it had got seriously like a band calling itself The Pretty Things and going off to do things in Ibiza and in Majorca again for that terrible Richard person.'

As Dick suggested, at this stage it seemed that any collection of individuals fronted by Phil May was being passed off as 'The Pretty Things' and whilst offering excellent value and plenty of fodder for sentimentalists and R&B fans in general it clearly was not *The* Pretty Things. Never, throughout the previous twenty years, had they been content to settle back on their laurels and milk the name or reputation like many of their fellow 60s and 70s survivors. No cabaret circuits like The Hollies or The Rockin' Berries, no nostalgia circuses like The Bay City Rollers and The Searchers. The Pretty Things had always been at the cutting edge, always searching for more, never content to rest on reputation and past success but striving always to create. It is abundantly clear that they do it for the love of the music, the expectation and creation, not the money. The mid to late 1980s saw this creativity temporarily stymied due to volatile line-ups and an inability to build a base and plan ahead.

Years later in an interview with *Channel 4 Teletext* Phil expounded on this ambition. 'The band's continually been at the sharp movements. It's important for any band to progress, not stick with a formula. It would drive me bonkers, I wouldn't even do it for the money. Unless you get some kind of self-stimulation, there's no point, so you have to evolve.'

Whilst recording *Cross Talk*, Dick had met up with Tom Greenhalgh from the Leeds based band The Mekons and Tom invited him to play a gig with them. He recalled it was good fun but also weird because they used a drum machine, which John Langford programmed. Dick played with them on and off for the next ten years, recording a number of albums and three radio sessions. He also contributed guitar to an album by Tom Newman, sessions which also involved Newman's good friend Mike Oldfield as well as Joe Shaw, Dave Gilmour, Steve Broughton, Snowy White and the Blues Band's Paul Jones. Ultimately the studio impounded the tapes because session fees remained unpaid and the recordings have yet to be released.

As Alan Clayson stated, early in 1983 The Bridge House pub in Little Venice, North London became a base for regular Tuesday night music sessions run by Phil. He used an upstairs room where a small bar was also sited. Effectively a jam session, friends and acquaintances would turn up and perform standards and old Pretties R&B numbers.

Phil also had an opportunity to resurrect his former acting ambitions when he appeared on hit TV show *Minder*, playing rock star Zac Zolar. The Fallen Angels song, 'Take Me Home', was used in the programme and as a result Butt Records issued a single, 'Take Me Home/James Marshall' and credited it to Zac Zolar and the Electric Banana. Both songs had previously been issued on the final De Wolfe album, *Return of the Electric Banana*.

Phil continued gigging with a 'Pretty Things' line up that included former Doll By Doll guitarist Joe Shaw. A new single was announced, 'One of the Survivors', and although it was never released it did appear on the Austrian bootleg, *Live at the Insel*.

It was during 1984 that Mark St John journeyed to Phil's place in Talbot Road and returned the tapes that comprised the 1981 Freerange sessions. 'Three years to the day, as per the contract,' he explained. Apparently Phil was busy and was indifferent to him. He did not have time to talk. Greatly pissed off, St John stalked away, having had a gutfull of the band. He would not reappear in The Pretty Things story for another three years.

Later that year, at the suggestion of friend and ex-Atlantic Records boss Phil Carson, Phil decided to cut a live album using many of the friends and regulars who played at The Bridge House. The album was recorded at The Heartbreak Hotel and consisted of standards such as 'Mona', 'Big Boss Man' and 'Shakin' All Over' plus some early Pretty Things material. He wasn't overjoyed with the results, particularly singling out John Clark's drumming as being too stiff. He recalled everybody being conscious that they had only one shot at it and consequently being uptight.

The same band played Frankfurt in late 1984 and the concert was taped and bootlegged as *Fun Tango*, a double album on the Italian Metropol label. The dual guitar line up of Shaw and Taylor seemed to be dominated by Shaw who took the majority of the leads. The itinerary included several songs not normally associated with the Pretties such as 'In The Midnight Hour' and 'Gimme Some Loving'.

Full circle then for Phil who in 1966 complained that the fans only wanted soul music. He asserted that although he didn't know what he wanted to sing he knew that it wasn't soul. 'In The Midnight Hour' was Wilson Pickett's big Atlantic hit from that same period, the very antithesis of the music that Phil preferred.

During 1985 this same line-up also played in Poland but a degree of internal strife was brewing, as Dick explained. 'It was all starting to get a bit funny with personalities in the band and Phil. At that point Rudi came along and said, 'Look, you can work. Without putting a fine point on it you and Phil are the important thing here. It doesn't matter who else is with you because the other people aren't authentic guys who people want to see from either the old days or the psychedelic band, they are just people basically who you are with.' Really, he said, what you should do is start a thing where Phil and me are the main characters and the others are just adjuncts to us.'

Phil and Dick met up with musicians Bertram Engel and Roelf ter Veld. 'We did a few gigs in Holland with that line up and eventually Bertie couldn't do it and Roelf's brother played drums and that turned into the Dutch line up and eventually Hans Waterman, came in and played drums.'

The next few years saw Phil and Dick based in Holland where they operated what Dick called 'The Pretty Things Project'.

In July of 1987 Phil and Dick agreed to travel to Munster, Germany to record an album at the Jovel-Tonstudio using a two-track digital recorder. This meant that the recordings couldn't be mixed and it afforded a freshness to the exercise as it became essentially a live album. Jo Shaw was again on guitar with Roelf Ter Veld on bass and Bertram Engel on drums. Although he was no longer a band member Engel had been specifically requested by the German record company so Roelf's brother reluctantly stepped down. By all accounts Steffi Stephan, a top German session bass player and owner of the studio, insisted on being involved and he took the place of Roelf on 'Well Known Blues' and also shook a tambourine on 'You Don't Believe Me'.

The resulting album, *Out Of The Island*, has received scant praise possibly because a number of Pretties classics are re-worked, but the versions actually worked extremely well in the context of a band having fun. The real delight can be found in the three new songs unveiled. 'Can't Stop', credited to May/Engel, was a typical Phil May song, jerky rhythm, adult lyrics and sustaining chorus. 'Cause And Effect', a May solo effort, echoed the 1966 Pretties with harsh almost guttural vocals. Phil's voice displayed a strangely pleasing, empathetic hoarseness which is at one with the tune and arrangement. As often seen with ageing bluesmen like James Cotton, Phil's voice had weathered into an instrument harsh, husky and occasionally sibilant. The third original, 'Well Known Blues,' was a group composition using standard blues chords and served as a back-drop for some fine Taylor/Shaw blues-guitar wailing.

The album received a German release in June 1988 on the Inak label but, as with virtually every phase of their career, another wheel came off the wagon just as it approached the fort. Dick Taylor explained, 'It was supposed to be called *Off The Island*, which is quite amusing, because I asked John Langford out of the Mekons to do a cover and I gave him the specification of what it was. For some reason he managed to translate *Off The Island* into *Out Of The Island*. Anyway, I sent off the thing and I liked the cover, he does funny things with photocopiers, which that is. He sent it straight to the record company and I only saw it after it had been approved. I said hold on, it all looks very well but it's actually the wrong title, they went 'Sorry…we didn't notice.' Most peculiar, we had referred to the title as *Off The Island*, we had discussed the title with the record company, it just shows how easy it is for things to get through.'

Rudi now introduced Phil and Dick to Robbie Acterr who assumed the function of tour manager. Acterr also took on the role of booking agent and they became very busy in Holland as well as touring France and various European cities. 'Rudi disappeared up a bag of coke or something,' explained Dick. 'Rudi was a remarkable character, you could make a film about Rudi cause he was a complete caricature of a loony Dutchman.'

Throughout the late '80s Dick became extensively involved with The Mekons and fitted in Pretties gigs whenever they arose. After Jo Shaw left to pursue his own ambitions, an American, Perry Alexander, was drafted in to provide support guitar. 'We never used to rehearse,' explained Dick, 'we did a couple of rehearsals but they never seemed to come to much.'

Perry's involvement had a further consequence. His guitar was an ESP Electro and Dick was most impressed by its ease and the fact that it stayed in tune longer than most others. Dick decided to switch from his regular Gibson and to this day continues to favour the make.

It was at this juncture that Mark St John reappeared, as swiftly as he had disappeared. It seems he was entertaining a blonde object of passion (on his birthday in the latter half of 1987, according to his submission in *Ugly Things*, or in 1988 at Break For The Border, as he proffered in the *Anthology* notes). His carefully planned evening was devastated by a seriously drunken

Phil May who staggered up, ruining the liaison, and chattering away as if the Freerange sessions had been just the other week. The not-so-surprising outcome of this casual re-acquaintance was a second meeting the next day during which it was agreed that Phil and Dick would record an album at St John's new studio at Wardour Street.

The capacity for attempting any valid chronological account of the Pretties history is doomed by the contrasting recollections of the participants and their manager. Over the following three years a number of new songs were committed to tape. Quite who produced and played on these is a matter of conjecture as are the dates and details.

Mark St John advised the *13 Chester Street* fanzine readers that during March 1987 a number of new songs were recorded, six of these have since been released – 'Not Givin' In', 'Eve of Destruction', 'Play With Fire', 'Love Keeps Hanging On', 'Passion of Love' and 'Mony Mony'. This time frame contradicts both of his previous assertions and is clearly wrong. Bass player Steve Browning, who played on 'Love Keeps Hanging On', stated that this was the first song he played on and that it was in 1989.

At one stage Phil and St John entertained the notion of reforming the original Pretty Things' line up, a difficult task, given John Stax's Australian domicile. They started with Viv Prince and journeyed to Devon where Viv was living amongst the fishermen. Since leaving the Things Viv had bounced from one venture to another. Joining the Hells Angels he became, allegedly, the only person in the Angels' history to be ejected for bad behaviour. He ran a building firm, engaged in painting and decorating and had his own night-club. Various musical projects foundered, such as temporary membership of the Jeff Beck Band and the unsuccessful single, 'Light of the Charge Brigade'. St John explained that Viv couldn't even play the 'toy drum set' he had and kept falling off his stool, embarrassed and embarrassing, but laughing nonetheless. The idea of a reformation suddenly seemed less appealing.

Phil and Dick began recording in the studio with producer Denny Bridges as St John related to *Ugly Things* readers, 'We got almost a whole album done in a few months in '87 and '88. I wasn't producing; that was being done by a guy who engineered in the studio called Denny Bridges. He was working with this pick-up "Cloggies" band and he was just running down through the bands' songbook. I was hardly involved at all.'

American Bridges had previously worked with Joe Cocker and Alex Harvey and later became involved with Annie Haslam's Renaissance. St John maintained he was steering clear of too much close contact having been 'dumped on' before. Rather disagreeably he commented that the group contained various 'bolt-ons' and 'idiots'. 'I fucking hated that band and line-up,' he seethed. Possible 'bolt-ons' and 'idiots' include Joe Shaw, the ter Veld brothers, Bertram Engel, and other well-respected musicians.

A number of sources have also listed Glen Matlock as interacting with the band around this time but this interesting possibility was put to death by Glen himself, 'I only played with The Pretty Things for a laugh one night at Dave Gilmour's gaff many moons ago.'

Did they record at Soho with St John before the Denny Bridges sessions? Definitely not, so did the Denny Bridges recordings occur in 1987 or were the sessions at the tail of 1988? If we believe St John's account of events, as opposed to the conflicting dates, it would seem likely that late 1987 through early 1988 saw the Denny Bridges recordings this would also endorse St John's earlier stories about reuniting with Phil in 1987/88. Bridges own diary shows that he finished working at The Basement in April 1988.

Denny Bridges remembered events somewhat differently to Mark. Like Dick Taylor he is adamant that St John drummed on all the tracks. Whilst St John claimed almost a whole album was recorded Denny recollected only four songs being completed – 'The Young Pretenders', 'Can't Stop', 'That Face' and 'Play With Fire', although he concedes that a few run-throughs and backing tracks may have been attempted. Denny also recalled that his then girlfriend, Dashiell Rae, added various piano and organ parts and that Frank Holland played some guitar.

The four tracks completed were new to the band and certainly didn't form part of the Euro-Pretties live set.

'The Young Pretenders' was a completely different version to that recorded at Freerange in 1981 although it was the Freerange version that eventually received a release as a bonus track on *Cross Talk* in 2000. Similarly, 'Play With Fire' is not the version released on *Rage Before Beauty*, although it did form the template for the later release. 'Can't Stop' had already been recorded as part of the *Out Of The Island* album and the Bridges sessions allowed another stab at it, although Dick felt that his guitar had a dated '80s sound.

Dick couldn't recall Denny too well, neither could he recall Dashiell Rae, but he vaguely remembered that Denny's version of 'The Young Pretenders' didn't work too well, particularly the middle eight. St John insisted that members of The Ramones, Aerosmith, Paul McCartney Band, Procol Harum and some former Yardbirds were also turning up saying, 'it was generally London's longest running free party. I was watching all this shit going down from a floor or two up and I wasn't getting the feeling that anything real was taking place.' He says he listened to the tapes and they were, 'Total shit. It sounded like nothing: too produced, no 'Pretties' vibe, no attitude and worst of all, no fucking balls.'

Denny found St John's views 'incomprehensible' and recalled that the tracks sounded, 'absolutely fantastic… every track is as clear as a bell and the individual sounds, sound huge. The mixes are dynamic and also three-dimensional. Mark should be happy that his drums sound so gigantic yet so real'. Denny remains sorry that the public has never had an opportunity to hear them. 'I'm not ashamed of this work, no way. I am sorry for those who aren't or weren't able to get it. I have been accused of being too subtle for my own good, but what the hell.' The 'longest running free party?' 'I certainly would have remembered the Aerosmith guys as I got to know them when they were at Air Studios in, say 1977,' continued Denny. 'I don't recall any horrendous long sessions and/or late nights/early mornings. All very civilised. The sessions were in 'down time' but there was plenty of that at The Basement in those days.'

At this stage the Pretties did not have a record contract, neither did they have a manager. There hadn't been any formal arrangement since the Judy Knight days. St John was renting office space to Shannon O'Shea, an American who was managing record producers, including Jimmy Miller. As a result of their regular studio proximity Phil, Dick and Shannon became friends and as a result of St John's persistence she agreed a deal whereby she would receive free office space and commission on the band if she took over as their manager. This offered Shannon a doorway into artiste management. 'I had no direct experience with managing bands, so it was an opportunity to diversify my professional palate. I have Mark to thank for practically forcing the issue with me, and giving me the experience that afforded future opportunities.'

Shannon's recollection of that nebulous period adds yet another twist, she remembered a studio line up of Phil & Dick, St John on drums, Frank Holland on guitar and Steve Browning on bass. She also believed that St John and Bridges actually co-produced the sessions.

It was late 1988, Shannon began looking into the band's contracts with Phonogram and EMI and entered into unproductive dialogue with both organisations. Matters reached a stalemate and it became clear that only legal action would force the issue.

After the 'unacceptable' Denny Bridges recordings St John was provided with a route forward when Phil's long time friend Dave Gilmour asked Phil and Dick to play as The Pretty Things at August's Wembley homecoming gigs on the Pink Floyd's *Momentary Lapse of Reason* world tour. With the band presumably free of 'bolt-ons' and 'idiots', Phil suggested to St John that he should play the drums. To complete the 'new and improved Pretty Things' they drew on two other studio guys – Frank Holland on second guitar and Steve Browning on bass. Browning had been seen by St John when playing near Brighton in the Desperate Dan Band, whose leader Rob Brookes was a friend of Frank Holland's from way back. Some time later St John persuaded Browning to become a studio session man and Browning left the Desperate Dan Band.

St John claimed that this line-up appeared more successful than the previous bands and as a result called a meeting of interested parties to announce that the 'new album' would be scrapped. 'It was a piece of crap and wasn't fit to hear.' He said that Dick tried to make out a case for the band members he had been working with but Phil agreed with St John and wanted to know where they went from there.

Dick was suitably diplomatic about defending his friends, 'I think it's not something I would get in to conflict with Mark about because it was something that wasn't going to continue.' Dick did feel that the previous members were important to the band. 'In some ways it did us very good stead because we continued to work through the '80s and into the start of the '90s whereas we wouldn't have worked were it not for those people.'

St John's overall recollection of events is at odds with Denny Bridges and on occasions Dick Taylor's and again it can be seen that dodgy memories contrive to place question marks over the chronology and the reality. Denny has retained a cassette of the sessions and his memory is unclouded.

Shannon O'Shea felt the post-Denny recordings were 'sonically dated' but 'good if you like The Pretty Things.' A number of labels were interested in the band but 'they were not prepared to pay the kind of money that Mark was asking,' she advised.

Although Steve Browning played the occasional gig with the band it was made clear that although he would be used for studio work they would continue with previous adjunct, Roelf ter Veld, for the live gigs.

St John concluded that up to £60,000 had been used, in fact wasted, on the recordings thus far and that he himself would produce a Pretty Things album using the Floyd concert line-up. The Floyd concert was in August 1988 and the chronology now seems to be settling into place. Early 1988 saw the Denny Bridges sessions, and the first St John recordings took place in the winter of 1988 and spring of 1989 when two 'key tracks' as St John described them were first committed to tape.

The Ronnie Lane Mobile Studio was sited at St John and Frank Holland's country house at Mayfield, Sussex, and the new improved Pretty Things laid down the basic tracks for 'God Give Me Strength To Carry On' and 'Pure Cold Stone'. Phil's relationship with wife Electra was falling apart around this time and he was bedding down at 'various low-life locations' with old friend Jack Daniels and his mates.

The recordings developed into a set formula, pretty much carried on to this day, whereby backing tracks would be cut using Phil, Mark and Frank

Holland and, if he was available from his van driving job, Dick. By this time Dick was finding it difficult to manage his day job and be alert enough to concentrate on the recording sessions.

Stuck on the M25 one day with his Acton property about to be repossessed he decided that he didn't want to live in London anymore. His mother had moved from her cottage on the Isle of Wight and moved in with Dick's sister in Leeds and after discussing matters with wife Michelle it was decided they would move down to his mother's cottage.

The event provided yet another chapter for the Pretties' big bumper book of adversity. The cottage, which was picturesquely situated at the top of a cliff, was declared structurally unsound. Not long afterwards it collapsed into the sea!

In October 1989 'Eve Of Destruction' would appear on a twelve inch maxi-single. Previously a 1965 hit for Barry McGuire, this PF Sloan penned anti-war hit was joined with 'Can't Stop', the May/Taylor song previously released on *Out Of The Island* and 'Goin' Downhill' a May/Tolson song written and recorded at the troubled 1981 Freerange sessions. This version of the Pretties comprised Phil and Dick, Mark St John on drums, Frank Holland on guitar, Steve Browning on bass and Bobby Webb on keyboards. A seven inch version was also released. The maxi-single showed May/Taylor as co-writers of 'Goin' Downhill', and when he discovered this some years later, Tolson was disgusted. It served to confirm his opinion of the fundamental corruption within the industry.

Out of the blue Peter Tolson was contacted. Could he travel down to the precisely draped basement that comprised St John's Wardour Street Studio? Again working on the remains of the Freerange material it had been decided that a new middle-eight was needed for 'The Young Pretenders'. Pete turned up one evening to do his thing with Phil, St John and Frank Holland around to greet him. This new middle eight was never used and when 'The Young Pretenders' eventually emerged as a bonus track on the reissued *Cross Talk,* it was in the form of the original 1981 version.

Thus began the first concerted effort to market The Pretty Things since the 1980 *Cross Talk* deal. In addition to the two singles an 'Eve Of Destruction' video was produced by Vivid Productions, although this has never been shown in the UK. Another version of 'Play With Fire' was also started at this time.

In September, just before the singles release, *The Sun* newspaper ran an article headed 'The Pretty Things are back... and looking pretty terrible.' Dick was understandably irritated, having provided *The Sun* with a selection of photographs they had chosen the 'Very worst one'. They should by now have been wise to the foulness of Fleet Street, or in this instance the wickedness of Wapping. Phil was philosophical, 'That's what happens when you get into bed with these people. If you get into bed with a nasty woman the chances are you are more likely to catch something. When you deal with newspapers like *The Sun*, the chances are that you will definitely catch something. *The Sun* is a slaggish newspaper. I doubt if they would ever be interested in writing a decent article. It did get the main point across so really we wasn't that worried about it.'

The Sun advised, incorrectly as events played out, that the band would be supporting the Stones during a 1990 UK tour. The Pretties had never played on the same bill as the Stones and this unlikely eventuality has remained a non-starter.

It was during this period, as St John tells it, that Phil and Dick began touring Europe with a band that he hated and which 'Stunk the fucking place out.' It was also around this time that Ronnie Spector was invited to duet with Phil on a version of the Tommy James & The Shondells number one hit, 'Mony Mony'. In describing the event St John reverted to the affectations of his youth and gushed, 'I am the world's biggest Phil Spector fan.' He has also alluded to being the number one Pretty Things fan and number one Peter Grant fan. Definitely a big, big fan. No argument.

The 'Mony Mony' sessions didn't work out as planned. Phil's original vocals were trashed because he didn't know the words, such as they were, and Spector's piece was laid down a whole year later. Only Frank Holland played guitar on this track as Dick was otherwise engaged.

Whilst the sessions held out promise for the future they were not bringing in any money and Phil kept busy looking for gigs to boost his income. He began issuing 'gig samples' cassettes highlighting Pretties material. These poor quality tapings, on St John's Basement Studio cassettes, contained the 'Eve of Destruction' single and two previously unheard songs, 'Not Givin' In' and 'Passion of Love', both of which would eventually emerge, with different mixes, on *the Rage Before Beauty* CD in 1999. Also on the cassette were versions of 'She's Fine She's Mine', 'Loneliest Person/L.S.D' and 'Havana Bound' from the *Out Of The Island* album. Three tracks from *Cross Talk* plus that excellent B-side 'Cold Stone' concluded the tape.

Rudimentary plans had been made for St John's Basement Studio to operate its own record label but these foundered, possibly due to cash-flow restrictions.

Phil and Dick now became involved in one of those 'dodgy extra-curricular activities' as St John politely described them, or 'various bullshit; fucked up little side deals to make various no-brain records, which continue to haunt them to this day' as he more offensively put it. The British Invasion All-Stars, an aggregation combining former members of The Yardbirds, Creation, Downliners Sect, Nashville Teens and Procol Harum were preparing to record their second CD at RMS Studios. Phil and Dick, as well as ex-Pirate Mick Green were invited to guest on some tracks. Phil provided the vocals for four of the thirteen tracks, 'Shakin' All Over', 'Shapes of Things', 'I Can Tell' and 'Promised Land', whilst Dick played guitar on six different numbers.

Released in 1991 on the Promised Land label, the album, *United*, was available by mail order or from specialist outlets. This was definitely a collector's only issue. The songs with Phil singing definitely benefited from his voice, which had improved with age and displayed a sympathetic and subtle phrasing. The other tracks were eminently forgettable sounding like a sub-species of the bland formulaic fodder that Rainbow, Whitesnake and Bon Jovi all contrived careers out of.

Fontana decided it was an appropriate time to re-issue the first two Pretty Things releases as CD singles – 'Rosalyn' and 'Don't Bring Me Down', each with their original b-sides.

Twink resurfaced in April 1990 when a new solo album, *Mr Rainbow*, was released on the Twink label. Forsaking the drum-kit for the microphone he reprised various songs from his days of yore including, from *SF Sorrow*, 'Baron Saturday' and 'Balloon Burning'. Twink also chose to include the abominable 'Three Jolly Little Dwarfs'. 'It's a comic rock 'n' roll masterpiece,' he declared, but few were listening and those that did probably regretted it. In the early 90s Twink became involved with The Bevis Frond whose motive force Nick Saloman was a great fan of the Pretties. Nick even named a track, 'Cries **From** The Inner Marshland', in deference to *Parachute's* 'Cries From The Midnight Circus'.

Plans were made for a European tour as Nick related. 'For our next European jaunt we were going to employ the services of ex-Pretty Things/Pink Fairies drum legend, Twink, otherwise known as John C Alder. However, shortly before leaving for Copenhagen, he began to show worrying portents of what may well have been to come. An insistence on a months supply of bottled water (in case he got spiked), and a private bathroom at every gig caused us sufficient anxiety to enquire whether or not he was really that keen on going. With a couple of days to spare, we replaced him with Ric Gunther.'

Nick Saloman declared that Twink was actually 'Charming and great fun' and that he very much enjoyed working with him. He considered him a really good drummer and felt that his legendary status as a difficult person probably related only to the financial aspects of his career. Like many who partied long and hard in the 60s Twink seems to reflect the consequences of those chemical excesses but is clearly a survivor.

Shannon O'Shea faded from the scene during the latter half of 1990 and five years later would successfully rebase herself and her management company Shannon O'Shea Management in Los Angeles. Throughout this period St John says he was increasingly involving himself in the legal situation with the record companies, something he did during the day whilst concentrating on the new album by night.

'I don't think she actually did get very much done for us,' stated Dick. 'I'm not sure if she was the right person for the job but I liked her, she was fine. It didn't work out.'

The nature of St John, his interest in, and friendship with the band, was always likely to cause difficulties for any manager as Shannon found out. 'Mark and I had creative and strategic differences of opinion. He had also insisted that I pay for some production costs amongst other things, which was placing me increasingly in debt. I was too naive to realise that this was not part of my responsibility. As time went on. I realised that I might not get repaid unless I took control of the band's strategy and did things differently. Mark and I both had strong personalities and clashed at this point, but I will say we both had the band's best interests at heart. Mark was a passionate and unorthodox character. He had a big heart, but he was difficult for me to work with as he had control issues.'

St Georges Records is a US based blues label owned by George Paulus. Back in 1990 it boasted Andre Williams, Tail Dragger and Little Mack Simmons amongst its roster of artists. In September 1990 George met with Jim McCarty, drummer with the seminal British blues band The Yardbirds, and talked up a recording deal stateside. A few days later George telephoned Phil May and over a couple of drinks they agreed a series of sessions in downtown Chicago with McCarty, Dick Taylor and a host of St Georges label artists.

January 1991 found the four of them ensconced in the Seagrape Recording Studio, Chicago with a band line-up that included local blues veteran, Studebaker John. The assembled clan ran through a covey of blues/R&B standards – Bo Diddley, Willie Dixon, Jimmy Reed, etc. The sessions were spread over eight days and Dick, in particular, was most pleased with the results. It must be every bluesman's dream to record authentic R&B on the West Side where such icons as Muddy Waters and Howlin' Wolf recorded some of their most enduring material.

The *Chicago Blues Tapes 1991* album by The Pretty Things/Yardbirds Blues Band was issued in the UK on Demon records in December 1991 and received a lukewarm response particularly from blues historian Neil Slaven. Writing in *Vox* magazine he suggested, 'The need to recreate stifles what new life might have been breathed into the originals.' In truth he had a point as the 'Fifteen blues chestnuts' as he called them, hardly broke any new ground which is a definite departure for Phil and Dick. Pleasant though it is, the album merely highlighted how excellent the original recordings were and how difficult it is for any artist to successfully take a fresh look at such dependables.

Another release of interest to Pretty Things fans was *Before The Fall – The Peel Sessions*. This 1992 album of BBC sessions on the Strange Fruit label included a May 64 version of 'Rosalyn' which was the earliest track amongst a throng of legends such as Hendrix, Free, Queen and T-Rex. For trainspotters this represented the earliest known live recording of the band, preceding the release of their debut single by a month.

There were further sessions at Seagrape over the following eighteen months and in 1993 another Pretties/Yardbirds collaboration appeared. The album entitled *Wine, Women & Whiskey* was a mix of standards and originals that covered little new ground. Dick also assisted on albums by two other St Georges acts – Andre Williams and The Eldorados. 'We can't really do The Pretty Things/Yardbirds Blues Band any more, but it was a kind of interesting little project to do,' explained Dick.

'There's still some stuff in the can,' advised Dick. 'Some of which, actually, is rather good so I don't know what will eventually happen. I know that George has been in contact with Mark, maybe some of that stuff can be dug out at some point. I know the thing we don't want to do is put out a rag bag of 'oh, this is what's left', but it might be nice to combine some of the side projects together.' One of the tracks hanging around is 'Art School Blues', which would be a temporary staple of the 1993-95 live act.

In early 1992 Phil decided to place the Pretty Things and miscellaneous projects on hold and joined a seriously funded attempt to launch a new group, John Coughlan's Diesel. Structured around ex-Status Quo drummer Coughlan, the line up comprised Bob Young on harp and vocals, Ray Minhinnett guitars and vocals, Billy Briggs on keyboards, Pete Tolson's ex-Eire Apparent colleague Chrissie Stewart on bass and one Phillip May on vocals and acoustic guitar.

Between January and March a number of tracks were recorded at Tuff Studios in Gothenburg. Two of them emerged on a single, 'River of Tears', credited to May/Engel/Carlton and a rocking number called 'No Moon Shines' with the whole band receiving writing and production credits.

Around £150,000 was used in support of the group but, for various reasons, it failed to spark and subsided unrealised into failure. 'We did an album,' said Phil. 'A couple of singles and two videos and nothing has come out. It's not been released yet. It's the story of my life.'

At the same time Band of Joy, a label which specialised in licensing and releasing BBC archive recordings, contacted Phil regarding the Pretties extensive session history. Agreement was reached and Phil selected fifteen tracks showcasing the band's work from the mid sixties R&B period through to the *Freeway Madness* material from 1973. Missing from the resulting *On Air* CD was the 1968 to 1969 output featuring Twink. Phil explained that Twink wanted some degree of control and had the potential to cause contractual problems and delays. Rather than include material Twink had drummed on, Phil and Project Manager Clive Selwood, played safe and selected around them.

The album suffered a torrent of scornful reviews with one US retailer awarding it one star out of a possible five due to the disgraceful lack of information. Session dates were not provided, not even the year, and the credits proved nonsensical. They appeared to list the band members on each particular track although, equally, they could have been indicating the writers of each track. Either way they got it wrong, Skip had never co-written a song let alone the ten indicated, and the band members did not write Bo Diddley's 'Mama Keep Your Big Mouth Shut'. If the listings are intended to denote musicians then it appears that only Dickson (sic) & Smith played on 'Big Boss Man'. Band members surnames are used throughout apart from Wally Waller who is noted as Wally. In all a cheap looking job with a nasty cover that screamed out 'low budget' and denigrated the wealth of excellent music within.

It was another Pretty Things' own goal, because the album actually show-cased the band at its best, as the blazing versions of 'Cold Stone', 'Cries From The Midnight Circus' and 'Onion Soup' attest. These three songs are the turbo-charged live versions that had developed after the band had grown comfortable playing them and introduced various changes and improvements. As an album it was musically excellent and illustrated the various band incarnations over the ten year period. Unfortunately it was also a missed opportunity. Phil played safe and kept to the more well-known and previously recorded material. The CD represented a tremendous opportunity to include those live favourites like 'Slow Beginnings', 'Spider Woman' and 'Turn My Head'. The CD was less than 53 minutes long so there was ample room to fit these and other songs. Talking in 1995 to Terry Coates, Phil conceded that there was 'More than enough tracks for a second album', a point proven by the *Forgotten Beebs* bootleg that appeared on the Tendolar label. This patchy release contained seventeen tracks from the 1967-1974 period including five with Twink drumming. Also included were two tracks by Eire Apparent from an April 1969 broadcast, presumably due to the Peter Tolson connection. Unfortunately, Tolson did not join Eire Apparent until May 1969 and these two tracks actually showcased the guitarwork of Mick Cox.

The liner notes allowed Phil to provide a perspective of the BBC sessions. He explained that in the early days the band met stern-faced indifference, an attitude that altered when producers such as Bernie Andrews lavished time and effort on their later sessions.

Record Collector savaged the release. The knowledgeable Peter Doggett railed against the lack of information, the way that song titles had been altered ('Buzz the Jerks'!) and the unsympathetic artwork. As he said, 'A case of style over content. There comes a point where a badly executed archive product is worth less than no project at all; and this is that point.'

Regrouping after the Diesel false start Phil got together with Dick and Jim McCarty to form a Pretty Things/Yardbirds gigging band. Assisted by Dick's friend Barkley McKay on guitar and old friend Chrissie Stewart on bass they played a few low key gigs. Jim McCarty explained that none of them were busy and it offered an opportunity to make some money.

In September 1992 Phil and Dick became involved in yet another non-Pretties project. Record producer, Mike Ober, who had pioneered the British Invasion All-Stars albums, harboured a long-standing plan to record an album around ex-Procol Harum organist Matthew Fisher. The idea was to use members of rock band The Inmates as backing musicians. The project needed a lead singer and Mike approached Phil who agreed and suggested that Dick should be involved, something that Ober, a long-time Pretties fan, was more than happy to agree to.

The recording sessions took place at the E7 Studios, Forest Gate and were pretty much live with occasional guitar overdubs. Phil laid down some guide vocals, which then had to be recut at RMS Studios. Barklay McKay also surfaced during the sessions adding some guitar.

The resulting album *A Whiter Shade of Dirty Water* was released as by The Pretty Things 'n Mates on the Kingdom label, although it was quickly withdrawn when Mark St John objected to the use of 'The Pretty Things' moniker. The label refused to reissue it without The Pretty Things byline and curently it remains unavailable.

A Pretty Things night was held in November at the Scala Cinema, in the Pentonville Road, organised by Slim Chance who ran the St John's Tavern at Archway. It had been intended that the all-nighter would show the three Pretty Things films – the 1966 *Pretty Things On Film*, 1969's *What's Good For The Goose* and *The Monster Club* from 1980. The band, comprising Phil, Dick, Jim McCarty and Chrissie Stewart played and were supported by The Mystreated and Dog. As it turned out the *Pretty Things On Film* was unavailable and time did not permit *The Monster Club* to be shown.

At the tail-end of 1992 The Pretty Things 'new album' was virtually finished, and the band begun pursuing EMI and Phonogram for unpaid royalties, a sum that with compound interest was believed to run to six figures. Plans were drawn up yet again to reform the 'original Pretty Things.' With John Stax in Australia and Brian Pendleton still on the missing list these plans had to be adjusted somewhat and according to Dick, even ex-temporary Thing, Mitch Mitchell was considered. It came to nothing due to the logistical difficulties.

In March 1993 Phil and Dick met up with Skip, Wally and Jon Povey to discuss the band's claims against EMI. It was the first time the old band members had got together for over eleven years and it was at this meeting that the seeds of a future reunion were sown. Meanwhile, Dick was again involving himself in production, this time for an Amsterdam-based band called Built For Comfort.

Phil busied himself with a project of a different kind. By paying careful attention to the television adverts one would have heard a bon vivant May extolling the virtues of Insignia deodorant by singing to the tune of 'All Over Now', the Bobby Womack song made famous by the Stones.

June 1993 presented yet another Pretty Things line-up – Phil, Dick, Steve Browning, Hans Waterman and the added ingredient of Barklay McKay on guitar – undertaking a 9-date tour of Germany and Austria. The same line up toured Germany and Holland September during October and 'Art School Blues' was given its first live airing.

Prior to the tour Phil had advertised in the *SF Sorrow* fanzine inviting commissions for a series of 10 paintings which he entitled 'Road Pictures.' Painted in acrylic on A3 and A4 canvas they each cost £135 and depicted backstage, dressing-room and other non-concert scenes. A few quid for the old boy, why not?

Speaking to Terry Coates, Phil gave his views on the then current music scene and his favoured artists. He named U2 and REM as excellent but opined, 'A lot of it is completely cosmetic. I don't mind Guns 'n' Roses, only for the fact that they have some rock and roll spirit about them, but I do find their music hard to take.' He considered The Black Crowes 'very substandard, rather like a watered down Rolling Stones, Pretty Things and Yardbirds.'

Throughout this period the Pretties remained busy in the studio with St John preparing the album. Doug Smith and Eve Carr came on board to deal with general administration and logistics through Doug's company Gell Tone Productions, which had been set up specifically for Pretty Things projects. Doug had been a founder of Clearwater Productions, the Management Company which looked after Hawkwind, Cochise and Skin Alley, and was the man responsible for kickstarting Dick Taylor's production career back in 1969/70.

The legal assault on EMI came to an end when towards the end of 1993 EMI agreed an out of court settlement rather than suffer the publicity and possible loss of a court action. This provided a substantial cash sum for the band plus the return of their back catalogue. The cash infusion was also welcome for Mark St John who was 'flat broke' and had lost ownership of his recording studio in June, due to the cost of financing the ongoing actions. Recalling this period in 1999 Phil confirmed, 'We had to go to the High Court, and if we had lost that case we would have lost everything, our houses, the whole thing. It was very scary, and there were days when I thought that we couldn't win against these big guys. It was only thanks to our manager Mark St John's resilience that we won.'

Artists who own their back-catalogue of recordings are a rarity. It is something that The Beatles, Stones and Pink Floyd cannot lay claim to and full credit must be given to St John for his persistence and refusal to back down against the big battalions. Many less committed individuals would have succumbed to the legal obfuscations of a major player like EMI and its expensive advisers.

The settlement involved the usual free speech restraint known as a confidentiality clause, which meant that no band member, spokesperson or adviser was able to talk about the case.

The settlement removed the frustration of the previous twenty five years as Phil explained to Peter Innes. 'It got to the point sometimes when you wondered, why even go on recording? We were robbed blind and obviously it gets to you. When you're in the dressing room and it hits you that you've not earned a penny from maybe thirty different albums you're autographing for a fan. Of course, it's not his fault, he's a fan and he's just buying your music. So yeah, frustration did set in.'

Chapter 16 – The EMI Debacle

The seeds of The Pretty Things legal dispute with EMI were sown when they signed a 'Penny contract' back on September 28, 1967. The apparent non-promotion of their output worldwide and EMI's failure or disinterest in policing Motown's US sales ensured that the band stayed poor.

The one year contract allowed EMI up to six annual extensions and obligated The Pretty Things to record two double-sided 45 rpm singles each year for which they would be paid three old pence, just over one penny in today's currency. Overseas sales would merit only half of these figures and 'low price series' releases, one sixth. Once sales exceeded 250,000 the rate would be increased according to a scale. Only 85% of the sale figures would be used for this calculation so as to account for promo's and other non-sales.

A twelve track LP would generate eighteen pence in pre-decimal money (around seven and a half pence now) as it would be considered the equivalent of six double-sided singles. The sales target for increased royalties would consequently be one sixth of the figure for a single. The contract included a clause that allowed EMI to recoup any unearned portion of the advance if the band split up. It also promised that a quarterly statement of sales would be furnished to the Bryan Morrison Agency and that royalties for sales outside the UK would be paid only after receipt by the company. EMI advanced a sum of £3,500 via the Bryan Morrison Agency and, apart from various small amounts, this would be the total of their royalty payments until 1994.

The band had always been uncomfortable with the way EMI had handled the marketing of *SF Sorrow* and, after the initial euphoria, had argued against the agreement with Motown which allowed that company to distribute the band via their Rare Earth label.

EMI were sufficiently happy with matters to sign a new contract with Motown in 1975 which specifically allowed the marketing of the *SF Sorrow/ Parachute* double album, *Real Pretty*. Like the previous contract it obliged Motown to provide EMI with half yearly sales statements within two months of the period in question. It further allowed for EMI to terminate the contract if Motown failed to account after a thirty day warning period. Like the previous contract EMI would receive a 10% royalty.

At this point, The Pretty Things and their various managers had not received proper UK territory sales figures or any funds beyond the 1967 signing advance. Remarkably, they had never received any sales figures whatsoever for the United States.

Back 1971, Phil May had telephoned EMI, asking them to switch the band to another US distributor. In September 1980 he again telephoned complaining about the continued marketing by Motown of Pretty Things records in the US and also touched on the matter of their outdated royalty terms.

EMI showed little interest in the complaints of a commercially unsuccessful band who were no longer signed to them. Like most sixties bands they were unable to pursue the matter due to financial constraints.

In 1981, when at rock bottom both financially and musically, Phil and Dick instructed London solicitors, Russells, to deal with the matter of unpaid royalties from the EMI recordings. Russells wrote to EMI in July contending that the company had failed to properly account to the band and had sent only irregular royalty statements for the non-US sales. They requested copies of all royalty statements with the threat that failure would invite legal consequences. EMI managed to obfuscate and Phil and Dick's resolve faltered in the face of the potentially prohibitive legal costs.

Russells' approach spurred EMI's business affairs manager, Roger Drage, into chasing both the royalties and contracts departments regarding the bands US royalty situation. Oliver Drake, in the contracts department, advised Drage that he couldn't find details of any sales figures received from Motown. He suggested to Drage that he explain to Russells that EMI was not responsible for accounting to The Pretty Things when no accounting had been made to them.

This response, which would be repeated continually throughout the saga, formed the basis of EMI's defence. Drage felt the US position was unsatisfactory, admitting in an internal memo that EMI's failure to investigate might result in litigation.

EMI issued yet another band compilation in March 1982, a mid-price release of *Pretty Things 1967-1971,* and they clearly saw the value in churning old product.

The situation reached an impasse until October 1986 when Russells, who had been receiving non-US royalty statements, advised EMI that they no longer represented the band.

About the same time Twink attempted yet another claim for royalty payments for his work on the *SF Sorrow* album and also in relation to work with his former band Tomorrow. During an October 1986 correspondence, Stephen Daglish, the EMI royalty administration manager, informed Twink that he was unable to furnish him with a copy of the EMI-Pretty Things contract without the permission of the contracting signatories. This was a repeat of their response to a similar request in 1977.

Twink persevered and in November 1987 asked EMI for £2,000 as a full settlement figure. Daglish explained to EMI's Legal Department that Twink had not been a signatory to the original Pretty Things' contract in 1967 and that Twink's claim was based upon him not having received a share of the £3,500 advance paid through the Bryan Morrison Agency. Daglish also touched on Motown's failure to account, which, Twink claimed, would have placed The Pretty Things account in credit.

Dick Taylor remained concerned about the lack of US royalties and during July 1988 made his own attempt. EMI's royalty department responded that enquiries revealed they had never received any US sales reports for the albums.

The following January, Dick was informed by Mark Taylor in the royalty department that they were currently holding royalties for The Pretty Things and asked him who these payments and future earnings should be sent to.

Revealingly, Mark Taylor had penned a memo two years earlier in which he confirmed that Motown had provided sales reports for the June 1976–June 1978 period. The reports showed that the income had been offset against losses from the entire EMI catalogue in respect of the 1969 contract. Daglish told Mark Taylor that this was not allowed, stating that he had checked The Pretty Things' royalty statements, and that no earnings arising from Motown sales under the 1969 agreement has been passed on to them.

During September 1989, EMI received correspondence from solicitors Butch Burns Balin & Co, on behalf of Twink. They requested a proper accounting and payment of royalties. EMI responded in its usual way and some four months later Twink instructed another firm, Cyril Cox & Co. They attempted a different tack proposing that although Twink was not a signatory to The Pretty Things original contract, he was a signatory to the 1968 and 1969 contract extensions. They pursued a logical course stating that if EMI was correct that Twink had no contractual agreement with them, then on what basis did they consider they had the rights to his performances, name or photographs?

By now Ian Hanson had taken over at EMI's business affairs department. Hanson immediately went on the offensive declaring that either Twink or Bryan Morrison had replaced Alan Skipper's name with Twink's on the 1968 contract extension document. Hanson also advised that in any event Twink's claim was now time barred.

This served to halt Twink's arguments for a while although, if he had been aware of Mark Taylor's December 1989 letter to Shannon O'Shea he would have kept close to the scent. Taylor had advised Shannon that he would not pay Phil or Dick their one fifth share 'As we do not know which members played on which tracks.' This seemed to support Twink's contention that he deserved payment.

Taylor's letter also advised that, until January 1989, the 1967 advance of

£3,500 had not been recouped. He stated that a small credit now existed and that the royalties were for all of the original contracted band-members, not just Phil and Dick whom she represented.

Ian Hanson then proceeded to successfully derail an attempt by Shannon O'Shea to renegotiate the band's royalty rate. In respect of the US royalty claim he explained that if any claim existed, which in any event he denied, it would now be time barred.

Hanson also responded to a query from EMI's legal department again advising that The Pretty Things claim was out of time. Quite remarkably he also confirmed the position, first stated by Stephen Daglish in a 1986 internal memo to Martin Haxby, that EMI had indeed received accounting from Motown. Daglish's memo explained that Motown had offset The Pretty Things royalties against losses sustained on sales by Love Sculpture, Toe Fat, the Virgil Brothers and Sounds Nice. This type of financial juggling is rather innocently entitled cross-collateralisation. The band and their advisers were presumably unaware of this. Hanson was obviously hoping that the time bar response would push the problem away.

Shannon attempted to pursue matters with EMI's chief executive officer Rupert Perry, whilst simultaneously asking Ian Hanson for copies of EMI's licensing agreements for Pretty Things product.

Perry confirmed EMI's position as previously stated by Hanson and suggested that she continue any future dialogue via Hanson. However, with his mind alerted to The Pretty Things' back catalogue Perry penned an internal memo stating that he had read in *Rolling Stone* that Polygram was planning to release some early Pretty Things CDs. He asked what had happened to EMI's Pretty Things albums and was anybody interested in them?

Shannon's involvement dismayed Twink and he instructed Lori Pompon, the manager of Twink Records, to write to EMI making it absolutely clear that Shannon did not have any authority to act in respect of him. Shannon recollected that Phil and Twink had fallen out, apparently Twink believed that Phil owed him money – £48 she recalled – and unless Phil paid him he refused to be involved in negotiations via Shannon.

Having exhausted all attempts to negotiate with EMI, Shannon re-instructed Russells Solicitors who, during March 1990, duly dispatched a five page letter to Rupert Perry. A number of issues were raised, the unpaid US royalties, the failure to account for US sales, an alleged under-accounting for non US sales and also the 1967 contract which they considered unsustainable as it was in restraint of trade. Russells stated that no evidence had been received indicating that EMI was pursuing the Motown matter and alleged that this was because it would have acted against EMI's own business interests. Mention was made of EMI's failure to provide a copy of the 1969 agreement with Motown and that Phil and Dick had written directly to Motown who had responded indicating that EMI was in a position to answer their enquiries. Russells further claimed that Ian Hanson had told Shannon that *SF Sorrow* and *Parachute* had jointly achieved sales of between 400,000 and 500,000 outside of North America suggesting an under-accounting of £45,000. A proper and detailed response was requested. Russells concluded by advising that Phil and Dick felt that over the years EMI had misled them.

The author, Tony English, pointed out that EMI was under a fiduciary obligation to The Pretty Things because they were an inexperienced group of musicians who placed all their trust in them when entering into the recording agreement. That they had relied on EMI's ability and integrity to properly promote and exploit their recordings throughout the world. He suggested that to resolve matters a meeting between all parties might prove useful. He allowed EMI fourteen days to reply and stated that in view of his clients lack of financial resources they would have no alternative but to apply for legal aid in pursuing such a claim.

EMI took their time in considering the letter. Before responding Ian Hanson sent a memo to Gareth Hopkins in the legal department, saying that the more he looked at the matter the more confident he was. He suggested that their claim should be countered by offering them an increased royalty rate. He reminded Hopkins that EMI had not actually received any money from Motown.

Hanson's response to Tony English at Russells was far from conciliatory. He began by stating that the position remained unchanged from their 1981 correspondence, and that he failed to see why the situation now was any different, save for Phil and Dick's current willingness to apply for legal aid, when, in 1981, they were unable or unprepared to. In relation to the 1967 contract he advised that the Agreement was signed in 1967 and not 1990. By the recording industry standards of 1967, the Agreement was neither onerous, unfair or in restraint of trade. 'Effectively the only argument that you are putting forward on this issue is that the terms of the Agreement are not now to your client's liking or commercial advantage, but with the greatest respect, that is totally irrelevant.'

It is perhaps worth contrasting The Pretty Things' 1967 contract with that of The Beatles. The Pretty Things' potential earnings were a stated monetary figure per sale. This contrasts with The Beatles percentage rate of 8.50%, a figure that Allen Klein managed to swell in 1968. The EMI contract also compared unfavourably with the Pretties' Fontana one, which at least had the ability to respond to inflation.

Hanson ably refuted Russells' allegation that EMI was trying to keep in with Motown by advising that EMI were Motown's licensees in various territories between 1964 and 1981. He also countered Russells' point relating to the band's inability to fully understand the implications of the EMI agreement. He pointed out that this 'inexperienced group' were, at the time, advised by The Bryan Morrison Agency who were far from inexperienced. Hanson finished with a flourish condemning the band's allegations as vexatious. He again refused sight of the EMI-Motown contract although he was prepared to confirm that it did not provide for an advance to be paid to EMI.

Hanson had further cause to write to Tony English in November, this time regarding Dick Taylor who had made direct contact with EMI. Dick had tried to speak with Rupert Perry but had been passed across to Hanson with whom Dick again raised the issue of unpaid royalties. Upon receiving no joy from Hanson he made allegations that EMI and Motown had entered into some illicit and covert arrangement which he planned to make public. Hanson advised Tony English that he had warned Taylor of the danger of making defamatory statements.

Dick's phone call seemed to shake the tree because in August 1991 Hanson authorised a payment to him of one fifth of the outstanding royalties. A cheque for £270.62 was sent in October with the caveat that payment would indemnify EMI against any third party claim that may be made. One can assume he was thinking of Twink. Although small, it was a welcome infusion of money although it was quite obvious to Dick and Phil that it didn't represent any of the unpaid US royalties.

In July 1992, Phil and Dick replaced Russells with a new firm, Hackett-Jones and Foley, who promptly wrote to EMI. Their letter repeated previous complaints affirming that EMI was in flagrant breach of its fiduciary obligations and describing them as wholly obstructive in the matter of the US licence. EMI, it was said, conducted themselves in their dealings with Phil and Dick solely in the promotion of their own interests and with a total disregard to their careers. Citing gross negligence, Hackett-Jones & Foley requested full accounting throughout the world, a copy of the US licence and all file correspondence between EMI and Motown. A period of fourteen days was allowed before the institution of court proceedings.

Hanson expressed his surprise at the letter's content. He sent them copies of his correspondence with Russells and formally denied all of the allegations. He invited the band to audit them and stated that having been threatened with court action in 1981 EMI didn't see a threat some eleven years later as adding anything to the situation.

Hanson was now reconciled to the threatened legal action and duly corresponded with EMI's solicitor, David Davies at Clintons. Less bullish than before, he confided to Davies that he was unsure of EMI's position. He explained that although EMI had properly accounted for non-US sales they had not done so for US sales. This, he said, was because Motown had failed to account to EMI. He then suggested that EMI ought to terminate their agreement with Motown in order to lessen their exposure.

Hanson also arranged for royalty statements to be sent from the Hayes office. These went back only to December 1987. It showed that Motown had reported net sales of 3,659 for *SF Sorrow*, 977 for *Parachute* and 5,186 for *Real Pretty*, the *SF Sorrow/Parachute* double package released in the mid 70s to cash in on the Swansong push.

Neither Phil nor Dick were able to obtain the Legal Aid necessary and Mark St John took it upon himself to bankroll the action. A gesture both magnanimous and supportive and one that few other managers would have contemplated.

Neil Peakall, the solicitor who had been dealing with the matter, left Hackett-Jones & Foley to join Kearns & Co whose Wardour Street offices were conveniently close to St John's studio. Phil and Dick switched to Kearns & Co who initiated High Court proceedings. In September 1992 EMI received a copy of the summons. It would be dealt with in the chancery division of the High Court in front of Master Winegarten. The summons alleged that:

EMI had failed to honour its fiduciary duty to the group to use reasonable care to promote the sale of the said recordings and recover the revenues earned by reason of such sales.

EMI had failed consistently throughout the term of the said agreement to account to the Plaintiffs and other members of the group in the UK;

EMI had failed properly or at all to account for the sales of such recordings made outside the UK and in particular had failed to account to the Plaintiffs at all for sale sin the USA;

That EMI had taken no steps whatsoever to terminate the aforesaid licensing agreement or to seek to stop the unauthorised release of the recordings;

That the EMI Agreement was voidable as it constituted an unreasonable restraint of trade.

Clintons retained the counsel of Ian Mill of Blackstone Chambers and after discussion with him, David Davies advised Hanson that two of the band's contentions would be thrown out – those relating to restraint of trade and the obligation to exploit the recordings.

Davies then issued a grave warning relating to the claim for a proper accounting. He advised that the claim in respect of accounting was limited to the previous six years. However, he then cautioned that there was a potential claim for damages for breach of the fiduciary duty and the total claim could amount to 12 years royalties in all.

However, the point that will have done most to alarm Hanson was in relation to EMI's failure to account for US sales. The implications for EMI were catastrophic. Davies explained that if EMI had not received an accounting and payment of royalties from Motown and if the group had been made aware of this, the claim would be limited to six years. He then reminded Hanson about the cross-collateralisation. That if Motown had accounted in respect of the group, but recouped advances paid on other contracts, it was likely that the court would conclude that payment had been received by EMI. Davies felt it arguable that EMI had received an account and concealed the fact from the group – a misrepresentation. Davies explained that it would enable the group to claim all royalties accounted for by Motown in this way. He reminded Hanson of Stephen Daglish's memo of 9th May 1986.

Daglish's memorandum was precise. It confirmed that the royalty department files contained sales reports received from Motown for the period December 1973 to June 1978, although some periods were missing. That during the early periods, Motown had offset any Pretty Things earnings against other recordings by Love Sculpture, Toe Fat, The Virgil Brothers and Sounds Nice with the result that the overall account was always in a debit position during this time.

After the Court hearing on 2nd March 1993, David Davies wrote to Ian Hanson advising that all parts of The Pretty Things' case relating to restraint of trade and the purported implied term to exploit, had been struck out.

Davies confirmed that EMI were entitled to institute proceedings against Motown and Hanson now became busy in requesting full information from them. He engaged in correspondence with Tonik Mizell, business and legal affairs vice president of The Motown Record Company who in turn made enquiries of Vincent Perrone, executive vice president of The Gordy Company, which was previously The Motown Record Corporation. EMI's licensing agreement was with the latter company.

During May, Hanson contacted Cora Barnes at Lupus Music, part of the Bryan Morrison Music Ltd, and asked whether Lupus had received any publishing royalties from the USA in respect of Pretty Things recordings. She replied that other than two very small amounts referring to a song named 'Spider Woman' (a song the band never actually recorded) they had not received any royalty payments.

In June, Jon Povey chose to enquire whether EMI were holding any royalties due to him. He may have been galvanised by the paragraph in *Music Week*, which reported that The Pretty Things were suing EMI. This article enraged Ian Hanson who consequently wrote a letter of rebuke to *Music Week's* editor, Steve Redmond.

Hanson was becoming exasperated by his failure to obtain information from the US. He wrote to Vincent Perrone in June 1993 confirming that EMI was being sued by The Pretty Things in respect of North American exploitation. He warned that unless he was able to answer their questions, he would be forced to join both The Gordy Company and Motown to the action. To avoid this he requested confirmation of whether The Gordy Company had been exploiting The Pretty Things recordings. If so he required details of the sales, prices sold and royalties accruing.

David Davies's cautionary words regarding concealed fraud had hit home and EMI's chief executive officer, Rupert Perry now became personally involved. Perry had noted the potential for financial loss and the attendant negative publicity and, unlike Hanson, was keen for an out of court settlement which he asked both the business affairs and legal departments to look into.

Hanson explained to Perry that whilst The Pretty Things' contract was fixed, EMI's contract with Motown was based on a percentage royalty. He explained that it was therefore difficult to compute a pro-rata figure. He confirmed that attempts were being made to obtain royalty information from Motown but they didn't seem very interested in an issue that was over 20 years old. Hanson was canny enough to note that although only Phil and Dick were the litigants any settlement would have to involve the other three signatories to the 1967 contract waiving their claims. In defending his actions, Hanson pointed out that his strategy was to provide evidence to the court that there had been no exploitation of these recordings in North America for the last six years which would result in the entirety of their claim being struck out.

Hanson's tone indicated that he was not yet reconciled to a settlement; he still hoped to have the claim thrown out on the six years time bar technicality. Nonetheless, he yielded to Perry's conciliatory stance and suggested paying the band between £8,000 and £10,000 and also offering a new royalty deal. In return, he wanted a waiver of all claims by all band members and a confidentiality clause. Furthermore, each side would be responsible for its own legal costs.

At this stage, August 1993, EMI had already paid out over £7,000 to Clintons in legal fees. The Pretty Things own costs are likely to have been higher if Russells' unsuccessful attempt in 1981 is taken into account. The settlement that Hanson proposed would have left the band in debt, albeit with an increased royalty relating to their old recordings. This, however, would not have offered any real financial reward as the albums were not being actively marketed. Additionally, the claims waiver would have rendered EMI safe from any future litigation.

At Perry's request Hanson penned an urgent memo to royalties depart-ment asking them to recalculate The Pretty Things royalties over the pre-vious six years on an enhanced basis. This would be a percentage royalty rather than the penny deal applied over the previous twenty-six years. He also requested the total post-recoupment royalties to date.

Hanson persevered with his enquiries of Motown and faxed Tonik Mizell. He pointed out that his President was now involved who planned to approach Mizell's superiors at Motown and Polygram, which would lead to unpleasant-ness.

A week later Hanson received an acerbic response from Mizell explaining the relationship between Motown, The Motown Record Company and the Motown Record Corporation which had been renamed The Gordy Com-pany. She insisted that he contact Vince Perrone at The Gordy Company for any further information.

On August 26 Hanson spoke over the telephone with Perrone who explained that he didn't care about the situation. He told Hanson that The Pretty Things couldn't sue him, but if they did he would defend. He expressed outrage that they should even consider such a course of action. According to Hanson's hand-written notes he informed Perrone that he agreed with him, from a legal point of view, but he had practical considera-tions to think about. The notes indicate that Perrone promised to provide information on Pretty Things sales but feared that the records may have been destroyed.

The following week Shirley Hairston of the Gordy subsidiary Jobette Music Co. faxed Hanson with Motown's producer reserve report. She con-firmed that royalty statements relating to The Pretty Things couldn't be found.

Armed with Motown's available figures Hanson produced a detailed mem-orandum to Rupert Perry. It confirmed that total sales across the two albums and the box set that Motown released amounted to 9,822 units which had accrued royalties amounting to £1,126, had EMI accounted to them at the time in accordance with the terms of the contract.

Hanson had established that the recalculated royalty figure for the previ-ous six years amounted to £13,884. He suggested two possible courses of action. Each involved paying the sum of £1,126 and inviting an audit for non-North American sales over the previous six years. He proposed giving them £5,000 as down payment for any audit claims, if they found less than this they could keep the £5,000.

The first option offered to return the masters for North America, the second required the return of the masters for world exploitation. Hanson indicated that the audit for sale outside North America was unlikely to find very much, and in both cases the band would have to waive all claims to date, except for claims that might arise out of the audit. EMI would seek a confidentiality clause and an agreed press statement. He suggested that EMI retain ownership of the Masters, 'On the basis that we are here to exploit catalogue rather than give it away.'

The total US sales figure of 9,822 for *SF Sorrow, Parachute* and the reissued double album seems farcical. It suggested that earlier sales records were missing, sales records that would have indicated substantially higher sales if only because they related to the initial release periods.

During August The Pretty Things played an ace card by granting power of attorney to their manager Mark St John. Whilst no legal eagle, St John was well versed in the ways of the recording industry. He also recognised the intrinsic value of the catalogue in the burgeoning CD age and the level of royalties that ought to have flowed into the Pretties' coffers. St John immediately arranged an August 24 meeting with Rupert Perry during which a frank exchange of views took place, as confirmed in his letter to Perry of September 20.

St John wrote on behalf of his Golden Recording Company Ltd, which he had started a year earlier. He crafted a wonderfully phrased letter reminding Perry that he had promised to revert to him with proposals based upon researches into the historic files. It stated that for him, the meeting had been held in a conciliatory spirit with a view to an amicable settlement.

He described the EMI contract as poorly devised and inappropriate and reminded Perry that he was looking for the return of the Pretties' copyrights.

St John's letter suggested that album and CD sales for the non-North American area had amounted to 500,000, which he felt should be historically fiscally adjusted and subjected to a reasonable percentage based on the entire term of their contract.

He also explored the North American shambles stating that they had both agreed that an accurate calculation of units sold would prove impossible as a result of the breaches practised by Motown.

St John also pointed out that North America was the largest and most lucrative market, that the second license granted to Motown coincided with Swansong's big US push and the subsequent re-release of *SF Sorrow* and *Parachute*, as the double album *Real Pretty* undoubtedly ate into the Swansong sales. He also made the valid point that it was Motown's fault that the US market perceived *SF Sorrow* as derivative of *Tommy* when it was actually the reverse. He reminded Perry that *Tommy* had been critically acclaimed in North America as revolutionary and this had elevated The Who's career. He suggested that these accolades and the attendant career elevation would have been accorded to The Pretty Things had Motown initially released and promoted *SF Sorrow* efficiently.

St John's reference to the Swansong period was relevant because in January 1976 EMI signed a further contract, which allowed Motown to take advantage of the increased interest in the Pretties due to Swansong's marketing drive.

It was now clear to EMI that the litigants couldn't be bought off with a mere £10,000 or an audit ruse. On October 19, Ian Hanson scribbled a memo to Rupert Perry suggesting an offer of £50,000 and the return of the band's masters. He also proposed that if after fourteen days the offer had not been accepted EMI should make a payment into the court which would be less than £50,000 and they wouldn't get their Masters back. This common and often unpleasant feature of litigation may have worked but Perry was acutely aware that the court hearing might unearth evidence of the concealed fraud and he decided to continue the bargaining.

During October, St John met with Rupert Perry again and this time brought with him the imposing figure of Peter Grant, The Pretty Things former manager. St John was asked to name his settlement figure for the North American issue and stated £250,000, Perry countered that EMI was thinking of £50,000. The meeting turned to the rest of the world sales and St John asserted that his calculations, based on 500,000 units sold, indicated an under-accounting of £16,500, although he failed to rationalise the figures. This figure was substantially less than Russells had suggested in March 1990. Perry may have seen this as an escape route and didn't question the veracity of the calculation.

After the meeting Perry asked Ian Hanson to calculate the interest on £16,500 from 1970 to date. He also asked for a calculation of the actual sales for the last six years based upon an assumed 10% royalty rate. Hanson seemed concerned that Perry might be weakening and might agree to a hefty settlement figure and he advised Perry that Phil and Dick's legal position was very weak and that there might be a method of stopping them using the press again. Hanson suggested that they should spend fifteen minutes together on the issue. Nonetheless, within a week he reported back that using an average compounded interest rate of 10.72%, the £16,500 would have grown to £171,666. This calculation was actually based on 23 complete years and did not include 1993. He also advised that the recalculated royalty figure for the previous six years was £13,884.

Three weeks later, on November 5, 1993, Ian Hanson wrote to St John at his company's Maidstone address, confirming an earlier telephone conversation. The Without Prejudice letter, suggested a settlement based on four precepts.

1.   A sum of £50,000 would be paid.
2.   The Pretty Things' catalogue would be assigned to them.
3.   All band members would waive all past, current and future claims or rights of action.
4.   The terms of the agreement would remain confidential.

In a surprisingly conciliatory tone, possibly because both he and the band were now financially constrained, St John responded expressing pleasure at the agreement to restore the band's copyrights. The sum offered, he suggested, was far too low. His counter suggestion was a simplification of the accounting procedures which appeared to be concerning EMI. He proposed that in full and final settlement the sum of £225,000 would be acceptable in respect of the entire, worldwide claim. This would of course be in addition to the return of the copyrights.

Kearns & Co had meanwhile lodged an amended summons before the Court. This added Motown as a co-defendant along with EMI.

Regardless of St John's accommodating words and much reduced settlement figure an agreement couldn't be reached and, on December 3, St John telephoned hoping to reach Rupert Perry. He explained that he was due to meet with representatives of *World In Action*, a current affairs television programme. EMI responded that his financial demands were unattractive but added that they were keen to settle. St John requested a meeting the following week. If not, the matter would proceed to court.

These actions implied a degree of desperation on St John's part. Either financial pressures were now forcing the issue or maybe he was entertaining doubts about their ability to win in court.

On December 6, St John and Hanson met at EMI's offices and, finally, a settlement acceptable to both sides was hammered out. Effectively it was the same deal that Hanson had offered on November 5 other than an increase to the cash figure. The final figure was a compromise between St John's demands and Hanson's offer.

The subsequent Agreement, dated January 1st 1994, and signed by all of the original contracted band members contained a number of precise clauses.

1 (a)   All contracted band members to give up any past, current or future claims against EMI

1 (b)   Phil and Dick to instruct their solicitors to gain an order to dismiss proceedings. Each side to meet its own costs.

1 (c)   The band and their advisors (professional or otherwise) promise not to disclose the terms of the Agreement or seek to publish, reveal, communicate or give to any person, firm or company any information relating to the dismissal of the Proceedings. If questioned, they or their advisors to

state only – "the proceedings against EMI have been dismissed and we/I have nothing further to add or say about the matter." The band and advisors to sign a letter of confidentiality.

2   In consideration of the above a sum of xxx to be paid to the Golden Recording Company within seven days of the date of execution.

3 (a)   EMI to assign to the artists all proprietary rights to the Recordings

3 (b)   EMI to make the masters available for collection

3 (c)   EMI to desist from manufacturing further band recordings but have the right to sell off stock for six months and then destroy all remaining stock. Additionally, EMI must contact its associates (licensees) and request them to comply with the above.

3 (d)   EMI to use all reasonable endeavours to provide band with a list detailing the third-party licenses that exist and to use all reasonable endeavours to seek to terminate the Third Party Licenses.

3 (e)   The band to be responsible for any third party royalty obligations and, additionally, shall hold EMI harmless from any loss or damage in respect of claims made against EMI.

4   From the date of assignment The Pretty Things-EMI Agreement to be terminated.

The settlement papers required the band member's signatures, which according to the typed document included those well known artistes Jon Dovey and Alan Shipper. To avoid potential embarrassment to the band members the actual figure has not been revealed, although one does not need a calculator to arrive at an approximation.

EMI had originally signed the band to a contract that rapidly lost value as inflation ravaged the financial landscape of the 1970s. They also failed to account properly for UK and European sales and failed to account for any US sales. Although able to void the contract with Motown due to repeated breaches, they failed to do so. Whilst they had received royalties on Pretty Things sales they used the technicality of cross-collateralisation to avoid any actual payments. As QC Ian Mill advised, this was concealed fraud, and Hanson and colleagues were completely aware of it.

The relatively low settlement figure bought EMI out of a potentially disastrous court admission with the subsequent bad press that such a public admission could engender. By insisting on the gagging clause EMI also ensured that those few people who were in possession of the facts and who wished for them to be revealed, in other words the band and their advisers, were debarred from any public comment whatsoever.

Hanson made sure that the letters of confidentiality were signed according to his requirements with Neil Peakall signing on behalf of Kearns and St John, Doug Smith and Amanda Thwaites doing likewise on behalf of the

Golden Recording Company Ltd. In early February the settlement in the form of two cheques was finally sent by EMI.

Hanson tried to ensure that all parts of the EMI empire were made aware of the settlement and that the bands copyrights would revert in July 1994. The settlement also allowed EMI to cease allocating royalties and Hanson's memo to Mark Taylor confirmed that no further royalties should be sent.

The legal action was officially dismissed on 28th April and each side became responsible for its own legal costs. The Pretty Things' outlay remains unknown but file copies show that Clinton's quarterly invoices to EMI had by now totalled £10,800.

During May, Hanson advised St John that the masters were available for collection and he confirmed that after July 26 all surplus stock would be destroyed. He confirmed that See For Miles and Demon had been contacted requesting that the licence agreements be terminated. He made clear that EMI could not force termination but added that in any event, following end of July all royalty earnings due under that licence agreement would flow through to the band. The letter also revealed that Polygram, EMI's German associate, had included 'Defecting Grey' on their *The Psychedelic Years* compilation and that Polygram had asked for an extension.

Hanson sent St John a list of the current licences, It showed that Demon were marketing *SF Sorrow* and *Parachute* and that the licences were due to terminate in August and December 1994 respectively. He explained that Demon was not prepared to delete the item. See For Miles was marketing *Singles A & B's* and again they were not prepared to relinquish. Their licence to market '1967-1971' and two early Pretty Things tracks on their *British Psychedelic Vol 2* had already expired. As Hanson had already pointed out Sequel, the Polygram subsidiary, had been including 'Defecting Grey' on their *The Psychedelic Years* album. This licence was due to end on July 31.

Hanson was busy searching out the band's original artwork as he was concerned to stick to the precise letter of the agreement. In a June memo to John Ashley he explained that he had to assemble the artwork for collection and that they were very litigious. He didn't want to give them an opportunity to sue EMI again. Despite his best endeavours Hanson had to write to St John confessing that the artwork couldn't be located and suggested that Demon and See For Miles probably had the originals.

Despite the settlement, Twink persisted in his own attempts to gain funds. Twink had not signed any waiver, and in an August 1997 missive he persevered with his argument that he had a contractual relationship with EMI vis-à-vis the *SF Sorrow* recordings and further correspondence ensued.

During February and April 1998 Twink continued with his assertion that by signing an April 1967 contract as part of Tomorrow he was individually contracted to EMI. In the face of EMI's continued rebuttals Twink was moved to write to them warning that due to their continued non-payment of royalties he intended to exploit all EMI recordings that featured him.

Presumably due to a lack of internal communication within the organisation, EMI's response cautioned Twink that as they were the exclusive copyright owner of the recordings they would vigorously pursue any infringement of their rights and seek penal damages and costs, obviously unaware that The Pretty Things' copyrights had been restored. Also unaware was the archives department and when Mark St John contacted them in August 1998 asking for all of the negatives, transparencies and photographs taken at various sessions they contacted Nigel Reeve asking for clarification.

So, The Pretty Things assumed control of their EMI copyrights. Fairly rare in the industry and 'pretty groundbreaking shit' as St John announced, but did they win the day? From this observers viewpoint EMI came out with a fairly conclusive points victory. The value of the copyrights was not worth all that much to them in 1994 and their apparent disinterest can be gauged by their preferred route of licensing out much of the catalogue.

St John's calculation of units shifted seemed somewhat optimistic when he suggested net sales of 400,000/500,000 but, if approximately correct, then the historically recalculated figure of £171,666, as supplied by Ian Hanson, indicated the real value of the unpaid royalties. Additional to this was the figure for the previous six years, an EMI internal memo from 1997 showed that £4,000 of Pretty Things royalties remained in a suspense account.

If St John's figures were even approximately right then The Pretty Things were owed considerably more than they settled for. A strict interpretation of the original EMI contract implied an under-accounting of around £76,000. Using Hanson's reading of inflation between 1970 and 1994 the fiscally adjusted figure comes to £760,000.

Neither do these sums include an amount relating to damages, loss and legal expenses. Had they been successful in court it is possible that a fairly substantial sum by way of damages could have filtered the bands' way. St John may have been unaware of the strength of their position. The loss of his recording studio in 1993 had probably shaken both his and the band's resolve. If he had kept to the April 1994 court date, rather than accepting an out-of-court settlement, who knows what may have been the outcome?

In retrospect, Ian Hanson did an exemplary job. He outmanoevered St John and potentially saved EMI a considerable sum and much corporate embarrassment. It proved yet again how those in possession of the facts invariably win the arguments, legal or otherwise.

CHAPTER 17 – Out With The New And In With The Old

The EMI constituents of the Pretty Things, Wally Waller, Jon Povey, Skip Alan and Peter Tolson had been approached regarding the prospective court action against EMI, and the intended *Anthology* covering the bands career. Since the abortive Freerange recording sessions they had mostly worked outside the music industry. Wally had done the De Wolfe solo album and a few jingles but had also been driving minicabs down in Sussex. 'I can't really remember doing much after (Freerange). I did all kinds of things – everybody's got to eat! I did drive a cab for a while, I sold advertising over the phone, I even stood in the middle of Selfridges selling vegetable shredders. I did everything, but in the end I thought I've just got to get back to music.' Jon Povey had been working as a sales manager for C P Hart for over eight years. Peter Tolson had, as the Chinese say, been living in interesting times. He and long term partner Gilly had parted a while back and she retained custody of their two children, Jesse and Aidan. A brief and unsuccessful marriage followed and in 1988 he decided on a major career change and undertook a degree in Computer Science at Hertfordshire University. Times were hard and financial constraints forced him to sell most of his collection of guitars, the exception being his favourite, the ex-Hendrix white Stratocaster. Skip was in a different situation altogether, he had continued to manage the business built up by his father, The Mastergroup, based at Thornton Heath. From a shaky early 80s position the business had prospered and Skip is generally considered a very rich man, possibly a millionaire.

The Pretty Things *Anthology*, *'Unrepentant'*, was planned for release in 1994 which, according to St John, was intended to coincide with the band's 30th Anniversary (although by 1994 it was actually 31 years). However, this could only be achieved if the legal arguments with Phonogram could be resolved. St John believed the band had a stronger case against Phonogram than against EMI, and in view of this he expected them to behave in a suitably contrite manner but, as he informed in the *Anthology* booklet, 'They were unreasonable, deliberately difficult and totally arrogant.' He also considered that a resolution to the matter was purposely held up by Phonogram just to ensure that the planned release date would be missed.

The band had to decide whether to persevere with the case against Phonogram, which could stretch across many years at great cost, or whether to agree a deal with them. They reluctantly chose the latter and received a figure described as 'a pittance'. The terms of the out of court settlement ensured that the band's cited complaints, the defendants' responses and the exact terms of the settlement cannot be disclosed, surprise, surprise. However, it is understood that they received their costs, the return of their masters and a cash sum. St John stated that the cost of the two actions had by then reached £150,000. This seems an unbelievable figure and we must assume it includes not just legal costs but all expenses defrayed, possibly including the loss of his recording studio.

The group had never received royalty payments from Fontana and as it was the Fontana days that saw all the hits and presumably the greatest corporate profit, this was no small rip off. Additionally, the buy-back arrangement brokered with the Inland Revenue ensured a further stream of profit from the sales impetus of the cassette tape revolution. The matter of disadvantageous contracts for naive bands in the sixties was not anything new, however most of the other bands were financially unable or psychologically unwilling to pursue the matter.

As with EMI it seemed that the considerable cost of continuing a court action against a multi-million pound conglomerate with very deep pockets was a bridge too far. Only the rich can afford justice in the civil courts and the band had to accept beer money in order to pursue the *Anthology* project.

The 'victories' against the music leviathans and recovery of their catalogue was big news. St John boasted that the whole music industry was looking at him and The Pretty Things as crusading leaders for a generation of unpaid bands and added that he was receiving numerous calls from artists in a similar position. It is known that he has assisted Adam Faith and David Courtney in tracking down royalty payments from their work on the first two Roger Daltrey albums. He has also represented Chumbawamba in their argument with One Little Indian, their original label, The Bay City Rollers with their claim against Arista/BMG, Arthur Brown, who stated that he never received royalties on his hit 'Fire'. Eddie Grant, Hawkwind, Tim Rose and Kenny Denton are also known to have used St John and additionally it is believed he is supporting the remaining Small Faces in their attempts to right the financial wrongs of their unfortunate past.

Like the EMI litigation, the action against Phonogram was only pursued by Phil and Dick. However, unlike the canny Ian Hanson, who had insisted that all the contracted band members sign away future claims, Phonogram neglected to include Viv Prince, John Stax or Brian Pendleton in the settlement and this opened the way for St John to pursue further claims on their behalf some four years later. John Stax explained that by settling with Phil and Dick Phonogram had effectively admitted liability and would have to pay the others.

St John now took over formally as the band's manager, a function which he claims Phil and Dick had wanted him to fulfil for years and which, to a greater or lesser degree, he had been.

The EMI settlement had brought the *Cross Talk* version of the band together and talking to each other properly for the first time in years. From these uneasy beginnings, made palatable by the EMI funds, plans were made to reform the band as a working and recording unit. Peter Tolson recalled that Phil telephoned him about the possibility. He entertained doubts about the sense, commercial and otherwise, of a reunion and a persuasive Phil came and stayed with him for a couple of days to try and get the feel of things again. Rehearsals started in April 1994 and went on for five months, which was difficult for many of them. Dick living on the Isle of Wight had to commute and both Jon and Wally had to fit around work commitments. For Peter, living in Harlow without any means of transport, the travel arrangements were an additional burden to the grief of being out of work and broke.

St John exclaimed, 'After the first half hour in a sweaty rehearsal room in West London it was clear that the magic was still there', however it is indisputable that the early rehearsals were difficult and fraught with tensions. Tolson expressed his disappointment at the rustiness of the band. Skip couldn't keep time and kept dropping his sticks and for a while was unsure whether he would make it back. Jon Povey had lost his touch and Peter who had not played guitar for six years was depressed by his own efforts. He used a borrowed guitar and recalled that the calluses built up from years of continual playing had gone, and how sliding down the frets on the 'shit-covered strings' he split his finger wide open.

During this period Phil and Dick continued to gig as The Pretty Things and it is apparent that the other group members were unaware of the rehearsals taking place with past band members. Dick himself felt uneasy about a situation where one version of the band was gigging, oblivious to the fact that another, admittedly more relevant version, was busy rehearsing for a planned comeback.

St John had previously decided that the band should attempt to licence back their old Swansong and Warners material and he made contact with former manager, and head of Swansong, Peter Grant. Grant was especially helpful and he smoothed the way via his network of friends and contacts. Sadly, Peter Grant died later that year and numerous tributes to him appeared in magazines and their letters pages. Grant's death allowed St John to gush in tribute, 'The finest man I ever met'…etc. This about the man who forged a managerial career out of the implication of violence and the threat of physical retribution.

He also made sure that when the 'new album' eventually emerged it carried a dedication to Peter Grant. 'So would every album be if I had my way' he persisted. St John usually gets his own way so one sits back in anticipation.

It should be noted amongst the blather of publicity regarding the reversion of their copyrights that whilst The Pretty Things own the Polygram/ EMI material they only control the Warners/Swansong material by virtue of these licence deals.

With all of the band's official material under their control, re-issue deals were now being discussed and brokered. It was said that Creation was to be the new UK label and a deal was planned with German label SPV for the European markets. The Creation 'deal' didn't last long, they pulled out of negotiations in May 1995 citing the band and St John as too troublesome. 'I don't need to be involved with people who are more difficult to deal with than Oasis & Primal Scream, especially when this is supposed to be a catalogue item,' announced Creation's James Kyllo. 'It didn't go ahead because we felt that their expectations were unrealistic and didn't want to go ahead with a project that seemed likely to end in a lot of ill feeling.' It is evident that Creation's views of anticipated sales did not match St Johns and they withdrew their interest.

St John lambasted them. He berated Oasis as 'pussycats' stating that Creation had said they were 'too fucking difficult to deal with'. A feather in The Pretty Things cap, apparently.

Various booking agents and journalists have taken the same view and it is clear that The Pretty Things image problem continues to this day. Old adversary Tony Calder would have liked the *Anthology* reissued on Immediate, but, 'The trouble is they are looked after by a nice guy called Mark St John and he drives us crazy.'

Fragile Records was quickly roped in to replace Creation, and the *Anthology*, finally, was on course.

The gigging band, soon to be known as 'The Discarded Pretty Things' played at the Brian Jones Memorial Concert, a dismal festival held at Cheltenham racecourse on June 2nd. Additionally they played a series of shows in the South West of England later in the month. Steve Browning's future wife Heather added violin at two concerts, contributing to 'Loneliest Person' and 'Art School Blues'.

In an interview with Terry Coates for the *SF Sorrow* fanzine, bassist Steve Browning had spoken optimistically about his position in the band. 'This line up feels right. I think that the other members feel the same. I realise that a lot of people have the impression that the Pretty Things are Phil and Dick plus a load of other guys, but that's definitely not what Phil and Dick think.'

Actually it was, and with St John's urging they were determined to resurrect the 'old brigade'.

On August 24th drummer Hans Waterman telephoned Dick Taylor and after 10 minutes of animated discussion he was an ex-Pretty Thing. Hans had discovered that Phil and Dick had been rehearsing with Skip Alan and understandably he was pissed off and hurt. Additionally he felt angry that these things were happening behind his back and that he had discovered the truth from the August issue of *Record Collector*. Hans quite rightly felt that Phil, Dick and Mark St John owed him some kind of explanation and apology. 'You have to draw the line somewhere. This had just gone too far.' Rather than be discarded he left with his dignity intact.

'Hans was very upset,' confirmed Dick. 'Hans did put a load of energy into it, a lot of work, and was a very professional musician, and he was just cheesed off at the end, unfortunately. I have no quarrel with Hans over that, I see no reason for him not to be upset. Barkley was upset but Barkley understood. I've known Barkley long enough to be able to talk, you know, Barkley and I still remain friends.' Dick did seem rather embarrassed by the charade, which was clearly at odds with his sense of fair play.

It is quite clear that apart from Phil and Dick the other constituents of the current band were completely unaware that rehearsals were in hand designed to supplant them with previous band members. This subterfuge placed a big black mark in the Pretties' book of honour, a book once flawless but now increasingly spotted with ink.

Speaking in 1995 Mark St John avowed, 'One of the strongest and longest running disputes was my insistence that I wanted to see a 'real' Pretties line-up in place. For me, the recent European based R&B formats have never reflected the band which I have always loved and devoted my time and efforts to.'

For this task alone St John deserves to enjoy the eternal appreciation and respect of Pretty Things fans world-wide. The *Cross Talk* line up was quite simply the strongest, meatiest and most creative of their varied and magnificently flawed career. It's just a shame that the methodology behind its return was so machiavellian.

September 7th saw the formation of The Melville Corporation Ltd, a private limited liability company that boasted two directors, Phillip Denis Arthur May and Richard Clifford Taylor, and an official address given as the Hendon offices of accountants Pyliotis Associates. When the See For Miles label released the *EP Collection Plus…* CD, the back cover trumpeted that the songs had been licensed from the Melville Corporation. In May 1997 Dick resigned leaving Phil as sole director although Craven Secretarial Services Ltd were added later.

This is a subject that the band does not like to talk about. Of course, questions concerning financial arrangements often have this kind of effect. It is probable that the limited company was set up purely to licence the band's back catalogue although it appears not to be involved in any of the later Snapper reissues. Did it mean that only Phil and Dick benefited financially from the Fontana back catalogue? Were Skip Alan, Brian Pendleton, John Stax and Viv Prince entitled to any income generated by this licensing? The band is not telling although John Stax confirmed that since the Snapper reissues in 1998 he has received money via Mark St John, which is not necessarily the same as from Melville. The Snapper reissues did not actually involve the Melville Corporation so apart from those few with all the answers – Mark, Dick and Phil – we may never know.

The Melville Corporation Ltd did not post any profits until 1998 when it disclosed a turnover of £63,000, a gross profit of £8,000 and a pre-tax profit of £1,000. A figure of £55,000 had been deducted under the heading 'cost of sales', an accountancy term that could refer to almost anything from consultancy fees to third party expenses. The 1999 accounts showed a reduced turnover of £42,000 and this time a pre-tax loss of £3,000. The following year saw an additional £42,000 turnover with a pre-tax profit of £4,000. Even the £147,000 total income represented a negligible sum considering that in net terms the Fontana years were the highest earning periods of their career.

The planned comeback gig for the 'new' Pretties was fast approaching but at this point, October 1994, the band suffered a massive haemorrhage with the defection of Peter Tolson. Beset by various pressures he was finding it financially and psychologically difficult to get back into the business. A drink-driving ban in 1992 forced him to rely on public transport and having insufficient money to take the train into rehearsals he decided to hitchhike from Harlow. He got as far as Cheshunt but had to walk the remaining forty miles to the Fulham rehearsal studio. He arrived over six hours late, his shoes in tatters and physically devastated. It was shortly after this that he bailed out.

St John stated, it was for the best, but was it? Peter Tolson had been responsible for the bulk of The Pretty Things music since 1971. Could his loss have been avoided? Musically it was definitely not for the best because, despite Frank Holland's increasing prowess, he was no replacement for Tolson the virtuoso guitarist or Tolson the composer. From St John's perspective a band without the strong-willed Tolson, a Tolson no longer prepared to give in on musical policy, was far more manageable. Wally, Skip and Jon have always been prepared to defer to Phil but that would not have been the Tolson way.

As well as the outside pressures and a deep-seated distrust of the music business in general, Peter had been increasingly concerned and unhappy at the Phil & Dick format, upon which St John had based the reformed band. He recalled a rehearsal that didn't go too well where afterwards they all went to a restaurant which levied exorbitant prices. Peter announced he wasn't paying those prices and went off to get a burger. St John tracked him down and they went back for a pint. He was so pissed off that he started on the whisky, and that was fatal. Peter and whisky are fine individually but together are a volatile mix and make for trouble. He remembered ending up flat on his back at Phil's place.

These were bad times for Peter. He stayed indoors and couldn't bring himself to answer the door or the telephone. He had not told the other band members he had left and they made numerous frantic attempts to contact him, even pestering his partner Pauline at her workplace. In desperation, St John journeyed around in an attempt to persuade him back. Peter was not for returning. He was diagnosed as suffering from a nervous breakdown and for a period was prescribed anti-depressants.

This crisis occurred just a week before the comeback gig. Jon Povey recalled the period and the problems it caused. 'We tried to play with him and then he disappeared and we couldn't risk it. We rehearsed for six months and we were gonna do a gig for Joanna Lumley's charity in a hotel as a kick-off gig after all these years and five days before the gig he was due in for a meeting and we couldn't find him. So Frank, who happened to be listening to all this stuff and knew the material and was a guitarist as well, in five days went away and learned all the solos. Came back and played them note for note. Peter was a brilliant guitarist, but a man with problems, a man with dark secrets in cupboards in his mind who couldn't relate to what was going on really.'

'He totally lost it, he just snapped,' said Phil.

Clearly Tolson was disillusioned with the new set up, which he called 'The Phil and Dick show'. 'The only people that were ever consulted by Mark were Phil and Dick, and it was the same as the old days, at a rehearsal the only ones that'd get heard were the ones with a bloody mike. Me, I don't sing, but if I didn't have a mike, and I didn't, I didn't get heard.' He also recalled a disagreement over the Pretties' sound, he wanted some of the songs to be less cluttered, to have periods where not everybody was playing at the same time. When he suggested this, St John responded, 'That's The Pretty Things sound.'

At the start of the rehearsals when the need for new material was discussed Peter had introduced a home-made tape of songs he had written and recorded in the early 80s. The band expressed great interest in them, one in particular that had a reggae inflection. This time around he was not going to accept his songs being moulded into standard Pretty Things fare as had happened under Norman Smith. Peter told them that they couldn't use any of the songs unless they recorded them the way he wanted. 'I said if you don't, you're not having them.' Apparently this was not to St John or the band's liking and nothing further was said about them.

Peter also shrank away from the way forward as prescribed by St John. 'He said no new stuff for three years. This is the set, this is how we will play it.' The parameters were set. St John ran things and Phil was the main man with back up from Dick. Although the other Pretty Things had been re-introduced they had also been disenfranchised. Tolson couldn't commit under those circumstances, his philosophy is to be fully involved or forget it.

Jon outlined his view of the pressures and responsibilities that came from being in a band like The Pretty Things. 'You have to realise that being in a successful band musically, but an unsuccessful band commercially, is very hard because at the end of the day there are pressures on with family. As time goes on, family gets bigger and proportionally everything else gets more difficult and one has to do it for something. At the end of the day there wasn't much around so Peter would like some money, obviously, and he had all those kinds of pressures with a young family and I think it got to him. He did come back and we had some great sessions, we did have some very, very good rehearsal sessions.'

Perhaps Peter's problems were exacerbated by St John, whose managerial approach has never benefited from a surfeit of Kissinger-style diplomacy. Jon: 'Well, I think Mark is a man you either love or hate, basically. If you are in a slightly unstable mental situation he's not the sort of bloke you want to be talking to really. Cause he's very direct, knows what he wants. Peter was heavily into drugs, and heavily into drink.'

Since this experience Peter has completely abandoned the music scene to the extent that he hardly even listens to music any longer. I questioned this drastic about-face. 'I've had a gut-full,' he explained, 'I put a lot of me into what I did and to have been shit on and had the piss taken…' His voice fell away and he shook his head. 'I don't classify myself as a musician anymore.'

Jon Povey continued his assessment of The Pretty Things in terms of responsibility and commitment. 'Phil tried to put together where we used as many original members as possible and to that degree they went and saw Viv Prince who was completely off his trolley and couldn't even play a note (sic) he couldn't even play his drums without falling off his drum-stool. You can't really base any kind of future on somebody like that unfortunately, as much as you would emotionally love them to play for old times sake. You have to draw the line somewhere where you're gonna be able to turn up and play for people who've paid good money and to take it further.'

Jon then explained the rationale of the 'new look' Pretties. 'The idea of doing this was to take it further, not just the old stuff, and take it into the nineties and into new music, which is what it's done to a degree. But Tolson, I think the nature of his.... I mean, anybody slightly rational would have sat down with everybody and said, 'Look, I can't get on with Mark, him and I are just not kicking it off at all. What can we actually do to resolve it?' 'Can we sit around a table and sort out the difficulties', find out what the difficulties are and sort them out, but just to run off... It was more than just Mark. My feeling is that he was influenced by the girl he was living with and all sorts of stuff like that. He was drinking a lot and he was taking all sorts of funny stuff, living out in the sticks somewhere and all those contributing factors didn't make for a healthy relationship really. Love him as I do as a guitarist, absolutely brilliant, if he was together and playing he could come back and play anytime, if he was basically straight or wanting to do it.

If you see the state of Skip – after we've played for an hour and a half you have to shovel him back into his bag and take him home. We don't say we're gonna do it and do it, it's natural it just happens like that. That's the unusual thing about The Pretty Things, it's a chemistry when all the ingredients are bubbling away, it's a very unique thing and I don't know of any other band that's like that. The Rolling Stones, you watch them, they go through it all but they don't do it with the energy The Pretty Things do. The Pretty Things energy is way, way above that of the Rolling Stones or any other band of that era. It's six energies if you like, that join together and shoot out the front of the stage in one massive... it comes across and people are very surprised. It's always maintained that level of energy.'

Dick viewed the Tolson situation similarly. 'He had stopped really... I think he was annoyed with himself cause he'd lost it a bit in terms of his ability. Also, I think he did have a few personal problems and he also got into other areas cause he was doing all the computer stuff. At the time he was doing it he wasn't actually working, I think he was very disillusioned with the music business full stop. I think that was what basically was behind it. As in all these things, I don't think it was just one thing which stopped him playing. He has an artistic temperament, I mean the fact is, he's one of the few people I know, in terms of manual dexterity and musical ability he is able to translate music out of his brain into his fingers. He's the most talented person I think I've met. He's one of those people, you know, darts, snooker, he's extraordinary. I think he's one of those people who can be classed as a bit of a genius.'

Phil contended that Peter did not have the constitution necessary for survival in the business, recounting tales of Tolson's drinking whisky after rehearsals and collapsing on the floor. It is clear however that Phil has the greatest respect for Tolson the guitarist and his virtuoso abilities. He said that both Jimmy Page and Dave Gilmour considered him top notch.

Peter accepts that he can't handle whisky, but considered that a side issue. He has no regrets about leaving the current incarnation. 'As far as Mark's concerned I think he's a brilliant, brilliant drummer but a control freak. He's made a huge investment in the band and he needs to see it back. They can't shit without asking him first and I don't live my life like that.'

'Pete never let us down when I was in the band,' Gordon Edwards told Terry Coates, 'I think he realised that whatever black mood he got into, that it was quite something special to be in a band like The Pretty Things. Everyone got on well, on stage, at rehearsals and after the gig, when we'd all go backstage and relax. I certainly can't consciously remember ever thinking, 'Oh God, we can't depend upon Pete, he's going to disappear,' because, to tell you the truth, the only one who ever walked out was Phil.'

'Yeah, that's true' agreed Jack Green. 'Phil was like that too. Phil brought Pete up, musically. Pete learned his trade in The Pretty Things, he played with them for a long time from when he was quite young and he learned a lot of that from Phil cause that's what Phil used to do, disappear for a while.'

Frank Holland deputised for Peter and did a good job of imitating his solos virtually note for note but this was never the way in the Tolson era where no two solos were alike, each gig a variation. A quest for spontaneity without the tedium of mindless repetition of the vinyl experience.

The grand return concert was held at the Marriott Hotel, London on 21st October and was billed as the 'Attack on Ataxia Benefit.' Tickets went for £45 and the evening comprised a four-course dinner and being entertained by an acoustic set from Donovan. At 11.30 the *real* Pretty Things took the stage and they ran through a two-hour set, which was a veritable history of the band. Starting as always with 'Roadrunner', they played tracks from eight of their nine studio albums, ignoring only the lamentable *Emotions* material. After sixteen numbers they left the stage but swiftly returned for the encore – what else, 'Route 66'. Skip lumbered to the front to belt out the song with Phil whilst Mark St John bounded on stage to take over behind the drum kit, slightly different from the old days when Jon Povey used to deputise. 'He just likes playing with us,' joked Povey. 'It's a bit of a perk, being a manager and earning no money you have to get him playing the drums, poor sod.'

Other changes were in evidence from the performances of their vintage days. Phil now sang lead on every song and Jon Povey who used to bounce from keyboards to congas to bass (when Wally switched to rhythm guitar) now played as much harmonica as keyboards.

After Peter Tolson's departure the band needed to confront the issue of a replacement guitarist. Frank Holland had other plans and was not prepared to make the necessary commitment. Overtures were made to Jack Green who lived on the Isle of Wight, less than ten miles from Dick. Jack's story is that after meeting Dick on the Isle he was contacted by Mark St John who said, 'Come and play with us and maybe you can be in the band.' Jack travelled from Ryde to London, at his own expense, and arranged to stay the night at Skip's house. Jack says that Dick implied it was a formality and that he was in.

Due to tonsillitis Jack was unable to sing but felt that overall things went okay. Whilst there St John asked if he had any photos of the band that could be used for the *Anthology* project. Jack mentioned he had quite a few which he and Gordon had liberated from the Swansong offices in the mid '70s, and yes, the band was welcome to use them.

A few weeks later St John telephoned and said, 'Sorry we can't use you, you play too much like Dick... but can we still use the photographs?' Needless to say, Jack's response was not the 'of course' that St John may have anticipated. There is very little similarity in their styles. Dick tends toward blues stylings whilst Jack plays in a more conventional rock vein, less histrionic than Frank Holland but stronger and more assured.

Four years later Dick explained what really happened that day. 'You know at one point Frank wasn't gonna do the gig after Tolson left and we actually, for want of a better word, auditioned Jack. It was a very curious event cause he came and auditioned and he decided that he'd got such a sore throat that he couldn't do any vocals and then he went out for dinner with Mark and Skip and Phil or something like that. It wasn't exactly acrimonious but he was not very complimentary about Peter Grant, and Mark of course was very, very friendly with Peter Grant and I think that upset Mark and to a certain extent Skip.'

'They made that decision without me. I wasn't involved in it at all,' explained Povey.

Dick explained that they auditioned one other guitarist, a friend of St John's whose name he couldn't recall, and then settled on Frank Holland who finally felt able to commit to the band.

Whilst all this was going on a single was released in Europe credited to Dick Taylor and Memphis. It comprised four songs, 'Roadrunner', 'Little Red Rooster', 'Little Queenie' and 'Baron Saturday' and was recorded back in November 1990 at a concert organised by *Dreamboat*, the then fanzine of the Dutch Pretty Things' fanclub. Memphis was a backing group made up of Dutch musicians including guitarist Henk Haanraads from the band Shoreline.

Another collection of songs featuring Dick Taylor became available in May 1995. This was the assortment of thirteen covers by Little Boy Blue & The Blue Boys which came up for auction at Christies in London. The tape was reportedly bought for a considerable sum by Mick Jagger to avoid the public release of what was essentially a rehearsal session.

It was also during this period that an advert appeared in the *SF Sorrow* fan-zine inviting readers to book a Mediterranean holiday amongst the orange groves of Fuzeta in Portugal, courtesy of Viv Prince Holidays Ltd.

A CD tribute to The Pretty Things arrived during the latter part of the year. *Not So Pretty* was a cosmopolitan collection of 22 artists playing songs associated with the Pretties. Released on the Australian label Corduroy Records it was available on import in the UK for a short period. The sleeve contained a eulogy to Viv Prince by *Ugly Things* editor Mike Stax. The CD opened with the Pretties themselves singing 'Midnight To Six Man', taken from a 1966 BBC radio session.

Various small gigs occupied the summer months before in late August, they performed on the Isle of Wight at the Smallbrook Stadium, Ryde. This was their first appearance there since the 1969 festival and proved to be a daft event for them as the headliners were Ant & Dec, children's TV stars who, as is often the pitiable way of things, had metamorphosed into a pop act. The evening ended on a more positive note when Dick and Phil sat in with old mate Pete Hogman and his Blues Band at the Winter Gardens, Ventnor.

With the line-up settled the band was able to concentrate on the release of the *Anthology*. Put back for over a year due to the legal problems and the difficulty in finding a sympathetic label the 2 CD package titled *Unrepentant* was finally made available on September 15th.

The anthology concept had originated back in 1990 but the contractual battles with EMI and Phonogram ensured it was placed on the back burner whilst the legal matters were addressed. Phil also explained that the record companies had been suggesting the original master tapes no longer existed, although apart from *Freeway Madness* all of the masters were returned in time for remastering and inclusion.

The combined playing time of two hours thirty four minutes represented superb value and the album provided a chronological history of the band from 1964 through to the final track, 'God Give Me The Strength (To Carry On)', previewed from the long anticipated 'new' album. The *Anthology* oozed care and professionalism, a real tribute to the band. The booklet included rare photographs, excellent graphics and artwork, an informative history provided by *Rolling Stone*'s Ken Kessler and an informative piece by Mark St John explaining his part in their mottled history.

Perhaps, best of all, the tracks had been painstakingly re-mastered by St John who succeeded in enhancing the clarity whilst holding true to the original music and resisting any temptation to add to the sound.

The cover picture, chosen by St John, showed the bruised and swollen face of Viv Prince after the beating administered during a tour of Denmark. As the caption stated, 'Bloody but unbowed.'

The band and St John had selected the tracks although Phil felt that they almost chose themselves. The *Anthology* represented every period of the band's official recording career so the De Wolfe material, *Out Of The Island*, the BBC sessions and the various spin-off recordings were naturally absent.

The twenty-seven tracks on CD 1 covered the 1964-71 period whilst the second CD showcased 1972 through to 1980 with a further seventeen cuts.

Originally Phil had suggested that a colour-coded system be used to highlight different band periods but this was over-ruled by Fragile who were looking for a career thread without too much complication. Phil also confessed that they were worried about the *Emotions* material but after hearing 'Growing In My Mind' he was pleasantly surprised. He was positively effusive about the remastering. 'All the layers of cellophane were stripped away and minus all that high echo sound crap that existed on our earlier stuff.'

Apart from the 'new' album preview track, *Anthology* included two other unreleased songs – the original EMI acetate demo version of 'Defecting Grey' which lasted just over five minutes and 'Get Yourself Home' the song recorded but then discarded as a follow up to 'Don't Bring Me Down'. Phil stated that he received the acetate from John Stax, but John recalled that he didn't know anything about its inclusion explaining they must have lifted the track from one of his limited edition pressings. 'They certainly haven't got the acetate.'

In an uncommonly rare interview granted to Peter Innes for the *SF Sorrow* fanzine, Mark St John referred to the addition of the new track, 'God Give Me The Strength (To Carry On)' which he wrote. He described it as 'a contender for an all-time classic Pretties track.' To these ears it is the weakest track on the *Anthology*. It featured The Inspirational Choir and sounded like slowed down Mahalia Jackson complete with Euro-friendly accordion. The track, which featured only Phil, Frank Holland and St John was recorded in Soho, early one Saturday morning during 1994 and is not a classic Pretty Things song.

'Now', said Mark St John to Innes, 'You tell me – have the last few gigs featuring our reconstituted line-up seen a total change in the band, an edge, aggression and belief that was absent before…or am I fucking deaf!'

He wasn't fucking deaf. He was fucking right. This was the *real* Pretty Things. Not some European format based around Phil and Dick, not some temporary holding venture where friends and out-of-a-gig musicians banded together under the Pretty Things umbrella. A true Pretty Things without Skip, Jon and Wally was unthinkable, one without the added ingredient of Tolson significantly less vital.

The Guardian made *Unrepentant* retrospective CD of the week. 'Disparage them if you will,' warned Adam Sweeting, 'but the staying power of The Pretty Things can never be called into question.' He eulogised about the packaging going on to say that 'they never delivered a keynote single (or album) by which we shall forever remember them.' He finished saying, 'the finale is 'God Give Me The Strength', a taster for the new album. It's ornate and gospelly and lasts seven minutes. It should be loud, stroppy and very short.'

The *Anthology* was formally launched with a gig at the 100 Club in London on September 26th and was marked by a reversion to 1964 ticket prices, four shillings in the old currency, and entrance was therefore £0.20p. A lengthy queue formed outside and many were turned away.

Among the many special guests were Peter Grant and Brian Pendleton. Peter was introduced on stage and thanked sincerely by Phil for all his past efforts. As a finale, Pendleton joined them for a rendition of 'Rosalyn'. Terry Coates had invited Brian along and it had been agreed beforehand that he would join the band on stage but he was left waiting until the very end. He felt he had been cold-shouldered and was only introduced during the encore almost as an afterthought for a reprise of 'Rosalyn'.

This prestigious launch of the *Anthology* also signalled another change, the introduction of 'The Men in Black.' Attired in best *Reservoir Dogs* gear – black suits, black socks, black ties and shades – they took to the stage with a typical over the top introduction by St John, who forsaking his cultured public school tone effected his 'East End Lad' voice and introduced them as 'Old bastards'. A grin from Phil, then straight into the perennial 'Roadrunner'. The sight of Phil dangling a black tie around his neck indicated how much his attitudes had changed since his late teens when he listed ties as one of his pet hates, something that 'greys' wore.

Where did this idea come from? 'Suits and black ties? Mark and Phil's idea,' explained Jon Povey. '*Reservoir Dogs* kind of thing but at least it's given us a cohesive identity. If you look at most middle-aged bands they all come in jeans and their old cowboy shirts on, that's not gonna happen. At least people remember you and they remember you for the suits. Now they may not like the suits but they remember.'

Back in the 70s Phil used to take the stage draped in best leopard-skin suit, toss his shoulder length hair and pace about with the grin of a man being paid for doing what he loved best. Gone is the leopard-skin, gone is much of the hair but the grin remains. What's with the suits and shades? Well, it is somewhat tacky and derivative, just the sort of charge levelled at their music back in 1964, but that's progress in the music business for you.

The concert was filmed with talk of video releases and a showing on Channel 4's *The White Room*. The video never materialised as it seemed that the television producers didn't feel the band fitted their viewers' tastes. If this latter suggestion is true then it does seem misguided because *The White Room* had made a point of regularly featuring 60s and 70s icons such as Ray Davies and Lou Reed. The Pretties would have gone down a storm.

At this stage, unaware of the story behind Peter Tolson's walkout, I innocently asked St John where Peter was. 'He's gone fucking mad!' he bellowed at me, before striding off.

For once there was quite a media response to a Pretties' album. St John and the management team had ensured a major media initiative and TV station Channel 4 included an interview with Phil on *Teletext*. Just a few days later they reviewed the album saying, 'All you could ever dream of is here – 'Don't Bring Me Down', their finest hour – and much, much more.' They awarded it four out of a possible five. Appearances on cable and satellite television also boosted their profile.

Jon Savage in *Mojo* enthused about Disc 1 saying, 'It's all you need. Disc 2 is not an inspiring experience: fine if you like the slack temp of '70s rock, dull if you do not. I hope they make some money out of this box, but wouldn't you prefer great 45s like 'Come See Me' or 'Mr Evasion' – neither selected here – to 'Singapore Silk Torpedo'?'

In September the *Daily Star* quoted Phil as saying, 'I've never done a proper job in my life, and I wouldn't know where to start. I live off the royalties from our records… I'm not a millionaire but I'm not broke.' The usual wind-up from Phil, which was not quite the truth as he did work once on a building site, occasionally gave tennis lessons and for some years had worked at an art gallery in Westbourne Grove.

Mojo magazine's November issue carried a fine article complemented by a colour photo from The 100 Club launch gig. It reported that the night's bar takings were the highest in nine years – and that was without Phil's help! The article reported how, in 1965, Phil and Brian Jones spent an evening with Rudolf Nureyev and Judy Garland. They suggested that Brian had coupled with Garland whilst Phil slept with Nureyev! 'Phil always said he was bisexual, but we never believed him' recalled John Stax. 'We thought he only did it because it was sort of…cool.'

The Sunday Times, Christmas Eve edition, carried an end of year A-Z feature. The Pretties surfaced under 'L for Louts' next to a recreation of the famous July 1964 colour supplement. The column carried an all too brief history that only mentioned one song, 'Rosalyn', but reminded us that they were 'long-haired louts with songs about hard drugs, homosexuality and masturbation.' It added that Phil 'lives alone with his bicycle in West London' and Skip Alan 'invented the Swivelwalker, a mobility aid for paraplegics.' Was Jon Povey really a Buddhist? 'No. You've read that in the *Sunday Times* colour supplement,' he sneered. 'It said 'Jon Povey lives in Clapham and is a Buddhist', its bullshit. I don't even live in Clapham, I live in Battersea, I'm not a Buddhist, I'm a vegetarian.' The article also advised Jon's age as 50, when it was actually 53. They left the final words to Phil, 'We may be parking the zimmer frames next to the Harley's, but the gang's still here.'

Peter Grant died on November 21st, only eight weeks after his last public appearance at the 100 Club. On the day of his funeral, December 10th, Phil, Skip, Jon and Mark St John were interviewed by 'Whispering' Bob Harris for his GLR radio show. Phil expressed surprise at how draining and affecting the day had been and told Bob that 'Peter really put the artist first.' Jon explained, 'He kept everybody else away from the band, so they could do their thing, so they could be creative. He kept all that stuff away from them so they could just be themselves.' St John, in his cool way added, 'It's glib to sum up in just a few sentences just what he brought to the party… he was the first guy to make it possible for an act to tour in a major territory like the States and make money.'

When questioned about Grant's 'hard man' reputation St John said, 'He was an absolute gentleman and as long as you were straightforward and honest, he was with you. But the moment any guile entered the picture, particularly in respect of anybody he managed, he could be devastating.'

Skip asserted that Grant was instrumental in them getting their catalogue back and remarked how he had stayed at the 100 Club right to the end even though he was clearly very tired.

Ed Bicknell who also greatly admired Grant explained that his 'hard man' reputation was exaggerated. 'All this stuff about holding people out of windows. He told me he'd never dropped anyone.'

'He made so many enemies, making his way to the top, he died an old man with no friends,' countered Gordon Edwards. 'I was told that by Jimmy Page.' Grant was a character who provoked extremes of opinion.

What had been an extremely eventful year ended with a December 11th charity gig at The Borderline, in London. The fairly small venue was a bit of a dive where everything seemed the opposite of how it should be – Shiny carpets and cloudy toilet mirrors. Perversely, this grimy downmarket venue was exactly the setting to best experience a band like The Pretty Things. The mix of low-ceilinged acoustics, smoke veiled bar queues and the typical congestion that a haunt like this extends provided a peculiar intimacy that larger venues, particularly rock arenas, can never hope to duplicate.

After a formidable delay Mr Pink and his friends clambered onto the tiny stage. The highlight of the set for many was the reintroduction of the song 'Come See Me', a cracking number which should have been a top ten entry back in 1966 and had not been played since. For the usual encore, 'Route 66', not one but two non-members jumped up on stage. Mark St John took his now customary place behind the skins whilst behind the keyboards stood Gordon Edwards, although then aged 49 he looked a full decade younger than the rest and much healthier than he had any right to.

Writing in the following day's *Guardian*, Robin Denselow got it just right. 'At the Borderline they came on in dark suits, white shirts and black ties, like a bunch of ageing villains on parole to attend a gangland funeral. Elegantly battered old rockers, the lot of them, and they still sounded terrific as they bashed into their R&B anthems from the sixties, 'Roadrunner' and 'Don't Bring Me Down'. They could have played safe and stuck to early rock and blues material, but instead they offered the full Pretties history. The *Tommy*-like *SF Sorrow* was mixed with bursts of elaborate, gentle pieces from the early seventies, driven along by the wonderful Dick Taylor. Singer Phil May still camped it up like Jagger but showed he's an underestimated performer with considerable range, as on their overlooked classic from the punk era, 'Office Love'.'

1996 was a fairly quiet year for the band although it started with a bang when the Pretties returned to the 100 Club in January. 'I'm not gonna introduce these guys, you know who the fuck they are,' in best affected barrow-boy cant, Mark St John, the compere for the evening, introduced the band who sailed straight into 'Roadrunner' followed by their now constant set.

It was clear that the band had a problem finding suitable venues in the UK. The pub circuit was inappropriate and would not pay enough to make playing financially viable. Larger venues tended to cater for those bands able to squeeze in a thousand or more paying punters. The Pretties fell somewhere between the two and little was available. Phil had bemoaned the changes since the '60s. 'We had clubs like the Middle Earth and the Round-house in London. You had Mothers in Birmingham, you had a place in Manchester. Not many, but there were about six or seven places where a certain kind of music, which in those days was psychedelic, could be played. We had the universities as well. We were playing very odd places and wherever you played you got six or seven hundred people in that area who were interested in it. These days it doesn't seem to happen that way in England any more and it's strange. I don't know why.'

A tour of Holland, Germany and Switzerland took place in May, although this was without Jon Povey who due to work commitments was unable to go. His replacement was Russell Keefe, previously with the Bay City Rollers, another act under the tutelage of St John. The tour opened with a concert at the Paradiso in Amsterdam. At Frankenthal, on the 16th May, the heat was such that a shaking and dehydrated Skip left the stage between numbers. A nonplussed Phil had to ask a roadie to deputise on 'Judgement Day', as their manager was unusually absent. Skip eventually returned for the usual encore of 'Route 66', a song they have never recorded. I asked Dick Taylor why this was and he confessed to being unsure, but maybe, 'Because Chuck Berry did the ultimate version and the Stones did their version and it never seemed to have much relevance.' He did say that they continued playing it because, 'It's also the thing which Skip can sing. Well…' deliberated Dick, 'the thing that Skip can be behind the microphone for.'

The first ever Pretty Things picture disc was released in June. 'Eve of Destruction' backed with the original 'Rosalyn' and 'Passion of Love', the song recorded at the 'Eve of Destruction' sessions back in 1989 and only previously heard on Phil's gig sample tape. With a limited release of 5,000 copies it was never intended as a chart contender, merely support product for the European tour.

Mid July found them playing an open-air festival at Burg Herzberg in Germany. Topping the bill was Hawkwind and supporting bands included Rainbirds and Guru Guru. This is the type of scenario The Pretty Things love most and it showed, with a performance lasting over two and half-hours.

Towards the end of 1996 the band was invited to join a host of 60s stars on an album celebrating the birth of British blues. Jack Bruce, Mick Jagger, Paul Jones, Phil's old friend Maggie Bell and many, many more recorded an album of standards at London's Church Studios under the watchful eye of producer Pete Brown. The Pretties re-recorded 'Judgement Day', the perennial favourite that retains a place in their repertoire.

The relationship with Fragile disintegrated, which St John attributed to problems with SPV Records in Germany. This again put back the release of the new album to everyone's consternation.

Throughout the previous 28 years, with the occasional hiatus and a few hiccups, a Pretty Things fan club had been operating out of Holland. Back in the 70s a version was run by Robert Gerretson, then in the 1980's Sjo Zeitzen controlled operations before handing over to Joop de Ligt in the early 1990's.

Operated within very limited budgets the resulting fanzines, *SF Sorrow* being the last incarnation, were cheap reproductions but provided Pretties fans throughout the world with details of the band including in depth interviews with group members and reviews of all concerts, product releases and associated matters. Support by the band and management ensured that the news was up to date.

On December 12th, *SF Sorrow* editor, Joop de Ligt, wrote to all fanzine subscribers with the news that he had, 'Received a very disturbing telephone call' from The Pretty Things management. As a result of accusations made, he felt he had no option but to close the fanclub down. Continuing without the support of both band and management would have been virtually impossible.

What could have caused this schism? The problem originated back in 1994 when Joop had an idea of promoting a one-off concert involving the reformation of the original 1964 band. In Issue 71 of the fanzine Joop described what transpired. May 1997 would have been the 10th anniversary of the *SF Sorrow* fanzine and in anticipation of this he spoke to Dick and Phil in 1994 about a possible reunion of the 1967/68 band. His ambition was for *SF Sorrow* to be played in its entirety, a seed of an idea that would later bear fruit. Dick and Phil gave a guarded okay, Joop didn't know at this stage that the band members plus Peter Tolson were actually engaged in rehearsals.

Over the following months Joop's ambitions widened and he turned his attentions to a reunion of the 1964 Fontana band. Joop contacted Brian Pendleton, John Stax and Viv Prince and posed the idea of a reunion concert to them. They all agreed, subject quite naturally to expenses. At this stage he wrote to Mark St John explaining his idea for a reunion of the original 1964 band.

St John responded indicating that it would be a good idea but pointing out the practical difficulties – funds, rehearsals, preparation and other logistical problems. St John was also concerned that he and the band would not have control because it would require record company funds to support it. Although these points were imbued with a sense of pessimism St John sounded an optimistic note by suggesting he and Joop work together to explore the possibilities.

Phil, Dick and Viv Prince all gave a conditional assent at this stage and John Stax also indicated that he was prepared to come over. Joop's original intention was to arrange it for April 19th 1995, the 30th anniversary of the famous Blokker concert. Financial considerations were paramount, for eighteen months he had little success in raising the necessary funding, and this date passed by. However in July 1996 he met up with a Delft record shop owner who agreed to provide at least £10,000 toward a reunion. There were two conditions tied to this, all of the original members had to turn up, and it had to be held in Delft.

An option was taken on a suitable venue for the gig. Rehearsal rooms, PA system, lightshow and hotel accommodation was arranged. The idea was to hold a Pretty Things fan club day together with a record fair. The *SF Sorrow* line up would play then, after a one-hour gap, the 1964 band would perform.

Joop wrote to Mark St John, enclosing as usual a post-paid return envelope and waited, and waited... Eventually St John was contacted, and claimed to have not received the letter. The option on the venue was close to expiring and Joop frantically tried to contact St John who had also changed his telephone number.

Just one hour before the deadline St John telephoned and told Joop that he had to cancel plans for the reunion concert. He advised him that it was due to trouble with SPV, their German record company.

Joop could not understand why this German record company business should affect a Dutch concert and decided to contact SPV to find out what was happening. Their representative, Mr Edlefsen, told him that in 1995 they signed a contract with St John which allowed them to re-issue the entire Pretty Things back catalogue including the *A's & B's* album and the planned new album. He said they paid St John £75,000 but he had not provided them with the master tapes. Edlefsen advised that SPV would be taking legal action.

Writing in *Ugly Things* four years later St John recalled that SPV, the German Record Company, had fucked them up in the biggest way. Apparently they wouldn't answer phone calls and wouldn't respond to faxes or letters. He claimed that despite having fought to sign The Pretty Things, SPV made it impossible to release the new album. He advised that legal action against them was imminent.

Whatever the merits of the conflicting viewpoints, the dispute was St John's rationale for not proceeding with Joop's planned reunion. To have achieved such a reunion in tandem with the rejuvenated 1967 line-up would have been remarkable and with hindsight can be seen as highly doubtful from the outset. Of course, had St John not sounded an optimistic note in his 1994 correspondence with Joop the conflict might never have arisen.

Both band and management were disturbed by Joop's contact with SPV, they believed it jeopardised the negotiations that were taking place. The band members were adamant that Joop should never have involved himself in these matters and they were firmly behind St John's blackballing of Joop and the fanzine.

The demise of the *SF Sorrow* fanzine meant the only magazine to regularly provide a forum for Pretty Things fans and information on the band was *Ugly Things*, edited by Mike Stax. The publication catered for fans of 60s garage bands, particularly The Pretties, Creation, Mick Farren and the Deviants and the Downliners Sect, and had been published once or twice a year since 1983.

Talking to Terry Coates in 1995 Phil had avowed his support for the fan club and commented on how much work and effort the fanzine organisers put into the publications – a labour of love. A shame then that despite Joop's idiosyncrasies the band and management felt it necessary to withdraw their support. Joop almost certainly subsidised the magazine and clearly loved the band. This hard-nosed attitude would not have been prevalent amongst the 1960/70s band which took a more circumspect view of such matters.

Years later Joop remained bitter about the whole situation, especially St John. He explained that St John told him he always went by the book but Joop was dismayed to find his *SF Sorrow* fanzine artwork taken and repro-duced within the re-issued *Get The Picture*.

Joop revealed that Dick had tried to persuade him to reconsider his deci-sion regarding the fanzine, 'But I said, no way. I had too much trouble with this guy. I'm happy it's all behind me. Even after I stopped this man gave me a very bad headache. This person probably thinks he is like God himself and therefore stands above the law.'

In due course St John approached Mike Stax suggesting that as he was already operating a semi-official Pretty Things fanzine within the *Ugly Things* magazine he should set up an official fan club. The magazine would naturally receive the full backing of band and management. Stax was even approached to write the sleeve notes for future Snapper releases and assisted in selecting the tracks on the *Latest Writs – Greatest Hits* CD issued in February 2000.

See For Miles, the specialist reissue label set up by Colin Miles, released the *EP Collection…Plus*, containing tracks from all three UK EP's as well as four France-only release EP's, all Fontana stuff. To fill out the album, St John and the band added six additional numbers, which were singles or album tracks. Brian Hogg who had also written the exhaustive notes to *Closed Res-taurant Blues* penned the excellent biographical liner notes within.

Mark St John now guided the band towards Snapper Music, whose man-agement he had met and 'bonded with'. Jon Beecher had set up Snapper in 1996 after his previous stint as managing director and co-founder of Castle Communications. Snapper was able to boast Peter Green and Porcupine Tree amongst its roster of artists and the contract enabled Snapper to reissue the whole of the Pretties official output and additionally provided for up to three new releases.

Interestingly the new album deal soley applied to Phil and Dick as only these two were signed to Snapper, with the rest of the band appearing to be peripheral. As with the 1980 *Cross Talk* deal this seemed odd for a band that over the decades had evinced such integrity. Alongside The Melville Corporation saga it raised a number of questions, which Dick was asked. He was caught off-guard, hesitant and somewhat taken aback. 'Err...I don't think I'd better get into that quite honestly. I think that's something we could deal with later, possibly.'

Jon Povey confirmed the situation and appeared fatalistic about the matter. 'I don't get too involved in all that, when they want me they call me up and I go and do whatever I've got to do.'

During the year, St John wound up his Golden Recording Company Ltd choosing to relinquish the much coveted limited liability status, an act that coincidentally ensured that accounts would not be a matter of public record.

The word in late 1997 was of a new single. Phil had written a song about the late Princess Diana, predictably portraying her as a victim and attacking the establishment. The single never happened and probably due to lack of topicality, it never made the album. Talk of a possible Channel 4 TV documentary also came to nothing.

During the summer The Pretty Things recorded their first batch of songs in the new resurrected format. Three of these eventually made it onto the new album 'Vivian Prince', 'Blue Turns To Red' and 'Everlasting Flame'.

Phil and wife Electra had parted some years before and the marital rupture concluded at this time with the formality of a divorce, although matters were sufficiently amicable that Phil would regularly join her, Sorrel and Paris for holidays at her Norfolk property.

Talking to *Ugly Things* magazine Phil was blunt in his assessment of the band's future. 'All being well, if the ship's sailing and the weather's not too bad, it's easy. If suddenly the fuckin' ship starts getting a few holes in it and the weather turns shitty, who knows what will happen.'

The Snapper contract provided for the release of remastered versions of the bands nine official LP's plus the 'new' album. The reissues would be treated with care and respect offering bonus tracks, in-depth liner notes often by the group who had lived it or by St John who had heard about it. They also included rare and previously unseen photographs. The eponymous debut album and *Get The Picture?* began the reissue schedule, followed by *Emotions*.

All three were released as mid-price items, as all the re-issues would be and this made them great value for money. Arguably all reissues should be mid or budget price items but many are not and in any event few of them are as carefully conceived and as painstakingly pieced together as the Snapper releases. The debut album, *The Pretty Things*, contained six bonus tracks and a video of the 100 Club launch gig with the original 'Rosalyn' blasting away in the background and 100 Club live footage teasingly crafted on as if the band were singing the original song.

The bonus tracks comprised the first two singles, 'Rosalyn' and 'Don't Bring Me Down', together with their respective B-sides, 'Big Boss Man' and 'We'll Be Together'. The rejected single, 'Get Yourself Home' and 'I Can Never Say', the B-side of 'Honey I Need', completed the eighteen track package.

Get The Picture? followed a similar theme, six bonus tracks plus the 1966 video of *Pretty Things On Film*. Bonus tracks were 'Get A Buzz', 'Sittin' All Alone', 'Midnight To Six Man', 'Me Needing You', 'Come See Me' and 'L.S.D.' Both CDs had been painstakingly re-mastered by Mark St John and Andy Pearce in February of the previous year.

The reissue of *Emotions* continued the chronological progression and contained seven additional tracks, 'House in the Country' and 'Progress', the last two non-album singles issued on Fontana, and four of the *Emotions* songs with the orchestration removed. Additionally a non-orchestrated version of 'Progress' was also included. This provided listeners with an opportunity to assess the recordings without the hated Reg Tilsley arrangements. Sad to say, many of the numbers sounded empty with the guitar/bass/drums arrangements sounding fairly bland and the whole thing lacked the urgency of the two previous albums. Some tracks such as 'My Time' retained a faint orchestral residue, and this bleed-through sounded better for being understated. 'Photographer' seemed rather naked without the brass but towards the end a marvellously inventive bass line was revealed, something that the orchestration had obliterated on the original.

Sleeve notes for the three re-releases were drafted by leading pop scribe Paul Du Noyer who made an excellent case for them being ambassadors for punk and the plague of garage bands that had emerged during the previous three decades. Unfortunately his commitment to the band did not extend as far as including any of their singles or albums in the books he penned listing the 1000 best singles and 1000 best albums.

Trevor Hodgett reviewed the three releases for *Rock 'n' Reel* magazine and felt that the debut album lacked 'The depth and compelling power of the R&B greats who inspired the band.' Like many a listener he ventured the opinion that on *Emotions* 'The songs are not distinguished enough and the orchestral arrangements are frequently intrusive.'

One odd feature of the reissues was the apparent ability of publishers, Peer Music, to assume ownership of the entire *Get The Picture?* material. It was not unreasonable for The Pretty Things own songs to have been diverted from Jimbo or Dumno Music but it seemed quite remarkable that Peer managed to acquire the rights to material written by Ray Charles Slim Harpo, JJ Jackson, and others.

With the 'new album' still bubbling away on the stove, in May 1998 the Pretties recorded one final track. Phil's delicate melody 'Fly Away' was recorded in one take without overdubbed harmonies or guitar. Its wistful cadence recalled 'Loneliest Person', the coda on *SF Sorrow*. With the first three albums having been re-packaged and released it was now the turn of *SF Sorrow*, still considered by many to be the bands' finest hour.

CHAPTER 18 – Resurrection

Phil May had long regarded *SF Sorrow* as the jewel in The Pretty Things' crown and the band had always harboured ambitions to perform the rock opera in its entirety. Back in the late 60s this proved impossible due to their reliance on the mellotron, an instrument that was difficult to transport due to a loss of calibration. Back then they had neither the technique nor the technology to perform the entire work and Dick suggested that they also lacked the confidence.

Tentative plans were made for a performance at the Chalk Farm Round-house where they had mimed versions in the late 60s but this proved implausible because Camden Council continually objected, due primarily to the building's woeful state of repair. Reluctantly the idea was dropped.

Dougie Dudgeon at Snapper then suggested that they perform the entire *SF Sorrow* 'opera' live on the Internet. Having been involved in a similar US based project with label act Ozric Tentacles he knew that the technical capability of the Internet was now proven and that it would prove to be a landmark.

An advertisement for a July 1998 Worcester Park Club appearance, contrived it as the band's final R&B gig and on the evening a packed crowd included the late, lamented Screaming Lord Sutch, who repeatedly punched the air as he propped up the bar. Was it the end of R&B for the Pretties? Could it really be that the Pretties would stop performing the very music that inspired them back in 1963 and still does to this day? Not very likely, Phil has resolved not to make the same mistake as The Byrds who upon reformation played a set that failed to include even one of their hits. Nonetheless as a marketing pitch it probably worked as the slogan conspired to produce a higher than usual turn out.

The following month saw two UK concerts. One was at Chiselhurst Caves, scene of the *Silk Torpedo* bash back in 1974 and the other was at Ronnie Scott's, in London where all became clear. With the live Internet broadcast of *SF Sorrow* barely two weeks away they were taking the opportunity to perfect songs from the album that had never been played live in its entirety. Arthur Brown was on hand to practice his narration, providing a quite forbidding aspect, like the brooding re-incarnation of Rasputin, fresh from execrable acts and intent on further abominations.

A promotional release maxi-single containing 'Defecting Grey', 'SF Sorrow Is Born', 'Balloon Burning' and 'Everlasting Flame' was distributed in August with a press release promoting the re-enactment of *SF Sorrow*. The release advertised the Chiselhurst Caves concert saying that The Pretty Things will show you something of the magic of this masterpiece. It advised that the only performance ever of *SF Sorrow* would be at 8.00 p.m. on Sunday September 6th at Abbey Road Studios with the added ingredient of Pink Floyd's Dave Gilmour. 'Everlasting Flame' was a new item for Pretties followers and would later appear on the new album when it eventually gained a release.

The Ronnie Scott's performance was a great success. Wally in particular considered it his favourite gig in recent years citing the intimacy and the reception accorded them. 'Standing on that stage was like standing on hallowed ground,' he confessed.

Held on the 23rd of August, it was a virtual dress rehearsal. Arthur Brown provided narration between a medley of *Sorrow* songs and Skip's son Dov assisted with the percussion, which on the album was extensive. The poster advertising the Ronnie Scott's appearance showed the band in full *Reservoir Dogs* regalia – black ties, black suits, black shades, black expressions – except for Dick. He chose to add open-toed sandals to his sartorial repertoire, and pretty damn fine it looked too.

So it happened, Sunday September 6th 1998. The Pretty Things, Dave Gilmour, Arthur Brown, Mark St John, Dov Skipper and various friends, family and scribes filled the legendary Abbey Road Studio 2. Nearly thirty years after its conception the world witnessed the maiden performance of the rock opera *SF Sorrow*.

Recently re-released by Snapper Records in the original mono and faithfully remastered by St John, the world's first rock opera was performed live and simultaneously broadcast over the Internet.

The broadcast could not be termed a resounding success for UK viewers as the signal was bounced from St Johns Wood across to the States and back again. The web traffic was such that UK viewers received at best broken images and dodgy sound, at worst they failed to obtain any transmission.

Those able to view would have seen the Master of Ceremonies, the ubiquitous Mark St John, regaling the audience with tales of the Pretties 'history of fucking up' and 'Earning pennies when others were earning thousands'. He again promulgated the myth that Norman Smith was bouncing from studio to studio producing *Piper At The Gates Of Dawn* and *SF Sorrow* whilst simultaneously engineering *Sgt Pepper*. It made good copy, sure, but quite simply was wrong. History did not need re-writing for The Pretty Things, the band's reputation stood on its merits and The Pretty Things place in the pantheon of R&B, psychedelic and rock history was secure.

This regularly promoted fable requires an appropriate rebuttal as already it is being accepted by scribes and interviewers and if left unchallenged will devolve into 'fact'. An exploration of the wealth of archive material detailing The Beatles recording sessions easily refutes the myth, and of course The Pretty Things didn't even sign to EMI until October 2 1967, four months after *Pepper's* release. It was actually the sessions for *Emotions* that paralleled the *Pepper* recordings.

Producer Norman Smith agreed. Was he involved in *Sgt Pepper*? 'Nothing to do with it at all,' he confirmed and went on to explain that *Piper At The Gates Of Dawn* and *SF Sorrow* had not been recorded simultaneously either. 'Well it's incorrect in terms of those two albums as well. You could never concurrently run two albums of such significance at the same time. For me at any rate it would have been impossible to run those two things concurrently. They were both pretty difficult to produce in different ways.'

Research confirms that The Pretty Things earliest EMI sessions were at Sound Techniques studio where 'Defecting Grey' and 'Mr Evasion' were laid down. The Abbey Road sessions for *SF Sorrow* commenced in November 1967, five months after the Floyd completed *Piper*.

Phil has since altered stance and stated that *SF Sorrow* was recorded whilst 'Pink Floyd was on the one side recording *Saucerful Of Secrets* and The Beatles on the other side with their *Sgt Peppers Lonely Hearts Club Band*.' Well, his recollection is half-right, an improvement on the St John inspired myth.

Thankfully Wally chose to put the record straight in his sleeve notes to the re-issued *Freeway Madness* when he outlined the contribution of Norman Smith. 'Perhaps his most famous works as an engineer were all the Beatles records right up till *Rubber Soul*.'

The *Sorrow* introduction continued and, after a joke about ageing trapeze artists attempting triples, St John introduced Dave Gilmour, who guested on guitar on four numbers, and 'Great fellow' Arthur Brown, who he also represented at the time. From there he handed over to Brown who performed a deliciously over-the-top narration which told the life story of Sebastian F Sorrow and which also served to separate the songs.

'Brown underpants time,' stated Phil describing the full day spent preparing for the evening's broadcast. It had been intended to run through the entire performance to iron out any rough edges and also to do a proper sound check but time spent allowing the cameras to obtain correct angles and other technical stuff ruined that plan. On the night they had to wing it having played all the numbers individually but never consecutively.

'It sounds fucking amazing,' emoted Phil. 'Especially as we didn't even have a chance to get everyone to do it all the way through once beforehand. We got Dave's sound, we got Dick's sound, we got Arthur's sound, but it was all piecemeal.'

The concert went better than anybody could have anticipated. Yes there is a bum note from Dick somewhere and Povey's voice did quaver a bit on 'I

See You' and Phil did confuse the lyrics on 'Death', but what the hell, that's just a typical gig isn't it?

The author, Jenny Fabian, reported the event for *Mojo* and was given the five star treatment by St John, being led backstage to visit with the band and dignitaries. In her subsequent article she recalled seeing the performance before, in the 60s, but she was mistaken. Several of the songs were performed but never the whole opera in its entirety. Of course she may have seen the Twink inspired mime affairs where they paraded around whilst the album was played.

Norman Smith and Peter Mew, respectively the original producer and engineer of the *Sorrow* recording sessions, were conspicuously absent from the extravaganza. Peter would have loved an invite and only heard about the concert when he checked in for work at Abbey Road Studios the following day. Norman Smith assured me that he did not receive an invitation although Phil had mentioned some weeks before the concert that they were trying to contact him. The band confirmed that they extended an invitation via Norman's son, Nick and Phil later suggested that Nick, the man originally responsible for unleashing St John on The Pretty Things, was being protective due to Norman's failing health.

'I think Nick did say something to me about it but it didn't mean there was a forthcoming thing at Abbey Road,' sighed Norman. 'I would certainly have gone had I received that kind of invitation but no, I never did. I didn't even know it was going to be at Abbey Road. I heard later that Phil was very upset that I didn't turn up, would you believe, I couldn't turn up if I didn't receive an invitation. I had no idea or I would most certainly have been there.'

The resurrection of *SF Sorrow* generated media interest from all the entertainment monthlys and *Record Collector's* November 1998 issue ran half a page detailing the performance and describing it as 'Faultless, inspired and, if possible, even more wonderful than the album itself.' Unfortunately the piece ended with a grouse, 'Which is why the pointless encore of 'Route 66' shattered an otherwise magical evening: a sweaty drummer belting out Chuck Berry was an unnecessary awakening from one of rock's great dreams.'

Dave Gilmour's participation was of course down to Phil. Great mates for many years, Phil considers Dave 'family', a word denoting true band members and long-time associates. Temporary and passing members like Simon Fox, Willie Wilson and Barklay McKay presumably being considered the equivalent of third cousins twice removed. 'Family' is a big thing with the band, Phil and Skip in particular, and indicates not only the 'true' band members but also the 'true' friends who have given support and succour over the years. By this definition Peter Tolson is family but Vic Unitt is not. Dave

Gilmour and Mike Stax qualify whilst Steve Browning fails the test. Twink and Jack Green qualify as family but have been consigned to the black sheep category and therefore fail to meet the stringent criteria.

Like most families, The Pretty Things have feuded and like many families have split up, reformed, fractured and somehow found themselves back together again at the end. Jon has engaged in punch-ups with Skip and Phil, whilst Wally has fired blows at Twink, yet, Twink apart, they still enjoy each other's company and clearly gel as a musical unit. Jack and Gordon retain fond memories of their stay in the band and Peter Tolson, whilst disgusted by the rock 'n' roll depravity, remembers most periods with genuine pleasure.

Snapper rushed out the *Resurrection* CD in October in a limited edition of 10,000. The recording ignored the 'Sweaty drummer' encore concentrating on the songs and narration of *SF Sorrow* with St John's measured introduction thrown in by way of a preface. In its review of the CD, *Record Collector* reported it 'An unqualified triumph.'

The CD benefited from adjustments which enabled some of the cock-ups to be eliminated. Gilmour's guitarwork on 'She Says Good Morning' and 'Old Man Going' was particularly memorable as was Skip's powerful drumming, the beats ricocheting off the wall of assisted percussion.

SF Sorrow was now in the spotlight again, not least for the re-issue of the original mono version together with four bonus tracks including the original acetate of the pre-EMI 'Defecting Grey', rescued from Jon Povey's mother's loft. The mono version sounded noticeably different from the stereo versions which most will have previously bought. The gong on 'Death' obliterated the following few seconds of the song and the exploding guitar solo on 'She Says Good Morning' is subdued, lacking the punch and vitality of the stereo version.

Attention was again brought by band, management and the media to it being the first rock opera. Comments abounded regarding its influence on Pete Townshend during the creation of *Tommy*.

Shortly after the broadcast Phil was contacted by Townshend as Dick recounted. 'Phil received a letter saying as far as he was aware Pete Townshend had never heard *SF Sorrow* and it certainly wasn't the inspiration for *Tommy* and could Phil please refrain from ever mentioning this again otherwise legal things would happen. What really cheesed me off, it was such a friendly letter but it was really being quite heavy about it, I wish you all the best and good luck old boy and all this and then saying, 'I'll sue you you bastard if you say this again'.'

Dick considered one specific song as clearly being influenced, 'I haven't seen him for goodness knows how long but I think it would be pretty hard to say 'Pinball Wizard' wasn't influenced by 'Old Man Going', it's there, the intro, it's amazing. You just think, hang on, it's straight off it. We had a guy called 'H' working for us – Howard – a roadie who is now unfortunately dead. He took *SF Sorrow*, either a tape or one of the first test pressings, to a party which they were at and he was very friendly with them and he did say, and I have no reason to think he was lying, that they kept playing it over and over again and were rather intrigued by it. Also people have told me they've read quotes from Pete Townshend saying, 'Yes it was certainly the inspiration for *Tommy*.'

Dick reasoned the matter out. 'If he hadn't said it before and if 'H' hadn't said it as well I would think fair enough, we've maybe got it wrong. I read the other week in *Record Collector* that we were inspired by the original Nirvana, one which I never heard. But he has said it and there is more than a passing resemblance, certainly the intro of 'Pinball Wizard'. What I actually think happened, he was boozing a lot at the time, I think he probably did hear it and was inspired and he's forgotten or he heard it a few times forgot that he heard it and did the classical thing of writing something that was pretty similar and forgotten what the source is. We've all done that, we've all written someone else's song and gone 'Oh shit' that's so and so afterwards.'

Derek Boltwood recalled, 'I remember at the time that Pete Townshend was widely quoted by saying that *SF Sorrow* had influenced *Tommy*. It may be that he doesn't like to be reminded of that.'

Patrick Humphries reported Procol Harum's Gary Brooker as saying, 'We were talking to Pete Townshend once and he said *Tommy* only happened because we'd done 'Held 'Twas In 'I.' This was the suite of songs on *Shine On Brightly*, Procol's second album, which was released in December 1968, the same month as *SF Sorrow*. Perhaps Townshend took inspiration from many sources, some remembered some forgotten.

Sorrow was swept along with a publicity blast that ensured its reappearance was reported in every worthwhile magazine, journal and newspaper. The reviews were most favourable. After thirty years the media was waking up to the lost gem and making up for their collective sin in neglecting to champion it first time around.

Michael Heatley writing in *Magpie* suggested that, 'The Pretty Things must wonder where they took the wrong turning on rock's long and winding road. Heard of *Tommy*? Well this preceded it by a full year, Pete Townshend admitting its influence in a *Billboard* magazine article.'

Uncut got it wrong straight away saying that *SF Sorrow* was on CD for the first time, a stereo version had appeared on Edsel in 1987. Scribe Nigel Williamson thought that, 'As an opera, the story was a messy and confused anti-war diatribe but much of the music was glorious.'

The Sunday Times confirmed that, 'It beat *Tommy* and most po-faced concept albums out of sight', and the *Freak Emporium* magazine announced that its readers poll had voted *SF Sorrow* the second greatest psychedelic album of all time, only Floyd's *Piper At The Gates Of Dawn* gaining more votes. *Record Collector's* January 2000 edition highlighted the ten best albums of every genre. Unsurprisingly *SF Sorrow* made the psychedelic ten and was described as a 'Consummate and oft overlooked masterpiece... the spirit of unbridled experimentation came together in one successful collage before the term "concept album" struck terror into the hearts of any sane individual.'

Classic Rock magazine took a different stance with reviewer Jerry Ewing rubbishing the album. The condemnation caused outrage and the magazine was telephoned by somebody who threatened Ewing. Acting editor Dave Ling who took the call, was told by the caller that he was the Pretties' manager Mark St John. The caller said he was a bit tasty, had heavy friends and used to hang around with Peter Grant and that Ewing had better be careful or else.

Understandable rage? Perhaps, but foot-shooting in the very best Pretty Things tradition because, unknown to either St John or the band, an in depth Pretties article was under consideration by *Classic Rock*. Not surprisingly the idea was swiftly dropped.

November was judged the appropriate time to re-issue *Silk Torpedo* and *Savage Eye*, again with bonus tracks. Snapper, who thus far had issued the CD's in chronological order, jumped two albums because they were receiving interest from the outlets for the Swansong material. *Silk Torpedo* included live versions of 'Singapore Silk Torpedo' and 'Dream/Joey' from a 1975 Santa Monica concert. The live cuts highlighted how the Pretties always played songs a tad faster live than when in the studio. Peter Tolson found this slightly irritating and recalled how the other band members overruled him because they felt it added excitement to the songs. In the liner notes Mark St John got it wrong when he commented on the track 'Joey' and volunteered that the song showed how closely Phil and Jon Povey were working at that time. The song was of course the work of Gordon Edwards.

The *Savage Eye* re-issue was the more interesting. Three bonus tracks were included, 'Tonight', that excellent failed single from May 1976 and two demo tracks recorded by Metropolis, 'Love Me A Little' and 'Dance All Night'. When 'Tonight' was originally released Swansong credited it to Gordon Edwards. Phil hated the song and, as the CD liner notes inform, he thinks the song a 'total piece of shit.' On the re-issued CD the composer has been forgotten.

The two Metropolis tracks were presumably also licensed from Swansong and included as an item of historical interest. Jack Green was somewhat unimpressed, and I asked Peter Tolson if he felt the same. 'Yeah, cause it's not The Pretty Things. Why the fuck have they got it on there?'

Gordon recalled 'Dance All Night' and the high vocal range required. ''Dance All Night' was so fucking high you wouldn't believe it. I was singing top C sharp, half a note higher than Pavarotti can hit. You didn't have the computer stuff you've got today but I used to say 'can you slow it down so I'm singing a note lower than normal', then we could speed it back later. The only people I heard sing that high before were people like Steve Winwood.'

Of the 1998 line-up only Skip played on the two Metropolis tracks. Tolson, Green and Edwards wrote the songs, although there is no reason why Snapper should know that, and, guess what? The credits are omitted for these two as well. Will they receive royalties? Neither Jack nor Gordon has received royalties for any of the Pretties material they composed, so why should matters change at this late stage? It also raises the question of why were these tracks added to the album? Why not some of the tracks from the abortive Dogs of War sessions at Rockfield? These included Peter, Wally and Skip and are clearly more representative of 'The Pretty Things' than the Metropolis material and it seems reasonable that these cuts would be available under licence.

Record Collector reviewed both reissues and also the *SF Sorrow Resurrection* in its June '99 issue. Reviewer, John Sturdy, considered it debatable whether the re-releases would 'Add to band members' pension funds.' He felt that *Silk Torpedo's* success in America was more due 'To Peter Grant's marketing muscle than any inherent musical quality.' Sturdy took issue with St John's liner notes stating, 'All too often, though, *Silk Torpedo* struggles to break free of the stifling conventionality that made the mid-70s UK Rock scene such a dreary animal and when current Pretties manager Mark St John asserts in a counter-productively hyperbolic sleevenote that the album is a perfect encapsulation of the era, cynics among us will claim that's not necessarily a recommendation.'

Savage Eye is castigated for 'The distressing anonymity of the hard rock tracks' with Sturdy expressing a preference for the wistful 'Sad Eye' and 'My Song'.

Dick kept musically healthy during this non-gigging period by playing on three tracks on ex-Savoy Brown vocalist Jackie Lynton's solo release. The album on New Day Records included many current and ex-members of Jethro Tull as well as Rick Parfitt, Status Quo's rhythm guitarist.

In November the Pretties performed a one-off show, headlining Cavestomp '98 in New York. The club was full beyond capacity and the gig was lauded as best of the year by the following day's New York Times. The three-day show provided a mix of new bands and garage originals and introduced the Pretty Things to America for the first time since the combustion days of 1976.

December saw the Pretties play an increasingly rare UK gig at the Torrington Arms, North Finchley. The gig was intended as a warm-up for the upcoming German TV extravaganza with Van Morrison. The practice was needed as it was the sloppiest I had ever seen them play. The harmonies were frequently out of tune and out of synch and Skip's drumming, so often the engine driving the band, was ragged and lacked timing. After the usual riotous 'Route 66' encore St John was accosted by the promoter who complained about the bent mike-stand which Skip had been wielding. St John had a word with Skip who looked suitably disgusted. He picked up the offending item and promptly bent it back into shape.

The German Van Morrison concert was held just before Christmas. The bill also included rising teenage blues star Jonny Lang, and the entire concert was broadcast on German TV and across Europe. As a support act they played an abridged set leaving out regulars such as 'Rosalyn' and in view of the TV cameras Phil abstained from shouting his usual 'Don't bring me down, motherfucker!' After the concert Phil, Dick and Skip were interviewed and Skip mentioned that his son Dov drummed with ex-Motown hitmaker Edwin Starr. Skip then decided to stand on his head!

CHAPTER 19 – All The Rage

'Albatross,' announced Dick. He was describing the weight of eighteen years of recordings, expectations and grief that had been absorbed by the new CD. Reputedly it had cost more than £200,000, hardly any of which would be recouped when, finally, it gained a release in March 1999 on the Snapper subsidiary Madfish. The original working title was *Paradise Lost* a description pertinent to the band's flirtation with mainstream success. This was discarded and Phil came up with *Cruel Britannia*, another title seemingly born of the Thatcher years, a period that coincided with the band's low point and a time when they, as with much of Britain, experienced both worry and despair. Spookily another Snapper band, The Selector, came up with the same title for their new album so once again a suitable name was sought. St John suggested, surely tongue-in-cheek, that he wanted to call it 'Fuck Oasis and Fuck You', partly in response to Skip's hatred of that derivative band's media fascination. The actual title, *Rage Before Beauty*, also coined by St John, perfectly summed up the continuing anger and edge that separated the Pretties music from their peers and indeed most of the youth bands. An edge that age, thankfully, had failed to blunt.

A 1999 *Mail On Sunday* music article commented, 'It's a sad truism that bands and stars tend to run out of steam long before they and their labels are prepared to call it a day.' This statement runs true for virtually all acts. Pink Floyd started their downhill trek after *Animals* whilst Yes have continually failed to move forward since *Close To The Edge*. Status Quo have tended to reconstitute the same old riffs and chord changes whilst some would argue that the Stones have turned out only the occasional track of note since *Exile On Main Street*.

The Pretty Things have never suffered from this creative malaise and it is worth touching on why this might be. In many instances success blunts the musical edge, removes the urge to succeed and diminishes the hunger that drives younger, fresher bands. Numerous acts have had one or two interesting things to say but have then carried on saying them across a hatful of releases to the point where it lurched into parody (Status Quo?). Similarly many acts seek to parade the range of their abilities by manoeuvring into different musical areas, a move that often backfires leaving a legacy of vacuity or embarrassment, one thinks of the Stones bandwagon excursion into psychedelia and The Tremeloes attempt at being progressive.

Ignoring their formative years, The Pretty Things have never quite reached the stage where money and fame has had an opportunity to strangle the creativity. It may be no coincidence that their closest brush with mainstream success, the Swansong period, mirrored their least convincing and enduring musical period. With something still to say and something to prove they persevered over a period far longer than the typical lifespan of most bands.

Rage, was the culmination of eighteen years of stop-start recording sessions. Beginning with the *Cross Talk* band (with Simon Fox in place of Skip and Willie Wilson) and extending across numerous combinations of players brought in at various points, Steve Browning, Bobby Webb, Mark St John, Nigel Ross-Scott, Matt Owen and Fulva Juste's troop.

Many songs were re-recorded or snipped, poked or otherwise tampered with to provide the desired end result.

The band's attitude to recording had altered over the years. In the 60s and 70s they laid down the bass and drum tracks then added guitar, harmony and vocals. Now they spend time getting the right feel and getting to know the song, then it is played 'live' with occasional overdubs. This is best personified by the recording of 'Fly Away' which was achieved in one take, without overdubs and, as St John says in the CD notes, if you listen carefully you can hear the bars being counted off.

A great many recordings were discarded during the tortured birth process of *Rage*, including three of the five tracks originally recorded at Freerange in 1981, 'The Young Pretenders', 'Wish Fulfilment' and 'Sea About Me'. Phil's Princess Diana tribute and various others also failed to make the grade.

Dave Gilmour guested on 'Love Keeps Hanging On', an extravaganza with the added assistance of the Bach Chorale, Gilmour's tremolo heavy guitar patterns and Mark St John's heaving drum rhythms. Lamenting the fracturing of his relationship with Electra it is heavy on the Shakespearian allegories and St John claims he shed tears after the emotional vocal session. Bassist Steve Browning related how Gilmour became caught up in the recordings. 'Phil was borrowing guitars off him to use on the new album and in the end, of course, he ended up coming in and doing a track. His guitar playing on that is just phenomenal. The song is really a vehicle for his playing.' The Bach Chorale added a strange ambience, not unlike the keening chorus on the Stones 'You Can't Always Get What You Want'.

The CD also contained a re-mixed version of 'Goin' Downhill' which commendably put the record straight and credited Peter Tolson's writing input although it was missing the coda tagged on to the original recording. It is unclear whether any of Tolson's guitarwork survived, Dick recalled St John using a guitar piece he had uncovered, but the musicianship couldn't be verified.

'Mony Mony' was a considerable disappointment. Unlike the other two covers it offered nothing new and compared unfavourably with Tommy

James and the Shondells version. Messy and cluttered it staggered along for just over four and a half minutes and represented a waste of valuable CD time. The version is not even liked by many in the band.

Dick felt it had flavours of blues and psychedelia, whilst Phil told American Internet site, Allstar, that it was a back-to-basics affair that went for a first take vibe rather than grand production. 'We always wanted to come back as a writing force. We never intended to get back together to play old stuff; rather, we've always wanted to go forward. Things are good. Everybody's writing, and in fact we've already got enough material for another two albums.'

When pressed for a favourite track Dick proffered 'God Give Me The Strength', the dismal song originally tagged on as the final track on the *Anthology*. Excepting some *Emotions* material and 'I Can Never Say', this is the least Pretty Thingsish track ever committed to tape and without Phil's vocal it would sound like Klaus Wunderlich Plays Gospel. Believe me, never trust a rock song if it contains a synthesised accordion.

The inclusion of the revved up version of P F Sloans 'Eve of Destruction' was something of a surprise given Phil's preference for new, freshly recorded material. He reasoned that the song's message remained particularly apt and retained its relevance, and he has a point. Although it has been doing the rounds since its 1989 single release it is still a great rocking version.

'Play With Fire', the 1965 Stones B-side has been seen by some as unnecessary. However this criticism is unfair, as the Things' version does not attempt to ape the Stones but embellishes the song with harmonies and stop-start rhythms. Phil explained that they had always wanted to do a Jagger/Richards song and that this, one of his favourites, was evocative of the mid-sixties London scene. Like 'Eve Of Destruction' it was recorded in 1989 with Steve Browning on bass although the harmonies suggest that Wally and Jon Povey were dubbed on later. Dick impishly explained to interviewers that they recorded it to help Mick Jagger pay for his 'divorce' from Jerry Hall.

The originals were more interesting however with the albums opening track, a ripping 'Passion Of Love', betraying a hint of Dylans' 'Tombstone Blues', the 1965 song that namechecked the Pretties. This late 1980s recording fairly bristles and sounds sufficiently commercial to have been a possible hit single.

'Vivian Prince', homage to the maniac ex-drummer, reverted to the patented Bo Diddley beat complete with acoustic guitars, plenty of percussion and a chorus that also acclaimed Skip. The third track, 'Everlasting Flame', wrongly suggested by some to be the Princess Diana tribute, was considered strong enough to be the album's single although Dougie at Snapper disagreed and vetoed the idea.

249

Not a great album, but a very good one. It contained gems like 'Goin' Downhill', 'Blue Turns To Red' and 'Pure Cold Stone' and benefited from a brisk start and strong middle section. Unfortunately it petered out and the final two tracks, 'Mony Mony' and 'God Give Me The Strength' are a sub-standard coda, like a champion racehorse limping across the finishing line.

An inspection of the liner-notes showed that Phil was credited or co-credited on all of the eleven original songs. Frank Holland was co-credited on four songs and St John on three. By contrast Jon Povey was only on two and Dick on one. Wally Waller who was so prolific in the '60s and '70s failed to receive even one credit.

'Yes it is Phil and Dick and Mark running the whole thing,' stated Jon Povey. 'We're doing other things as well. I'd like to be involved more but the parameters are already set so we just leave it at that. We like playing and we're trying to get The Pretty Things more recognition if you like. It's never been managed properly before, even in Peter Grant's days it really wasn't managed properly because the main focus was Led Zeppelin, of course. We were just like a subsidiary.'

Wally accepted that St John was basing everything around Phil and Dick. 'I think he has a vision of how to market the band, and who's to say he's wrong? He's done very well. His vision seems to hold true. We get on and it's not a big problem, in my opinion the best is still to come.'

Is it the Phil and Dick Show? 'I think that's the current perception,' conceded Wally. 'I mean they are the two originals and I think with the current regime that's what's going on, that's something where all you can do is do your stuff and if people don't like it, it's too bad. There's always other avenues, people always need songs. There are loads of recording artists who don't write their own material and there's a dearth of good material about, so I'm not too disappointed. I mean some of the stuff I write is obviously not Pretty Things material, some of it I consider is, but that's something else. But you know, when we come to look at the new album we'll have to sort out who's doing what then.'

Jon looked at the positive aspects. 'Oh yes, we're certainly getting some royalties coming through now, which is fine. They've done a fantastic job, Snapper Music and Mark, however their style of doing it. They've put us in a far stronger position than anybody has ever done, ever. It's a great shame that we didn't know them 25 years ago cause they've actually rooted for us and supported us all the way through and tried very hard to lick it into shape, put it into some sort of professional direction including suits and black ties.'

Why was it that St John seemed to be pushing Phil and Dick to the fore? Jon: 'Dunno, no idea. The problems we had with EMI were basically sorted out with Phil and Dick being the main thrusts against those companies as being the major signees if you like, so that's the way its continued. It makes it easier in terms of papers and contracts and all the rest of it. So we're associated with it – we're a 100% behind it. On paper it's easier to manage I guess, from an administrative point of view, and its done through Phil and Dick's company.' This, presumably is a reference to The Melville Corporation Ltd.

Dick made it very clear that he has the utmost faith in St John's governership. 'He's always had our welfare at heart,' he told me. 'Often he's done things and taken no commission or whatever.' Like me, Dick had heard many stories about St John and, initially, was somewhat wary. He explained however that whenever he heard Mark's version of things it always turned out that he was right.

Wally's apparent inability to get his songs recorded may be due to the attitude that Phil now adopts towards recording. 'I hate finished demos with harmonies and stuff all worked out, I want spontaneity. I tell the guys not to bring this stuff in because we're not doing it.' Phil believes that the freshness of a song is more important than its quality. This seems an odd viewpoint. If a song of the calibre of 'Grass' or 'The Good Mr Square' had been lying around for a few years and was then dusted off and brought in by Wally or another band member with harmonies and bass lines already worked out surely it would not be discarded. Phil said he advised the band that they should not start writing until two months before recording.

In the liner notes to the re-issued *Get The Picture?* Phil explained his philosophy. 'Good rock 'n' roll is about getting to the edge and bad rock 'n' roll is something that's been thought about too much: so much market research goes into it that it's not worth doing. All the great rock 'n' roll bands have been dangerous. All the great stuff I've ever been thrilled by has an element of falling off the wire. The excitement is that it doesn't. It's somebody taking a Grand Prix corner five miles faster than the corner is meant to be taken.'

Say what you will about Mark St John, his production of the album is exemplary. It is quite impossible to tell purely from the recorded sounds just which tracks are eighteen years old and which are new. The clarity of the vocals and guitars and crispness of the drums and percussion is first rate.

April's *Uncut* magazine awarded it three stars, calling it a halfway decent album and suggested that 'Vivian Prince' was the highlight. The following month *Classic Rock*, who clearly didn't hold a grudge, called it their best album since *Silk Torpedo* and informed its readers that it, 'Cleverly fuses state-of-the-art technology with an essential organic subjectivity – i.e., late 60s psychedelia – but with a world weary passion that screams 1999.'

Johnny Black for *Mojo* described it as 'garage punk R&B par excellence that would stand out as a classic even in the middle of a *Nuggets* compilation.' He pointed out that unlike other sixties survivors they still retained relevance. 'Of the few still functioning 60s rock codgers, most strive pathetically to regain cool by aping contemporary musical modes. Only the Pretties have the gall not to fix what ain't broke, and retain their cool by sounding almost exactly as they always did.'

St John had by now sold much of the publishing to Lupus Music, which had been the band's publishing company during the golden EMI and first Warner Brothers period. This re-established the link with Bryan Morrison, ex-manager, publisher and now ensconced with the gentry as owner of the Royal Berkshire Polo Club where he brushes shoulders with Prince Charles.

Dick was quite evasive about the new album and which tracks had been cut with the reconstituted 1967 line-up. 'Quite a few were actually done with them. Quite a few songs, I'm not gonna go into details which ones are which, you may have noticed that in the sleeve notes themselves there's not any details of who played on what. We basically want to leave it as a bit of a mystery, as to who played on what.' Fortunately in issue 2 of the Pretties fanzine, 13 Chester Street, St John put the record straighter and itemised the record with chronological details, although if you have read thus far you will be aware that St John's chronology is not always completely reliable.

Dick had now married again to Anne who was running a pub in Ventnor. Anne confided that when she was eleven, and lived in Melbourne, Australia, she used to have a poster of the Pretty Things on her bedroom wall. 'And here I am married to one.'

Work commitments precluded Jon Povey from agreeing to a Spring 1999 tour of Europe and the band turned to ex-member Gordon Edwards who presumably was glad of the offer. Gordon attended several rehearsals where Povey taught him the songs and arrangements but, with the tour just days away, he disappeared and couldn't be traced.

Povey was scathing in his criticism at this lack of professionalism. 'Another one who's brain damaged unfortunately. A man who means well but isn't focused and you can't really go on a day to day basis. You can't pay for all the equipment and the travel and then turn up with no pianist. He's gone off somewhere, he's out of his brain… he's irresponsible really. People like that tend to be locked in a time warp unfortunately and haven't come out of it. They're still in that kind of 60s/70s drug hazed life which isn't bad, maybe it's a great life to be in, but it when it comes to being responsible and not letting other people down and not being selfish then Gordon, brilliant guy though he is… I was amazed at Gordon because I always looked up to him as a pianist, apart from anything else, because I'm a pianist and he was a very unusual pianist, very, very clever. He came round to my house 18 months ago and we did some work for a little while and he'd lost it totally. He couldn't even remember half the stuff. I was playing the intro for 'Singapore Silk Torpedo', he couldn't even remember writing it. That, unfortunately, is the sad thing about it. One feels for him probably even more than he feels for himself. He probably doesn't even realise where he's gone to or never moved from. He doesn't really want to step over that threshold. There's a threshold of his life as it was which he's now in still, locked in that warp. He just doesn't want to take the risk of not being able to do it, he'd rather be into his previous incarnation, if you like, and be happy and safer there.'

Phil was much less verbose, 'He's fucked up, like Viv.'

Gordon explained his side of it. 'The impression I got is they weren't that together. I was afraid that if I went on the tour with them it would be a really bad experience. Also at the time I had a problem with my older brother who'd just died from a heart attack, my father six months later died from a heart attack and all that.'

Gordon is something of an enigma, all agree that he is a brilliant musician but he has conspicuously under-achieved during the latter part of his life. Since the Kinks days, and an emotionally crippling split with a girlfriend, he has wallowed in an underworld of drink and drug related personal chaos. He'd done a bit of painting and decorating and 'slagging off the old unemployment people for a few years' but nothing of any musical consequence. These days Gordon doesn't possess a keyboard or guitar, just memories that seem like yesterday but in reality date back to the mid 70s. His friends have confided that Gordon has battled with a drug habit for well over 20 years and they fear for his future.

June 1999 saw Snapper finally re-issue *Parachute*, complete with the bonus of the five Harvest tracks that made up EMI's two post-*Parachute* singles. In the same month The Pretty Things made another 100 Club appearance, but one with a difference. An enterprising German promoter arranged a tour package and twinned the Pretties appearance with The Rolling Stones Wembley concerts, which were spread over that week. The concert marked the introduction of material from *Rage Before Beauty*. Three tracks were aired, 'Vivian Prince', 'Passion of Love' and 'Goin' Downhill'.

Press that announced the 'Original 1966 line-up' was inaccurate in that Wally Waller and Jon Povey didn't join until 1967. However publicity about the band has always been prone to exaggeration. Even the 'sixty one convictions' that St John claims the band has racked up is an accumulation of matters relating to both current and ex-band members and include the massive Viv Prince legacy, the Povey drug bust, as well as Peter Tolson's drink-drive and ABH fiascos. Presumably they also include the Freerange era slugfest that kept Phil, Jon and St John safely in custody for the night.

As Jon Povey has said, 'Mr Exaggeration'.

CHAPTER 20 – New Single, New Writs, No Hits

During the mid 60s The Pretty Things didn't give a toss who they might upset – the press, the establishment, even other bands. Throughout that period and the 70s they ingested copious quantities of alcohol and dope and sneered at the burgeoning punk poseurs. Although the 80s found them unable, for financial reasons, to continue hell-raising on such a vast scale it found them neither apologetic nor contrite. No real surprise then that during the last year of the millennium they yet again excited press comment regarding their behaviour and, reminiscent of that infamous New Zealand tour, for corrupting the minds of children.

As July moved towards August, The Pretty Things, gnarled and combative, could be found in the confines of a converted church known as Wessex Studios looking for that most unlikely of holy grails – a hit single. St John felt that the band really could score a hit although he conceded that their reputation would stand in the way. His answer? The single would be released under an assumed name, '4.20 p.m.' and for TV and video appearances they would play (mime) in masks. Only when the single hit the charts would they be unmasked as…gasp…The Pretty Things!!

St John and Frank Holland had initiated the writing sessions assisted later on by Phil. Frank's kernel of an idea evolved into the song 'All Light Up' and with the added ingredient of Dick Taylor on guitar they played around with it until a song proper emerged. During a break in the sessions St John heard the sounds of children playing at the nearby Highbury Quadrant School and sent Frank Holland and his guitar outside to persuade them to chant, "All light up" while he taped it. At the weekend Wally and Jon arrived to add bass, mellotron and backing vocals through a Leslie cabinet. Three days later and a single was recorded but the b-side, St John's idea called 'Pretty Beat', had to be completed in the remaining hours of Sunday evening, and remarkably it was. Skip, Wally and Jon all had work commitments the following morning and adjusted to this extremely tight schedule. St John mixed the tracks during the following two days and on Wednesday presented them, as the Pretties new hit single, to a suitably startled Snapper Records.

'All Light Up' was released on Sep 24th, but only in the States. This should have been a major event but seemed to ripple rather than splash. The big idea to release it under an assumed name was dropped so the new big idea was to tie it in with the forthcoming US tour. Unhappily, the release date coincided with the end of the tour, so much of the impact was lost. Some months later Phil assured me the single would receive a UK release in the Spring of 2000. 'It's a summer song,' he advised, cryptically.

The recording returned the ageing recidivists to the newspaper columns when staff at the school complained that the band had failed to obtain permission to record the children. Frank had approached to the school gates, guitar in hand, and persuaded the children to chant the title chorus but he had not actually entered the school precincts, so nothing could be done. Islington Council was 'very angry' and stated, pompously and some-what pointlessly, that the taping was 'totally unauthorised'. Their spokesman explained, 'They never sought permission. If they had we would have looked into it to check what it was being used for.'

Permission was not needed and not one law had been transgressed, which of course was beside the point. Are we seriously to believe that Islington Council would have granted permission for a band as notorious as The Pretty Things to record children singing a chorus applauding the smoking of marijuana? We are not talking Boyzone here, no toothy grins and shal-low muzak, no consumer friendly pap that retards and impressionable young girls can smile and gently sway to. 'All Light Up' recalled the violence of the 60s, murderous Manson, the Vietnam War, the French riots and the assassination of Martin Luther King, with a binding chorus of "All light up". The band's 'anthem to marijuana' as Phil described it. The psychedelic cover depicted a big-haired Jon Povey lighting what appeared to be a mega-joint.

The song oozed 1960s musical references with keyboard and flute effects, recalling The Beatles' golden 1967 period, before it surged into the title-chant chorus. Much heavier than 'Strawberry Fields' it reverberated with the sounds of St John and the band hammering the studio walls with their fists to achieve the required boom effect. Phil's vocal, evoking the husky, world-weary quality of the old bluesman retained both phrasing and delivery without sacrificing any of the old power. As Lofty Riches commented when comparing the 1964 band with the present version, 'When I last heard them, and I've heard them play a few times, Phil's voice was one thousand percent better.'

Phil considered the song a cross between 'Strawberry Fields' and 'Another Brick In The Wall', although the sounds of school children playing were not new to the band, the device having been used previously on 'Children' on the *Emotions* album. The single contained three other tracks, 'Love Keeps Hanging On' and 'Goin' Downhill', both from the *Rage Before Beauty* CD, and the other new track 'Pretty Beat'. Both new songs were credited to the now prolific writing team of St John/Holland/May although Dick Taylor received a co-credit on Pretty Beat.

'I can't say we object to any publicity about the kids being on it,' essayed

255

Dick. This publicity represented a fine opportunity for the band to capitalise on their historic bad boy image. The red banner newspapers, with their commitment to traditional UK family values, would have loved an excuse to expose decrepit rock 'n' rollers tainting innocent schoolchildren with their vile drug message, but it didn't happen. For whatever reason the band's management and label chose or were otherwise unable to issue the single whilst the initial furore smoked and kindled. Another opportunity squandered, perhaps. How often had the band and its legion of fans complained about a lack of publicity and disinterest from the media. Regardless of how trivial and ludicrous the incident may have been it would have allowed them to play the press for their own purposes rather than the usual reverse process.

Meanwhile, writing in the new Pretty Things fanzine, *13 Chester Street*, St John announced his intention to sue James De Wolfe, head of the De Wolfe record label, who he denounced as 'a shit.' His angry outburst was because De Wolfe had consistently allowed or arranged for the *Electric Banana* product to be sold with a 'Pretty Things' byline. As with the banning of Mike Ober's Pretty Things 'n' Mates volume, St John was intent on restricting use of the Pretty Things name on 'non-authorised' recordings. He had asked De Wolfe not to do this but had been ignored. De Wolfe also stands accused of reneging on an agreement to return the master tapes. James De Wolfe issued a terse statement, 'Apart from the fact that as session musicians individual members of the group known as "The Pretty Things" recorded several albums for our production music library, there is nothing further that I can add that would be of any help to you. The albums were released as *Electric Bananas* and their release is confined for library use though in later years some titles were commercially released.'

The new Pretty Things fanzine had been launched in August as part of a new US based fan club run by Mike Stax, and future wife Anja. The newsletter was heavily supported by both band and management and in a much more committed manner than previously accorded Joop de Ligt.

A US tour took place in September 1999, the first proper tour for over 23 years, starting in Vancouver, on through Seattle, San Francisco and ending nineteen days later in Philadelphia. Utilising the services and comforts of a 12-sleeper bus they raced across the States picking up sleep as best they could. By mutual agreement the bus toilet was not used in a major way and the occasional stops were welcomed.

Whilst there, they met up with Twink, who a couple of years before had married and moved to the States. In spite of rumours to the contrary Dick Taylor insisted that Twink didn't play with the Pretties. 'No he didn't guest with us in the States, what happened was we went and played at the Whiskey-A-Go-Go. Twink was guesting with a band who were playing with us and we all said hello to him and what have you. Not only from certain areas he wouldn't have been welcome but also it would have been very difficult. For reasons best known to himself Skip really dislikes him. I think the real reason Skip dislikes him is because he was 'the other drummer' whereas Viv was the original. He's got a certain resentment about Twink where on the other hand it was Skip who left the band so I can't think quite why he hates the man who replaced him so much.'

Twink actually sang one of his few good songs '10,000 Words In A Cardboard Box' with the band Smallstone which he joined for what turned out to be a very short period.

The sound system at the Whiskey was poor and apparently, the too-cool sound guy was not fussed about righting matters. The four hundred strong audience included Slash and Gene Simmons but overall the band was disappointed. Roadie Jon Hart reported St John complaining, 'God took a dump and they all landed in LA.'

Pretty Things tours are now much less frantic than during the 1970s. No groupies buying their way in with chemical allures. The wall-to-wall shagging has also subdued as Jon Povey explained. 'Yeah, in those days you're a young guy and you had your eye on everything that was running around and therefore it was not a great time to be married or have children because in America, particularly, when they're knocking at your door at three o'clock in the morning thirteen deep trying to jump in your bed it's very difficult to say no. It doesn't make for any lasting relationships. These days, when you're getting close to 60, one doesn't really feel the same way about that side of it, flattering as it would be.'

The Pretty Things played to crowds of between 100 and 300 in most instances but they comprised numerous hard-core fans, many of whom had travelled hundreds of miles. In Vancouver dedicated fan Eric obtained a wall poster, which the band signed for him. At this point the club's five bouncers forced him to hand it back. When the Pretties got wind of this, they made' a new poster. Phil drew a winged guitar and the rest of the band signed it. Skip signed his name under a short statement "A new Pretties poster 'cause some cunt took the other one but this is better."

In San Francisco Skip was nearly arrested. He was involved in an altercation at a restaurant, something to do with a crab and two bottles of wine. St John has commented on how Skip seems determined to live up to the maniac legacy of Viv Prince and this episode evoked memories of Viv's escapades in New Zealand with his lobster.

Phil's voice gave him problems during the tour and he consumed large quantities of honey, often on stage between numbers. Skip, having recovered from the crab escapade, was brought down by a virulent flu and at The

Garage in Washington had to leave part way through the set and St John took over for the remainder of the gig.

The Chicago gig at House of the Blues proved somewhat disappointing with only two hundred fans in attendance, about 10% of capacity. However Rick Roger, reporting for the *Chicago Tribune* was most impressed. 'Compared to recent live sets by contemporaries like the Stones and The Who, The Pretty Things acquitted themselves brilliantly. Where the Stones threw a great party and The Who produced a grand spectacle, The Pretty Things – unaided by extra singers and musicians – pounded out rock 'n' roll that bristled and writhed with youthful energy and a hint of mayhem. It was the real thing.'

Phil described The Grog Shop in Cleveland as the worst venue he had ever played, disgusting sound, tiny stage and foul toilet area. The Virginia concert had to be cancelled. It seemed that the band's publicity machine was not too clever in the run up to the tour and this contributed to several disappointing turnouts. At Denver, with one hour to gig time, only 17 tickets had gone and the band played to their smallest audience since art school.

Skip was in trouble yet again at the Bowery Ballroom in New York when he involved himself in a scuffle with a security guard and had to exit before it became serious. He was missing his wife at this point and spent most of his journeys at the back of the bus with Wally. As St John observed, 'He is a violent, middle-aged man'.

The tour must be considered something of a disappointment. Venues were not filled and the American public displayed a surprising indifference. Financially it was not a winner either. T-shirt and CD sales generated a worthwhile income but 25% had to be given to the venues with the band's cut in San Francisco being a mere $300.

Simultaneously available in the States, courtesy of Norton Records, were five vinyl EP's originally released between 1964-67 containing all the singles from that era except 'Cry To Me'. As *Record Collector* informed, 'The records themselves are minus the push-out centre, which completes the authentic feel.' The final EP, 'House In The Country', contained a demo version of that forgettable pop ditty, 'Progress'.

'The thing about this band,' said Phil to *T Max*, 'is we've always believed and cared in what we've done. We know a lot of people in the business, not mentioning any names, who've milked the same bloody album for ten years. Fine, but I don't know how they can go on stage at night, knowing every single one of their numbers, from album one to album ten, are pretty similar, all in the same mould. I guess they don't have a lot to say.'

'We are semi-professionals', he proclaimed on Snapper's Pretty Things website. 'We've never considered ourselves entertainers, and I haven't got anything to go onstage with as a message. I don't even want to be in show business. I want to be in The Pretty Things, and that's very different.' A very different assessment from the opinions espoused to Derek Boltwood in 1969 when he declared that the band was in showbiz and needed to entertain.

During October, St John sent a fax formally declining a request for an interview for this book. Dipping into Phil's box of mixed metaphors he explained, 'We all march to the tune of our own drum. The Pretty Things don't follow the basic trends set by the rest of the civilians out there.'

Like many before me I find it difficult to warm to the man. However, to give him his due, he seems to have the band's best interests at heart, albeit in a manner where he seemingly dictates the terms. The Pretty Things appear content to fall in behind and leave the decision-making to him. Like Peter Grant he can be considered a good friend and an awful enemy.

St John has made the Pretties much more financially aware. Not a difficult task perhaps given their history of fiscal irresponsibility. He was responsible for the formation of The Melville Corporation Ltd and also introduced the band to Craven Secretarial Services. This sea change has also served to reduce the numbers of gigs, particularly in the UK. No longer do they pop out for a quick pub gig or social club jaunt. Work commitments have reduced the opportunities and often these do not pay enough and balance sheet aware-ness is the name of the game under his governorship.

The Pretties have always played for the love of the music and the quick fix of the concert or free festival. Financial rewards always appeared of second-ary interest to them so it was a surprise to read the interview in *SF Sorrow* fanzine where Phil expressed interest in his songs being used for television advertising. He felt that 'Get The Picture?' would be a great song for Kodak to use and clearly the man would like some money.

For six days in the middle of November 1999, The Boston Rock Opera presented *SF Sorrow* in its entirety supported by a cast of 14, a six piece rock band and a multi-image light show. The BRO was a non-profit organisation dedicated to presenting original adaptations of classic rock opera, conceptual rock and new works, concentrating on works 'that never got the staging they deserved'. Previous adaptations included *Happiness Stan* drawn from the Small Faces classic *Ogden's* album, *Preservation* – a version of The Kinks *Village Green* epic, although they've avoided the over-presented *Tommy*.

Peter Moore, frontman with that excellent and under appreciated band Count Zero, took the role of Sorrow whilst Gene Dante performed the nar-ration. The BRO decided to augment Phil's story and fabricated tendrils of storyline from the song lyrics. They introduced the character 'Grey' and named 'the girl next door', Sally.

Phil was decidedly unimpressed saying, 'They thought the band would jump up saying hooray when they decided to stage *SF Sorrow*. Look what happened to *Tommy*, they made it pop. We said look, it's in the public domain, we can't stop you but we won't be giving you any assistance and if you mess with it we'll be pissed off. Ray Davies had given the BRO his blessing to interpret *Preservation* as they saw fit but Phil did not wish to be involved.

Perplexing, because years earlier Phil had proved effusive and supportive when Lynn Seymour of the Canadian Ballet Company wanted to perform *SF Sorrow* as a ballet. 'We were at the point of finalising it when she had a breakdown and pulled out. So it was shelved.'

Eleanor explained that during the US Tour she had dinner with the band and explained her plans. Although Phil appeared slightly nervous about the possibility of 'a watered down Broadway-type show' she received assent from Mark St John on the basis that it was not promoted as a band-sponsored project. Eleanor made clear that the production would not have gone ahead had it been seen as contentious.

The British film, *Best*, based on the early life story of soccer genius George Best received a general release and boasted a varied soundtrack which included two Pretty Things songs, 'Don't Bring Me Down' and 'Buzz The Jerk'. It is said their inclusion was at the insistence of George Best himself, apparently a staunch Pretty Things fan.

Dick had been keeping busy on the Isle of Wight playing in The Sparkle Bothers duo, and when ex-Family guitarist Charlie Whitney decided to leave local band The Blues MD's Dick was asked to replace him, a position he continues to hold alongside his Pretty Things duties. Later in the year Dick would turn up as supporting guitarist for a series of humorous but bizarre gigs featuring rock journalist Alan Clayson.

February 2000 saw the UK and US release of a Pretty Things best of, *Latest Writs – Greatest Hits*, again on Snapper's Madfish label. The CD contained nineteen tracks and highlighted the band's output from 1964's 'Rosalyn' through to 'Vivian Prince' off *Rage Before Beauty* and also included the intended single, 'All Light Up'. Perversely the Stateside CD was an abridged version with only fifteen tracks compared to the UK's nineteen, something to do with licensing problems perhaps, although the missing songs, from the 1966-71 period, do not appear to share any label or publishing similarities.

The compilation was originally selected by Mike Stax who took a leftfield approach and skipped several of the expected songs whilst including a few lesser-known tracks. This method was over-ruled by the band and/or their label/management and the unusual was duly replaced by the expected. Mike had chosen 'Miss Fay Regrets', 'Come Home Momma' and 'The Sun' but these were replaced by 'Defecting Grey', 'Singapore Silk Torpedo' and 'Cries

From The Midnight Circus'. These changes must have been a last minute decision because the Snapper website and UK Virgin stores displayed advertising material enthusing about 'Miss Fay Regrets'.

As a primer it offered excellent value for a taste of their varied career but it failed to hit the mark as a greatest hits collection. When a band has managed only seven UK chart entries, a Greatest Hits CD is difficult enough, leaving out three of them, 'Honey I Need', 'Cry To Me' and 'House In The Country', beggars belief. *Mojo* confirmed this view and suggested that the first two albums would have been preferable. *Q* opined that 'As a retrospective the selection of tracks is found wanting.' However they did congratulate Phil on the 'great sleeve notes', a view not shared by *Record Collector*, 'Phil May's sleevenotes are awash with spelling and punctuation mistakes... reinforcing the Things' reputation as dope-crazed boozers.' *Record Collector* also criticised the packaging, 'No dates or original album sources are listed for any of the 19 non-chronologically ordered songs' and they finished with the caution 'a band this important deserves a more thoughtful approach.' *Uncut's* Gavin Martin awarded the CD 4 stars. 'This terrific collection loses a star for not matching frontman Phil May's priceless sleevenotes with time line and session details.'

Phil was most irritated by *Record Collector's* comments. 'It wasn't meant to be punctuated,' he told me, 'it was stream of consciousness stuff. The office did that and they should have done the spelling. I can't spell.' A fact easily established by glancing at Phil's notes on the back sleeve of the *Live at the Heartbreak Hotel* album.

Snapper showed a strong commitment to new technology by creating a corporate website dedicated to The Pretty Things. They included a Pretty Things message board, links page, discography and other sub pages. The pages provided a wealth of information to the surfer that was only slightly spoiled by the misinformation lurking amongst the history page. Viv Prince was not beaten up by Ingemar Johannsen, the assault was allegedly carried out by his brother. Ingemar Johannsen never fought Muhammad Ali, as the page states, luckily for him.

Any chance that 'All Light Up' would receive a UK release disappeared when it was included on a free CD given with the April edition of *Classic Rock*. What were the band and their management up to? 'All Light Up' represented a marvellous opportunity for them to capitalise on the bad press occasioned by the playground-recording incident.

Snapper had sent advance copies of the single to various DJ's to sound out the anticipated response. The omens were not good, without airplay it would not sell and if it did not sell then Snapper would be a charity not a business.

Early in 2000, a new Pretties bootleg appeared, *Hyde & Psych*. The CD included four tracks from a 1968 Hyde Park concert where they played a very ragged set sounding poorly rehearsed and featuring off-key harmonies. Dick has admitted that in those days they didn't rehearse all that often and the Hyde Park concert highlighted this artistic laziness, for instance on 'Alexander' John Povey bursts in for a non-existent chorus. The remainder of the CD comprised a March 1969 concert at the Paradiso in Amsterdam, which sounds much more together.

May 2000 should have seen the final two instalments in Snapper's re-issue programme, *Freeway Madness* and *Cross Talk*. Instead *Cross Talk* initially surfaced as part of a three CD box set also containing the eponymous debut album and *Parachute* – an album each from the 60s, 70s and 80s. The entire Pretties back-catalogue was due to be re-reissued simultaneously in limited edition (of 3,000 but 5,000 for *SF Sorrow*) digipack format however, as always, matters went adrift and the digipacks were not made available for a further five weeks.

In *Record Buyer* magazine Alan Clayson reviewed the stereo version of *SF Sorrow* and trumpeted its credentials as one of the 60s most important recordings. 'A world at large cannot justify remaining deaf to *SF Sorrow* if it still listens to lesser works like *Tommy* and, as far as I'm concerned, *Sgt. Pepper*.' To my ears the stereo version is more enjoyable than the mono but even the remastering skills of St John cannot remove the crackles and noises from the more obvious third and fourth generation dubbings.

The *Anthology* was scheduled to be hauled out again, although on Snapper for the first time, with the release due during 2002 and this will have completed the entire reissue process. Proper European availability of the remastered albums was also agreed thanks to a conclusion of the feud with SPV. Snapper involved themselves in a distribution arrangement with SPV and this ended the legal nastiness.

Cross Talk was a welcome release for all Pretty Things fans. Regularly overlooked by industry pundits it served as the Pretties Things punk album. Spitting disdain it gave the finger to those who had consigned them to the footnotes of rock history as outdated. But the Pretties were still out of luck and when originally released the album sank like a cold stone.

The remastered version sounded crisper than the original vinyl issue, whose muddy sound the band disliked. Phil was hoping to have the album remixed but funds did not allow that luxury. As with all things Pretty the release arrived with a touch of controversy, not least the fact that initially to obtain a copy one had to purchase the other two albums in the three CD pack. Albums that Pretty Things fans will already have bought.

As bonus items it included the three previously unreleased tracks from

St John's initial Freerange sessions – 'Wish Fulfilment', 'Sea About Me' and 'The Young'. Writing credits were given as May/Tolson, May/Waller and May/Povey respectively. The incorrect allocation of song-writing credits has historically been a Pretty Things trait and clearly nothing had changed. 'Wish Fulfilment' was written in its entirety by Peter Tolson both lyrics and music, whilst Peter and Phil were jointly responsible for 'Sea About Me' with Wally contributing the middle eight. Peter also recalled writing the middle eight and chorus for 'The Young Pretenders'. Jon Povey's recollection of the song he was credited with co-writing was somewhat vague, 'That's some song Phil and Wally wrote for one of them spurious albums under some guise, Phil and the Pirates or something.'

Unlike 'Goin' Downhill' and 'Goodbye Goodbye' on the *Rage* CD the three bonus tracks from the difficult Freerange sessions were largely unaltered with the only obvious differences being due to mixing. No monster Zulu drum rhythms like those welded onto 'Goin' Downhill'.

As he is no longer in the band Tolson has no means of fighting his own corner when it comes to righting wrongs about writing songs. In reality he can't even be bothered. It is situations like this that have pushed him away from the business. As you will have gathered by now, ensuring the correct writing credits has never been a particularly strong point with the band and other tracks on the reissue bear this out. On the original vinyl release 'Bitter End' was stated to be a May/Stuart composition, we are now advised that it was actually a May/Povey joint effort. I asked Electra May (Stuart) about her composing skills and she seemed nonplussed and suggested I speak with Phil about such matters. Obviously with the divorce from Phil has come the loss of writing credits. Jesse Tolson has also been removed as joint writer of 'She Don't', with Phil reclaiming the credit and presumably the trickle of royalties involved. Phil's justification may be that he did, after all, co-write the song. The very same arguments Jack Green and Gordon Edwards have ventured.

This continued game-playing over writing credits, which filters down to subsequent royalty payments or lack of, poses the question of how does one end up with a writing credit? What is fair? What is deserving? What is a rip off? Jon Povey has a clear view of the matter. 'If you are into it and you are there adding to it as the song is being written then you become part of it. When it's somebody who comes in with a song in its entirety it's their song.' Not everybody will agree with him.

It may be worth scrutinising the writings within the sleevenotes. Starting with 'spitting blood but still defiant' St John argues their case during the punk era using pugilistic imagery. The band members are characterised in that overly ornate, semi-abusive style that Pretties fans have come to expect. Dick is sinking 'deeper into a debt mountain' a desperate aphorism at best. Povey was 'delivering himself from evil… driven by excess and ultra-habitual drug abuse.' Wally was described as spiralling 'downward into an ever-increasing round of post 'Persuaders' celebrity Euro-bullshit and inappropriate recording projects.' Phil is subjected to a psychological analysis with the prognosis 'incendiary.' Peter Tolson 'was seriously adrift in Harlow high-rise hell.'

St John mentioned the episode where Peter 'auditioned' for The Scorpions, although, being unusually coy, he failed to mention the name of the band in question. He also transferred the audition from Hanover to Munich and misreported the actual conversation.

Was Peter Tolson adrift in 'Harlow high-rise hell'? 'I did live in a flat but not in a high-rise block.' Well at least the Harlow bit was right.

Correctly, he described *Cross Talk* as a 'flawed masterpiece' and propositioned that 'Lost That Girl', 'Sea Of Blue' and 'Edge Of The Night' were merely okay. 'Edge Of The Night', is a pop song, admittedly a good one. With 'Sea Of Blue' he is on the nail, it fails to ignite and Tolson himself suggested that it was 'filler, because we had nothing else.' It sat uneasily with the petulance and irritation that comprised the bulk of the album. I questioned whether it might have been expedient to use some of the excellent but unrecorded songs that the band wrote in the early 70s, such as 'Spider Woman' and 'Slow Beginnings'. 'We forgot all about them,' he confessed.

St John related a 'set-to' that supposedly occurred between Peter and Phil concerning May's reluctance to sing the lyrics of 'Wish Fulfilment'. St John contested that Phil 'didn't feel he was young enough to do it.' Tolson remembered matters differently recalling that Phil simply didn't like singing lyrics that he hadn't penned and that he didn't understand them anyway. He said he suggested that Phil try to come up with something better, 'but he didn't try, got pissed and sang it anyway.' The listener can plainly hear May's unease at the lyrics and his inability, or lack of interest, in perfecting the phrasing.

So, is the idea of *Phil May's Pretty Things* a truly bad thing? After all, most people will associate Phil May with The Pretty Things and he has been the only constant during their many phases. However from these quarters it seems to be a wrong move. As St John might say it doesn't have a 'rightness' about it. From their snarling debut in 1963 to their final fling during 1981 the band continually shared the burdens of writing, singing and musical direction to such an extent that Jack Green sincerely believed there were 'too many chiefs.' This group responsibility displayed a sign of a deeper morality and sense of fair play than normally seen in group situations. Of course, no band is truly democratic and both Jon Povey and Skip have historically been content to accept lesser roles, but to see Wally Waller marginalised in the new format Pretty Things is sad.

Without St John's intervention, persistence and financial support the ship would have sunk many years previous. St John effectively runs The Pretty Things by virtue of his ubiquity. As well as managing the band he produces them, involves himself in the writing and creating process, lays down the initial drum tracks, beats a tambourine/maraca/wall and attempts backing vocals. He is effectively an all-singing, all-dancing seventh member. He radiates attitude and at concerts is seen striding around like a disqualified biker anxious for a redeeming argument. In recent years, by design or otherwise he almost exhibits the remarkable facility to physically metamorphose into a resemblance of Peter Grant.

The reissued *Freeway Madness* displayed a welcome crispness of sound, which had been missing from the previous American CD release. The original mastertapes had finally been located and St John was able to remaster from source and this skill indicated his true vocation. The four bonus tracks, 'Religion's Dead', 'Havana Bound', 'Love Is Good' and 'Onion Soup' highlighted the band at its best, extemporising and fitting the songs into a different form that allowed spontaneity and freeform playing. The CD insert announced that the live tracks came from a Lyceum concert in the summer of 1973, but this was incorrect, the recordings were lifted from a BBC *In Concert* appearance at the Golders Green Hippodrome in August 1973. This concert concluded with an encore of 'Route 66', which was excluded, presumably because it did not fit in with the *Freeway Madness* timescale. Also removed was DJ Pete Drummond's introduction and spoken song links.

Throughout the early part of the year the band contented themselves with the occasional interview and liner sleeve note. Phil worked on his own book on the band – sex, drugs, rock & roll and tennis – and Dick played occasional gigs locally. During May and June they wandered around Europe playing two gigs in France, one of them at Eurodisney, which were the precursor to a short tour of Germany and Switzerland.

As usual things failed to go exactly to plan and in Germany concerns for Phil's whereabouts were allayed, shortly before a gig, when he was finally traced having spent the night in a transvestite bar.

When *Cross Talk* eventually surfaced in digipack format, inside a hard clear plastic sleeve, it contained a quote from Phil. '*Crosstalk*. Long nights – cocaine fuel – great tracks.' Each digipack release was 'enhanced' by a suitably pithy phrase from a Thing, emblazoned on the inside sleeve.

A December gig in Spain sharpened them for a return to the 100 Club where they held a Christmas Party supported by Arthur Brown. The raucous two hour set included the first ever performance of 'Defecting Grey' where the band augmented their sound by using recordings of the swirling sounds that characterised the original. 'Roadrunner' was dropped and the

265

set opened with an unconvincing version of 'Remember That Boy' complete with obligatory vocal fuck-up when Phil continued singing the chorus into the second verse. A broken rib, sustained the day before the Spanish jaunt bothered Phil throughout the set which he managed with the assistance of pain-killers and red wine. Other oldies reprised were 'Onion Soup' and 'Dream/Joey'. The gig also confirmed the inability of members to recall details of their past. Phil introduced 'Come See Me' as a 'b-side or album track' until corrected by Dick. Jon Povey suggested 'Defecting Grey' was a 1966 record and that *Silk Torpedo* originated in 1972.

In March 2001 Catfish Records, the specialist blues subsidiary of Snapper, announced that it would shortly be releasing a new Pretties album of blues tracks, a release date later amended to August 2002. Although to be credited as The Pretty Things it would only be Phil, Dick with intermittent Jon Povey and would be an acoustic 'back to the roots' blues covers album with versions of Muddy Waters and Bo Diddley songs. Later information indicated that the current fad of 'guest stars' would abound with Keith Richards, Marianne Faithfull and the ubiqitous Dave Gilmour being mentioned. It was also announced that Repertoire Records planned to release a number of Pretty Things albums in Germany, including the BBC sessions album and *The Singles – A's & B's*. Repertoire had previously issued the De Wolfe catalogue under the Pretty Things name thus incurring the St John wrath. Also in the works is a DVD release of the Abbey Road *SF Sorrow* netcast.

Later that March, as their pension ages approached, the band received the first of a number of unsettling reminders that even they couldn't go on forever and that a kind of retirement is forced on all of us.

Chapter 21 – ill's Well That Ends Well

At the start of 2001 all of The Pretty Things, apart from Frank Holland, were in their mid to late fifties. Although toughened by a life spent on the road, the very same rigours have a habit of catching up sometime. Even Peter Tolson who is firmly out of the music industry quagmire considers he's living on borrowed time.

In late March, whilst rehearsing for a short tour of France, Skip Alan complained of breathlessness and chest pains. A hurried visit to the hospital diagnosed high blood pressure and an elevated cholesterol count which fortunately are both treatable by medication. Skip cannot play without one hundred percent commitment, which may well be medically undesirable, and question marks must have been in his and the bands minds. No doubt St John is able to deputise for their relatively few gigging dates and he already lays down the basic track when recording sessions arise. Most people agree that technically he is a far better drummer than Skip although whether his commitment to other matters allows him to be a full time Pretty Thing is doubtful. Also in doubt is whether the band would wish to continue as The Pretty Things without Skip.

During April, St John issued a statement on the internet regarding Skip and the band's future. Although the statement carried The Pretty Things appellation, Phil and Dick confirmed that it was issued without their knowledge. The statement claimed to answer speculation concerning Skip's health and the band's future but also served as an attack on the author for posting details of Skip's condition on the internet. These postings were described by St John as 'usually inaccurate', a fine condemnation from a man whose rewriting of Pretty Things history strides way beyond hyperbole.

The statement was sent via Mike Stax at the fan club because St John did not have internet access. In fact neither does he have an e-mail facility because, as St John told one Snapper employee, he would always get mail from "absolute nutters".

What does the future hold, Skip's health withstanding? Very occasional UK and US gigs interspersed with short European tours seems the likely scenario. Phil cannot envisage continuing after age 60, which gives less than three years. Jon Povey, who is two years older than Phil, considered the matter carefully. 'It's very much a family thing, I think if one of us was to leave or die then basically that would be the end of it. I don't think anybody wants to do it without anybody else and that's one of the strengths of it that we do collectively feel very positive about playing and we know we play well, we know that what we do is unique to us.'

May 2001 provided a further grim reminder that the onslaught of age and insidious decrepitude stalks amongst us all. Original rhythm guitarist, Brian Pendleton was discovered dead by the door of his Maidstone flat. He had been battling lung cancer for a number of years, was financially bereft and was living in DSS accommodation. Dick was moved to comment that, 'Whilst plenty of people can play guitar like Jimi Hendrix, few could play like Brian Pendleton.'

Pendleton's death also had possible repercussions for the legal action against Polygram. Brian was going to be the main thrust because he didn't have any money and, unlike the others, was UK based. The possibility of the action being legally aided was slipping away.

Tentative plans were made for gigs with the reconstituted Yardbirds and ex-Animal Eric Burden. Ominously, this sounded a tad like a dressed up version of the holiday camp package tours that previously had been greeted with disdain. Skip's health problems meant that the plans came to nothing and The Yardbirds set off on a nationwide tour with the Spencer Davis band and The Troggs.

Some fans would have embraced this type of gig but for many it would have been hard to stomach. Not the music of course, that's always very welcome, but the vibe. The whiff of sell out and the faint odour of burning integrity. The worry that it might have signalled the end of the inspiration. That they are driven like other bands after all, simply chasing the dollar. Time will tell.

Although St John stated that they were 'committed to working with their specific original line-up' the Pretties undertook a short tour of Germany in July 2001 with St John rattling away on the kit. Maybe this is the way forward?

Nuggets 11: Original Artyfacts From the British Empire and Beyond was accorded record of the week status by the *Sunday Times* during July and the review was reflective. 'Four tracks by The Pretty Things makes you wonder why they haven't been canonised alongside The Beatles'. Actually only three Pretty Things recordings were used – 'Midnight To Six Man', 'Rosalyn' and 'Walking Through My Dreams' 'although The Fairies version of 'Get Yourself Home' was also included. The 4-CD box set included an essay by Greg Shaw and track by track notes from Mike Stax.

The album notes failed to credit Ian Sterling as co-writer of 'Midnight To Six Man' and incorrectly suggested that Viv Prince drummed on 'Rosalyn', nonetheless it accorded an excellent introduction to mainly UK R&B and the Pretties in particular.

Another slice of psychedelic nostalgia in the form of *Acid Drops, Spacedust & Flying Saucers: Psychedelic Confectionery from the UK Underground 1965-69* was released. Like the *Psychedelia At Abbey Road* issue, this four-CD offering from EMI allowed the Pretties the ironic pleasure of licensing their back catalogue to the previous owners.

Snapper took another stab at marketing the back catalogue with two double CD releases *The Rhythm & Blues Years* and *The Psychedelic Years* issued on their Recall label. With thirty four and thirty five tracks respectively and a £10.99 tag they represented excellent value. The first CD claimed to be 'the rhythm and blues years' but oddly included 'It's Been So Long', the Gordon Edwards ballad from 1975's *Savage Eye*. After the perplexing publishing credits on previous releases the issue was resolved with Jewel Music resuming their ownership of the Bo Diddley material and Tristian Music being credited with Jimmy Reed's 'The Moon Is Rising'. Mike Stax, again provided detailed liner-notes awash with information and asides from Phil and Dick.

The Psychedelic Years proved the more interesting with three previously unreleased tracks. From a March 1969 Amsterdam gig came live versions of 'Alexander' and 'She Says Good Morning' and from an earlier *Emotions* session an amazingly excellent version of 'Children' complete with superior Phil vocal and minus most of the harmonies and that irritating kazoo.

In June, John Stax paid a visit to England as part of a worldwide holiday. He met up with his old buddies again and discussed with St John the ongoing legal action. Not long after returning to his Menzies Creek home John suffered a severe heart attack that resulted in him undergoing a quadruple by-pass operation. Thankfully he is on the road to recovery and as I write this is looking forward to Christmas, a glass of beer and a return to work in early 2002.

At the same time the death was announced of Richard Hite who assisted on both of the Chicago Blues releases in the early 1990s. All in all a sad year for The Pretty Things and their cohorts.

October 2001 witnessed the first ever, and probably last ever, performance of *SF Sorrow* before a paying audience when the band, complete with a much slimmer Skip, took the stage at the Royal Festival Hall. Aided again by Arthur Brown, Dave Gilmour and Skip's son Dov. The evening was a total success with a faultless performance and an extended encore, which included 'Fire', with Arthur Brown's flaming helmet. *The Daily Telegraph's* Clark Collis considered the evening less than successful. 'It soon became clear why *Sorrow* never achieved greater success, its highly competent but less than psychedelic rock songs clashing horribly with narrator Brown's almost Tolkien-esque script.'

Skip again made noises about it being his last gig. Like an ageing boxer on the interminable title trail, the spirit may have outlasted the body. This time it looks like the end for Skip although, no official announcement from the management because bad news is bad for business.

Phil and Dick have both commented on the international attitudes to music and age. Only in the UK is age a consideration. Blues and jazz artists play until they drop, nobody laughs at them or points at the wrinkles and receding hairlines. The problem, according to Phil, is that rock is about youth. Jack Green holds a similar view. 'My main musical influences were rock 'n' roll and R&B. From Elvis, Muddy Waters, anything with roots I liked. I didn't like rock music I find it's for kids. I find older guys standing up playing rock music is a bit sad, it's a youthful thing. It's for young men, I find at my age if you're gonna stand up on stage and play you should really play something with roots to it and you'll probably be accepted playing that.'

Where to now? It was said that they (Phil & Dick) had a three album deal with Snapper although it is now known that it was a one album deal with Snapper holding an option for two more. Snapper themselves seemed to be pulling away from further involvement and it is increasingly unlikely that the option will be exercised. They were disappointed with the sales figures for *Rage Before Beauty* which, although quite extensively promoted, only sold around 15,000 copies. This is considerably less than either *SF Sorrow*, which achieved over 30,000 or the eponymous first album that sold well over the 20,000 mark. CD releases must make a profit for the label and the Pretties didn't seem to be profitable. The digipac releases were quite expensive to put out and even in limited editions of 3,000/5,000 they are still hanging around. In total the Snapper releases sold over 120,000 worldwide.

Well, The Pretty Things are still here, still defiant and still starved of any worthwhile material rewards from their thirty-eight years of endeavour. You really have to admire the steely resolve and sheer bloody-mindedness of such people. Dick, who has to hold down a full time work as a driver to make ends meet, has lost numerous jobs because he always puts The Pretty Things, The Tour or The Gig before anything else. It's what he does.

'I don't think we really had our hearts set on buying a Rolls Royce,' Dick told Richie Unterberger. 'We did it because we liked doing it. We're certainly not doing it for the money.'

Too many people have trod a musical path where the monetary aspect was the only goal. The Pretty Things transcended this, not always on purpose of course because they tried on many occasions to break into the singles and albums charts. Their aim, however, has always been the artistic merit of the music before the financial reward of the hit.

It is all too easy to sound pompous when arguing the relative merits of different music. Notwithstanding this it seems clear that music can be classified in two ways – it is either good or bad, and the definition is subjective. It can also be assessed in terms of raison d'être, does the music have any reason for existence other than as a money making tool? Does it have any intrinsic worth? This again is subjective but in a world where increasingly every item seems temporary or with a built-in obsolescence few would argue that the majority of the music product purchased or played on radio is a quick-fix response from an industry anxious to shift units.

The Pretty Things do not have Swiss bank accounts or disgustingly healthy trust funds. Unlike Troggs leader Reg Presley their songs have not been unearthed and used in blockbuster films. Unlike numerous versions of their '60s peers they do not inhabit the financially rewarding holiday camp/pseudo-cabaret circuit and, unlike the majority of their rivals, they have retained their self-respect and inner drive.

The final word to Jon Povey. 'I would have liked the band to be more successful really. Sold more records, got more recognition for their art.' Regrets? 'The industry for its apathy, not just for not recognising The Pretty Things but other bands as well, who did some amazing stuff which because of commercial pressures with commercial radio such as it is today won't be played for one reason or another which is absolute nonsense. The industry has changed a lot, not necessarily for the better.

'It's a crap business really, I mean it's a real shit business. But you do it… something makes you do it. There ain't no money in it really, I always tend to feel that you feed people you're putting food into other people's mouths. You either accept that you're gonna do it or say bollocks, I'm not gonna do it. I think you gain through your own creativity. If you're a creative person you can't stop that creativity you can't put a block on the tap. It's nice to have. Something makes you do it.'

Appendix A – Where are they now?

PHIL MAY shares his time between the Pretty Things and his art interest at the Caelt Gallery in Westbourne Grove. Able to survive on his royalties he appears remarkably sanguine regarding the Pretties lack of commercial success. Phil has added cycling to his obsession with tennis and loves cycling across Europe.

DICK TAYLOR lives at Ventnor on the Isle of Wight. Unlike Phil he doesn't have sufficient royalties to survive and he and wife Anne get by with income from her school dinner lady job and various lightweight gigs and occasional sessions that Dick is involved with as well as his occasional driving jobs.

JON POVEY and wife Rogie live happily on the Clapham/Battersea border where he manages an outlet specialising in high quality bathroom ware. Jon is philosophical about life and concludes that not many people close to age 60 can be fortunate enough to still enjoy a creative musical career.

WALLY WALLER lives near Arundel, Sussex with wife Sarah and children. He works as an electrician and spends much of his time writing and recording music in his home studio. Wally intends to continue writing music, accepting that not much of it will be used by the Pretty Things, and intends marketing the songs to other performers.

SKIP ALAN lives with wife and son Dov in South London. He heads the Mastergroup based in Thornton Heath. Still curmudgeonly he retains his love of live performances although high blood pressure and a high cholesterol level have now ended his drumming career. Cruising round Cowes in a motor launch is his preferred leisure activity.

FRANK HOLLAND plays guitar in the Pretty Things and forms part of the tri-axial writing partnership with Phil and Mark St John.

JOHN ALDER (Twink) now lives in Beverley Hills and continues to play with various bands such as Small Stone. He's announced that he has an incurable disease which is now controlled.

JOHN STAX lives in Australia with wife Wendy and daughter Naomi. John makes musical instruments such as guitars and dulcimers and occasionally plays bass in the Paramount Trio, who specialise in 60s R&B. Fortunately his heart attack in September 2001 has prompted by-pass surgery which should allow him to continue with his enjoyable family lifestyle.

STUART BROOKS apparently lives in the Los Angeles area. No more is known

GORDON EDWARDS lives in West London and continues to pursue a musical career, which he still hopes will be in tandem with Jack Green.

JACK GREEN lives on the Isle of Wight with wife Jacqueline. During the late 90s he played guitar in the reconstituted T-Rex before leaving in early 2000. Like Peter Tolson he is disenchanted with the music industry and now pursues a career in video production and public relations.

VIV PRINCE lives in Portugal where he breeds alsation dogs and grows oranges. He is now pretty much recovered from the hit and run incident that nearly cost him his life.

PETER TOLSON lives in Harlow with partner Pauline. He works in the City of London as a QA Manager. He rarely plays guitar and has turned his back on the musical rat-race.

BRIAN PENDLETON sadly died in May 2001 from lung cancer

STEVE BROWNING still lives in the Gosport area and continues to play bass guitar in various blues-rock bands.

VIC UNITT is rumoured to be back in the UK, after a period in the States. No other info is available.

MARK ST JOHN is alive and is currently The Pretty Things manager. He also spends his time looking into the 'penny contracts' that continue to haunt other 60s bands.

DEREK BOLTWOOD lives in Dorchester where he writes.

BRYAN MORRISON retains his Pretty connection through his ownership of publishing company Lupus Music, He retains fingers in pies and most recently became involved in an Internet company that intends relaying rock concerts.

NORMAN SMITH is now retired and lives with his wife in Sussex.

PETER MEW remains at Abbey Road after 36 years. He specialises in re-mastering and among he many works has been the Tomorrow back catalogue.

TONY CLARKE lives in Bromley. As well as production work he is involved in writing and performing his own music.

'LOFTY' RICHES is close to retirement and looking forward to living somewhere in the sun.

MIKE OBER remains involved in music distribution particularly those with Yardbirds connections.

IAN HANSON'S success in fending off the Pretty Things legal manoeuvres led him to join Virgin Records as Commercial Director. Six years later, November 2000 he rejoined EMI as Executive Vice President of EMI Europe

DENNY BRIDGES lives and works in New Jersey and is still involved in production and engineering.

JIM MCCARTY drums in the 'new' Yardbirds.

SHANNON O'SHEA runs a SOS, a very successful management company based in Los Angeles.

Appendix B – Thank you's

DICK TAYLOR: For his patience and complete honesty

JON POVEY: For allowing me to ruin his lunch hour by asking him silly questions and for forgetting to buy him the pint that I promised

WALLY WALLER (ALLEN): For his frankness and for letting me intrude on evenings better spent with his family

ELECTRA MAY: For replying to my letter after I had given up all hope of tracking her down

PETER TOLSON: For his absolute openness and sincerity. Like Nick Drake, Peter is too sensitive for the machiavellian music industry. A great loss.

JACK GREEN: Jack has spent hours talking on the telephone, although being a Scotsman he didn't pay. A really nice guy who has found an enjoyable niche outside of music.

GORDON EDWARDS: Like Peter and Jack, Gordon was adamant that the 'true story' be told, not the dodgy, factually incorrect and exaggerated nonsense's often perpetuated in the album sleevenotes.

JOHN AND WENDY STAX: John and Wendy took time out from the UK segment of their world holiday to share their memories which was much more than I could ever have expected, a big thank you to both of you. I hope you get well soon John.

TERRY COATES: Fan, and long-time archivist has provided invaluable assistance and use of information and quotes from interviews he has carried out with current and ex-band members. Also the odd photo, sorry Terry.

JORGEN ANGEL: Whose photographs of musicians and bands from the 1960s inwards provide a veritable goldmine of captured history. Jorgen's web site www.angel.dk provides many more examples of these.

JOOP DE LIGT: Who for no profit and at great personal expense ran the *SF Sorrow fanzine* for a number of years until he fell foul of The Pretty Things Management. Thanks for all of your help and support Joop. Keep enjoying the music

PETER INNES: Had been contemplating his own book on the band, and in a spirit of true Pretty Things camaraderie provided valuable insights and advice. Peter's various interviews for *Rock 'n' Reel* magazine and the *SF Sorrow* fanzine have proved a wonderful source of information. Best wishes Peter.

NORMAN SMITH: Legendary producer Norman was gracious in allowing me to intrude upon his time and fire numerous questions at him regarding the band (it probably made a change from questions about The Beatles and the Floyd) and I am beholden to him.

PETER MEW AND TONY CLARKE: Current and past Abbey Road engineers have also given freely of their time and opinions for which I am greatly obliged.

BRYAN MORRISON: The Pretty Things manager back in the tabloid horror days has been extremely generous with both his time and his memories. A thank you also to Cora Barnes.

SHANNON O'SHEA: Band manager during the late 1980s made time to correspond from her LA Management Company base and was particularly candid.

DEREK BOLTWOOD: Managed them during the latter part of the EMI period and has extremely frank and helpful and polite.

LOFTY RICHES: The bands original roadie has also taken time to recount various stories. Thanks Lofty.

DENNY BRIDGES: Produced of a number of 1988 tracks at The Basement Studio and was also extremely congenial to the point of sending a tape of those sessions. Thanks Denny, it was much appreciated.

MIKE STAX: The Editor of *Ugly Things* magazine who also runs the official Pretty Things Fan Club. Mike has kindly allowed me to quote from articles in *Ugly Things* and I am indebted. Keep up the excellent work Mike, and Anja.

DAVID BLAKEY: Controller of Bo Diddley – The Originator website, who proved extremely helpful. David's site is a veritable encyclopaedia of Bo knowledge. http://members.com/-Originator_2/index.html

JON KIRKMAN: Runs a great rock website 'Rock Ahead' and his interview with Phil May, which can be heard on the site, provided much useful info.

ED DEANE: 'Fallen Angel' and guitarist par excellence provided a number of useful insights into those often memory clouded late 70s days.

DAVE WILKIE: Live At The Heartbreak Hotel keyboard player who also proved helpful and accommodating.

DAVE EMLEN: Runs the unbelievably exhaustive Kinks website has been extremely generous with his time, information and contacts.

DOUG HINMAN: Kinks and Yardbirds archivist has been especially informative and supportive and I look forward to his imminent Kinks tome.

MIKE OBER: Produced two albums, United and A Whiter Shade of Muddy Water that had a Pretty content. Thanks for the assistance.

JAMES KYLLO: Was most helpful in providing background to the band's brief dalliance with Creation Records, cheers James.

ANDREW LOOG OLDHAM: Kindly responded with a message after an e-mail enquiry, Ta.

MICK AVORY: The former Kinks drummer who assisted with some useful background information

NICK SALOMAN (THE BEVIS FROND) AND PHIL MCMULLEN: Were both extremely friendly and with details of Twink's interview for Ptolemaic Terrascope magazine and a big thank you to you both.

ARTHUR BROWN: The God of Hellfire kindly spared the time to discuss his memories and opinions, particularly in relation to the SF Sorrow v Tommy controversy.

JIM MCCARTY: Who took the trouble to respond to my questions without guile. Best wishes Jim.

ED BICKNELL: Supplied numerous informative and often hilarious insights, plus one cracking quote. Thanks Ed.

JON ASTLEY AND PHIL CHAPMAN: Both recalled their production work and associated trials working on the Cross Talk album. Thank you for sparing the time.

GLEN MATLOCK: Put the record straight regarding his 'membership' of the band, nice one Glen.

PHILIP PENDLETON: Spoke freely about his late father. (I hope you like the book Philip).

RICK HOFFMAN: Has worked tirelessly to keep the band alive via his website and internet discussion group. A thankless task and one that I know the band and their many fans appreciate.

ED MABE AND PERFECT SOUND FOREVER: Thanks for the information. There is more of it at www.furious.com/perfect

ALAN CLAYSON: Journalist, author and eccentric singer has written many articles and reviews about The Pretty Things and these have proved a very useful source. Thanks Alan. P.S Your Cabbage Patch gig was awful.

ROB BROOKS: Frontman for the Desperate Dan Band, thanks for your help and strong opinions Rob. Read and enjoy.

ROBERT GERRETSON: Ran a European Pretty Things fanclub back in the early 1970s and was a generous and warm natured guy.

JON HART: Who acted as roadie on the 1999 US tour and wrote perceptively and honestly about the tribulations of those three and a bit weeks.

MELODY MAKER: Now sadly defunct, allowed unrestricted access to the archives of both that paper and Disc, and for this I am extremely grateful.

THE BRITISH LIBRARY: Who were able to accommodate my wishes and allowed full access to their fabulous archived collection of magazines and papers at both Kings Cross and Colindale.

EMI: Which allowed unrestricted access to their invaluable and amazingly exhaustive archives at Hayes.

Appendix C – Bibliography and Sources

BBC In Concert
Blueprint magazine
Disc
The Guardian
Melody Maker
NME
Pop Weekly
Record Mirror
Rough Guide To Rock
SF Sorrow fanzine
The Sunday Times
13 Chester Street fanzine
Ugly Things magazine
Perfect Sound Forever http://www.furious.com/perfect
Ruth & Gregg at the EMI Archives in Hayes
Green Magazine
Jorgen Angel – music photographer
Pete Anderson – Crazy Diamond Syd Barrett
Mark Andrews – Progression
Jon Astley – Co-producer of Cross Talk
Mick Avory – ex Kinks drummer
Ed Bicknell – former Circle Agency booker and ex-Dire Straits Manager
Derek Boltwood – 1969/70 manager
Denny Bridges – Producer and engineer
Arthur Brown – performer
Tony Clarke – engineer on Parachute/Freeway Madness
Alan Clayson – journalist, author and wannabe singer
Terry Coates – long time fan and archivist
James de Wolfe
Ed Deane – guitarist
Joop De Ligt – former editor of SF Sorrow fanzine
Roger Dopson
Gordon Edwards – ex Pretty Thing & ex-Kink
Dave Emlen – Kinks website guru
Allan Evans – journalist
George Evers – journalist
Marianne Faithfull – female singer and muse
Jack Green – ex Pretty Thing, ex-T.Rex and successful solo artist
Tony Harris and Alison – Snapper Records
Jon Hart – US tour roadie
Doug Hinman – Kinks and Yardbirds archivist
Trevor Hodgett – journalist
Peter Innes – Pretty Things archivist
DJ Johnson – journalist
Alan Jones – journalist
Jon Kirkman – journalist
James Kyllo ex-Creation records now at Go Pop
Carol Ledger – 1960s fan & fellow partygoer
Andrew Loog-Oldham – Manager Rolling Stones and boss of Immediate Records
Ed Mabe – journalist
T Max – of Noise Magazine
Electra May – Phil's ex-wife

The Pretty Things

Phil May – perennial Pretty Thing
Jim McCarty – Yardbirds drummer
Phil McMullen of Ptolemaic Terrascope magazine
Peter Mew – engineer on SF Sorrow
Emily Moore – The Guardian
Peter Moore – singer, composer, etc. with Count Zero
Bryan Morrison – original manager
Mike Ober – ex producer
Siouxsie O'Neill – ex Snapper Records
Shannon O'Shea – ex-Manager
Jon Povey – Pretty Thing
Eleanor Ramsay – Boston Rock Opera
Lofty Riches – original roadie
Mark St John – Pretty Things current manager
Nick Saloman (The Bevis Frond)
Charles Shaar-Murray – Blues On CD
Norman Smith – producer 1967/75
John Stax – original Pretty Things bassist
Dick Taylor – Pretty Thing
Peter Tolson – ex-Pretty Thing guitarist and computer
Wally Waller – Pretty Thing
Mike Watkins – Crazy Diamond Syd Barrett
Chris Welch – Peter Grant The Man Who Led Zeppelin
Dave Wilkie – keyboard player
Ritchie Yorke (Led Zeppelin – From early days to Plant and Page)
All the others who wished to remain anonymous.

Appendix D – UK DISCOGRAPHY

Singles

Rosalyn/Big Boss Man: June 1964
Don't Bring Me Down/We'll Be Together: October 1964
Honey I Need/I Can Never Say: February 1965
Cry To Me/Get A Buzz: July 1965
Midnight To Six Man/Can't Stand The Pain: December 1965
Come See Me/L.S.D.: April 1966
A House In The Country/Me Needing You: July 1966
Progress/Buzz The Jerk: December 1966
Children/My Time: April 1967
Defecting Grey/Mr Evasion: November 1967
Talking About The Good Times/Walking Through My Dreams: February 1968
Private Sorrow/Balloon Burning: November 1968
The Good Mr Square/Blue Serge Blues: April 1970
October 26/Cold Stone: October 1970
Stone Hearted Mama/Summertime/Circus Mind: May 1971
Over The Moon/Havana Bound: January 1973
Is It Only Love/Joey: January 1975
I'm Keeping/Atlanta: June 1975
Joey/Come Home Mamma: September 1975
Sad Eye/ Remember That Boy: February 1976
Tonight/It Isn't Rock 'n Roll: May 1976
I'm Calling/Sea Of Blue: August 1980
Falling Again/She Don't: October 1980
Eve Of Destruction/Goin' Downhill/Can't Stop: September 1989
Defecting Grey, SF Sorrow Is Born, Balloon Burning and Everlasting Flame: August 1998

Albums/CDs

The Pretty Things
Release Date : March 1965
Producer : Jack Baverstock & Bobby Graham
Engineer : unknown
Tracks: Roadrunner, Judgement Day, 13 Chester Street, Big City, Unknown Blues, Mama, Keep Your Big Mouth Shut, Honey I Need, Oh Baby Doll, She's Fine She's Mine, Don't Lie To Me, The Moon Is Rising, Pretty Thing

Get The Picture
Release Date : December 1965
Producer : Bobby Graham
Engineer : unknown
Tracks: You Don't Believe Me, Buzz The Jerk, Get The Picture, Can't Stand The Pain, Rainin' In My Heart, We'll Play House, You'll Never Do It To Me Baby, I Had A Dream, I Want Your Love, London Town, Cry To Me, Gonna Find Me A Substitute

Emotions
Release Date : May 1967
Producer : Steve Rowland
Engineer : unknown
Tracks: Death Of A Socialite, Children, The Sun, There Will Never Be Another Day, House Of Ten, Out In The Night, One Long Glance, Growing In My Mind, Photographer, Bright Lights Of The City, Tripping, My Time

The Pretty Things

S. F. Sorrow
Release Date : December 1968
Producer : Norman Smith
Engineer : Peter Mew (also Ken Scott, Phil McDonald, Mike Sheedy)
Tracks: S. F. Sorrow Is Born, Bracelets Of Fingers, She Says Good Morning, Private Sorrow, Balloon Burning, Death, Baron Saturday, The Journey, I See You, Well Of Destiny, Trust, Old Man Going, Loneliest Person
Parachute
Release Date : June 1970
Producer : Norman Smith
Engineers : Tony Clark & Nick Webb
Tracks: Scene One, The Good Mr Square, She Was Tall, She Was High, In The Square, The Letter, Rain, Miss Fay Regrets, Cries From The Midnight Circus, Grass, Sickle Clowns, She's A Lover, What's The Use, Parachute

Freeway Madness
Release Date : December 1972
Producer : Asa Briggs (AKA Wally Waller)
Engineer : Tony Clarke
Tracks: Love Is Good, Havana Bound, Peter, Rip Off Train, Over The Moon, Religion's Dead, Country Road, Allnight Sailor, Onion Soup, Another Bowl?

Silk Torpedo
Release Date : October 1974
Producer : Norman Smith
Engineer : Keith Harwood
Tracks: Dream/Joey, Maybe You Tried, Atlanta, L.A.N.T.A, Is It Only Love, Come Home Mamma, Bridge Of God, Singapore Silk Torpedo, Belfast Cowboys

Savage Eye
Release Date : May 1976
Producer : Norman Smith
Engineer : Keith Harwood
Tracks: Under The Volcano, My Song, Sad Eye, Remember That Boy, It Isn't Rock n' Roll, I'm Keeping, It's Been So Long, Drowned Man, Theme For Michelle

Cross Talk
Release Date : August 1980
Producer : Jon Astley & Phil Chapman
Engineer : Astley & Chapman
Tracks: I'm Calling, Edge Of The Night, Sea Of Blue, Lost That Girl, Bitter End, Office Love, Falling Again, It's So Hard, She Don't, No Future

Rage Before Beauty
Release Date : March 1999
Producer : Mark St John
Engineer : Marc Francs (on some)
Tracks: Passion Of Love, Vivian Prince, Everlasting Flame, Love Keeps Hanging On, Eve Of Destruction, Not Givin' In, Pure Cold Stone, Blue Turns To Red, Goodbye Goodbye, Goin' Downhill, Play With Fire, Fly Away, Mony Mony, God Give Me The Strength

Other album/CD releases of interest
Electric Banana: De Wolfe 1967
More Electric Banana: De Wolfe 1968
Even More Electric Banana: De Wolfe 1969
Phillipe Debarge: 1969
Hot Licks: De Wolfe 1973
Il Barritz: 1974
Greatest Hits 64-57 (compilation): Fontana October 1975
Singles As & Bs (compilation): See For Miles October 1977
The Return Of The Electric Banana: De Wolfe 1978

Phil May And The Fallen Angels : Butt 1978
The Pretty Things 1967-1971 (compilation): Harvest March 1982
Live At Heartbreak Hotel: August 1984
Let Me Hear The Choir Sing (compilation): Bam Caruso October 1984
Closed Restaurant Blues (compilation): Bam Caruso February 1985
Cries From The Midnight Circus (compilation): Harvest May 1986
Out Of The Island: Intak June 1988
Pretty Things/Yardbirds Blues Band – The Chicago Blues Tapes: St Georges December 1991
On Air: Band of Joy April 1992
John Coghlans Diesel – River Of Tears/No Moon Shines (Single): 1992
Pretty Things/Yardbirds Blues Band – Wine Women & Whiskey: St Georges1993
Unrepentant – The Anthology: Fragile September 1995
EP Collection: See For Miles 1996
S. F. Sorrow – Resurrection: Snapper October 1998

The Snapper Re-issues:

The Pretty Things
April 1998
Bonus tracks: Rosalyn, Big Boss Man, Don't Bring Me Down, We'll Be Together, I Can Never Say, Get Yourself Home.

Get The Picture
April 1998
Bonus tracks: Sitting All Alone, Midnight To Six Man, Me Needing You, Come See Me, Get A Buzz, £SD,

Emotions
April 1998
Bonus Tracks: Progress, A House In The Country, Progress (alt version), Photographer, There Will Never Be Another Day Like Today, My Time, The Sun

Silk Torpedo
October 1998
Bonus Tracks: Singapore Silk Torpedo, Dream/Joey,

Savage Eye
October 1998
Bonus Tracks: Tonight, Love Me A Little (Metropolis), Dance All Night (Metropolis)

SF Sorrow (mono)
October 1998
Bonus Tracks: Defecting Grey, Mr Evasion, Talking About The Good Times, Walking Through My Dreams

SF Sorrow Resurrection
October 1998
Live Internet broadcast

Parachute
June 1999
Bonus Tracks: Blue Serge Blues, October 26, Cold Stone, Stone Hearted Mama, Summertime: Circus Mind,

Latest Writs Greatest Hits
February 2000
Tracks: Come See Me: Don't Bring Me Down: Defecting Grey (Original single version): SF Sorrow Is Born: £.S.D: All Light Up: Midnight To Six Man: Remember That Boy: Rosalyn: Singapore Silk Torpedo: Old Man Going: Vivian Prince: Roadrunner: Talkin' About The Good Times: Summertime: Tripping: Havana Bound: Cries From The Midnight Circus: Bitter End

Freeway Madness
June 2000
Bonus Tracks: Religion's Dead: Havana Bound: Love Is Good: Onion Soup (all live 1973)

The Pretty Things

Cross Talk
June 2000
Bonus Tracks: Wish Fulfilment: Sea About Me: The Young Pretenders

The Rhythm & Blues Years
July 2001
Tracks:
CD1
Judgement Day: The Moon Is Rising: I'm Gonna Find Me A Substitute: 13 Chester Street: Oh Baby Doll: Get A Buzz: Don't Bring Me Down: Sitting All Alone: You'll Never Do It Baby: Come See Me: Rosalyn: She's Fine, She's Mine: I Can Never Say: Get Yourself Home: I Had A Dream: Me Needing You: It's Been So Long
CD2
Mama Keep Your Big Mouth Shut: Rainin' In My Heart: Big Boss Man: Unknown Blues: We" Play House: Don't Lie To Me: I Want Your Love: Roadrunner: We'll Be Together: Honey I Need: Cry To Me: Buxx The Jerk: Big City: London Town: Out In The Night: Vivian Prince: Pretty Thing

The Psychedelic Years
October 2001
Tracks:
CD1
Scene One: She Says Good Morning (live '69): Talkin' About The Good Times: L.S.D.: Old Man Going: My Time: SF Sorrow Is Born: Trust: October 26th: There Will Never Be Another Day: Mr Evasion: Death: Can't Stand The Pain: The Journey: I See You: Well Of Destiny: Alexander (live '69)
CD2
Defecting Grey: In The Square/The Letter/Rain: Walking Through My Dreams: Bracelets Of Fingers: Growing In My Mind: Baron Saturday: She's A Lover: Bright Lights Of The City: Blue Serge Blues: Children (alternate version): One Long Glance: Private Sorrow: Balloon Burning: The Sun: Grass: What's The Use: Parachute: Loneliest Person

Appendix E – Useful Information

Mark St John can be contacted on Tel: 07050 169210 or Fax: 07010 700 808

Snapper Records 0207 610 0330

Bryan Morrison/Lupus Music 0207 706 7304

Jorgen Angel photographs can be viewed and ordered at www.angel.dk

Ugly Things magazine www.ugly-things.com/

The Pretty Things Fan Club www.ugly-things.com/fanclub.htm

Electric Banana Pretty Things website www.aimcommunity.de/pretties/index.htm

Rick Hoffman's Mindspring website http://bkonwh.topcities.com//pretties.htm

Perfect Sound Forever magazine www.furious.com/perfect

Georgie The Midnite www.koeln.netsurf.de/~juergen.schuette/pretty/pretty.html

Ptolemaic Terrascope www.terrascope.org/home.html

Jon Kirkman's 'Rock Ahead'www.themusicindex.com/rockahead/intro1.htm

David Blakey's Bo Diddley website http://members.com/~Originator_2/index.html

Dave Emlens Kinks site: http://kinks.it.rit.edu/kontents.html

Appendix F – Further notes

Wally Allen also produced *Kes – A Major Fancy*, the solo album by the Barclay James Harvest guitarist John Lees. It was recorded, primarily at Abbey Road, between December 1972 and January 1973. Skip Alan and Sunshine's Gordon Edwards were roped in for the sessions as was Rod Argent.

Wally became involved with Country Joe MacDonald, and produced the song 'Fantasy' for him. 'I needed some musicians so I got Sunshine in. So it's Sunshine & Country Joe on it. It was Country Joe and Sunshine with a Pretty Thing producing. I might have sung something on the chorus.' During October 'Fantasy' was issued as a single on the Vanguard label to promote the album it came from, *Paris Sessions*. Close listening detects the silky harmonies of Gordon Edwards and Jack Green that would show to such advantage on later Pretties albums. Years later the CD, *Best Of Country Joe – The Vanguard Years* would contain sleeve notes claiming that 'Fantasy' had help from The Pretty Things!

Jack Green expressed great surprise when he heard that 'Fantasy' had been released. He hadn't realised that the session was for real, he had been told that they were just demoing a song and turned up to be paid lower than normal rates.

Wally also became involved with the Marcus Hook Roll Band and Fogg, and was asked to produce a number of tracks by Bees Make Honey. He ended up producing half the album with Nick Lowe producing the other half. This was Wally's introduction to guitarist Ed Deane and drummer Fran Byrne who some years later would both feature in the story.

From Wally's perspective, the politics at EMI was beginning to turn creativity into disillusion. 'I found it very frustrating working at EMI. I thought I made some quite good records but the organisation was so big you kind of got lost in it. I mean, to try and get a good budget out of somebody for promotion and stuff. Because it was an 'in-house' production nobody thought it was that good to start with. They'd much rather put their faith in an inherited hit from America – like all the Tamla-Motown stuff.'

What sort of person is Phil May? Under St John's governorship he has become the central focus of interviewers and the controller who vets the re-issues, new recordings and tour schedules. The interviews given to various music journalists over the last thirty-five years enable a reasonably accurate picture to be drawn. He conspires to assume various 'identities' ensuring a confusing amalgam of personalities. 'Bigheaded and a name dropper' is how one ex-Pretty Thing described him. He loves to be with and to be seen with music and showbiz names and has acquired a reputation for name-dropping and often throws a 'Van', a 'Gilmour' or a 'Crispian' into the conversation whilst also claiming that he likes to be around non-musos.

Like most singers he is considered a prima donna, not least by fellow band members. John Stax offered this view in an interview published by *SF Sorrow* fanzine and Peter Tolson confirmed it. Phil's preference and sometimes insistence on only singing his own lyrics has also ensured that he receives a writing credit, and subsequent royalties, on much of the band's output including many of those songs composed by Gordon Edwards and Jack Green.

Clearly a vivid and insightful writer he has yet to master the nuances of punctuation, spelling and grammar, a victory perhaps for the artist over the artisan. Also, like many a performer he can be moody and quickly switch from an attitude of extreme friendliness to one of curt dismissal as St John found to his dismay when he returned the Freerange tapes in 1994.

Since splitting from Electra Phil lives with his close friend, Colin Graham, in a small flat on the Kensington-Chelsea border. It seems he has reduced his alcoholic intake, which threatened to get out of hand in the early 90s, although fellow band members take care to ensure he doesn't drink, or at least not too much, before performances.

I have always found him approachable and have never been subjected to bad temper or curt dismissal in all the years I have telephoned and bothered him. Clearly a complex fellow and, ignoring the usual human idiosyncrasies, a pretty decent guy.

The drumming of Skip Alan is seldom mentioned. Like Viv Prince he is more often considered in the light of outrageous behaviour and stage destruction, whereas the reality is that he's a vital component of The Pretty Things sound. His drumming and camaraderie spark the band and drive the songs relentlessly down the track. Often he drums himself to the brink of exhaustion as Peter Tolson recalled. 'Once, we had done the *Silk Torpedo* album and we were hot and we played at the Marquee. The place was packed, John Paul Jones and Noel Redding were there and if any fire regulation people had been there it would have been shut down. In the middle of the third number Skip had sweated so much that he got cramp and couldn't hit the snare and we had to send out for salt tablets and pour a load of water down him so he could finish the gig.'

This was the June 1976 Marquee gig where a London evening paper trumpeted the likely guest appearance of Led Zeppelin. Consequently queues stretched for hundreds of yards. The concert certainly improved the band's profile and, apart from the one Zeppelin turn out, John Paul Jones assisting with a boogie-woogie encore, it was particularly memorable for the band's acerbic digs at then current teenybop idols The Bay City Rollers.

Skip's style involves a much greater use of crash cymbal and high-hat than most rock drummers, falling into line with the Pretties historical dependence on maracas, tambourines, handclaps, ashtrays and other forms of percussion. Skip was inspired by the great jazz drummers such as Gene Krupa and because of this he doesn't drum in the traditional rock beast manner but tends to play over everything. In truth he uses the drums like an instrument, laying rhythms and fills across the melody and driving the songs often in a time-lapse, staccato manner. His tendency to play all over the song with a free-form jazzy style has often irritated his fellow musicians. Pete Tolson confessed that he finds it easier to have a solid player like Ian Pace or John Bonham behind him and Jack Green confirmed that Skip's jazzy playing made it a nightmare to keep a rhythm going. Gordon Edwards didn't really care, saying contemptuously 'drummers are ten a penny.'

Peter also remembered the famous Skip temper. 'Skip could lose it real quick. Once we played a gig at this old pub and we had a new drum roadie and he didn't set up the drums as Skip liked it. Always fatal. Anyway, about four or five songs in the crash cymbal came off. He picked it up and whoosh, like a Frisbee. Now, this is a 23-inch crash cymbal that would take some buggers head off. One bloke just ducked and it hit the wall and stayed there, quivering in the wall…just because it came off.'

Peter also recalled the day Skip dressed up in a gorilla suit and on the way to a gig leered out of the vehicle window terrifying passers-by. Apparently Skip was so taken with the outfit that he decided he would keep it on and his wife had to bring him bananas to eat!

With Skip you can never rationalise whether he is serious or incredibly subtle. In a Swansong press release for the *Silk Torpedo* album he claimed, 'I spent hours thinking about the new album while we were recording it, even though I didn't write any of it.'

John Povey provided a remarkably pithy description: 'Skip's a hot and cold guy. He's actually a very intelligent bloke who pretends to be very thick.'

Norman Smith remembered Skip with great fondness. 'I got on very well with Skip, we had an awful lot of laughs. He was always interested in life, Skipper. I always used to take the piss out of him quite a bit, to be honest with you, I probably would agree with John. It did seem he was putting on a bit of an act, his thickness, but I liked him very much indeed.'

Derek Boltwood recalled being on an aeroplane with the band heading for a gig in Amsterdam and being approached by Skip. 'I was sitting down and reading a book and Skip came up to me and he said 'we're really lucky' and I said 'how's that Skip?' He said 'well, we've got a manager who reads books.' He wasn't being sarcastic or anything like that'

Jack recounted another tale. 'We were in a club in Paris called the Cheetah club. It's on three floors and there's a sort of river running through it. It was full of celebrities – Mike McCartney, Joan Collins – and Skip would get undressed at the drop of a hat, he would be down to his pants if you blinked. I turned round and there was Skip down to his purple Y-fronts and he had his arm around this enormous stuffed ostrich. He was trying to get into this river, wanting to go for a swim. There was the club manager holding onto the back of his y-fronts, Skip was right over the water and there was somebody holding onto the manager and Richard Cole went up and kicked the last person and they were straight in the water and Skip was floating around with this stuffed ostrich.'

Gordon Edwards: 'We were in the states, somewhere like the Hyatt Hotel on Sunset Strip. Because Skip had heard about people tossing televisions out of windows I saw him pick up this television and make a bee-line for the window to throw it out into the pool, about sixty feet below. I turned round and said 'if you toss that out the window the money's coming out of your pocket not mine'. So after telling him that he would have to pay for it he decided he wouldn't do it, ha ha.'

SAF, Helter Skelter and Firefly Books

Mail Order

All SAF, Helter Skelter and Firefly titles are available by mail order from the world-famous Helter Skelter bookshop.

Telephone: +44 (0)20 7836 1151
or Fax: +44 (0)20 7240 9880

Office hours: Mon-Fri 10:00am – 7:00pm,
Sat: 10:00am – 6:00pm, Sun: closed.

**Helter Skelter Bookshop, 4 Denmark Street, London,
WC2H 8LL, United Kingdom.**

If you are in London come and visit us and browse the titles in person.

Order Online

For the latest on SAF, Helter Skelter and Firefly titles, or to order books online, check the SAF or Helter Skelter websites.

You can also browse the full range of rock, pop, jazz and experimental music books we have available, as well as keeping up with our latest releases and special offers.

You can also contact us via email, and request a catalogue.

info@safpublishing.com
helter@skelter.demon.co.uk

**www.safpublishing.com
www.skelter.demon.co.uk**